THE KREMLIN *AND* WORLD POLITICS

Studies in Soviet Policy and Action

Vintage *RUSSIAN* Library

THE KREMLIN *AND* WORLD POLITICS

Studies in Soviet Policy and Action

BY

PHILIP E. MOSELY

VINTAGE BOOKS

A DIVISION OF RANDOM HOUSE

New York

VINTAGE BOOKS
are published by ALFRED A. KNOPF, INC.
and RANDOM HOUSE, INC.

Library of Congress Catalog Card Number: 60-9146

Manufactured in the United States of America

Preface

WHEN LENIN led the war-tortured people of Russia into the October Revolution, he also took them out of the main line of western democratic evolution. His revolution, and the new system of ideology and power which he built upon it, drove a deep chasm between the Bolshevist regime and the liberal traditions of western Europe and North America. The consequences of this profound rift have grown in import to be the major preoccupation of both leaders and citizens. This collection of essays is a selection among a variety of efforts I have made over the past quarter-century to understand the "Russian problem" and to interpret both the constant and the changing features that the Soviet system presents to its own people and to the outside world.

Ever since the beginning of 1940 a succession of urgent responsibilities to others more than to myself—policy research and planning, negotiation, intensive teaching at the graduate level, planning and administration of research programs on the Soviet Union and more recently on American foreign policy—have frustrated my desire to complete a more extensive and unified study of Soviet policy, but in the meantime some of my observations and recommendations have appeared in periodical form. The idea of bringing together some of the more pertinent of these partial studies was suggested to me by a number of friends and warmly encouraged by Morris Philipson, Editor of Vintage Books. *The Kremlin and World Politics* is a consequence of these urgings.

I take special pleasure in acknowledging the gracious permission of the editors or other holders of copyright to republish the twenty-five articles I have selected. Specific acknowledgment of this permission is made at the beginning of each article. Each article has been reprinted in its original wording except for a few minor changes designed to avoid certain verbal repetitions or to make the original thought slightly more precise. In Essay Two, "Aspects of Russian Expansion," however, I have found it necessary to make a number of clarifying changes because its wording was too close to its original form of a lecture. For Essays One through Fourteen I have prepared brief introductory notes designed either to make clear the continuing significance of these earlier studies or to summarize pertinent information of more recent date. Some new information has also been inserted in several footnotes identified as "Author's Note 1959." To provide uniformity of presentation, subheadings have been omitted and footnotes have been renumbered according to the publisher's style, and a number of changes have been made throughout, for example, substituting "Formosa" for "Taiwan." No changes have been made, I feel, that modify the meaning of the original study at the time it was written. Finally, I take great pleasure in expressing my appreciation to Cynthia Cooper, who has copyedited this volume so ably, to Lorna Brennan for her careful reading of the proofs, and to Elizabeth Valkenier for preparing the index.

PHILIP E. MOSELY

November 30, 1959

Contents

PART I

Continuities in Soviet Outlook

:1:

SOME SOVIET TECHNIQUES OF NEGOTIATION[1]

[*July 1951*]

INTRODUCTORY NOTE · Since this essay was written in 1951, and, more importantly, since Khrushchev's consolidation of the succession to Stalin, a number of changes have taken place in the Soviet conduct of negotiation. Instead of remaining inaccessible and oracularly mysterious within the Kremlin walls, Khrushchev has shown himself eager to visit, however formally and superficially, many different countries. Whether he has thereby come to understand much of their diverse cultures, aspirations, and strengths remains obscure; in any case he appears to weave into his day-to-day decisions and his frequent pronouncements a somewhat larger proportion of factual data, even though they are inserted into a rigorously Bolshevik framework of doctrine.

Stalin was reluctant to inject his person and his prestige directly into negotiations unless he held a very strong hand, as he did in the wartime negotiations with his Western allies. Whether or not Khrushchev overestimates the Soviet power position and his personal powers of persuasion, he has shown a constant eagerness, since the consolidation of his own position in January 1955, to enter into direct dealings with foreign leaders. At the same time

[1] *Negotiating with the Russians,* edited by Raymond Dennett and Joseph E. Johnson (Boston: World Peace Foundation; 1951), pp. 271–303. Copyright 1951 by the World Peace Foundation.

these contacts have so far reinforced, rather than watered down, the arrogance of Soviet dogma and of Soviet demands.

With the removal of Stalin's hand and the eclipse of Molotov, Soviet second-rank negotiators have emerged much better acquainted with the languages, politics, and internal divisions of the West, though they still adhere closely to the doctrinal core and rigid techniques described in this essay. True, the traditional dogma of the "capitalist encirclement" of the Soviet Union has been replaced by a new one—that of the triumphant "socialist encirclement" of the "imperialist" powers. This reversal of dogmas describes but does not account for the new emphasis in Soviet policy on the use of specific and graphic nuclear threats, or its boldness in leaping over a resistant periphery to win political friends in the Middle East and in Asia. Most ominous, since 1958, has been Khrushchev's new practice of the "rolling crisis," moving the seat of tension rapidly from Lebanon to the Formosa Strait, then to Berlin, and so on. From his position of caution Stalin, at least, preferred to stir up one crisis at a time, milking each of all possible advantages before leading over a bridge of "coexistence" propaganda to the next major crisis.

*

THERE is a deepseated tradition in Western diplomacy that an effective diplomat should be a two-way interpreter. He must present his own government's policy forcefully to the government to which he is accredited and defend the essential interests of his country. If he is to give intelligent advice to his government, he must also develop a keen insight into the policies of the government with which he deals, and become skilled in distinguishing basic interests and sentiments which it cannot disregard from secondary ones which it may adjust or limit for the broader purpose of reaching agreement. Occasionally, as instanced by Woodrow Wilson's criticism of Walter Hines Page, it has seemed as if individual ambassadors become too much penetrated by the viewpoint and interests of the country to which they were sent and less able to press contrary views of their own governments.

No such problem of delicate balance in functions arises to plague the Soviet negotiator. This has been especially true since the great purge of the Commissariat of Foreign Affairs in 1938–9 and the replacement of Litvinov by Molotov in 1939. The new foreign affairs staff was recruited among the middle ranks of Soviet officials, whose entire training had been based on rigid adherence to centralized decisions and who had rarely had informal contacts with life outside the Soviet Union. The present-day Soviet representative can hardly be called a "negotiator" in the customary sense. He is rather treated as a mechanical mouthpiece for views and demands formulated centrally in Moscow, and is deliberately isolated from the impact of views, interests, and sentiments which influence foreign governments and peoples. Probably the Soviet representative abroad, through fear of being accused of "falling captive to imperialist and cosmopolitan influences," serves as a block to the transmission of foreign views and sentiments, rather than as a channel for communicating them to his government.

This does not mean that Moscow is cut off from the flow of public opinion materials from abroad. On the contrary, it probably receives a very large volume of material, especially clippings of all kinds. On occasion Andrei Vyshinskii quotes triumphantly from some small local newspaper or some relatively obscure "public figure" to prove that the "ruling circles" in the United States are hatching some "imperialist," "warmongering" plot. This practice arouses bewilderment or uneasy merriment in American listeners, whose ears are attuned to the cacophony of conflicting views. In the Soviet way of thinking, the citing of such sources is perfectly logical since it is assumed that nothing happens "accidentally" and therefore all expressions of opinion are of equal value in exposing the underlying pattern of hostile intention. Incidentally, the diligent Soviet gathering of opinion data appears to rely primarily upon newspapers and their editorial expressions; from the indirect evidence available it seems that very little attention is paid to radio material and to the much more potent role of radio commentators in molding the thinking of the public.

The large amount of opinion material imported daily from abroad appears to be analyzed and digested in Moscow with two purposes in mind. One is to prove that, despite protestations of humanitarian and peace-loving intentions, the adversary is actually preparing an aggressive war of conquest. Thus, isolated expressions of a willingness to go to war in the near future or statements of ability to wage war are gladly built up into a confirmation of the "imperialist" and "aggressive" aims of the "ruling circles" in the United States. Other material is cited to prove that "the broad masses" in the enemy country are opposed both to war and to all preparation for defense, but are thwarted in giving effect to their attitude by the "dictatorship of big capital."

Some students of Soviet policy believe—in my opinion, far too hopefully—that this two-fold use of foreign press material is directed primarily towards molding public opinion within the Soviet Union, in satellite or, rather, "captive" states, and among the Communist or Communist-influenced faithful elsewhere, and that the Soviet leaders at the center of power have available an objective and factual analysis of foreign events and currents of opinion as a basis for their decisions. No doubt, the Politburo has available many facts and reports which do not enter into the controlled flow of information available to their subjects. And on occasion Stalin, less often Molotov or Vyshinskii, has shown an awareness of facts or opinions widely known abroad yet not imparted to their own people. On more rare occasions they have shown a willingness to make small concessions to those interests, alien as they are to the Soviet way of thinking.

At Potsdam President Truman and Secretary Byrnes presented with great earnestness the resentment felt by Americans at the complete censorship which was being exercised over news reporting from the former German satellites—Hungary, Rumania, and Bulgaria—with the connivance or by the orders of the Soviet occupation authorities. They protested that, since the United States was among the victors and was represented on the Allied Control Commissions, American opinion could not understand why American correspondents were prevented from reporting freely on developments in those countries. While Generalissimus Stalin undoubtedly continued to regard conscientious Western correspondents as "spies" and as a nuisance to be tolerated as little as possible, he accepted President Truman's arguments based on the power position of the victor and agreed, after relatively unacrimonious dispute, to the United States proposal for assuring Western correspondents of freedom to gather and transmit news from the three satellites. The leader of the Soviet regime could accept the Western contentions in this matter, particularly as they left untouched the central power positions of Soviet policy, while subordinate agents would have felt impelled, in harmony with the Soviet concept of centralized manipulation of "opinion," to reject them with vehement accusations of ill will.

In opening negotiations with any Soviet representatives except Stalin, the first problem is to discover whether the representatives have any instructions at all. To discover what (if any) those instructions are, requires sitting out the whole course of the negotiation, with its demands, insults, and rigidities and its always uncertain outcome. By comparison, Western representatives are often allowed to exercise a certain amount of discretion. They may facilitate the ultimate attainment of a workable compromise—a generally shared goal of both sides—by giving their "opposite number" some fairly clear intimation of the "hard" and "soft" spots in their instructions. A still further development of this flexible approach to the desired goal of adjustment, one based on a high level of intergovernmental and interpersonal trust, is to discuss in detail, at various stages in their formulation, instructions which are in process of preparation. For example, a staff officer may be able to tell his counterpart what recommendations on a given matter he proposes to make to his superiors and similarly to learn what ones will be made by his "opposite number" in the other government; if his recommendations are overruled "higher up," no reproach is made to him and no official reference can be made to his confidence.

A thorough knowledge on both sides of the respective instructions as they are being worked out enhances the mutual understanding of the interests and forces which underly the positions taken, eliminates many secondary points of friction and leaves the larger unagreed issues in clearer view. This pattern of "continuous" negotiation, preceding and following the principal and formal negotiation, requires continuing consultation and reporting on at least three levels—the expert or "recommending and drafting" level, the intermediate or "assistant secretary" level, and, finally, the "ministerial" level. Where, in addition to the ministry of foreign affairs, various other ministries or executive departments, dealing with military, financial, and other matters, are also concerned, there may emerge parallel three-level consultations with those departments on the same informal basis.

A similarly informal and highly effective approach is provided by the "working party," a technique which was first cultivated within the British civil service to deal with interdepartmental problems below the level of the cabinet and the cabinet secretariat, and which has been applied very successfully in interallied and even wider international negotiations. Under the "working party" technique the staffs of experts are given a broadly stated problem to work out, on which each national staff brings to bear a broad picture of the aims and interests of its own government. In the course of its work, facts are established, alternative solutions are considered, and an agreed recommendation may be reached, for presentation to the principal negotiators on both sides. Under this procedure the various staffs operate as experts as much or more than as national representatives, and it is understood that neither side is bound by anything said or tentatively drafted until the report and recommendations as a whole have been considered and approved "at a political level."

These and similar techniques or habits of "continuous negotiation" provide the daily adjustment or lubrication of policy among like-minded and like-purposed Western powers. They are, of course, not practiced by the Soviet government in its dealings with the West. Soviet experts and diplomats cannot participate in an informal day-to-day exchange of information, comments, and tentative recommendations concerning policy. Until Moscow has sent instructions they can say nothing at all, for they may fail to express the exact nuance of thinking or intention which has not yet been formulated at the center, and transmitted to them. After Moscow has spoken they can only repeat the exact formulation given to them, and no variation may be introduced into it unless Moscow has sent the necessary further instructions. The Western habit of continuous negotiation is baffling to the Soviet diplomats, who cannot understand that their Western colleagues have both the opportunity and the responsibility for presenting and even advocating policies within their own governmental operations and that, within a broadly agreed pattern of interests and purposes, they have considerable leeway in finding the most effective, and usually informal, methods of influencing their "opposite numbers" in foreign ministries or embassies.

The frequently noted woodenness of Soviet negotiation apparently applies in relations with satellite or captive regimes, at least with their governments. Thus President (then Premier) Gottwald, outwardly the principal leader of the Communist party of Czechoslovakia, was called on the carpet in Moscow, in early July 1947. He was told by Stalin in person that his government must withdraw its acceptance of the invitation to participate in the conference which was about to meet in Paris to prepare the groundwork for the Marshall Plan of economic aid to European economic recovery. Gottwald had assumed that the government of Czechoslovakia was free to accept this invitation and that the Communist members of the cabinet were free to vote for its acceptance. His dismay, on being confronted with Stalin's absolute and vehement veto, points to the absence, at least at that time, of informal daily exchanges between the two governments. Similarly, the period preceding the June 1948 break between Moscow and Belgrade was clearly marked by the failure of informal communication between Soviet and Yugoslav policy makers as well as by the failure of the Soviet embassy to inform Moscow of the probable effects of an attempt to overthrow the leadership of Marshal Tito.

The important network of informal communication among the Western powers, as well as the moderate latitude given to their representatives, makes for a swift pace of negotiation which arouses bewilderment and suspicion among their Soviet colleagues. Since Western foreign ministries are receiving daily a flow of confidential comment on foreign views and intentions, they are forearmed with current analyses and can often give necessary decisions rapidly. Western diplomats also have a substantial latitude to work out agreed positions and drafts, at least on secondary and procedural matters. Thus, their minor differences are often resolved with what seems to their Soviet colleagues like suspicious speed.

Not believing in or not understanding the system of informal communication and limited individual latitude, the Soviet representatives readily fall back on the theory of "American dictation." It is easier for them to assert that the United States government has exerted political, military, and financial pressure to force its will upon other governments than to take the trouble to analyze the complex and, to them, unfamiliar and unbelievable system of informal communication which usually lies behind the "automatic majorities" assembled around United States proposals. They are incredulous when told that such pressure is exerted only rarely and that more often agreement is reached through give and take of views, by which no side gets its full position and each gets a part of it.

Sometimes the sole instructions with which a Soviet delegation enters a conference are that it is not to commit itself to anything or sign anything. Oddly enough, the outcome may be fairly pleasant and even profitable. When the British and American governments decided to call a conference, held at Bretton Woods, for the creation of postwar institutions of financial and economic co-operation, the Soviet government at first decided to refrain from participation in it. Probably it saw, at best, no direct gain to itself through setting up international machinery to promote monetary stability and the flow of international investment. At the worst, in accordance with the Soviet philosophy of history, it must have regarded such efforts as a futile and undesirable attempt to stave off the long-predicted "general crisis of capitalism." When the Soviet government received the intimation that its refusal even to attend the Bretton Woods Conference would discourage the tenderly nurtured growth of inter-Allied co-operation and would provide Goebbels with valuable propaganda material, it reversed its position regarding participation in the conference, but not with respect to joining in arrangements and obligations which might emerge from it, and sent a small but able delegation.

Having no direct responsibility for the outcome and probably having no need to annoy "the center" in Moscow with requests for instructions, members of the Soviet delegation could devote their very considerable ingenuity to helping the progress of the conference, by making many minor but useful suggestions as they went along.

The usual experience with "uninstructed" Soviet delegations has been the reverse of this. In some negotiations it became clear, after delivery by it of numerous charges and accusations, that the Soviet delegation had no instructions except to "report back." In 1944, with the beginning of the liberation of western Europe, it became urgent to make provision for the orderly restoration of inland transportation, both by land and water, and it was hoped that these provisions would be applicable to all European belligerents except the Soviet Union and the United Kingdom. Some countries had been stripped of rolling stock and barges; others held plundered equipment in large quantities. Undestroyed repair facilities would be very unevenly distributed upon the cessation of hostilities; some countries would have considerably more than the necessary minimum of new rails, rolling stock and bridging material, while others would have none at all. And efficient allocation of urgently needed materials, which Great Britain, Canada, and the United States were preparing to supply, required the establishment of some European-wide agency for arriving at agreed but voluntary decisions on these matters. During the greater part of 1944 American, British, and Soviet delegations negotiated in London for the establishment of an emergency European Inland Transport Organization.

At least the American and British delegations negotiated with each other and with the Soviet delegation, with great zeal and energy, but the Soviet delegation failed to "negotiate back." The Western representatives explained over and over again that not only each great power but each member government would be free to accept or reject the recommendations of EITO, but that it was hoped that agreed recommendations, based on a joint study of the facts, would usually be reached. The Soviet delegates reiterated endlessly that their government could not agree to leave these decisions to any experts. Obviously, the concept that governments would merely ratify the "decisions" reached by experts was both unfamiliar and inconceivable to them. While the Western negotiators felt that the "European" character of the proposed organization was a positive factor, the Soviet delegates seemed to regard it with great suspicion, which was merely confirmed when the British delegation expressed a hope that currently neutral countries would also join EITO after the conclusion of hostilities. As the discussions with the Russians continued, the American and British drafts were clarified and gradually began to merge into a single draft, more or less by attrition. Naturally, this only increased the uneasiness of the Russians, who could not conceive of any representative daring to modify the sacrosanct text which had been handed down to him.

Days and weeks went by with constant meetings. When the Soviet representatives criticized some aspect of the American or British draft, the other delegations promptly offered some revision which appeared likely to meet that particular criticism. So many versions of the various articles flew around the table that the Russian interpreter was frankly unable to render them to his own delegation. Without attempting to grasp the fine nuances as between successive drafting texts the Soviet delegate proceeded to repeat this or that general criticism, accusation, or suspicion after each one of them. Firm in a consciousness both of good intentions and of a practical, functional approach to a vital problem, the Western delegates urged on their Soviet colleagues the importance of the early creation of EITO, in order that it could begin urgently needed planning for the recovery of the transportation system.

To this the Russian representative blandly retorted that "planning" was not possible under capitalism, anyway.

After several weeks of "negotiation" the American delegation came to the conclusion that the Soviet delegation was unable to present any proposals of its own or to accept any British or American proposals. On the other hand it was free to raise and repeat any number of criticisms of the other drafts, provided it did not allow itself to be pinned down to approval of any individual provision or textual wording. It was clear that the Soviet delegation had long since given up any effort to record in Russian or to transmit to its own government any of the numerous modified drafts which had been submitted by the other two delegations during the course of the negotiation. It was quite probable that the Soviet delegation had been hustled off to London with no proposals to present and with no detailed instructions except to report back. Once in London, its members were probably too timid to make any recommendations or even to ask for new instructions, and in Moscow the few people who were qualified to handle a question of this kind were too busy with matters of direct Soviet interest, such as transforming the Lublin Committee into the government of Poland or negotiating the Soviet terms for the armistice with Rumania, to bother their heads or Stalin's head about EITO.

What could be done about this impasse? In relations between Western countries, questions could be asked informally between middle-ranking members of an embassy and members of the foreign office; within a few days intentions could be clarified and decisions taken. Since the Soviet system permits communication only at the top and since the "top-level" channels of communication were badly overloaded with more urgent military and political questions, the negotiators for EITO had to find some way to "muddle through."

My own analysis of the situation was that the Soviet

delegation would report to its own government only when it had firm American and British proposals to transmit. Instead of devoting their full effort to persuading the Soviet delegation to take a position, which it was not empowered to do, the two Western delegations should now work out their differences and arrive at an agreed draft. But they should do this in front of the Russians, since otherwise the latter would regard Anglo-American consensus as a conspiracy against themselves. In arriving at a single draft the two delegations should take reasonable account of the various general Soviet objections and should point out to the Soviet delegation that they were doing so. The agreed draft should provide fully for Soviet adherence, then or in the future, to EITO, but it should provide for its coming into force without Soviet participation after a waiting period. If it required Soviet participation in order to come into force, and if the Soviet government saw no direct benefit for itself in joining it, it would block the entire agreement merely by not answering various notes and *démarches*. On the other hand, every effort should be made to secure Soviet participation since Soviet refusal would also mean that the Soviet zone in Germany and the countries occupied by the Soviet armies would also refrain from joining this useful co-operative effort. However, on balance it seemed that the Soviet government would be more likely to join EITO if it saw that the other Allies were prepared, eventually, to go ahead without it, after taking every precaution to keep the Soviet government informed at each point in the negotiation.

Neither the full hopes nor the entire fears which inspired the EITO negotiators were fulfilled. The question of Soviet participation dragged along until the Potsdam Conference of July 1945. Then, in one of the occasional moments of good feeling between the storms, the British delegation raised the question and urged Soviet participation in EITO. After some whispered consultations, in which Mr. Vyshinskii was seen to shake his head with some vigor despite an effort at impassivity, Generalissimus Stalin turned back to the table, and without further discussion or questions announced that the Soviet government would join EITO. This step, however, did not result in the Soviet government relaxing its demands for rolling stock, equipment, barges, tugs, cranes, repair tools, and so forth, in countries occupied or "liberated" by it; it also contributed nothing in the question of whether Germany would be treated as an economic unit or whether the Soviet zone would, as turned out to be the case, be regarded solely as a Soviet appendage.

By far the most frequent situation is one in which the Soviet negotiators are bound by detailed instructions rigidly pressed. Each point at issue, large or small, then becomes a test of will and nerves. Instead of striving to reduce the number of points of friction and to isolate and diminish the major conflicts of interest, the Soviet negotiator often appears to his exasperated Western colleague to take pride in finding the maximum number of disputes and in dwelling on each of them to the full. Even during the wartime period of relative cooperation, it was noticeable that each decision to convene a three-power conference was followed by the piling up of disputes and grievances, as well as by the rapid fabrication of Soviet accomplished facts. Thus the decision to hold the Yalta Conference was followed swiftly by the unilateral Soviet recognition of the Lublin Committee as the legitimate government of Poland. While arrangements were being made to hold the Potsdam Conference, at which Poland's territorial gains in the west would presumably be determined by three-power decision, the Soviet government proceeded to turn over to Polish administration a large part of the Soviet zone. This action was, of course, an assertion of the Soviet Union's exclusive role in eastern Europe, in disregard of a political agreement to determine the western boundary of Poland jointly, and in violation of the three-power agreement defining the zones of occupation in Germany.

The closely related technique of playing up grievances was also well illustrated at Potsdam. Bitter and prolonged Soviet attacks upon the presence of British troops in Greece, the Dodecanese, Syria, and Lebanon took up much time and energy. When the Western negotiators had been worn down by these wrangles the Soviet negotiators could face with greater equanimity the American and especially the British protests against the brutal assertion of Soviet hegemony in Hungary, Rumania, and Bulgaria. By their tactics the Soviet leaders had encouraged their militant supporters in Greece, had upheld their reputation for hostility to "colonialism" in the Middle East, and had fought off any co-ordinated Western program for loosening their grip on the three satellites.

At the same time, without fanfare, they secured what at the time promised to be a long extension of the occupation of Iranian Azerbaijan. In 1942, when the Soviet Union and Britain had promised Iran to withdraw their troops from Iranian soil "six months after the conclusion of hostilities," the Soviet Union had been at war with Germany and not with Japan. At Potsdam, when the Soviet Union was still not at war with Japan, it rejected the British assumption that the six months' period should be counted from the surrender of Germany and insisted, against Western objections, that the period should be counted from the surrender of Japan! The best military advice at the time was that the war with Japan might end late in 1946 or in 1947. By occupying Iranian Azerbaijan for so many additional months, the Soviet forces, which had already cut it off from control by Teheran, could expect to complete the assimilation of this area into the ranks of the "people's democracies." Thus the wrangles over the role of British troops in the eastern Mediterranean had effectively covered up a drastic and unreasonable reinterpretation of an international agreement, made without even consulting Iran, which was a signatory to it.

The treasuring of grievances, real or imaginary, within a cycle of themes for negotiation is paralleled within the individual negotiation by the use of disconcerting ripostes and of accusations of bad faith. One of the most important issues which confronted the Moscow Conference of Foreign Ministers in October 1943 was whether the Czechoslovak government in exile should conclude a twenty-year defensive alliance with the Soviet Union alone, or whether the building of any regional systems of postwar guarantees against a revival of German aggression should be postponed until the three major Allies could resolve the problem by joint decision. As early as February 1942, the Soviet government had proposed twenty-year bilateral treaties of mutual defense against Germany to the Polish, Czechoslovak, and Yugoslav governments in exile. Only the Beneš government had accepted the proposal, and of the three governments concerned it alone was allowed by the Soviet government to return to its homeland, only to be overthrown in its turn by a Communist seizure of power in February 1948. The British and American viewpoint was that this and similar regional problems should be postponed until after the defeat of Germany, until the governments in exile had returned to their countries and had received a direct mandate from their peoples to undertake long-range commitments, and until the postwar system of international security could be worked out on the basis of the contemplated organization of the United Nations.

The Czechoslovak government was eager to cooperate with both East and West and hoped to have the support of both. However, in accordance with military prospects, it looked to the Soviet forces to enable it to return to its country and it had a mandate from the underground at home to accept Soviet support for its postwar security. Enthusiasm for Slav solidarity, Russia's ambiguously encouraging support of Czechoslovakia at the Munich crisis, in contrast to its abandonment by Britain and France, the desire to dissociate itself from the Polish-Soviet territorial dispute and to avoid the kind of internecine struggle which was tearing Yugoslavia apart were factors which encouraged the Beneš government to sign the Soviet alliance. The treaty had been ready in draft form for many months, but Beneš wished to sign it only with the approval of the British and American governments, or at least with their express acquiescence.

It was against this background that the issue was taken up by the Conference of Foreign Ministers, but the issues were not threshed out in detail. Early in the discussion a concrete issue of fact arose between Eden and Molotov. In a conciliatory fashion Eden began by saying, "I may be mistaken, but . . ." Before he could complete his sentence Molotov broke in harshly, "You *are* mistaken." His abrupt riposte was effective. Eden's presentation was disrupted. By this tactic, and by constant accusations that the Western powers were trying to rebuild a *cordon sanitaire* in eastern Europe, Molotov succeeded in evading any probing discussion of the nature and purpose of the Soviet program of building up a security belt of its own and he won British approval and American acquiescence for the first step, the conclusion of the Soviet-Czechoslovak alliance, which was signed at Moscow two months later.

A similar attempt to use accusations of evil intentions to gain a Soviet point occurred during the negotiations of April–July 1945 over the arrangements for the occupation and control of Austria. In planning the zones of occupation the American, British, and French delegations maintained that, as had been arranged in the agreement on zones of occupation in Germany, zonal boundaries should follow existing provincial or *Länder* frontiers. Any other procedure would involve complicated and detailed reshufflings of administrative, police, rationing, housing, and other arrangements. The Soviet delegation, however, refused to follow the precedent which had been applied in the drawing of the German zones and insisted on cancelling all changes in administrative boundaries which had been made since the annexation by Germany in 1938.

The reason was simple enough. The *Land* of Vienna had undergone a long overdue expansion after the *Anschluss.* If the more extended post-1938 *Land* of Vienna were placed under four-power control, the province of Lower Austria, which was to be under Soviet occupation, would be reduced by that much in area, population, and resources. It must be said, in all fairness, that the Western position was genuinely based on the factor of administrative convenience and was not motivated directly by a desire to constrict the area of Soviet control. However, this was probably not appreciated by the Soviet negotiators, as the Western delegations were also insisting, and insisted successfully after many weeks of heated discussions, on rejecting the Soviet demand to occupy large parts of Styria and Carinthia and on limiting the Soviet zone to Lower Austria and Burgenland.

During the long and tedious debates over the question of adopting the pre-1938 or post-1938 boundaries of the *Land* of Vienna, the favored argument of the Soviet delegation was that by urging the use of the post-1938 provincial boundary the United States representative "was promoting fascism." After hearing the changes rung on this charge for several sessions and many hours I calmly pointed out that, unlike certain other governments, my government had not given political recognition to the Nazi seizure of Austria, that the Allied authorities in Austria would have enough to do in effecting the separation of Austria from Germany and in eradicating Nazism without wasting time in reshuffling minor administrative boundaries, and that I was unmoved by the charge of "promoting fascism" since I was on record as having pointed out the warlike and aggressive dangers of German fascism as early as 1930. This particular argument was thereupon dropped by the Soviet delegation, a factor which helped to improve the tone and quality of later deliberations on the arrangements for Austria. In the end the agreement established the *Land* of Vienna within its narrower pre-1938 boundaries, but it did so only in return for numerous concessions which were made by the Soviet delegation from its original and hard-fought demands.

During the course of negotiation it is often clear that the Soviet representatives are under compulsion to try for a certain number of times to secure each Soviet point, no matter how minor. After trying up to a certain limit and finding that the demand cannot be put through, the Soviet representative has often given in, only to turn to the next item in dispute, over which a similarly prolonged period of deadlock ensues. What is not clear, however, is whether the number or duration of these tries has been prescribed in advance by instruction or whether it is left to the judgment of the individual Soviet negotiator to decide when he has built up a sufficiently impressive and protective record of having beat his head against a stone wall.

A good example of the head-against-stone-wall technique developed rather early in the negotiations of 1945–6 over the Yugoslav-Italian boundary. At the first meeting of the Council of Foreign Ministers, held at London in September 1945, almost the only item of agreement was a brief instruction to the deputies to the effect that the boundary "should be in the main the ethnic line leaving a minimum under alien rule." When the deputies began their work at Lancaster House in January 1946, the Soviet delegation began a strong campaign, lasting for some six weeks of almost daily argument, to remove the words, "in the main." The issue was fought over in long meetings of the four-power Commission for the Investigation of the Yugoslav-Italian Boundary, and from there it was carried into long, numerous, and even more tense meetings of the deputies.

The three words which aroused Soviet ire were extremely important. If the boundary was to follow "the ethnic line," it would reach the sea between Monfalcone and Trieste, leaving Trieste with its large Italian majority and the coastal strip of western Istria within Yugoslavia. In the triangle Monfalcone-Gorizia-Trieste the ethnic boundary between Italian and Slovene villages is clearly marked and has hardly varied in several hundreds of years. On the other hand, if the boundary was to be "in the main the ethnic line," the commission would have to give considerable weight to the claims of the Italian majorities in Trieste and in the coastal strip of Istria, offsetting against them the Slovene national character of several small villages in the coastal strip between Monfalcone and Trieste. If the words "in the main" were omitted it was hardly necessary to send out an investigating commission at all, with its attendant wave of turbulence, terrorization, kidnappings, and murders, and the "ethnic line," pure and simple, could be drawn in Lancaster House.

During the weeks of intensive debate, tension mounted around the green-topped table. As usual, Soviet intransigence turned the dispute into a test of staying power. In view of the fact that public opinion still continued to regard any failure to reach speedy agreement with the Soviet government as primarily the fault of American or British "reactionaries," rather than attributing any part of it to the "all-or-nothing" Soviet attitude, it was not clear how long the Western delegations would hold out against the Soviet demand that the boundary issue be prejudged one hundred per cent in favor of the Soviet position. In an effort to win the Soviet delegation over to a compromise, the Western delegations offered to remove from the purview of the boundary commission Fiume, the islands of Quarnero and the primarily Yugoslav-inhabited parts of Venezia Giulia; they did insist that the formula "in the main" be retained and that the commission be free to investigate the Italian and mixed areas within the region. Finally, "enough was enough," even for Soviet negotiators enamored of indefinite repetition, and the deputies suspended their meetings without agreement on the terms of reference.

Now, at last, the Soviet delegation had, reluctantly, to inform Moscow that the Western deputies refused to budge on this basic issue of rewriting the formula which had been approved by the Council of Foreign Ministers. This put up to the Soviet government the question of taking the responsibility for an indefinite deadlock in the negotiation of the peace treaties. After two days of marking time the Soviet delegation asked to have a meeting of the deputies and proceeded, without apparent resentment, to approve the final Western-backed version of the commission's terms of reference, retaining the key words, "in the main the ethnic line." One basic factor in the Soviet decision to recede from its stubbornly pressed demand must have been that Anglo-American forces were stationed in Trieste, Pola, and the Isonzo valley. If Yugoslav or Soviet forces had been in possession the deadlock would probably have been allowed to continue indefinitely.

While Western representatives are usually given some leeway to negotiate and always may refer back to their governments with recommendations and suggestions which, they believe, may advance their task, they can sometimes arouse a sympathetic response, on minor matters, in their Soviet colleagues by making it clear that there are certain points on which they cannot budge. A situation of this kind arose during the discussions of 1944 in London concerning the terms of the armistice with Bulgaria. After the Soviet Union had declared war on Bulgaria and its troops had occupied the country, the initiative in drafting the terms of the armistice passed to the Soviet delegation to the European Advisory Commission. The Russian representatives now argued for extremely favorable terms for the Bulgarians, although the latter had inflicted great and needless sufferings on both Greece and Yugoslavia. It was clear that the Soviet negotiators considered every gain for Bulgaria, which they now regarded as a Soviet client, as a gain for the Soviet Union.

In particular, the Soviet representatives strongly opposed any suggestion that the Bulgarians, who were then eating very well and had, over the last few months, accumulated large supplies of foodstuffs which could no longer be shipped to Germany because of the breakdown in transportation, should be required to deliver reparations. On the other hand, all of Greece was suffering severely from lack of foodstuffs—some parts were on the verge of acute starvation—and the situation was serious in many parts of Yugoslavia. In order to provide a bare minimum of food, very tight Allied supplies and shipping were being diverted to Greece, and of course American, British, and Canadian taxpayers were meeting the bill for this aid. The Soviet negotiators brushed aside all these considerations, based on the community of the Allied war effort, and argued that since Bulgaria had declared war on Germany and was now fighting on the side of the Allies, it was wrong to discourage its new-found zeal by requiring the payment of reparations even through deliveries in kind. No such consideration had prevented the Soviet government, a few weeks before, from imposing vast and indefinite obligations of reparation and restitution upon Rumania, whose defection to the Allied side was a genuinely important contribution to the war against Germany.

Finding that debate around the table failed to budge the Soviet representatives, I sought them out for a private talk. I explained that if Bulgaria escaped the payment of all reparations in kind the burdens of the American government would be increased by just that much, that approval and review by the Congress of all appropriations was a basic part of our governmental procedure, that failure to impose on Bulgaria the payment of reparations might lead to an investigation, and that I might then be punished. At the word "punished," a sympathetic gleam of understanding came into the eyes of my Soviet colleagues, and on the following day they agreed to insert the provision for payment of reparation in kind into the terms of the armistice. It is hardly necessary to record that, in any case, the enforcement of the terms of the armistice lay primarily in the hands of "the Allied (Soviet) High Command" in Bulgaria, and that, according to one report, for the authenticity of which I cannot vouch, Bulgarian deliveries to Greece under the terms of the armistice amounted to one broken-down wagon and two slat-ribbed cows!

One of the main pitfalls in wartime Anglo-American negotiations with the Soviet Union was the tendency to rely upon reaching an "agreement in principle," without spelling out in sufficient detail all the steps in its execution. After long and strenuous debates, studded with charges, accusations, and suspicions, it was undoubtedly a great relief to reach a somewhat generally worded agreement and to go home. Prodded by manifold public and party duties, anxious to prove to themselves and to their people that current agreements and postwar co-operation with the Soviet government were genuinely possible, facing "deadlines" with regard to the expectations of legislatures and of public opinion, the Western leaders often approached these negotiations under serious disadvantages. Wooed rather than the wooer, able to deal at leisure with the manipulation of their public opinion at home, facing no deadlines, the Soviet leaders had many advantages. In this situation the Western powers sometimes gained the "principle" of their hopes, only to find that "in practice" the Soviet government continued to pursue its original aims.

At Yalta the Soviet government agreed, after very lengthy argument and stubborn resistance, to participate in a reconstruction of the Polish government which would, it appeared, permit the survival of some political freedom for the great non-Communist majority of the people. By delays and quibblings over the execution of the "agreement in principle" during the next few months, the Soviet government secured about ninety per cent of the original position with which it had come to Yalta and thus strengthened beyond challenge the small Communist minority in its dominant control of the country. At Yalta the Soviet government also agreed, in return for sweeping territorial and other concessions, to deal only with the Chinese National government as the representative of China. By turning over territory, administration, and Japanese arms to Chinese Communist forces, the Russians nullified, in the areas where their forces were dominant, the principal and vital *quid pro quo* which they had promised at Yalta. When British, Canadian, and American negotiators come to an "agreement in principle," they often haggle to a fare thee well over the implementation of an arrangement which may still be distasteful to each of them. However, they remain within the framework of the principle to which they have agreed, or else they frankly ask to reopen the "agreement in principle" and to renegotiate it on the grounds that further consideration has shown that they cannot carry it out. It has remained for the Soviet representatives to assert that they are carrying out an "agreement in principle" by doing just the reverse "in practice."

Except for a scant handful of legal consultants who were trained in general jurisprudence and international law prior to the great revolution of 1927–9 in Soviet academic life, Soviet representatives usually show little comprehension of the legal problems which arise in seeking agreements among nations, or in meeting the constitutional requirements of democratic states, and special obstacles have arisen not infrequently from this cause. During the Paris sessions of the Council of Foreign Ministers there was one amusing instance of this difficulty. The Soviet delegation appeared rather puzzled over the presence of Senator Tom Connally and the late Senator Arthur H. Vandenberg among the

American delegation. Senator Vandenberg upset them particularly. After some especially outrageous tirade by Molotov, he would take his unsmoked cigar from his mouth and grin across the table most engagingly, as if to say: "Well, well, that *is* a new angle!"

One afternoon, as we were leaving the conference hall for tea, a member of the Soviet delegation, taking me by the arm, asked, after one or two hurried preliminaries, why the Senators were there. I quickly gave him a three-minute sketch of the background and working of the bipartisan foreign policy and explained that the peace treaties, on which the council was working, could be ratified by the President only upon the advice and consent of the Senate, and of two thirds of the Senate, at that. And since (using Soviet terms for clarity) American parties were "undisciplined," affirmative action by the Senate would require approval and support by influential leaders of both parties. My Soviet colleague was frankly amazed to learn of this responsibility of the Senate. "You don't mean that the Senate would refuse to ratify a treaty that your government had signed?" he asked. To that I could only reply that the Senate had often refused to act at all or had acted negatively on treaties negotiated and submitted to it by the executive.

In 1944, in the work of the European Advisory Commission, a difficult legal problem arose during the preparation of the instrument of unconditional surrender which was to be imposed by the three, later four, powers at the time of the final surrender of the German government and the German High Command. Should those forces which would be surrendered in this final act, in distinction from those who surrendered or were captured during hostilities, be declared prisoners-of-war, or not? After detailed discussions with military and legal experts the American and British delegations were instructed to oppose declaring such German and other enemy personnel to be prisoners-of-war, while the Soviet government insisted that they be so declared.

From the American and British viewpoint there was a whole series of difficulties involved in this. The final surrender might suddenly place from three to six million German armed personnel in their custody, with the legal requirement to furnish them with food, housing, clothing, and medical care according to the respective standards applied by the American and British armies to their own troops on a garrison footing. This was not physically, financially, or politically feasible. Furthermore, in the unprecedented situation in which Germany would cease to be a sovereign state there was no way of knowing how long this tremendous burden might continue. It would also mean that the legally necessary provision for the German forces would place them in a greatly favored position as against the liberated populations of our own Allies in Europe. Finally, there was considerable legal doubt as to whether a prisoner-of-war could be tried for war crimes aside from the previously established crimes of war. It was clear that the Soviet Union was faced by no such difficulties. Its personnel had been subjected by the Nazis to great cruelty and even to mass extermination, and it was not bound by any international conventions in its treatment of German prisoners taken during or at the close of hostilities.

For some five months this problem was a serious block in the way of completing an agreed instrument of unconditional surrender. The Soviet delegation insisted day after day that the German forces must be declared prisoners-of-war. The American and British delegations explained over and over again why they were unwilling to do this, though they were willing, and proposed fairly early in the negotiation, that provision be made that each of the three, later four, Commanders in Chief be free to declare or not to declare prisoners-of-war those German forces which came under control at the final surrender. In attacking both the position of the two Western delegations and the compromise which they had offered, the Soviet representatives continually accused the latter of "promoting German militarism," "fostering Nazism," and so forth.

Finally, Soviet consent to the proposed compromise formula was secured by drawing up a fairly detailed statement of the difficulties which the Soviet proposal raised, translating it into Russian, and persuading the Soviet delegation to send it to Moscow, despite the reluctance of the Soviet negotiators to appear even to question the correctness of their original instructions to which they had held so stubbornly. Even at the very end the Soviet delegation remained unconvinced that there was any real legal difficulty involved for the Western powers but were persuaded finally that there was "nothing bad" in this final compromise for the Soviet position.

In this as in numerous other instances Soviet negotiators, even when under some pressure to reach agreement, have shown that they are in mortal terror of violating any part, minor or major, of their instructions, and are extremely reluctant to report to Moscow that they cannot get every point and every wording in their own drafts. Making recommendations for even slight changes in their instructions exposes them to serious risks. It means that they consider their own superiors slightly less than omniscient. It may mean that they can be accused of giving undue weight to the viewpoint of another government and thus of "falling captive to imperialist insinuations." The result is that, even when, in a given question, the Soviet negotiator is committed to the desirability of achieving agreement, he is unable to take any initiative in finding a reasonable meeting ground of viewpoints and he is usually extremely reluctant even to present to his own government suggestions for compromise or reconciliation of differences which originate in other delegations.

A widespread lack of ease in using English or French commonly adds a good deal to the difficulties of the Soviet negotiator. Russian linguists have done pioneer work in the development of effective teaching of languages. Most of the newer methods which have been developed in the United States during and since the war for the intensive teaching of languages were familiar twenty years ago in the best Soviet institutes. But relatively few Soviet representatives abroad have received adequate training in languages at a sufficiently early age, and almost none have had the experience of living informally in a foreign culture at an impressionable period of their development. Since the great purge of the Soviet foreign service at the end of the 1930's, the staff has been recruited primarily from among administrators and engineers, with a sprinkling of professors. Until they entered upon their new careers the newer Soviet diplomats had no need or incentive to learn a foreign language effectively, and once entered upon it they have no time or permission to relax and absorb not only a language but the culture or way of thought which is expressed in mastering it. This places a special burden on foreign negotiators to phrase their proposals and texts in a form which can be rendered exactly into Russian, if they wish their own positions to be understood.

Russian, particularly in its Soviet usage, lends itself even less readily than English to the disciplined clarity of French, the unequalled language of diplomacy. Dictionary renditions are often downright misleading. According to dictionaries and pre-Soviet usage, *predlagat'* means "to propose"; in Soviet usage, carried over from Communist party practice, it means "to direct," to give an instruction which cannot be disobeyed. On occasion I have seen a Soviet negotiator fall into a rage because an inoffensive "propose" was turned into *predlagat'* in the translation. The word *soyuz* in Russian means both an "alliance" between two independent states and a complete "union" into a single state. *Blagorazumnyi* is as near as Russian comes to "reasonable," and the Russian word has none of the overtones or undertones of its English meaning.

The Russian word *vlast'* is usually rendered as "authority," but *vlast'* connotes a complete power of disposal, not a limited "authority." This difficulty was illustrated in an abortive attempt, in April 1945, to negotiate an agreement concerning the future status of Allied newspaper and radio correspondents in Germany. The key provision of a draft agreement, which had been drawn up in the War Department for negotiation in the European Advisory Commission, was that the correspondent was to be subject "to the full authority" of the Commander in Chief who issued credentials to him in his own zone. When I received this draft, with the instruction to begin negotiations at once for its acceptance by the four governments, I pointed out to Washington that in the Soviet interpretation of this provision an American correspondent who entered the Soviet zone could be tried by a secret Soviet court and sentenced by purely administrative procedure to a term in a concentration camp because some article which he had written ten years earlier in America was regarded as "inimical to the security and strength" of the Soviet Union. My objections were overruled and my suggested redraftings, designed to avoid this risk, were brushed aside. I received a peremptory instruction to circulate the draft agreement and to urge its adoption.

For more than fifteen months the Soviet delegation had, time and again, been extremely slow in responding to American and British proposals, and it was usually unable to give any indication of whether it would ever be able to negotiate. In this case, however, Moscow acted with great alacrity. Within less than a week the Soviet delegation indicated that it wished to begin negotiations on the following day on the American draft agreement. It was clear that the Soviet foreign office liked the War Department's draft and that it was ready to accept it with minor changes. With no time for further argument with Washington about the dangerous draft, I wired that I expected to be asked to clarify some of the wording of the draft. If, for example, I should be asked to define "full authority," I proposed to state that its meaning was that the Commander in Chief had "full authority in matters of accrediting and disaccrediting" foreign correspondents in his zone.

A few hours later the European Advisory Commission began its first and only session on the draft agreement. The Soviet representative offered a few minor textual improvements in the American draft and then declared that he was prepared to conclude it at once. It was now my turn to explain that by "full authority" the draft meant only "full authority in matters of accrediting and disaccrediting" correspondents. After this the Soviet representative rapidly lost interest in the draft, and the subject was not discussed again in the commission, which had many other urgent matters to struggle with.

One of the difficulties of Soviet-Russian vocabulary is that the word "compromise" is not of native origin and carries with it no favorable empathy. It is habitually used only in combination with the adjective "putrid." "Compromise for the sake of getting on with the job" is natural to American and British people, but it is alien to the Bolshevist way of thinking and to the discipline which the Communist party has striven to inculcate in its members. To give up a demand once presented, even a very minor or formalistic point, makes a Bolshevik-trained negotiator feel that he is losing control of his own will and is becoming subject to an alien will. Therefore any point which has finally to be abandoned must be given up only after a most terrific struggle. The Soviet negotiator must first prove to himself and his superiors that he is up against an immovable force. Only then is he justified in abandoning a point which plainly cannot be gained and in moving on to the next item, which will again be debated in an cqually bittcr tug of wills.

The Soviet negotiator must try to force the acceptance of his entire proposal. Hence he regards each provision and phrase as equally important. The Bolshevik is trained to feel that ideology must be "monolithic" at any given time, even though it may change from time to time. In one period it may be wrong for a "good Bolshevik" to shave every day and to wear a necktie; at another time he will be reprimanded for neglecting these amenities. The important thing is to have a complete answer to past, present, and future and to insist, against all contrary evidence, that this answer is, always has been, and must ever be, the same. This attitude gives rise to an insistence (absurd to the Westerner) upon periodically rewriting the history of the party, of Russia, and of the world and of rewriting it each time to uphold some new "infallible" dogma.

The Western negotiator is usually able to envisage a series of minor shifts in his own and other positions. He is "pluralistic" in his approach to a solution, in the adjustments of democratic decision making at home and in seeking adjustments of interests and views among nations. The Soviet negotiator is worried, puzzled, scornful, and suspicious when the Western negotiator tries out a series of minor variations to see if the opposing positions cannot be brought closer together. To him it means only that the Western representative was "not serious" in the first place. If he is willing to shift so quickly from his original position it must mean that he did not hold it in earnest to begin with and that he can eventually be forced all the way over to the Soviet position, provided the Soviet negotiator will only display "principled steadfastness" long enough and vigorously enough.

The Western representative tends to assume that a minor concession here or there will facilitate achieving the common aim of co-operative action. He does not necessarily look for an immediate *quid pro quo* for each minor concession. At a later stage in the negotiation his partner will remember the facilitating concession and will yield something in turn. To him "good will" is both a lubricant of the negotiating process and a valuable intangible by-product. The Soviet negotiator takes a minor concession as a sign that his principles are stronger and his will is firmer than those of his opponent. He does not believe in "good will." He is trained to assume the ill will of the "capitalist environment." If an "imperialist" negotiator asserts his will for peace, it means, at the best, that he is consciously in favor of peace but is unconsciously a tool of uncontrollable forces which work for war and for the final clash between "two worlds." At the worst, it means that he is trying to deceive and gain time while mouthing words of "peace." To a Bolshevik even a momentary "loss of vigilance" may have fatal consequences. The Soviet diplomat feels himself like a traveler by night in the forest who must be constantly on the watch for the smallest sound or sight of treachery. He must be unceasingly on guard against his own human tendency to "fall into complacency" and thus to underestimate the dangers which surround both him and the regime which he serves.

Soviet diplomacy is also monolithic in its method of operation and in its reactions to outside events or internal changes of stress. The American practice is to subdivide authority extensively, both at home and in foreign dealings. A military mission in Moscow, trying to work out plans for military co-ordination, would have nothing to say about the arrangements or conditions for lend-lease. A political negotiation, aiming to preserve the freedom of choice for an East European nation, would have no relation to another mission which might be deciding which German ships should be transferred to the Soviet Union, and all of them would have no relation to a decision concerning military and economic aid to China. No such autonomy or fragmentation of authority is felt in the Soviet conduct of its foreign policy. While it is probable that little background information on policy is communicated by Moscow to its representatives abroad, beyond that which they need individually in order to carry out their instructions, it is pretty clear that underlying attitudes are communicated rapidly to them. Thus, a negotiation over the statute of Tangier bogs down in Paris; this may be a repercussion of a crisis which has arisen in Vienna or of a note delivered in Warsaw. Bolshevist mythology is full of "chain-reaction" concepts of causality. With the clumsy force of centralized wisdom it attempts to meet this assumed universal causal interdependence ("nothing is accidental") with its confidence in its own ability to manipulate events in accordance with its own Leninist-Stalinist dialectic, which it regards as a unique instrument for both foreseeing and bringing about the future.

This is a grim picture. The Soviet negotiator is tight as a spring, deeply suspicious, always trying to exert the Soviet will power outward and to avoid reflecting non-Soviet facts and aspirations inward, a rigid agent knowing only the segment of policy which he must carry out with mechanical precision. Does this mean that "negotiation" in any real sense of the term is impossible? Admitting that negotiation under these conditions is a very limited affair and very difficult and unrewarding, it may still be both possible and essential. But it requires a special approach. Naturally, a knowledge of Russian in its Soviet nuances is important. It is equally important to understand the role of the Soviet negotiator in relation to his own government and to its ideology. The Department of State has carried on a far-sighted policy of equipping a substantial number of its representatives through language and area training and through service in missions in the Soviet-dominated areas to deal with Soviet problems, and as these young men mature in experience they will fill an important need. The Army and Air Force have also done a good deal along this line.

In the absence of informal channels of communication with Soviet representatives it is important for an American delegation to be able to determine whether the Soviet negotiators have no instructions, have definite instructions, or merely have instructions to build up a propaganda position. A well-equipped negotiator can go much more thoroughly into the range of Soviet intentions if he follows the discussion in the original, without being handicapped by the opaque veil of translation. In addition he should review each document exchanged or each statement made in the light of its clear rendering into Russian. It is unfortunate, for example, that many American public figures continually speak of the need for an "aggressive policy" to counteract Soviet pressures, when they mean an "energetic" or "vigorous" policy. In Russian "aggressive" means only "intending to commit or engaged in committing aggression," and the colloquial American use of "aggressive" inevitably receives a sinister meaning in Russian translation, which is the form in which documents must be utilized by all but a handful of Soviet negotiators and policy makers.

In conducting negotiations with Soviet representatives it is important to adopt in the beginning a single clear position, one which can be upheld logically and politically during long discussions. The Soviet delegation will not report this position as the final and strongly held one until they have had a chance to attack it from all sides. Indefinite repetition of arguments must be accepted as an inevitable preparation to negotiate. The American negotiator is inclined to make a single presentation and then to become impatient when the Soviet response makes it plain that the Soviet representative either has not understood it or does not believe it. The Soviet negotiator, of course, does not believe what he hears, but he listens for undertones of firmness or uncertainty which tell him whether or not he is shaking the determination of his adversary. Strong but controlled feeling, rather than impatience or anger, is an effective way of giving him his answer to this question. When a position is firmly established it is often advantageous to prepare a special memorandum, accompanied by a clear and idiomatic translation into Russian, in order to be sure that one's own position is adequately reported to Moscow, the only spot at which new instructions are likely to be initiated. Oral statements of position may or may not be reported, but it is probable that every bit of written material is carefully transmitted. If some part of the English memorandum does not lend itself to clear rendering into Russian, it is useful to rewrite the English version until it can be rendered without ambiguity, for while Russian can express any thought, it does not lend itself flexibly to a literal rendering of an English concept or phrase.

Once a position has been worked out, the non-Soviet negotiator must be prepared to uphold it in detail, and for a long time. The technique of constantly trying out variant versions, which works well in the Western style of negotiation, only confuses the Soviet representative, who suspects some new trick in each new variant and must subject each in turn to exhaustive interpretation. Constantly modifying one's position or the way in which it is expressed means also that the Soviet negotiator is at a loss to know what version is based on bedrock and should therefore be reported to Moscow. Even slight shifts in position or wording increase his belief that the adversary's position is a shaky one and thus encourage him to hold out that much longer for the full Soviet position. Western negotiators are usually in a position to accept slight adaptations, but even the slightest variation must be reported back to Moscow for decision there.

Since Western negotiators are generally free, in the light of previous instructions and their knowledge of their governments' over-all policies, to comment at once on new proposals or statements made during the course of negotiation, they often assume that Soviet negotiators have a similar latitude and accordingly press them to express their views. When so pressed, the Soviet negotiator is always free to raise innumerable objections and criticisms. He is not free to express concordance with any part of a proposal on which he has not received instructions from Moscow. Even the "program statements" of Soviet negotiators must be reviewed or written in Moscow before they can be delivered, and therefore Soviet statements at conferences often seem to have little relation to the immediately preceding statements of other delegations.

When a negotiation is actually under way, it is useful to avoid pressing the Soviet delegation to commit itself on a new proposal or draft. During the active negotiations carried on in the European Advisory Commission, whenever a new proposal or even a redraft was first presented, it was my habit to ask questions which would clarify its meaning and implications and then to take the initiative, even if I had adequate instructions, in saying that I would have to consult my government before commenting on it, thus relieving the Soviet delegation of the onus of either declining to comment on it or else of building up a whole series of negative statements against the proposal. Then, on occasions when I had instructions on the new point at issue, I would go at once to the Soviet delegation and inform its members in detail of the American position. This meant that Moscow had before it, at the same time, the proposal and the American position on it. When there was a certain underlying desire to reach agreements, this procedure was often effective, or so it seemed, in reducing the number of divergences by providing full background on the problem before Moscow had taken a firm position, which could later be modified only by a long and exhausting tug of wills. Such informal discussions, conducted in Russian, also offered an occasion for learning or sensing the often unforeseen Russian objections and suspicions and for attempting to remove or alleviate them at an early stage.

When stating a position it is well to be sparing in the use of general or broadly stated principles, and when such principles are an essential part of the position it is necessary to remember that they are not shared by the Soviet negotiator. Broad statements of principle can, however, be effectively anchored in the historic experience of one's own people and, explained in that setting, they can have a certain impact on Soviet thinking. Soviet policy makers may then accept them as a fact which must be taken into account, even though they do not believe in them or share them.

Wherever possible it is more useful to state one's position in terms of a definite material interest, as in the case of the question of Bulgaria's obligation to provide reparation to Greece and Yugoslavia. Soviet-trained negotiators pride themselves on identifying material interests and can therefore more readily visualize them as facts to which a certain adjustment can be made.

This can be illustrated from the problem of the Soviet treatment of American prisoners-of-war who were overrun in the Soviet advance into eastern Germany. Despite the agreement for mutual assistance in collecting, caring for, and repatriating each other's prisoners-of-war, the agreement never received halfway adequate implementation on the Soviet side, and great and unnecessary hardships were inflicted by the Soviet attitude on American and other Western prisoners. The Soviet authorities could not understand that it was a normal and automatic principle, for Americans, to give every possible care, on an American standard, to fellow-countrymen who had been taken captive. Soviet prisoners, overrun by their own armies, were given only the meager standard of care which falls to the lot of the ordinary Soviet population, and in addition they were subjected to special disabilities until they could prove that they had not, in some measure, surrendered voluntarily to the Germans. If the American authorities had emphasized that liberated American prisoners must be well cared for because they were needed immediately in the war against Japan—which was not the case—the Soviet authorities would probably have given much better co-operation in caring for and transporting them, as they would have been impressed by the direct material interest involved.

Is it worthwhile to dwell on these experiences or to

talk about negotiating at all? Even during the wartime alliance against the common menaces of Germany and Japan, negotiations with the Soviet government were extremely difficult and frustrating, and, aside from the advantage of having established the United Nations, even before the end of the war, as a "forum for the opinions of mankind," none of the wartime agreements on postwar co-operation has worked out as was hoped, even against hope. Since the war the Soviet government has striven by all the means in its extensive arsenal to gain and retain every advantage for its side, regardless of the fact that thereby it quickly dissipated a very large reservoir of goodwill and aroused the deep alarm of all nations which lay beyond its direct control. In a period of Soviet expansion and of hope for further expansion, negotiation could have only the purpose of confusing and dividing the nations which opposed its pressure, and since the war the Soviet purpose in negotiating has not been to reach agreements with strong opponents but to intimidate weaker and adjacent countries and to undermine the stamina of its principal potential adversaries.

Protected by two oceans and remote from the direct origins of previous world wars, Americans have been accustomed to ignore the rising storm and then, once it has burst upon them, to work solely for victory over the immediate menace. Thus, they tend to feel a sharp dichotomy between "war" and "peace." When at peace they are reluctant to think of the possibility of war. When at war they concentrate solely on winning the war, as if it were a grim football match, and refuse to worry about the peace which is the goal of war. Through Lenin and Stalin, Soviet thinking has fully absorbed the Clausewitz maxims that national strength and strong alliances determine the effectiveness of national policy in peace, and that in war one must never lose sight of the aims of policy for which it is waged. To the Soviet way of thinking, conflict is inherent in the development of "capitalist" society, and cannot be wished out of existence by "subjective good will."

Within this ongoing history of conflict, however, Soviet tactics and techniques are not inflexible. Soviet policy towards the outside world has varied markedly during the past thirty-four years. True, the outward pressure of Soviet power has marked and seared the post-1945 years and the building of a reliable counterforce is only now under way in Europe. The outline of a similar counterforce cannot yet be discerned in Asia. In Western policy the building of "positions of strength" and the use of negotiation must go hand in hand. Building of strength and negotiating cannot be regarded as alternatives or as opposites. They must be teamed. Negotiation without strength and determination behind it is frustrating, dangerous, and may be suicidal. However, when strength has been built, refusal to negotiate may precipitate a colossal struggle, which would be fought as a cruel civil war in many parts of the world—the very conflict which Western strength is being fashioned to avert.

For the time being negotiation of those issues which are negotiable between the Soviet Union and the West is, generally speaking, in abeyance. But the art of policy will be to recognize, from a position of strength, future potentialities of negotiation, not with an expectation of bringing about a lasting or world-wide relaxation of Soviet ambitions, but as a means of alleviating individual sources of tension and thus of strengthening the free world. And if negotiation must go in harness with consistent and purposeful building of strength, the art and technique of international dealings must also be broadened to take full account of the peculiar character of the Soviet approach to negotiation.

:2:

ASPECTS OF RUSSIAN EXPANSION[1]

[*January 1948*]

INTRODUCTORY NOTE · Delivered first as a public lecture at Brown University, this essay explores rather briefly the commonly held assumption that the expansionism of Moscovite and Imperial Russia and that of the Soviet leadership represent basically the same ambitions, carried out under different ideological banners. This attempt to point up major continuities and contrasts over several centuries is useful if it stirs both author and reader to re-examine traditional Russian and revolutionary Soviet concepts of the political role of universal and national values and goals.

In recent years the complex nature of Soviet and Russian nationalism has been examined in a number of penetrating studies, particularly in *Soviet Russian Nationalism*, by Frederick C. Barghoorn (New York: Oxford University Press; 1956); *The Formation of the Soviet Union; Communism and Nationalism, 1917–1923*, by

[1] The *American Slavic and East European Review*, Vol. VII, No. 3 (October 1948), pp. 197–213. Copyright 1948 by the American Association for the Advancement of Slavic Studies, Inc.

Richard Pipes (Cambridge: Harvard University Press; 1954); *Ukrainian Nationalism, 1939–1945*, by John A. Armstrong (New York: Columbia University Press; 1955); *Literary Policies in the Soviet Ukraine, 1917–1934*, by George S. N. Luckyj (New York: Columbia University Press; 1956); and *Bolshevism in Turkestan, 1917–1927*, by Alexander G. Park (New York: Columbia University Press; 1957). Many problems remain obscure. To what degree has a supranational Soviet nationalism displaced or dulled the separate identities of the non-Russian peoples? How are the fluctuating limits set from above for the permitted expression of national cultures? What are the relations between the dominant Russian or Russianized minorities and the non-Russian peoples who form the majorities in thirteen out of the fifteen Union Republics?

The long and complex interactions among religions, cultures, and nationalities in East Central Europe have been brilliantly illuminated by two recent studies: *The Making of Central and Eastern Europe*, by Reverend František Dvorník (London: Polish Research Centre; 1949); and *Borderlands of Western Civilization, A History of East Central Europe*, by Oskar Halecki (New York: Ronald Press; 1952).

*

RUSSIAN imperialism under various regimes has often been denounced, and rarely praised. Even more seldom has it been defined. It is, in fact, more difficult to define than to condemn. From the beginning, in the 1450's, of the final unification of the Russian principalities around a single center of power—Moscow—the Muscovite state itself was constantly expanding across the East European plain, through the settlement of Russian peasants, and even in this earliest period various non-Russian peoples came under Muscovite rule. At what point does "expansion" end and "imperialism" begin?

One of the greatest of Russian historians, V. O. Kliuchevskii, prefaces his *History of Russia* by stating that "the principal fundamental factor in Russian history has been migration or colonization."[2] But his *History* had little to say about the expansion of Russia.

Rather than attempt to trace the history of Russian expansion century by century, it will perhaps be more fruitful to look at a few of the general characteristics which have left their imprint on this aspect of Russian development. One such striking feature is the absence of any clearly marked geographical boundaries defining the area of national settlement. While the Grand Principality of Moscow included, around 1460, a patchwork of territories lying mainly within two hundred miles of Moscow, it was still subject nominally to a greater and nonnational political entity, the Tartar Empire or Horde. In turn, Moscow controlled a Tartar vassal state of its own, the Tsardom of Kasimov, a buffer between Moscow and Kazan, the Tartar capital. A hundred years later, in the time of Ivan the Terrible, the greatly enlarged Tsardom of Moscow also included the Tartar areas of the middle and lower Volga, while large areas in the west, inhabited by Eastern Slavs of the Orthodox faith, were under Polish rule. Thus one can say that, strictly speaking, there was no period when Russia was both a unified and a purely national state.

The East European plain and its borderlands had historically been the meeting ground and frequently the battleground of several politically organized peoples. Whichever of them had the upper hand dominated the entire area and thus included alien peoples under its rule. The medieval Russian principalities had been under Tartar rule; the Muscovite state then took the place of the western Tartar *ulus*. This background makes it easier to understand that the concept of "one nation one state," which has come in modern times to play such a dominant role in the political feelings of

[2] V. O. Kliuchevskii: A *History of Russia,* (London: Dent & Sons; 1911–31), Vol. 1 (1911), p. 2. For an interesting study of the eastward movement in Russia see R. J. Kerner, *The Urge to the Sea; the Course of Russian History; the Role of Rivers, Portages, Ostrogs, Monasteries and Furs* (Berkeley: University of California Press; 1942).

most other European peoples, holds no special place in the historic memories of the Russian people.

This does not mean that the idea of the Russian people has not been of major importance in the expansion of the state. The national-religious concept of Russia as a distinctive entity was clearly formulated by the last decade of the fifteenth century. At that time the idea of "Moscow the Third Rome," the only independent center of the Orthodox faith, with a special duty to preserve and extend that faith, became a powerful element of official ideology and of popular feeling. This theory, while it served until the time of Peter the Great to justify a policy of excluding foreign cultural influences, was not, basically, a program of territorial expansion, except against Lithuania-Poland. It was much more a defensive weapon designed to eliminate any claim by the Greek Church, which had come under Ottoman control with the fall of Constantinople in 1453, to exert control over what was now, in fact if not yet in form, a fully independent Russian Church. It was at the same time a barrier against the efforts of the Papacy to extend its supremacy over the Russian Church.

The role of the religious factor in the formation of Russian nationality should not be underestimated. Allegiance to the Church was for a long time the test of nationality, particularly in the western borderlands of Russia—the regions which have been so often in dispute between Russia and Poland. It is curious to discover, for example, that in the exchange of populations which has taken place since 1945 between the Soviet Union and Poland, adherence to Catholicism has generally been taken as a token of Polish nationality, and membership in the Orthodox or Uniat churches as evidence of Ukrainian or Belorussian nationality.

Loyalty to the Russian Church and loyalty to the tsar were identical concepts in earlier Russian history. True, the expansion of Russia brought with it toleration of Lutheranism, after part of the Baltic provinces were incorporated under Peter the Great. Under Catherine II a special charter proclaimed toleration for Islam after the Tartars of Crimea were conquered. Yet, the supremacy of the Russian Church remained unchallenged, and it enjoyed many special advantages. Until 1905 persons of other religions could be converted to Orthodoxy, but it was forbidden for a person baptized in the Orthodox faith to pass to another religion. Proselytizing on behalf of Orthodoxy was an important though not always zealously performed function of the Church. In winning converts to Orthodoxy, the Church was adding to the numbers of those who were directly bound to the tsar, not only by the duty of civil loyalty, but by a religious duty of obedience, violation of which constituted a sin as well as a crime. Conversely, a non-Russian, of whatever origin, once converted to Orthodoxy, was accepted as a Russian in every sense of the word. The Russian concept of nationality had no place for a racial notion, for in colonizing eastern Europe and northern Asia it had absorbed into its religious, and hence cultural and political, sphere substantial numbers of persons of diverse racial and linguistic strains. The phenomenon of persons passing from one cultural group to another is even more widespread today, as illustrated in a provision of the Soviet census, which has special rubrics for recording "nationality by origin" and "nationality by culture." For example, a person born of Ukrainian or Georgian parents may consider himself a Russian by culture; and a person of Russian descent may identify himself with the culture of a people of a non-Russian nationality among whom he has grown up.

Particular stress is laid upon this notion of Russian nationality, because the Soviet idea of nationality, viewed as a nonnational loyalty to a system of ideas and to a common but nonnational fatherland, is closer to it in essential respects than to European definitions of nationality. The idea that a falling away from this loyalty is like deviating from the one true and unifying faith is illustrated by the prohibition placed upon the marriage of Soviet citizens with foreigners[3] and by the elaborate rules and taboos which regulate contacts between Soviet citizens and foreigners. The ideological, rather than national, content of Soviet thinking about loyalty is made clear by the extreme penalties which have been visited upon entire classes of citizens for their attachment to private cultivation of land and upon entire nationalities for their devotion to separate nationalist traditions. As illustrated by the behavior of Communist believers in many parts of the world, the Soviet conception of nationality is not necessarily bound to any particular geographical area. It is, theoretically speaking, a potentially universal concept; this was not true of the earlier Russian idea of nationality, despite certain messianic overtones expressed in the concept of "Moscow the Third Rome" or in the thinking of some of the nineteenth-century Slavophiles.

Community of religion was important in promoting the formation of Muscovite Russia, or Moscovia, and in facilitating its expansion to become the Russian state. It was the antagonism between Polish Catholicism and Ukrainian Orthodoxy which, in the middle of the seventeenth century, contributed more than any other one factor to the separation of the greater part of the Ukraine from Poland and to its gradual absorption into Russia. Uniformity of religion between Russians and Ukrainians also delayed the emergence of a self-conscious Ukrainian nationalism. It did not develop until the close of the nineteenth century when the spread of secular education produced an intelligentsia sprung directly from the village—the center of Ukrain-

[3] (Author's note, 1959) This statute was repealed in a decree of the Presidium of the U.S.S.R. Supreme Soviet of November 26, 1953, annulling the decree of the Presidium of the U.S.S.R. Supreme Soviet "On Forbidding Marriage Between U.S.S.R. Citizens and Foreigners," of February 15, 1947, *Vedomosti Verkhovnogo Soveta SSSR*, December 1, 1953, p. 26 however, marriage to a foreigner may or may not be followed by permission to leave the Soviet Union to accompany the foreign spouse to his or her own country.

ian speech and tradition—not from the Russianized towns of Ukraine. In the Russian Ukraine a distinctive Ukrainian consciousness emerged some two generations later than in Austrian-ruled Eastern Galicia, where the clash between the Uniat Church of the Ukrainians and the Catholic Church of the Poles stimulated the crystallization of a separate Ukrainian feeling of nationality.

Community of religion also facilitated the expansion of Russia into the Trans-Caucasus. By the late eighteenth century Georgia, or Gruziia, with its own national church which had been founded earlier than the Russian Church, looked to Russia for protection against the Moslem Tartars of neighboring Azerbaijan as well as against both Persian and Ottoman suzerainty. Again, in the Russian wars of the 1820's against Persia and Turkey the sympathy of the Armenians, a people of a related Christian church, was important in the expansion of Russian rule south of the Caucasus Mountains. After 1878 official Russian sympathy for the Armenians as fellow Christians was tempered by fear of the revolutionary and terrorist activities of the Armenian intelligentsia which were directed against both tsarist and Ottoman absolutism.

During World War I, in furtherance of its desire to be the protector of the Armenians, Russia staked out a claim, which was recognized by France and Britain, to annex the entire northeastern quarter of Anatolia, including the entire area inhabited then by an Armenian minority. Despite the almost complete absence of Armenians in this area today, the same territory has again been claimed by the Soviet Union as the homeland of Armenians, who are now being repatriated to Soviet Armenia from the Near East and even from the United States.[4]

Under tsarist Russia nationalities were, in a sense, "rated" in terms of their loyalty, and that rating was

[4] (Author's note, 1959) After Stalin's death in 1953 the Soviet government renounced its claim to Turkey's territory.

largely based on religion. Highest in the scale were the Orthodox, including Russians, Belorussians, and Ukrainians. Close behind came the Georgians and the Armenians. The Moslems of Central Asia, especially the Uzbeks of Bukhara, were not considered loyal and were normally exempted from military service. When in 1916 an attempt was made to conscript the Uzbeks into the Russian army, they broke out in a revolt which swept over a large part of Central Asia. The Moslem Tartars of the Volga, who had been under Russian rule since the mid-sixteenth century, were considered loyal, while the Tartars of the Crimea, under Russian rule only since 1784 and possessed of a stronger memory of their own former statehood, were not used on any front against the Turks.

Curiously enough, a similar rating has been observed as a by-product of World War II. At a victory celebration in 1945, Generalissimus Stalin raised his glass to "the Russian people"—emphasizing the word "Russian" — "which has borne the burden of victory." Simultaneously, the Soviet regime has shown great tenacity in unifying all the Ukrainians for the first time in modern history, including those of northern Bukovina, Eastern Galicia, and sub-Carpathian Ruthenia, areas which were not parts of the former Russian Empire; and it has similarly reunited the Belorussians, divided after 1920 between Soviet and Polish rule. As recognition of the importance of these two non-Russian nationalities, it has secured separate representation for the Ukrainian and Belorussian Republics in the United Nations and in a number of international conferences.

At the other end of the Soviet scale are several smaller nationalities which were found wanting in the test of war and which have been deprived of separate national existence within the Soviet Union. By a decree of 1946[6] the Crimean Tartar Republic was abolished. Its inhabitants have lost their identity by being scattered across the Russian land; even the Tartar place

[6] *Izvestiia*, June 27, 1946.

names in the Crimea have been eliminated, except for a few names of general historic significance. The Chechen-Ingush Autonomous Republic in the North Caucasus has been similarly abolished, while the autonomous republic of the Volga Germans was liquidated in 1941. The Kalmyk people, who live in the steppes near the lower Volga, have also been deprived of a separate national identity. As a punishment for "failure to resist the promptings of the Nazi-Fascist invaders" the republics, formerly inhabited by nearly three million of these peoples, have disappeared from the Soviet map.

In other important instances it was not community of religion and culture, but force of arms, or a combination of force and compromise, which facilitated the expansion of Russia. The outthrust to the Baltic under Peter the Great was the final stage in a long struggle between Russian determination to reach the nearby sea and the Baltic empire of Sweden. Its outcome was hastened by a timely compromise between Peter and the German nobility of the Baltic provinces, which assured the self-government of the nobility and safeguarded the special position of the Lutheran Church and of the German language. Within a generation the German Baltic nobility was playing a disproportionately large role in the Russian court and diplomacy, and in the administration. Here, then, was the case of a strategic necessity, recognized in good season by a local ruling group, which made favorable terms for itself and its local privileges while gaining access to the preferment and honors of a great empire.

The compromise between the Russian ruling house and the Baltic nobility lasted for nearly two centuries. It broke down only when the government of Alexander III, bent on Russianizing the borderlands and on making their institutions uniform with those of the rest of Russia, began to enforce Russian instead of German as the language of administration and education. As both languages were equally foreign to the mass of the native Balt peoples, which harbored deep social resentment against the German-speaking Baltic nobles and burghers, the Ests and Letts were glad to see the monopoly of German culture broken. It was not until 1905 that the native peoples of the area won the limited right to use their own languages—Estonian, Latvian, and Lithuanian—in the schools.

When defeat and revolution deprived the Russian center of power to maintain its control over the Baltic region, and defeat in the West removed German military force from the area, the native peoples were able to assert their right to national self-rule. While there was doubt from the beginning that they would be able to keep their independence when Russia revived, their downfall came, not from inner dissension, but from the new strategic situation created in eastern Europe by the co-operation of the two strongest powers, Germany and the Soviet Union. The reintegration of the Baltic states into the Soviet Union has been followed by migration to the west or by the forced removal to the interior of the Soviet Union of a large part of the educated class which formed the backbone of the Baltic states' independence. A new intelligentsia, trained in accordance with Soviet ideas of limited national rights, is being formed to administer the Baltic republics, while the peasants, long accustomed to working their individual farms on a high technical level, have apparently not been subjected to the collectivization enforced elsewhere in the Soviet Union.[6]

At the other extremity of the empire, in Central Asia, the expansion of the Russian state was carried through directly by military force, principally during the 1860's and 1870's. Here the effort to fill the vacuum of power which lay between the Russian frontier and the sphere of influence of British India met with no willingness to compromise, for it was dealing with peoples fanatically loyal to Islam and

[6] (Author's note, 1959) By 1949 and 1950 the full regime of collectivization was extended to the three Baltic republics.

attached to their own way of life. Once Russian power was established in Central Asia, it accomplished a number of incidental reforms which somewhat softened the opposition to it. Tsarist administration, arbitrary and inefficient as it might seem to its own critics at home, was still a vast improvement over the previous native rule. In place of the arbitrary authority of clan elders and local landlords, the peasantry in many districts came to be governed by elected elders. Slavery was abolished. While religious fanaticism, sullen resentment of the conquerors, and ignorance of the Russian language and customs prevented any large number of natives from benefiting from the transmission of Western culture in its Russian form, the way was opened, if only scantily and for a few, for direct communication with the world of modern knowledge and ideas. Business life came under the protection of a regular administration, and the interchange of the cotton of Central Asia for manufactured goods from European Russia stimulated a rapid economic development. Russian settlement here, like European settlement in the Near East, took the form of creating new European cities side by side with ancient native cities like Tashkent, Bukhara, and Samarkand.

If imperialism is defined as the rule of one nationality over other nationalities, then the tsarist Empire represented a remarkable type of imperialism among European states, for Great Russians, by language, comprised just over one half of the population in 1914. The Ukrainians and Belorussians had not developed a widespread mass movement of political self-determination, while several other nationalities looked to the tsarist government with loyalty for protection against antagonists closer at hand. In Finland, for example, the earliest development of Finnish cultural nationalism met with support from the Russian government, which was glad to see weakened the dominant cultural and political position of the Swedish-speaking upper class. It was only when the Finnish-speaking majority and

Swedish-speaking minority joined in defense of special political and administrative rights of the Duchy of Finland that the government in St. Petersburg became alarmed at the growth of Finnish nationalism. Similarly, in the Caucasus region both Georgians and Armenians were loyal supporters of the Russian connection against their Moslem neighbors.

Unless rule over a multinational empire is to be regarded in itself as sufficient proof of imperialism, then some more refined and complex criterion must be sought, such as the continued resistance to the aims of that governing state. Both Central Asia and Russian Poland come to mind as prime examples. The population of Central Asia, isolated from the main stream of Russian cultural development by a strong feeling of religious separation and by a recent memory of the cruelty of conquest, remained stubbornly hostile, though politically inert and divided by national rivalries within the area. Here a compact Russian minority of soldiers and administrators ruled an alien mass, usually returning to European Russia upon completion of their service. Small numbers of Russian workers and intellectuals settled permanently, without mingling with the native population.

In Russian Poland, the preservation of an unbroken cultural continuity, extending back to the Middle Ages and tempered in the Renaissance and the Enlightenment, was an unwavering purpose of the compact and unassimilable Polish nation. Its determination to restore national statehood, lost only in 1815, or rather in 1831, remained inextinguishable. In Poland, Russian rule showed many earmarks of imperialism, except that the Polish economy benefited from its competitive advantages within Russia; by 1914 Russian Poland contained about one fourth of the industry of the empire.

A special situation was presented by the Jewish population of the empire. Largely concentrated in Poland, Belorussia, and the Ukraine, this group did not form a compact territorial unity, as did the Poles or the Finns, but was everywhere a minority, a functional minority. Originally an interstitial body in a society of landlords and peasants, its function in providing the services of middlemen and artisans protected its special religious and cultural status for several centuries. Questions of equal rights and assimilation came to the fore as the old social structure gradually broke up in the nineteenth century. After wavering for a time between promoting assimilation of the Jews and pressing them within the narrow walls of restrictive territorial, professional, and economic limitations, the decaying tsarist government singled out the defenseless Jewish population as a scapegoat to deflect from itself the accumulated social and political discontents of the western parts of the empire. Official anti-Semitism, protected and even organized by the secret political police, culminated in pogroms in provinces of substantial Jewish settlement. It is only fair to add that liberal Russians objected to this as well as to other forms of bureaucratic oppression. As one example it may be mentioned that when a ritual murder trial was instigated at Kiev in 1913, a large number of Russian barristers volunteered their services for the defense, and the trial of Beilis turned into a trial of the police who had engineered this cruel farce.

The lack of national rights was made less painful to the non-Russian groups since the Russian people suffered just as much from unredressed social and political grievances. And the struggle to satisfy the widespread yearnings for social and political justice was led by the Russian intelligentsia. In fact, by definition, only those persons who were consciously critical of tsarist officialdom belonged to the intelligentsia.

Communion with the Russian intelligentsia marked the entrance into a world of free ideas for educated members of the non-Russian nationalities, except the Poles, who had their own traditions of the struggle for freedom. Membership in a fellowship of idealistic protest formed the intelligentsia, in which Russians and Jews, Georgians and Ukrainians mingled without distinction. It was the universal and humane appeal of Russian culture and literature and the common climate of democratic ideals which proved to be the strongest cement in reuniting most of the peoples of the old empire. By a curious irony of history, the empire, in its fumbling efforts to adapt itself to the modern world, almost destroyed the old habits of loyalty among the non-Russian peoples, while the intelligentsia, which took form in opposition to bureaucratic rule and social oppression, was reforging a community of cultural experience and shared ideals which was instrumental in recreating a multinational state on the ruins of the obsolescent empire.

The problem of regrouping the various peoples who had lived within the empire fell to the new Soviet regime. When the period of revolutionary upheaval was over, the new Soviet state emerged with somewhat shrunken boundaries on the west and in the Caucasus and with the prerevolutionary boundaries in the east. When one considers the complete breakdown of the old regime and the painful task of building a new state, in the face of the magic slogan of "self-determination" among the non-Russian nationalities, coupled with frequent interventions in the border regions, first of German, then of Allied and American forces, the reconstitution of nearly all the territory of the former multinational state appears as a major achievement. Austria-Hungary, which had a far better record, especially in its Austrian half, for the enlightened treatment of its nationalities, broke up entirely under a similar strain, while Turkey, which had failed to buttress its rule with advantages of economic and cultural progress, was reduced to its purely ethnic nucleus.

This is not the place in which to review the vicissitudes of Russian territory during the period of revolution, civil wars, and interventions.[7] Within a few months of the November revolution the new Soviet Russia was reduced to somewhat less than the area which Moscovia had ruled in 1580. The results of over three centuries of "gathering lands"—the favorite occupation of rulers—had been swept away.

At the time of the revolution the Socialist intelligentsia of Russia was of two minds concerning the future of the non-Russian areas. Most of them felt that national self-determination would benefit only the local landlords and the middle class, and they held to the general conviction that economic progress meant the formation of larger economic units rather than the subdivision of existing ones.

The program of what emerged as the dominant wing of the Socialist intelligentsia—the Bolsheviks—was rather more complicated and far more astute. This program owed a great deal to the insight of Joseph Stalin, himself a Georgian, who had devoted much of his effort to the problem of nationalities. While holding no brief for the breaking up of Russia, and believing that the victory of the proletariat in each part of it would, in the end, recreate Russia as a workers' and peasants' state, the Bolsheviks saw that nothing short of a dramatic proclamation of the complete equality of all nationalities within Russia, and of their right freely to secede, would satisfy the accumulated resentments of those national groups whose feelings and interests had been profoundly injured by the previous policies of Imperial Russia. This was the content of the decree of the Council of People's Commissars of November 15, 1917, on the "Rights of the Peoples of Russia to Self-Determination."[8]

The new Soviet government, which had just secured a precarious grip on the central regions of the country, did not want the dissolution of Russia's political and

[7] For a detailed account see William Henry Chamberlin: *The Russian Revolution, 1917–1921*, 2 vols. (New York: Macmillan; 1935).

[8] *Izvestiia*, November 16, 1917.

economic unity. However it recognized the political reality that any compact national group inhabiting an outlying part of the empire could, in fact, not be prevented from breaking away from Great Russia if it so desired. The new government gave prompt approval to the right of the Finns and the Poles to national independence, and somewhat less prompt recognition of Ukrainian independence.

The November revolution was brought about through the seizure of power by a minority party and was followed, in January 1918, by the forcible dispersion of the All-Russian Constituent Assembly. Thus the first effect of the revolution was to accelerate the dissolution of the former Russian state. During 1917, between the first and second revolutions, when the country seemed to be moving toward a system of political liberty and self-government, the leaders of the non-Russian groups thought generally in terms of satisfying the demands of their nationalities through the establishment of cultural and administrative autonomy within the framework of a federal state. The seizure of power by the Bolsheviks hastened the movement for national independence in the Ukraine and, soon after, in the Trans-Caucasus, which, in turn, broke into the republics of Georgia, Azerbaijan, and Armenia in the spring of 1918.

The new government in Petrograd quickly recognized the independence of the Ukrainian People's Republic, with its capital at Kiev, but it showed its real policy with regard to national self-determination by promptly setting up a rival Soviet Ukrainian government in Khar'kov. In the three years of struggle which followed, Kiev changed hands no less than thirteen times.

The history of Georgian independence was somewhat similar. Until the November revolution the Georgian Socialist leaders showed no signs of contemplating national independence. In fact, Georgian Mensheviks like Chkheidze and Tseretelli had played leading parts in the work of the Petrograd Soviet and the provisional government until the non-Communist parties were outlawed by the Bolsheviks. Consolidation of Bolshevik power in Great Russia was followed by a hesitant establishment of Georgian independence, tardily recognized by the Soviet government. Even when Soviet Russia had become an immediately adjoining neighbor of independent Georgia, it reaffirmed its recognition of the Republic of Georgia. Finally, in February 1921, Soviet forces entered its territory, to join hands with a pro-Soviet uprising, and Georgia was proclaimed a Soviet republic.

In its early years the Soviet government used the device of promoting "people's republics" as an intermediate status between full independence and a Soviet regime. A Far Eastern republic was set up in 1921 to govern the region between Lake Baikal and the Pacific in order to provide a buffer between Soviet Russia and Japanese imperialism. Power was exercised by a "united front" of all Socialist and democratic parties. A coalition cabinet conducted fair elections within the republic and carried on negotiations with outside powers for the evacuation of the remaining Japanese troops from the area. Once the latter had been removed from the mainland, the coalition cabinet came to an end; power was transferred to the Bolshevik party, which had all along held the key posts controlling the police and the armed militia, and the "republic" was integrated into Soviet Russia.

A similar evolution occurred in Central Asia, where the absence of a substantial Russian population, except along the railways, and of a native proletariat gave critical importance to the native peasantry and middle class. In 1920 two People's Soviet (but not Socialist) Republics were formed, in Bukhara and Khiva. The small Bolshevik elements co-operated with the non-Socialist representatives of the local population, led by the so-called "Young Bukharan" and "Young Khivan" parties. By 1924 the balance of power in the region had changed sufficiently so that these supposedly independent states could be joined to the Soviet Union as Soviet republics. By 1936 Central Asia was represented in the Soviet Union by five Union republics—Uzbekistan, Turkmenistan, Tadjikstan, Kazakhstan, and the Kirghiz Republic.

A more recent example is that of the Tannu-Tuva People's Republic, a small state lying between Soviet Siberia and the Mongolian People's Republic. This area had long been recognized by the Soviet government as an independent state, despite Chinese claims to suzerainty over it, although it maintained diplomatic relations only with the Soviet Union. Finally it was absorbed into the Soviet Union in 1943, but news of this change did not reach the outside world until 1945. Interestingly enough, Tannu-Tuva did not become a constituent republic of the Soviet Union, like other formerly independent regions, but simply a minor administrative subdivision within the Russian Federal Republic.

On the Soviet western border, however, the Moldavian Autonomous Republic, which had been a part of the Ukrainian Union Republic until 1940, was greatly enlarged in that year. Two thirds of Bessarabia, detached from Rumania under the terms of a Soviet ultimatum, were added to form the new Moldavian Union Republic, in which Moldavian, which is simply Rumanian written in a Russian-type alphabet, is the official language. A part of the original territory of the district was at that time transferred to the Ukraine, together with the extreme northern and southern strips of Bessarabia.

Theoretically, at least, the Soviet method of extension of frontiers—by coming with superior force to the defense of "oppressed" groups within neighboring states—is capable of very great and even world-wide application. In the first upsurge of revolutionary enthusiasm the hope for a "Soviet of the World" played a great part in sustaining the defenders of the beleaguered citadel of world revolution. In practice, however, the drawing of the western frontier of the Soviet Union shows a strong recognition of traditional barriers set by ethnic and cultural factors to the direct extension of Soviet rule. Although no immediate military or political issue could have prevented the Soviet government from incorporating Finland or Poland, Rumania or Bulgaria into its federal state at the close of World War II, it has refrained from doing so. The attempt made in 1939–40 to declare Finland a Soviet republic has not been repeated. Soviet territorial claims against Finland, apart from the lease of the naval base at Porkkala,[9] have been confined to strategic rectifications of the frontier; the withdrawal of the Finnish population from the ceded areas has again made the political boundary an ethnic one as well. The continued existence of a Karelo-Finnish Republic within the Soviet Union does not contradict this principle, since the Karelian population constitutes a minority within that republic.[1]

In general, the postwar boundaries of the Soviet Union in Europe are surprisingly close to those which the Imperial government and general staff had projected in 1915. The main difference is that the future relation of Poland and Russia had not been decided in 1915, although it was certain that if Russia won, Poland would remain attached through either a personal union or a military alliance. Unofficial Russian proposals of that time also included plans for re-establishing the Kingdom of Bohemia, with a Russian grand duke as ruler, while Yugoslavia, Rumania, and Greece were closely bound by dynastic ties to the ruling family of Russia, and, in varying degrees, to Russian policy.

What of Russian and Soviet imperialism beyond the borders of the state? The influence of Russia was pre-

[9] (Author's note, 1959) The Soviet-leased base at Porkkala was retroceded to Finland after Stalin's death.

[1] (Author's note, 1959) In 1956 the Karelo-Finnish Republic was demoted from being one of the sixteen Union Republics to a humble Autonomous Republic within the Russian Federal Republic.

ponderant in Outer Mongolia by 1912. In Manchuria it controlled the northern areas, through the special position of the Russian-operated Chinese Eastern Railway and through the growth of Russian business and settlement, after yielding southern Sakhalin, Korea, and southern Manchuria to Japanese control in 1905. In Persia, Russian influence prevailed in the fertile north; British influence was strong in the south. The Russian railway in northern Persia, the Russian Bank, the Russian monopoly of navigation on the Caspian, and Russian fishing concessions created a position of power, one which was beginning to be offset by the important development of British petroleum in the south. In the projected division of the spoils of Turkey in 1915, Imperial Russia had been promised full possession of the Straits of Constantinople as well as a large sphere of influence in nothern Anatolia.

Soviet power and influence abroad are more extensive than the Imperial government dreamed of. In the Far East the Soviet Union has reappropriated southern Sakhalin and has annexed the Kurile Islands which it had recognized as Japanese in 1875. It is in occupation of the northern half of Korea.[2] It has recovered control of the Chinese Eastern and South Manchurian railways, in nominal partnership with China, and it is again in possession of a naval base at Port Arthur and a free port at Dairen. China has renounced its sovereignty over the People's Republic of Mongolia, which is bound to the Soviet Union by an alliance and maintains diplomatic relations with it alone.[3]

The countries of Europe which border on the Soviet

[2] (Author's note, 1959) Soviet troops were withdrawn in 1949; subsequent events need not be recounted here.

[3] (Author's note, 1959) After Stalin's death the Soviet government sold its part-ownership in railroad, mining, and other joint-stock companies to Communist China, and withdrew from Dairen and Port Arthur. The Mongolian People's Republic now maintains diplomatic relations with eighteen countries including Communist China and the other members of the Communist bloc, India, Burma, Indonesia, and a number of states from the Asian-African group.

Union are intimately involved with Soviet policy. The impact of that policy is not the same in each of these countries. In Yugoslavia, for example, the impetus of a fervent Communist movement has swept the country into a dictatorship so closely modeled on the Soviet pattern that even the names of political subdivisions and administrative agencies are parallel with those of the Soviet Union.[4] In Bulgaria a strong native Communist movement has also established a monopoly of power. In Czechoslovakia, a Communist monopoly of power developed more gradually. A small and relatively unenthusiastic Communist party also has the dominant role in Poland, but in comparison with the movement in Yugoslavia, it has extended its control slowly from major levels of policy to details of living and thinking. Rumania showed much pliability to Soviet dominance, while Hungary had to be pushed about and threatened. Finland, despite the severe terms of the peace, has been able to manage its internal affairs to a remarkable degree.

One common feature of the border countries is the dominant position of the Communist party, without whose co-operation no major decision can be taken. Representatives of the party occupy key positions in control of the police, education, and economic life.

This strength rests on some very old and some very new factors. Among Orthodox populations much is made of the feeling of religious community, and representatives of the Russian clergy visit their Orthodox colleagues in the neighboring countries. In Yugoslavia, Bulgaria, and Czechoslovakia the appeal of pan-Slavism is strong. Hatred of Germany because of its oppressive and cruel policy makes these countries seek Soviet protection against a German revival, not now, but twenty or fifty years from now. For many peoples in this area the memory of

[4] (Author's note, 1959) There is no need to review the turbulent changes which have taken place in East Central Europe since this was written in February 1948.

German aggression dates back, not thirty, but a thousand years. Above all, the political dependence of these countries is cemented by the practical monopoly of power exercised by the Communist parties. The political alliances between the Soviet Union and each of the governments have been reinforced by military conventions whose published provisions assure close co-ordination between the Soviet army and the local army in equipment, training, and organization. Military loyalty seems assured by the important roles played by native officers who served in the Red Army before the war or co-operated closely with it during the war, and political loyalty of the armed forces to the new orientation has been strengthened by extensive purges of their personnel.

In the economic sphere the effects of the new Soviet dominance are far-reaching. The two extremes are represented by Czechoslovakia and Rumania. Since it has the largest heavy industries and best machine-tool production of the entire area, Czechoslovakia is particularly well situated to trade with the Soviet Union, from which it can obtain certain foodstuffs and raw materials. The degree to which the two economies supplement each other should not be exaggerated, however, for there are many types of imports which both countries need to seek elsewhere, while many of the best markets for Czechoslovak wares have been in overseas areas. In the first year after liberation one half of Czechoslovakia's trade was with the Soviet Union, one reason being that Czechoslovakia was unable to open up routes across the American zone in Germany. More recently, in the first half of 1947, trade with the Soviet Union amounted to about twenty-three per cent of the Czechoslovak total. A factor which has favored adjustment to the new relationship with the Soviet Union was the decision, made as early as November 1945, as to which German-owned factories were to be dismantled and transferred to the Soviet Union. This permitted the Czechs to put the remaining factories to work for their own account. Even after the Communist seizure of power in February 1948, trade between the two countries seemed to be conducted largely on commercial principles.

The opposite extreme is illustrated by Rumania, where Soviet economic pressure and control have been exerted in diverse ways. When the Soviet armies entered this country they claimed as war booty, under their unilateral definition, large amounts of commodities and equipment of all kinds. It was argued, for example, that a factory which had made uniforms for the army represented war booty, though it could readily be converted to peacetime production. A second source of immediate Soviet gain was through the collection of occupation costs; currency supplied by the defeated government on Soviet demand was not used solely to support the army of occupation but to buy up large quantities of materials for shipment to the Soviet Union. A third source of gain has been through restitution. The Western powers have defined restitution as the return of identifiable looted property; under Soviet practice similar or equivalent goods have been taken as well, and, in theory, Rumania has also been held responsible for German looting of Soviet property.

A fourth source of profit has been the transfer to Soviet ownership of German properties, as agreed at Potsdam. This has brought a large part of Rumania's manufacturing equipment into Soviet possession, for the term "German property" was often interpreted as any machine of German manufacture, even if bought and paid for by Rumanians before the war, and it has included, as well, business enterprises in which the Germans had, by whatever means, secured a substantial share of control. Thus there are factories which were forcibly taken from their former owners by the Germans and which have now become Soviet property. A fifth category covers Rumanian enterprises and some

German properties, which have been placed under joint Soviet-Rumanian ownership. More than fifty enterprises, including mining, banking, oil, machine making, lumbering, Danube navigation, and so forth, are thus, in practice, under Soviet control. It has been estimated that, apart from agriculture, some sixty to sixty-five per cent of the industrial capital of Rumania has by these means come into permanent Soviet possession at no cost to the Soviet Union.

A final source of Soviet advantage lies in the collection of $300 million in reparations. The actual amount is in reality greater than the sum officially credited to the account of Rumania, for such devices as basing valuation on prewar dollar prices and imposing penalties for incomplete or delayed deliveries have been applied on a considerable scale. If all these ingenious methods for gathering into Soviet hands both movable wealth and fixed capital are considered together, the picture which results is one of taking over the entire country's economic resources.

Soviet expansion in Europe is a direct outcome of the strategic conditions under which the war against Nazi Germany was fought. So far, Communist dominance has been established in those countries which were liberated by Soviet armies, and, except in the case of Albania, it has not been established in any country which had not undergone Soviet liberation or occupation.

Soviet influence in countries beyond its periphery of dependent governments is exerted both through the political and military weight of the Soviet Union, which is the strongest power in Europe or in Asia, and through the local activities of Communist parties. This latter is a unique phenomenon. The remarkable character of this influence and potential lever of power is shown by the fact that many forms of discontent—social, national, and spiritual—are focused in an overriding loyalty to a state whose own life is to an amazing degree closed off from direct observation and comparison by individuals not already converted to the faith.

Old Russia, through painful struggles, extended its rule over one sixth of the world. Its ideas were parochial, like those of other national states, despite occasional traces of messianic doctrine. Soviet Russia, which claims to offer a universal formula, is remarkably parochial in its way of life and its habits of thought. The directing of so much fervent loyalty toward Moscow, and the ability of the Soviet state to find devoted supporters and even willing martyrs to its cause in so many parts of the world, is a new phenomenon in world politics. Will the fervor and the power of attraction diminish with the burning down of revolutionary fire within the Soviet Union? Will other political and social faiths have the inner conviction and cohesion to meet and contain this urge to extend the realm of Soviet expansion? These are the paramount questions of the next few decades.

:3:

RECENT SOVIET TRIALS AND POLICIES[1]

[*April 1938*]

INTRODUCTORY NOTE · In its gathering momentum from Kirov's assassination in December 1934 to Yezhov's replacement by Beria in December 1938, the great purge marked the paroxysm and culmination of the Stalinist revolutionizing of Soviet society. The dissolution of the Society of Old Bolsheviks and the physical liquidation of most of those Communists who remembered an earlier milder rule within and over the party, merely symbolized the impatient emergence of the first post-revolutionary generation. This stratum of "new Soviet men" many of whom climbed to power over the corpses of the original revolutionaries, thereafter largely administered the Soviet system in Stalin's last fifteen years. Under a new leader, Khrushchev, who joined the revolution after it had succeeded, these new men largely set the tone for the governance of the country today.

The doctrinaire rigidities of the Soviet system, its authoritarian habits in management, and its aversion to

[1] *The Yale Review,* Vol. xxvii. No. 4 (Summer 1938), pp. 745–66. Copyright 1938 by The Yale Review.

intellectual inquiry except in technology combine with strong will power, habits of strenuous work, and strong party discipline to shape its style of work both at home and in world politics. In a sense Stalin strove, through purges, to break the last threads between traditional ethics and Bolshevik morality. His all-too-complete success in building a new instrument of rule largely determines Soviet top stratum reflexes today.

That is why it is useful to take a brief background look at the new ruling group as it was emerging in 1938 from the struggle to harness the country to the demands of the party, and to bind the party to the will of a single "all-wise" leader. The system of the purges, and the mentality which it reflected and implanted, have cut deep into Soviet thinking and feeling. To understand how the official apparatus looks out on world politics we must not lose sight of the twin experiences which have scarred its mind: the ruthless struggle by which it emerged victorious from Stalin's purges, and the equally desperate struggle to survive World War II and reap as fully as possible the fruits of survival and victory.

*

THE international prestige of the Soviet Union has stood at a low ebb in recent months. The failure of the Loyalists in Spain, Soviet unwillingness to assist China on a broad scale, the eclipse of the Popular Front in France, a growing tendency to ignore the Soviet alliances with France and Czechoslovakia, the seemingly definitive weakening of the League of Nations, whether in spite of or because of its temporary flare-up of vigor after it was joined by Russia—these and other recent shifts have registered the decline of Soviet influence in world affairs. The swing from an exaggerated view of Soviet might to the current underestimation of its potential strength has been fostered by a succession of domestic purges over the last three years. The spectacle of a great power denouncing and destroying numbers of its political, military, and industrial leaders under charges of espionage, treason, and sabotage has created in most foreign quarters a feeling of disbelief, mingled with perplexity and disgust.

If the official accusations are to be accepted literally, nearly all the outstanding leaders of the Bolshevist party, except those who had died before the present purges, have been guilty of trying to overthrow the Soviet regime, planning their government's defeat in case of war, selling state secrets to its enemies, hampering its economic progress, plotting Stalin's murder again and again, and other equally heinous crimes. The alternative to this conception is the belief that the trials of 1936–8 have been organized by Stalin and the "new men" around him through ambition, fear, and desire for revenge against earlier rivals and potential challengers for power. Both conceptions, by stressing the idea of personal "villainy," tend to obscure the conditions and trends in Soviet development which underlie these sensational events.

Before turning to a brief analysis of these trends, certain peculiar features in the trials should be pointed out. Each successive trial has brought to light a wider range of anti-Stalinist activities, larger circles of conspirators. The most recent of the great trials, associated with the name of Bukharin, lumped together conspiracy charges involving prominent diplomats, financial and industrial leaders, heads of several non-Russian republics, the military leaders shot so suddenly in June 1937, and the political police, represented by their former chief, Yagoda. Yet the persistent efforts of the prosecutor, Vyshinskii, failed to pull these many threads into a single coherent movement. The trial proved the existence of a variety of groups doubtful of and hostile to Stalin's policies, rather than a close-knit conspiracy.

Another striking feature of the trials has been the division of the accused into criminals of ideology and criminals of action. Bukharin, for instance, declared himself guilty even of actions of which he knew nothing, since they had been inspired by his ideas. In general, the Old Bolsheviks readily admitted their disagreements with the Stalinist line, but denied, or confessed with great reluctance to accusations of espionage and sabotage. On the other hand, obscure individuals, placed on trial with them, admitted with a certain glibness having committed or intended to commit, the most vile and detailed crimes, while their ideological foundation amounted to attributing to Bukharin, Zinoviev, and Trotskii the ideological paternity for their acts. While the line between the conduct of the two main types of defendants is not to be drawn too sharply, it was evident enough for Bukharin to refer to one of his fellow prisoners as a "*provocateur*." Whether they were *provocateurs* or not, the connection of the "obscure" wing with the "ideological" defendants was usually most tenuous, and backed only by their own assertions.

If it is fairly easy to guess why the obscure defendants denounce themselves and others so readily, the question still remains, why do the Old Bolshevik leaders confess? No single or simple answer can be given. Some may hope that their lives will be spared in return for co-operation with the prosecutor: that hope has been justified in the case of Radek and Rakovskii, to mention only two. Others may hope to protect their families from revenge. At the Bukharin trial Levin declared that he had poisoned Gorkii since Yagoda, then the all-powerful head of the political police, threatened, if he refused, to destroy him and his family. It would be rash to assume that the police have changed their methods radically under Yagoda's successor. The prisoners have been brought to public trial only after months of isolation and moral pressure. The prosecutor is free to select for trial those persons whose confessions will best fit into the picture which he proposes to draw; he can dispose of the recalcitrant by less public methods.

There are, moreover, other factors at work to bring

these former revolutionaries to public confession of real or alleged crimes. As Bolsheviks they have always upheld the party's right to exact complete obedience and conformity from its members; they themselves have been active in defining and enforcing Bolshevist orthodoxy. Now that the party, in turn, condemns their disagreements with its line, they have no moral ground on which to deny its claim to punish them. Their long-standing disagreements with Stalin have been public property; many had confessed publicly even earlier, some of them more than once. Finally, there is one other intangible of special significance. The Old Bolsheviks have spent their entire lives in the service of the party; looking back on a generation of struggle for their ideals under Lenin's leadership, they idealize "The Party" and its unity in a way scarcely comprehensible to those who have joined it since its triumph. Once convinced that their disagreements and intrigues had injured the party, persuaded of the error of their way by the incontestable fact of Stalin's victory over them, assured that their self-humiliation would serve the party's ends, some of the Old Bolsheviks could be brought not only to confess their ideological sins but to demand their own destruction. In their final statements the dominant note is one of despair at their break with the party.

The Old Bolsheviks have been particularly vulnerable because of their own obsolete conception of their function within the party. Beneath the outward unity of the party, functioning as an instrument of rule, there had long been an unstated but accepted "constitutional" right of free private discussion within the top ranks of the party, functioning as an oligarchical, policy-determining body. For example, during the shift from war communism to the New Economic Policy in 1921, there were seven or eight widely divergent views, advocated by as many groups within the party. With his genius for analysis, his sure judgment, and his strong personal hold over the party, Lenin always managed such difficult shifts of policy without shedding the blood of party members. But Stalin lacks certain of Lenin's advantages. Despite his strong native intelligence and an unbending will, Stalin was at first only one among Lenin's heirs; he could rely on neither an unquestioned intellectual supremacy nor strong personal devotion to swing the party his way. The Old Bolsheviks were bound to resent Stalin's gradual assumption of a dictatorship within the party, his suppression of their traditional influence over policy, and, since 1932, his growing willingness to shed Communist blood. Stalin, on the other hand, could maintain with complete sincerity that he knew Russia far better than his critics; that his policy was closer to the ordinary man in Russia than their abstract internationalism, mingled, as it was, with a scarcely concealed contempt for Russia's "Asiatic backwardness"; finally, that he had succeeded in consolidating his power while the Old Bolsheviks had gone on relying on past revolutionary services to maintain their prestige.

Against this background of potential, perhaps inevitable conflict, it is amazing what slight evidence of any coherent attempt to remove Stalin has been produced by the trials. Yet such attempts were certainly talked about and, in part, carried out. The more the party has been eclipsed by a single leader, the more strongly the party machine has been held in grip by Stalin and his "new men," the greater must have been the pressure to relax that grip by an act of individual terrorism. The logic of events over the last ten years has intensified the struggle for power within the upper ranks of the increasingly "monolithic" and subservient party. The logic of power has compelled Stalin not merely to destroy his opponents within the party but to discredit them completely by staging their public confessions of treason and sabotage.

Finally, it must be kept in mind that a public trial—called in Russia a "demonstration trial"—is always held for a political purpose. Anyone found guilty of treason or sabotage can be dispatched without publicity if that is preferable. An open trial is intended to discredit tendencies which have been working against the government's policy. In the Bukharin trial these tendencies were as numerous as the various groups lumped together on the prisoners' bench. The trial was intended to prove that both the party opposition and the eight military leaders, executed after secret judgment in June 1937, had plotted to break down Soviet alliances and friendships abroad, had been preparing the way for defeat and loss of territory in case of war, and had been carrying on espionage for the German, Polish, English, and Japanese secret services. It was also intended to paint the opposition, and not the Stalin government, as responsible for widespread and persistent economic difficulties, such as the mistreatment of the collectivized peasantry, unprofitable and inefficient operation of industry, abuse of labor, and failure to provide the consumer with a constant flow of sound and inexpensive commodities. The trial further attempted to prove that discontent within the various non-Russian republics of the Union was caused not by Moscow's policy towards them but through deliberate sabotage by the former leaders of the republics. In each of these spheres of policy, important changes have been made during the last four years, and it is safe to assume that they could not be effected without a bitter struggle within the highest Soviet circles. In this struggle the trials of 1936–8 stand out as a dramatic episode; but they cannot be rated at their true significance without a brief survey of recent shifts in Soviet diplomacy and strategy, in economic life, and in the nationalities problem.

For many years the Soviet government rejected on principle all military alliances with capitalist countries. It claimed to stand aside from their imperialist quarrels; it looked to an alliance with the revolutionary working class and peasantry within their countries to assure the ultimate triumph of the world revolution. The appearance of Nazi Germany as a definite danger to the Soviet Union led Stalin to revise his policy radically. Russia entered into alliances with France and Czechoslovakia. The Soviet army is now obligated to come to the defense of Czechoslovakia if the latter is attacked by Germany, provided the French army does the same. Russia's adherence to the League of Nations likewise increased the probability of her being embroiled in another European war. The realignment in Russia's international relations has necessitated recasting her strategic plans. It has generally been assumed that until four years ago Soviet strategy called for a war of defense, at least in its opening phases. In case of attack on their western frontier the Soviet forces were to withdraw to strongly prepared fortifications, allowing the invading army to occupy the frontier regions, and obliging it to give battle on Soviet soil. This strategy would, it was felt, increase considerably the advantage of the defending forces. The invading armies would have to extend their lines of supply into regions almost lacking in roads or railways. The Soviet forces would be fighting in a region in which they know every hill and brook, and could operate from carefully prepared bases. The claim of the Soviet government to be a victim of aggression would be strengthened; as the innocent party to the conflict, it could appeal more convincingly to its own people, to opinion in neutral countries, and to dissatisfied elements in the homeland of the invaders. Assuming, on the experience of the last war, that the final outcome of a new world struggle would be decided not by the impetus of the opening attack but by the patriotic endurance and economic efficiency of the countries engaged, this defensive strategy, to be pursued at least in the opening stages of war, would greatly improve Soviet prospects of ultimate victory.

Since 1934 the conclusion of alliances with France and Czechoslovakia has upset these assumptions. If the Soviet army were to adopt a defensive strategy and stay within its own borders, instead of crossing either Rumanian or Polish territory to assist Czechoslovakia against possible German aggression, the Czechoslovak army and state would be overwhelmed within a few weeks; the menace of German expansion would then roll close to Russia's own frontier. But even if Russia moved swiftly enough to save part of Czechoslovakia, she could rely only on the aid of France; the offensive value of French co-operation against Germany has, however, been more and more discounted of late. Since the refortification of the Rhineland, it is assumed that a French advance into Germany could be held back by a much smaller German force, while the main German army would be free to operate offensively to the east. Within France grim determination to defend the nation's territory against attack might give way to perplexity, hesitation, and even social strife if French boundaries remained intact, while French man power were sacrificed to rescue distant allies in eastern Europe. These considerations could not but have weight in some circles in Moscow. Some of the military and political leaders must have objected to surrendering the advantages of diplomatic neutrality and defensive strategy for the sake of helping Russia's new allies much more than those allies could help Russia. At the same time, the traditional contempt professed for the capitalist world and the refusal to participate in capitalist combinations of power diplomacy were abruptly discarded when Russia entered into her new alliances. The explanation that the Soviet government is now defending democracy everywhere against fascism has a hollow ring, compared with the old rejection of all obligations tending to uphold capitalist government anywhere; especially since the Soviet press even now never misses an opportunity to denounce the shams and deceits of "bourgeois democracy." The sudden change in the Soviet attitude towards its "capitalist encirclement" must have disturbed profoundly architects of Bolshevist orthodoxy, like Bukharin and Zinoviev.

Significant light has been thrown on this fundamental problem of Soviet policy by an amendment inserted in the new Soviet constitution in December 1936. The original wording, in accord with the older ideology, provided that Soviet troops would be used only to defend Soviet territory against attack. As a result of the intervention either of Russia's allies, or of some influential party leaders, this clause was revamped to read that Soviet forces would be used only to defend Soviet territory *and* to fulfil the international obligations of the government—a very significant addition. The question of a defensive versus an offensive strategy is a vital point in the Russian and European situation. Perhaps the dispute took such a serious form that some of the highest military leaders, such as Tukhachevskii, the leading strategist, Yakir, commander of the Kiev military district, Uborevich, commander of the White Russian district, diplomats like Karakhan and Krestinskii, had to be put out of the way physically to assure the triumph of the policy of co-operation with France and Czechoslovakia.

The conflict over the orientation of Soviet foreign policy must also be considered from a broader point of view. After crying "Wolf! Wolf!" on every possible pretext since the period of foreign intervention in 1918–22 left the new regime ridden by the nightmare of encirclement and partition, the Soviet regime is now faced by an undeniable menace. At such a crisis, domestic and foreign policy are more closely interdependent than ever. After building up the largest army ever kept under arms in peace time and equipping it with modern tools of war, drawn for the first time from an adequate native industry, the military leaders may have felt that their responsibility for assuring Soviet victory in case of war could not be confined to technical and strategic preparations. They may well have urged changes in domestic policy. Such interference beyond their "special" sphere may have led to a general conflict over Soviet policy, a conflict in which the military leaders were outmanoeuvred by Stalin and his supporters. This interpretation finds support in the evidence of the latest trial, at which Bukharin asserted that Stalin's policy was leading Russia to defeat. He denied the accusation that he had intended to hand over Soviet territory to Germany and Japan; but he admitted that defeat might force Russia to surrender some territory temporarily. At the same time, in order to revive the people's will to victory, important internal changes would have to be made after the defeat and Stalin's overthrow. What are the conditions which led the military leaders and the party opposition to despair of Russia's success in case of an early war?

During the term of the First Five-Year Plan, from 1928 to 1932, Russia was engaged in a piecemeal and undeclared civil war. Large groups of the peasantry were "liquidated"; others left the land; the remainder was forced into a collectivized system of agriculture, devised to satisfy the needs of the state, but repugnant to the bulk of the peasantry. Over the same period, partly as a retort to the skepticism of the intellectuals regarding the stupendous plans set forth by the government, partly as a punishment for actual sabotage by a small minority of technicians, but chiefly as a means for destroying the prestige and potential leadership of the intelligentsia, the thin but essential stratum of non-Communist intellectuals was treated with great severity. Many observers felt between 1929 and 1933 that the government was really aiming to exterminate the educated groups inherited from the old regime, even before their indispensable functions could be taken over by men trained under the new regime. At the same time, though every effort was made to secure the support of labor and it was continually assured that the Five-Year Plan was devoted to its advancement, the workers underwent very great hardships. Food was rationed through an elaborate system of distribution; the provision of housing lagged far behind the growth of the urban population; the prices of essential commodities in the free market, and even at government-controlled prices, rose far more rapidly than wages. The freedom of the workers to change jobs was considerably restricted. Only a small part of the workers improved their material position noticeably. The dissatisfaction of the bulk of the workers was expressed in a portentously high percentage of labor turnover, by "soldiering," by a high ratio of bad output, by the occasional assassination of the favored shock-brigade workers.

Faced by dissension, and even treason, within the ruling party, at grips with a real danger of foreign war, since 1934 Stalin has made one concession after another to satisfy these three main bodies of citizens—the peasantry, the workers, and the intelligentsia. The government has tried in many ways to stimulate the self-interest of the collectivized peasantry, which now cultivates about eighty per cent of the arable land. Fifty million acres of collectivized land have been parcelled out to the collective farm members for their individual use. On garden plots of half an acre to two acres, the collectivized peasant raises vegetables, pigs, chickens, and perhaps keeps a cow; he is allowed to sell on the market any surplus above his own needs. After the disastrous decline in cattle from 68,100,000 head in 1929 to 42,400,000 in 1934, the government realized that dairying had to be entrusted again to the individual interest of the peasant. It has promised each collectivized household a cow; about one fourth of the collective farm members are still unprovided for.

Within the collective farm system as well, the government has set about reawakening individual interest. The principle of distribution according to needs, or "by mouths," has been definitely condemned as "leftist," and replaced by distribution according to labor performed. Each member of the collective has a "labor book"; the brigadier, or overseer, enters each day the amount and quality of work performed in terms of so many "labor days." At the end of the year, after government taxes and payment for the services of the government-owned and -operated machine and tractor stations, seed, reserves, and so on, have been deducted, the balance is set off against the total number of labor days credited to all the members of the collective; the unit value of the labor day is thus determined, and each member is paid off in grain and rubles. This is individual piece-rate payment applied with a vengeance. Individual interest has also been stimulated by assigning a gang or brigade of forty to sixty members to a definite section of the collective. At first this was done for a single growing season; now it is, in theory, obligatory for the duration of the crop rotation cycle, varying from three to nine years. Obviously, this arouses a feeling of pseudo-proprietorship, especially since bonuses and fines of ten per cent have been established to reward or penalize the brigade for the quality of its work.

One of the chief complaints of the collectivized peasantry has been insecurity of title to the land. Frequently a collective was deprived of part or even all of its area for the benefit of a neighboring collective or of some state farm. As early as 1932, the government condemned this common practice; since 1936, deeds of perpetual use of the land have been issued to about forty per cent of the collectives. This, it is hoped, will raise the interest of the collectivized peasantry in making efficient use of its land and in effecting capital improvements. Instead of continuing its dangerous practice of taking land from the collectives, the government has broken up a large number of unprofitable state farms, more especially in the central and western regions, and turned over twenty-five million acres of this land to the collectives. By assuring more of the collectives a sufficiency of land, the government expects to strengthen the peasants' attachment to the collective system, to enable them to improve their rotation and pastures, and, tacitly, to remedy the continued land hunger.

During the process of collectivization, the government organized mechanical aid in agriculture on a large scale through the machine and tractor stations. About seventy per cent of the collectives are now assisted in some or most of their operations by these government-owned and -controlled organizations. In 1935 it was estimated that their charges for service amounted to eighteen or twenty per cent of the gross product of the collectives served. Since then the charges of the stations have been somewhat reduced; the operating deficit of the stations is, however, made good out of the state budget, which, in turn, is balanced by direct and indirect taxation of the peasantry. Needless to say, before the establishment of the stations (begun in 1929) this part of the agricultural output would have gone directly to the peasant as part of the reward for his labor and that of his animals; payments for mechanized cultivation represent, therefore, a deduction from the gross earnings of the peasant. Reduction of these charges is obviously only a palliative. The real problem is that of inciting the collectivized peasantry to improve agricultural productivity.

The most comprehensive effort to secure the active support of the collectivized peasantry for the new system is associated with the Collective Farm Charter of 1935, which codified the organization of farm labor, the piece-rate system of distribution, and the individual right of its members to "an acre and a cow." However, wholesale violations of the charter have recently been reported. In some districts the right of the collective to be consulted in drawing up its annual production plan has been ignored. In one county twenty-eight production plans were confirmed by the District Executive Committee in less than an hour; not one of the objections raised by the presidents of the collectives was given serious consideration. Another common abuse has been the wholesale expulsion of members from the collective, in violation of the charter.

One peasant was expelled by a local Communist tyrant, because he had acquired a gramophone and a bicycle, another because his grandfather had been a priest a hundred years before. An expelled peasant cannot recover his land from the collective, but may, in theory, be assigned land elsewhere. These wholesale and illegal expulsions embitter the victims, and arouse great anxiety among the remaining members of the collective. Needless to say, this mistreatment of the peasants is now officially laid at the door of the "traitors and wreckers." In general, however, the wholesale expulsions have occurred rather through government pressure to raise labor discipline in the collectives, and thus to assure the fulfilment of its plans.

Have the concessions of the last three years satisfied the peasantry? Have they assured the government of its enthusiastic support in case of foreign attack? That question could probably be settled only by the test of war. Side by side with collectives with a substantial income per household, there are others which have distributed no income to their members. In some, administrative expenses amount to twenty per cent of the gross income, instead of the two per cent allowed by the charter. In others, unwise or premature capital improvements eat up the income, leaving little or nothing to be divided among the members. Finally, there is, as always, the question of what the peasant can buy with his income, when he has one.

During the last three months, the Soviet newspapers have again echoed with indignant reports that such essentials as soap, matches, sugar, and cut tobacco are not to be had in many villages, and even in some cities. Overcharging and underweighing are reported to be widespread. When all is said and done, what the peasant and other consumers can buy, depends on the operation of industry and distribution. In this sphere, conditions are still poor, though much improved over the catastrophic situation of 1930–3. Since 1934 the distribution of consumers' goods to the villages has increased at a much more rapid rate than to the cities. The flow of goods is still very uneven, prices are high, quality is low. After several years of commodity famine, the peasant may be grateful for the recent improvement; if he looks back even to 1924–8 for comparison, he is not likely to be very enthusiastic over his present condition.

It is significant of the still continued struggle over collectivization that Bukharin asserted at his trial that the land must be returned to the use of the individual peasants, in order to assure the government of their support. When the peasants of Perm Province heard of the "freedom" proclaimed by the new constitution, they at once began to break up the collectives and to revert to individual cultivation, until stopped by the government. The problem of individual as against collective ownership of the land in Russia is now fundamentally a problem of raising agricultural productivity to support an ever-increasing population. The collective system must achieve this through efficient organization and specialization of labor, introduction of intensive crops, and improved rotations to enrich the soil and the diet, through capital improvements and the application of modern knowledge to every collective farm. This colossal task will require many years. Will the international situation allow the Soviet government the margin of time needed? If not, the Russian peasantry may yet reject this proposed collectivist escape from its blind alley, just as it rejected Stolypin's individualist solution in 1917.

In organizing and directing the village along its new path, the government has created a new mainstay of its power. From among the collectivized peasantry it has singled out a thin stratum of better-paid and loyal "leaders." Brigadiers, who oversee thc work of large groups, *zvenevye* in charge of smaller units, tractor drivers and presidents of collectives, exert much power locally and earn far more than the average members. When the government wishes to consult the peasantry, this responsible and privileged group speaks for the villages as a whole.

A similar tendency towards the creation of a new upper crust has been going on among the workers. Ever since 1930–1, there has been a growing emphasis on the payment of differential wages and piece-rate work, as incentives to labor discipline and efficiency. The culmination of this process came with the Stakhanovite movement of 1935–7, which established many new records of individual output and earnings. But instead of co-ordinating all stages in production, making the entire process run more smoothly, and thus raising efficiency all around, the Stakhanovite system placed chief stress on the setting of high individual records. In the Azov and Black Sea regions it was discovered that Stakhanovite records had been achieved by concentrating the best tractors, oil supply, repairmen, and drivers in one brigade; a record was achieved, but at the price of disorganizing and discouraging all the other tractor brigades. During the first months of 1938, a fresh start was made with Stakhanovism; now it is intended to represent genuine competition in efficiency, not the running up of useless individual records. The newspapers recently denounced the proclamation of a "Stakhanovite month," and declared that every month must be Stakhanovite.

This movement, as well as its forerunners, those of the "shock-brigade workers" and the "excellent workers," has left one permanent result—the creation of a labor aristocracy. Before the war a labor aristocracy had scarcely begun to emerge in Russia. The equalitarian emotions of the revolutionary upsurge, which persisted well into the term of the First Five-Year Plan, further delayed its development. It has been emerging rapidly during the 1930's. This thin layer of well-paid, skilled workers and overseers enjoys the highest standard of living attainable in Russia, except for a few handfuls of political, technical, and literary figures. This social process is a natural consequence of Russia's industrial expansion. The development of a large number of new industries, the demand for many new types of skill, the growing complexity of the industrial equipment, the discarding of foreign engineers and mechanics have stimulated the growth of a layer of skilled workers. This new stratum is firmly attached to the regime which has enabled it to rise out of the morass of the untrained and underpaid. At the same time, its emergence shows how far the country has moved from the equalitarian slogans and impulses of the revolution; many Old Bolsheviks still idealize proletarian solidarity, which is now receding into the past, so far as material conditions are concerned. The Stalinist conception of proletarian democracy is based not on "equality of reward" but on the "career open to talents."

The industrial problem of labor discipline and incentive has apparently been handled with increasing success through piecework and the creation of a labor aristocracy. The problem of financial stability has been less amenable to control. During the past four years, the reckless financing of industry has been abandoned, largely because the government has had to return a larger share of the national income to the collectivized peasantry; in part, because of the growing burden of military expenditure. The principle of making industry pay its own way has frequently come into conflict with the obligations of the government factories towards their workers. During the early months of 1938, the newspapers have bristled with reports of factories which owe their workers arrears of wages over several months, sometimes amounting to millions of rubles. When a factory fails to fulfil its financial plans, the government banks cut down its credits, and it is unable to pay its workers or to buy new raw materials from other government agencies. The principle of self-supporting industry has also collided with the institution of detailed, centralized planning. It was discovered, for example, that under the new profit principle the furniture industry was concentrating on the production of high-priced articles, which brought a substantial profit, to the neglect of cheap and unprofitable articles, required by the mass consumer and provided for by the plan. When volume was stressed in Soviet industry, cost was disregarded, and the loss was commonly made up out of the general budget, in other words, out of consumption. Now that the emphasis is on financial results, industry is inclined to shift its production to profitable lines, regardless of the central planning system. Significantly, at the trials the opposition leaders were accused of desiring to destroy the system of planning, and to revert to a concession system of industrial management.

In addition to favoring the development of its two new mainstays—the managers of collectivized agriculture and the new labor aristocracy—the Stalin government has been cultivating the good will of the new intelligentsia. The educated class in Russia today is very different from the prewar intelligentsia. It is much more numerous. Its training has been more technical and practical. It has no firsthand knowledge of the outside world, and is sincerely convinced that, however bad some conditions may be at home, things are much worse elsewhere. It is little disturbed over the "eternal questions" to which the older intelligentsia devoted sleepless nights of soul-searching discussion. Its prime concern is with a career and a comfortable living. Julien Benda would call it "Americanized," in a derogatory sense. The new intelligentsia is indifferent to abstractions. It is eager to enjoy whatever comfort or even prosperity may come its way; having risen directly from the masses, unlike a large part of the prewar intelligentsia, it has no uneasy feeling of prospering at the expense of the masses. Though devoid of the idealism and enthusiasms of the older intelligentsia, the new educated class is by no means indifferent to literature and history, to the theatre and music. In the future it may so far mature as to feel the need for a freely developing culture, for free inquiry and creation. Now, however, it seems quite accustomed to living within the walls of orthodoxy erected by the regime.

During the last four years, the government has made many efforts to assure itself of the support of the new intelligentsia. The very name, "intelligentsia," was one of contempt during the time of the First Five-Year Plan; now it connotes the highest praise. Stalin has frequently lauded the non-Communist intelligentsia as against the inefficient and heretical party members. The wooing of the educated class has been particularly felt in the rehabilitation of Great Russian culture and history. The renewed cult of Pushkin and Nekrasov, the revived veneration for Peter the Great and St. Alexander Nevskii, the rewriting of history to stress the positive contributions made by the Russian people, indicate this shift. With it has come a new stress on the importance of the Russian language as a common medium of all the peoples in the Union. The number of hours devoted to Russian has been sharply increased in the schools of the non-Russian republics, at the expense of the local languages. In large measure, this new emphasis on Russian language and culture represents a reaction against the long-continued depreciation of prerevolutionary Russian culture as a common Soviet heritage, and against the excessive glorification of the non-Russian cultures.

The growth of anti-Russian, local nationalism, even among the non-Russian Communists, was stressed by the recent trials; and during the past three years, repeated purges have been carried through in all the non-Russian republics. In a little over a year, the secretaryship of the Communist party of the Ukraine has changed hands three times. Half the Communists of the large Kiev organization were charged with counterrevolution, some falsely so. The head of the Belorussian Republic committed suicide, and many of his aids were shot as spies and traitors. Twenty party members were shot in Tiflis, allegedly for striving to separate

Georgia from the Soviet Union. Uzbek leaders were tried along with Bukharin. The strenuous years of industrialization and collectivization were bound to arouse strong local and national opposition to Stalin's policies. At the same time, the hothouse forcing of a new national intelligentsia among each of the many nationalities certainly created strong ambitions for power among the newly educated. The strongest centrifugal force, however, has been economic discontent. A uniform type of education, the conscious fostering of a supranational, Soviet loyalty, the increasing mingling of the different nationalities, and growth of economic interdependence should be listed among the centripetal forces in the Soviet nationalities policy.

If one were to accept literally the accusations made at the recent trials and purges of party, economic, and cultural life, the inevitable conclusion would be that the Soviet regime is passing through a dangerous, perhaps fatal crisis. Yet this conclusion can hardly be subscribed to. To the unaccustomed ear Bolshevist vocabulary is primitive and pungent; it disdains nuances. The meaning of Soviet trials and purges cannot be measured by the democratic yardstick. "Demonstration trials" have been staged at fairly recurrent intervals; purges and re-purges have been going on with a varying degree of intensity ever since the founding of the regime; the outpourings of "self-criticism," as exercised through the press, are regularly turned on and off, at the government's behest. In Soviet newspapers, loud boasting alternates with equally loud denunciation. For a dictator, spectacular purges are almost the only way of making sharp changes in policy, and of weeding out inefficient or stale figures in the apparatus.

The recent purges and trials have, however, surpassed any of their forerunners in their known range and intensity. In estimating their importance we are, of course, at the serious disadvantage of not knowing how many obscure people have been imprisoned or executed in connection with them. What is more, these purges have apparently caused a real shift in the apparatus of government. The party formerly eclipsed the government machine in actual power; the bureaucracy, with much creaking and inefficiency, carried out policies initiated by the party. With the growing concentration of its power in Stalin's hands, the party has gradually lost all voice in determining policy. After balancing for several years among the party, the political police, and the army, as instruments of his rule, Stalin has apparently put all his bets on the police system. In the rivalry between the army and the political police, the latter have won; they now dominate the army through the institution of two "military commissars" to supervise the work of the army commander of each military district. The triumph of the political police over the economic apparatus has been sealed with the appointment of police officials as heads of several important commissariats, such as water transport, communications, and timber. In addition, the police have long had a very large industrial, mining, and lumbering setup of their own, and have their representatives strategically placed within all government, economic, and cultural branches.

The political police, under Yezhov, now exercise direct control over the party organizations as well. Demoralized by the disgrace of its former idols, wracked by the purge, driven to distraction by the most recent "purge of the purgers," the party must have been an easy prey to the police system. On numerous occasions, Yezhov's office has condemned party organizations for wrongly expelling members under unsubstantiated charges of "wrecking" and "treason." Thus the political police have the final voice as to the right to belong to the party at all. Party membership is now less attractive than bcforc, especially when measured against the risks which it entails. During and since the election campaign of December 1937, the government has stressed its claim to represent the "bloc of the party and nonparty members," thus dropping at least the appearance of a

Communist "monopoly of power." In subjecting to the political police its rivals for influence over Soviet policy, Stalin has probably had in mind the danger of divided leadership in case of war, as well as the threat to his own power. Possibly the unified "police state" will work with less friction and inefficiency than the "party state"; perhaps not. In any case, the sensational process of transition to the police state has apparently dealt a fatal blow to the older conception of the function of the party, at the same time shaking Soviet prestige abroad.

For all its uncouth ways of doing things, the Soviet regime has been accomplishing a number of essential jobs, at an expense difficult to measure. It has given tremendous impetus to the industrialization of Russia and to the utilization of its natural resources; it has done so without mortgaging the future of the country to foreign creditors. The regime has outlined and in part set going a system of social welfare which may eventually create real social security, once the level of production permits it. It has created, to an unusual degree, equality of opportunity for the present generation of youth, thus preparing the way to use the country's best human resources. It has made great strides in combating political forms of exclusive nationalism, while leaving considerable leeway for cultural development among its many nationalities; it has been working toward a new kind of state, not one based primarily on nationalism.

This experiment is doubly significant at a time when exasperated national feeling is heaping up fresh dangers everywhere else in Europe. The Soviet regime has organized the defense of its territory in earnest; for the first time, Russian armies are backed by an adequate industrial system. However it may seek to preserve international peace, whether through isolation or through co-operation, the Soviet government is among the defenders of peace today, instead of being a factor of imperialist rivalry and diplomatic instability. Within these general lines of Soviet development, a sharp struggle has been going on over the concrete means of doing these jobs—a struggle between Stalin and other Old Bolsheviks, between the party as it was under Lenin and the party in its new subordinate role, between Soviet nationalism and local nationalism, between the political police and their rivals for control. On these struggles the recent trials have thrown a lurid, if fitful light. But these struggles did not begin with the trials, and they have not ended with them.

:4:

FREEDOM OF ARTISTIC EXPRESSION AND SCIENTIFIC INQUIRY IN RUSSIA[1]

[*January 1938*]

INTRODUCTORY NOTE · The role of party ideology and party controls is a determining one in Soviet science, literature, and art, and disputes within the Soviet apparatus relate to the intensity and manner of control, not to its central function and inevitability. Yet the relation between control and creativity defies solution. Artistic and scientific achievements can be encouraged, facilitated, and rewarded by political authorities, but they do not spring at the party's command from the brains of creative individuals. Can there be successes in science and art without failures? And who, except intelligent and tolerant "users" of the product, can serve as judges of success and failure?

Through an intensive exploration of Soviet published sources of 1936 and 1937, of which only a small part could be presented in article length, this study tried to delineate both the tragic impasse of Soviet scientific, literary, and artistic creativity and the continuing quandary of a totali-

[1] *Annals of the American Academy of Political and Social Science*, Vol. cc (December 1938), pp. 254–74. Copyright 1938 by the American Academy of Political and Social Science.

tarian regime which claims to foster creative "freedom" more effectively than the loosely organized, pluralistic societies of the democracies. Written halfway through the present lifetime of the Soviet regime, "Freedom of Artistic Expression and Scientific Inquiry in Russia" may serve to clarify the process by which the ruling party set about binding all intellectual life to its purposes.

Since that tragic era, in which even those who survived the "binding" were crippled intellectually, the natural sciences have, it is true, made great strides in some fields of abstract and applied research. In part this has been due to the increasing blending of party controls and scientific management. Because a larger number of vigorous scientific administrators are party members, they are better equipped to protect their institutes against day-to-day political interference. Because of the power and prestige they bring to the state, they are left free to work more or less unhindered within their specialized fields of research. In the political and social sciences, however, the "unbinding" of the researcher has been slow, tentative, and hesitant. (See below, Twenty-one, "Russia Revisited: Moscow Dialogues, 1956" for some impressions of Soviet social sciences in 1956.)

*

AGAINST any attempt to compress within the limits of an article a survey of intellectual freedom in the Soviet Union today, at least two objections will at once be raised. Such an effort will, with justification, be declared unhistorical. To measure freedom at any time and in any country is an ungrateful task. The laboratory has yet to produce a "freedom meter" to put beside its ingenious lie detector. In lieu of such a device, it would, no doubt, be instructive to turn back, for comparison with the present, to the intellectual life of sixteenth-century Moscovia, based as it was on a definite body of revelation and sacred commentaries, which controversialists such as Ivan the Terrible and the *émigré*

Prince Kurbskii hurled at each other's heads. The picture of a Nicholas I "guiding" the creative mind of a Pushkin and chastising his deviations from the official slogans of "autocracy, orthodoxy, and nationalism" would offer food for ironic reflection. The struggles of Leo Tolstoy against political censorship and ecclesiastical anathema are fresh in human memory. To this objection the following paper presents but one defense: it is frankly unhistorical. It limits its scope to conditions in the Soviet Union in 1936 and 1937. It is intended as a factual summary of Soviet practice, and leaves it to the reader to fill in the domestic and international background.

The second objection is equally serious. Marxism regards all intellectual activity as a part of the superstructure of social development taken as a whole, which is determined in turn by the emergent phases of the class struggle. Marxism is regarded by its advocates both as the only basis of scientific and artistic creation and as the most important weapon in the armory of the proletarian class struggle; hence it regards as scientifically and artistically "true" only that which aids the proletariat in its struggle to overthrow capitalism and to establish a classless society. As Academician Gubkin has recently reminded the world, Lenin considered "pure" or "classless" science to be an impossibility.[2] The classless society has supposedly been consummated in the main with the completion of the Second Five-Year Plan (December 31, 1937); thus, in a society which is now proclaimed to be neither capitalist nor proletarian, but Soviet in character, science and art should also be emerging, presumably, into a classless era. Since, however, class and political motives are still being sought in all expressions of scientific and artistic activity in the Soviet Union, the purpose of this article is not to argue the question of Marxist determinism, but to examine concretely recent phenomena in this

[2] Akademik I. Gubkin: "*Lenin i nauka*," *Pravda*, No. 21 (Jan. 21, 1937), p. 3.

sphere of life, no less important for the well-being and progress of a society than statistics of literacy or of grain production.

Despite the emphasis on Marxist orthodoxy which underlies the Bolshevist attitude toward intellectual inquiry and artistic creation, it is interesting to note that Soviet practice has varied widely during the first twenty years of the new regime. The years of revolution, civil war, and militant communism (1917–22) were years of relative liberty, even anarchy, in the intellectual sphere. Innumerable groups of poets and painters gave expression to the most varied and extravagant "isms." Except in matters directly affecting the country's political crisis, the censorship was fairly lax. Scholars, writers, and artists who were not connected with any anti-Bolshevist party were given a special ration; the new regime sought to win the co-operation of the intelligentsia, without, however, concealing or neglecting the weapons of coercion at its disposal.

Under the New Economic Policy (1922–7) the Bolshevist party began more actively to dominate the intellectual field. It developed its own leading institutions, such as the Communist Academy and the Lenin Institute, which came into being side by side with older universities and institutions like the Academy of Sciences. In the country at large and in the intellectual and artistic sphere, the old and the new existed together in unstable equilibrium.

The new drive for militant communism, associated with the First Five-Year Plan (1927–32), destroyed that temporary equilibrium. The emphasis was now placed on proletarian culture, proletarian literature, even proletarian science. Definite, organized groups, backed by unlimited government and party support, undertook to put these slogans into effect. The Academy of Sciences was overhauled; many of its older and non-Communist members, tolerated till then, were sent into exile or prison when the mild regime of Secretary Oldenburg gave way to that of Volgin and Gorbunov. Scientists were ordered to stop "daydreaming" and to buckle down to solving the pressing problems of socialist reconstruction. In literature, non-Communist "fellow travelers" were thrust aside and a hundred per cent Communist and proletarian literature was proclaimed as the goal. In every sphere, prerevolutionary figures were ruthlessly dispatched to the outer limbo by younger, militant, and sometimes unscrupulous successors.

After the severe strain of the First Plan, a certain relaxation set in, from 1933 to 1935. It has been attributed, in part at least, to the influence of Maxim Gorkii, who was eager to reconcile the government and the intelligentsia, and of Kirov, who, as political head of Leningrad, was particularly impressed by the cultural and scientific values preserved and produced in the former capital. Be its cause what it may, an important work of pacification was undertaken in those years. Writers and critics, previously terrorized by the activities of Averbach's group in control of the Russian Association of Proletarian Writers, were in 1934 united into a single Union of Soviet Writers. In literature an era of good feeling seemed to replace the spirit of mutual destruction. The same type of unification and reconciliation was effected in music, painting, sculpture, and architecture. The rivalry between the Communist Academy and the older Academy of Sciences was overcome by fusing the two into an Academy of Sciences of the U.S.S.R. This era of good feeling was marked by foreign recognition of Soviet scientific achievement (the Moscow Congress of Physiologists and the Arctic exploration for example), and by a new stress on "Soviet humanism" and "Soviet realism" in literature (the popularity of Sholokhov, Pavlenko, and Nicholas Ostrovskii).

However, after Kirov's murder in December 1934 by a disgruntled Communist, a fresh wave of tension set in. Month by month it spread throughout the party, the vast economic structure, and finally cultural life. Scientific and artistic creation was subjected to political scrutiny with a rigor unequaled even in earlier years of the regime. The relative "liberalism" of 1932–5 gave way to a relentless ferreting out of "deviations." Expression in the past of ideas identified with or tolerated by the party line of that time, but no longer consonant with its present tendencies, became a frequent cause of political disgrace and creative annihilation. In 1936 and 1937 every sphere of scientific and artistic life saw its existing standards and dogmas discarded, and its personnel drastically overhauled. Many of the standard-bearers of Bolshevist orthodoxy in intellectual life were relegated to the pariah status of "enemies of the people," and their ideas denounced as "counter-revolutionary." Science and art were required to adhere to the ever-shifting line of the ruling party even more closely than between 1929 and 1932.

The repercussions of this general tension within the party will now be traced in the arts—music, architecture, painting, sculpture, and literature; in the social sciences—history, ethnography, jurisprudence, and political science, economics, psychology, and philosophy; and in the physical and biological sciences, especially genetics. Only official Soviet material, drawn from newspapers, journals, and books of the years 1936 and 1937, has been used; hearsay evidence has been rigorously excluded. Although the multiplicity of names may at times be fatiguing, it is scarcely to be avoided if the reader is to be enabled to judge for himself the extent and severity of the purge which has been going on in almost every branch of art and science.

The signal for overhauling intellectual and artistic life was given by two events, neither of which was fully appreciated at the time. On January 27, 1936, the official press issued a government decree announcing a competition for the writing of a new textbook on the history of the U.S.S.R.[3] On the following day *Pravda* made a slashing attack on Dmitry Shostakovich, best

[3] Decree of Jan. 26, 1936, signed by Stalin and Molotov, *Izvestiia*, No. 23 (Jan. 27, 1936), p. 3; *Pravda*, No. 26 (Jan. 27, 1936), p. 2.

known as composer of *Lady Macbeth of Mtsensk.*[4] The decree for the reform in the teaching of history became the signal for a general "cleansing" of the theories and personnel throughout the social sciences—a process which will be traced in some detail in a later section of this article. The attack of the leading party organ against Shostakovich's "decadent bourgeois formalism and naturalism" in music marked the beginning of a drastic sifting of tendencies and persons in all branches of art and literature.

Since 1930 Dmitry Shostakovich had been widely hailed as a composer of genius, the first among the postwar generation to achieve general fame. As late as January 20, 1936, the government organ, *Izvestiia*, asserted that his work had "conquered the love of the mass spectator," and that his *Lady Macbeth* was "the most brilliant Soviet production in music."[5] But even then, signs of a change were visible. In the same issue *Izvestiia* published the official report of an interview of Stalin and Molotov with Dzerzhinskii, composer of the music for the opera *Quiet Flows the Don*, a work of slight musical originality but inspired by Soviet patriotism and Cossack folklore. At this time, *Izvestiia* had no foreboding of the impending purge, for, in its editorial comment on this interview, it listed Shostakovich first among five Soviet composers whom it singled out for highest praise.[6]

On January 28 *Pravda* struck. It denounced Shostakovich root and branch for destroying harmony and melody in music, for his alleged striving for innovation at the expense of intelligibility, for "leftist stress of ugliness," for naturalism and formalism, for sympathy

[4] *"Sumbur vmesto muzyki; ob opere 'Ledi Makbet Mtsenskogo uezda,'" Pravda*, No. 27 (Jan. 28, 1936), p. 3.

[5] A. Piotrovskii: *"Laboratoriia sovetskoi opery," Izvestiia*, No. 4 (Jan. 5, 1936), p. 4; V. Mlechin: *"Teatr smelykh iskanii,"* ibid., No. 17 (Jan. 20, 1936), p. 4.

[6] *"Beseda tovarishchei Stalina i Molotova s avtorami opernogo spektaklia 'Tikhii Don,'"* ibid., No. 17 (Jan. 20, 1936), p. 1; *"Vyshe znamia iskusstva sotsializma!"* ibid., p. 1.

with the bourgeois heroine of the opera and for being "unpolitical," and finally for the interest shown abroad in his music. On February 6 *Pravda* returned to the attack with an article annihilating Shostakovich's ballet, *Limpid Stream.* It accused (and accusation by *Pravda* is equivalent to condemnation without opportunity for appeal) the composer of failure to treat the collective farm and the Kuban Cossacks in realistic fashion. Another article denounced Shostakovich's musical compositions for the cinema, and also attacked L. Knipper for "crude naturalism," Leitsus for abstractness, and Pototskii for neglect of the folk song as the true basis of soviet music.[7]

The new favorite, Dzerzhinskii, smugly wrapped himself in the folds of official approval, expressed in the Stalin-Molotov interview, and hastened to inform the press of his own ideological orthodoxy. "I have never had to renounce, in oral or written form, any of my creative principles, and I have no need to do so now." In the meeting held by the Moscow Composer's Union to discuss the *Pravda* thunderbolt, it was sarcastically pointed out that, while musicians had flocked to first auditions of Shostakovich's works, scarcely any of them had attended the session devoted to Dzerzhinskii's opera. *Izvestiia* now discovered, contrary to its declaration of January 5, that "the broad opera-going public was dissatisfied with *Lady Macbeth.*"[8]

In the discussion held by the Leningrad Composers' Union one critic, A. S. Rabinovich, declared that he saw only "two possibilities: either I must discover the mistakes in my conception and bring it into harmony with the directions issued by *Pravda*, or, if I cannot see those mistakes, I must change my profession. . . .

[7] "*Baletnaia fal'sh,*" Pravda, No. 36 (Feb. 6, 1936), p. 3; D. Kabalevskii: "*Podenshchina v kinomuzyke i ee plody,*" ibid., No. 59 (Feb. 29, 1936), p. 4.

[8] I. Dzerzhinskii: "*Chto ia izvlek dlia sebia?*" *Izvestiia*, No. 38 (Feb. 14, 1936), p. 4; "*Tvorcheskaia diskussiia moskovskikh kompozitorov,*" ibid., No. 38 (Feb. 14, 1936), p. 4; N. Cheliapov: "*Diskussiia na muzykal'nom fronte,*" ibid., No. 49 (Feb. 27, 1936), p. 3.

The critic too has the right to demand careful treatment for himself. He too is a living being, with convictions which it is not so simple and easy to break and reset. . . ." Rabinovich was at once attacked and overwhelmed by the official leaders of the union as "an anti-Soviet preacher of militant formalism." In this atmosphere of denunciation and panic, special mention had to be made that Shostakovich was not to be regarded as "done for," as "a living corpse," or as an object for "demagogical annihilation." [9] However, his operas and ballets were automatically removed from the stage, as an immediate consequence of *Pravda's* attack. A list of fifteen composers at work on operas in March of 1937 did not include Shostakovich's name.[1]

The "creative discussion" in the Leningrad Union was also devoted to the "exposure of the concrete bearers of bourgeois formalistic music." Composers Popov, Shcherbachev, Kochurov, Zhelobinskii, and Arapov, together with critics Sollertinskii, Samosud, Rabinovich, and Druskin, were singled out for denunciation as hostile to Soviet realism, indifferent to the tastes and musical creations of the masses, and overmuch influenced by the "decadent" music of the West. Schönberg, Honegger, and Berg were anathematized; the atonal system was definitely banned as "un-Soviet" and as "a sign of the blind alley in which bourgeois music is caught, a sign of its hopeless crisis." [2]

Meanwhile the organization of musical work was also being subjected to severe criticism. *Izvestiia* denounced to the newly formed and omnipotent Commit-

[9] "*Protiv formalizma i fal'shi. Tvorcheskaia diskussiia v Leningradskom soiuze sovetskikh kompozitorov,*" *Sovetskaia Muzyka*, No. 5 (May 1936), pp. 50, 53; P. Riazanov: "*Zadachi sovetskogo kompozitora,*" ibid., p. 23, B. Asaf'ev: "*Volnuiushchie voprosy,*" ibid., p. 26.

[1] G. Khubov: "*Novye sovetskie opery,*" *Pravda*, No. 68 (Mar. 10, 1937), p. 6; "Composer Regains His Place in Soviet," *The New York Times*, Nov. 29, 1937, p. 24, reports the première of Shostakovich's Fifth Symphony.

[2] "*Protiv formalizma i fal'shi. Tvorcheskaia diskussiia v Leningradskom soiuze sovetskikh kompozitorov,*" *Sovetskaia Muzyka*, No. 5 (May 1936), pp. 28, 29, 30; P. Riazanov: "*Zadachi sovetskogo kompozitora,*" ibid., pp. 18, 19.

tee for the Affairs of the Arts widespread favoritism in the arranging of concerts. "Some far from first-class 'soloist' who is clever enough to arouse the material interest of the administrator receives a tremendous number of engagements, while an honest and modest artist seldom has a chance to appear in concerts." This is especially serious since the organization of concerts is the monopoly of a government bureau. The state of the Composers' Union in June 1937 was also far from satisfactory. The union was dominated by a clique.

> Shutting themselves off in a small group, looking after their own prosperity and not the advancement of Soviet music, they . . . have brought the Union to ruin. . . . They have laid hands on the monopoly right to accept, evaluate, and distribute musical output. They advertise and push compositions which are often very mediocre, but have been written by their toadies. They generously bestow numerous 'subsidies' on their friends. . . . The party group . . . does not permit them to be exposed and suppresses the criticism which had been begun. . . .[3]

Under such conditions it seems a slight exaggeration to declare, as did one Soviet critic, that "the party and the government, with the support of the broad masses of toilers, with remarkable love and care aid Soviet creative organizations and each individual creative worker." [4]

Pravda's attack on formalism in music was at once extended to the field of architecture. At a conference of Moscow architects Academician Alabian complained: "We all agree that formalism is in general alien to Soviet architecture; but when we begin to speak of concrete bearers of formalism, our disagreements and contradictions commence." Alabian remedied this lack by attacking the work of two outstanding architects,

[3] "*Bol'nye uchastki muzykal'nogo fronta,*" *Izvestiia,* No. 53 (Mar. 3, 1936), p. 4; A. Volozhenin: "*V Moskovskom soiuze kompozitorov,*" ibid., No. 149 (June 27, 1937), p. 3.

[4] V. Iokhel'son: "*Na poroge 4-i godovshchiny L.S.S.K.,*" *Sovetskaia Muzyka,* No. 11 (Nov. 1935), p. 9.

Mel'nikov and Leonidov. Right then and there Vesnin and Ginzburg renounced their former constructivist theories in architecture. In June 1937 the architects continued to denounce formalism, eclecticism, and constructivism, and to urge the combination of American technique with the classical style.[5]

The painters also had to be brought into harmony with the new line in art, as expressed in the *Pravda* article against Shostakovich. In June 1936 the all-powerful head of the Committee for the Affairs of the Arts, Comrade Kerzhentsev, attacked the existing system of buying new works for the famous Tret'iakov Museum of Russian Art.

> Its directors have acted on the liberal principle that the museum's task was to display . . . every tendency in painting, without any adequate criterion and without in the least considering whether the works were realistic or not. This supposed objectivity, in reality, masked encouragement given to all formalistic and crudely realistic tendencies in painting. . . .

The subdictator in the arts went on to denounce Larionov, Udal'tsov, Rozanov, and six other painters for depicting ugly children, formless lines, scarcely human figures, a broken violin, and so forth. His committee announced its decision to remove from the Tret'iakov Museum in Moscow and the Russian Museum in Leningrad all formalistic and naturalistic paintings of the last twenty-five years.

> Such paintings have no place in the public halls, but belong in special buildings to be used by art specialists or to illustrate the very coarse formalistic and naturalistic errors made by some of our artists. The Soviet section in these museums must be gone over with special care and supplemented by the princi-

[5] D. K.: "*Formalizm v arkhitekture*," *Izvestiia*, No. 51 (Feb. 29, 1936), p. 4; "*Rezoliutsiia I Vsesoiuznogo s'ezda sovetskikh arkhitektorov po dokladam o zadachakh sovetskoi arkhitektury*," ibid., No. 149 (June 27, 1937), p. 3; A Shchusev: "*Sovetskaia arkhitektura i klassicheskoe nasledstvo*," ibid., p. 3; "*Arkhitektor sovetskoi strany*," ibid., p. 1.

> pal works of Soviet realist artists. . . . Through understanding the artistic heritage of the masters of painting—the realists—through relentless struggle against formalism and crude naturalism, we will build the road for socialist pictorial art to flourish.[6]

Since private patronage has disappeared in the Soviet Union, this means that hereafter the only source of livelihood for painters—purchase by government museums—is to be reserved to those who can convince Comrade Kerzhentsev that they are realists.

The campaign against naturalism in art was carried a step further in September 1937. A collection of recent paintings and studies of the Soviet Ukraine was first exhibited in a dozen cities and praised by the local newspapers, only to meet with complete annihilation at the hands of *Pravda*. Some of the pictures represented mean huts, lopsided hovels, poorly clad mothers and children, gaunt cows. *Pravda* exclaimed with indignation:

> Where are the beautifully arranged streets, the gay houses of the Ukrainian collective farms? . . . Neither clubs, nor kindergartens, nor electrical stations of the collective farms are shown here. . . . This entire collection cannot be regarded as anything but an insolent sally of Ukrainian bourgeois nationalists. The Trotskyite-Bukharinist enemies, wreckers, at work in the Administration for the Affairs of the Arts, under the Council of People's Commissars of the Ukraine, have lauded this exhibition to the skies. They have deliberately guided the brush of some painters of the Ukraine along a hostile path. . . .[7]

In case painters still had any doubts concerning the difference between naturalism and realism, they now know that realism means depicting rosy-cheeked, pearly-toothed maidens against a background of model cot-

[6] P. Kerzhentsev: "*O tret'iakovskoi galleree*," Pravda, No. 155 (June 7, 1936), p. 3.

[7] T. Gorbunov: "*Kleveta na ukrainskuiu deistvitel'nost'*," ibid., No. 252 (Sept. 12, 1937), p. 4.

tages, power stations, and electric milking machines. Artists who ruthlessly expressed the ugly sides of life under Tsarism are now venerated as realists; but since life has become prosperous, gay, and free under the new regime, any artist who paints the less attractive sides of its life is obviously a "naturalist," a sabateur, and a "Trotskyite slanderer."

The Moscow Union of Soviet Artists owned and operated four sculpture workshops, a lithographic plant, a painting shop, four decoration plants, two shops for banners, one for artistic embroidery, a workshop for the production of artists' canvas, and so forth. All this activity would seem to be useful and necessary. However, *Pravda* was dissatisfied. When the Union of Soviet Artists was formed in 1932, over ten various groups were combined in it. But the previous groups continued to make themselves felt within the new union.

> Even in the party group of the administration the representatives of the various creative groups and groupings combat one another continually. All this holds back the development of artistic creativeness and creates a serious danger lest a number of artists, including Communists, be deflected from the very important political tasks confronting Soviet art. . . .[8]

Thus, from the official Soviet viewpoint, diversity and disagreement among artistic groups and tendencies represent a political danger, which can be overcome only by enforcing conformity through more intense supervision by the responsible political organs, such as the party group in the administration of the union and

[8] N. Denisovskii: "*Pis'mo v redaktsiiu. Khudozhnikam nuzhen edinyi soiuz*," ibid., No. 63 (Mar. 5, 1937), p. 3. Although this report is contained in a "Letter to the Editor," a Soviet editor is personally responsible not only for every line printed, but also for typographical errors and makeup. *Pravda* blasted the editors of *Komsomol'skaia Pravda* and *Sotsialisticheskaia Sviaz'* for printing satirical verses on the reverse page of a picture of a Soviet hero; "if one examines the paper against the light, the result is a pasquinade furnishing the class enemy occasion for evil exultation." "*Eshche o redaktorskoi bditel'nosti*," *Pravda*, No. 3 (Jan. 3, 1937), p. 6.

the "responsible representative" of the Committee for the Affairs of the Arts.

The attack on the inactivity of the Artists' Union was at once followed by a similar blast against the Moscow Union of Sculptors. The union had not convened for several years; it had not even been called together to pass a resolution denouncing the Trotskyite traitors of August 1936 and January 1937; it was disclosed that its Production Bureau had been in the hands of an unnamed "enemy of the people."[9] In June 1937, *Izvestiia* reported that the Moscow sculptors had not held a single general meeting since 1931, and that no new members had been admitted in over three years. When a general meeting was at last called, the government organ expressed disgust at the lack of "healthy criticism," of "thorough discussion of the future of Soviet sculpture."[1] Evidently, the Moscow sculptors were politically so "backward" that they failed to realize that their art could progress only by a constant search for, and denunciation of, "naturalism" and "formalism."

If such was the case, their complacency was to be rudely shattered. In July 1937, *Izvestiia* devastatingly condemned a large part of the current exhibition of sculpture in Moscow.

> Is this not an anatomical museum, in which the unheard-of uglinesses of the human body have been deliberately collected for the edification of posterity? . . . Bourgeois art has created great images of manly and womanly beauty, strengthening the victorious class of the *bourgeoisie*. Soviet sculpture must create, and will create, very great images of the beauty of the victorious Soviet people, images which will evoke emulation, which will fill with pride the hearts of Soviet people. . . .

[9] B. Sandomirskaia: "*Pis'mo v redaktsiiu. Ne tvorcheskii soiuz, a kantselariia*," ibid., No. 75 (Mar. 17, 1937), p. 4. The term "enemy of the people" implies that its bearer has been "liquidated' by the firing squad, prison, or exile to some remote part of the country.

[1] K.: "*Sobranie skul'ptorov Moskvy*," *Izvestiia*, No. 135 (June 10, 1937), p. 4; I. B.: "*U skul'ptorov*," ibid., No. 136 (June 11, 1937), p. 4.

In the discussion held at the opening of the exhibition "not a single voice had been raised in wrathful protest . . ." against counterrevolutionary formalism and naturalism. Even "the Responsible Representative of the Committee for the Affairs of the Arts," Comrade Neiman—the official champion of the party line in art—had made no objection to the exhibits.[2] Hereafter, Soviet sculptors, like Soviet painters and musicians, will know what is "art" and what is "anti-Soviet slander"—till the next shift in the party line.

The latest purge in literature did not get under way until early in 1937. The plenary session of the Administration of the Writers' Union met in February 1937 in an atmosphere very different from that of February 1936. In 1936 there had been few recriminations among the writers. As a matter of fact, *Izvestiia* reproached the union for talking continually about the works of the past instead of "discussing in concrete and businesslike fashion what has been accomplished in Soviet literature over the last year and a half." At this session the recent *Pravda* attack on formalism in music was carried over to the field of poetry. Pasternak, one of the most talented Soviet poets, was severely denounced for his alleged tendency to "formalism"; however, to the accompaniment of loud applause, he was defended by several prominent critics against the charge of being merely a lyrical and "intimate" poet.[3] By February 1937 the official attitude toward Pasternak had changed radically, and for the worse. Bukharin, his chief advocate at the Writers' Congress of 1934, was by 1937 in prison; in 1938 he was to be tried and executed as a counterrevolutionary, anti-Stalinist conspirator. Comrade Surkov, one of the pamphleteer war horses of the party line, proclaimed to the plenary session of February 1937 that

[2] V. Burevoi: "*Sub'ekty i ob'ekty*," ibid., No. 157 (July 6, 1937), p. 3.

[3] D. Kal'm: "*Na plenume v Minske*," ibid., No. 38 (Feb. 14, 1936), p. 3; Kal'm: "*Na plenume v Minske*," ibid., No. 39 (Feb. 15, 1936), p. 5.

> Pushkin summons us away from the mysticism and "complicated" unintelligibility of Pasternak, Sel'vinskii, and the rest, to elevated, clear language and verse, to the creation of images of the genuine heroes of our time, the Bolsheviks, the people of the working class.

Pasternak was now accused of "slandering Soviet reality."

> The role of the restorers of bourgeois decadence in the Soviet state is becoming truly dangerous, for the Soviet people has grown to a point where it understands who is its friend and who is its enemy even in such a delicate sphere as poetry.

In opposition to Pasternak's "intimate" poetry, *Pravda* now bestowed its official blessing on the "political poetry" of Surkov, Bezymenskii, and several others, with their day-to-day treatment of government and party slogans in verse.[4]

The plenary session of February 1937 was not content with denouncing certain general tendencies in literature. Its "Responsible Secretary," Comrade Stavskii, got down to cases. "Trotskyite enemies of the people and their agents have succeeded in penetrating various units of the literary organizations. . . ." Ter-Vaganian and Friedliand had been published in the journals *Novyi Mir* and *Okt'iabr'*. The first-named journal had also printed works of "enemies of the people" such as Pikel' and Pavel Vasilev.

> The Gorbachev group has been machinating in Leningrad. The Trotskyite Senchenko has been at the head of the Ukrainian Writers' Union. A group of Dashnag [Armenian nationalist, anti-Soviet revolutionaries] and Trotskyites . . . has been at work in the Armenian Union. . . .

[4] "*Pushkinskii plenum pravleniia soiuza pisatelei*," Pravda, No. 55 (Feb. 25, 1937), p. 6; "*O politicheskoi poezii*," ibid., No. 58 (Feb. 28, 1937), p. 4.

The "Responsible Secretary" proclaimed: "We have been and are cleansing our ranks."[5]

In April 1937 a meeting of the Moscow Writers' Union denounced the work of its own secretariat. Comrade Liashko complained that it had "assembled the writers from time to time and lectured them about their backwardness" instead of examining concretely the work of individual writers. Comrade Nakoriakov attacked the union for "not guiding the creative work of the writers and not having a collective creative plan." Comrade Berezovskii accused the Literary Fund (the government fund for assistance to favored authors) and the Administration for the Protection of Authors' Rights of squandering "tens of thousands of rubles in loans and bonuses to the employees of these institutions," and of assisting various "enemies of the people."[6]

The "cleansing" of literature, already well under way during the winter of 1936–7 as a concomitant of the trials of the Old Bolsheviks, became much more intense in the spring, with the downfall of Henry Yagoda, for many years all-powerful head of the G.P.U. (General Political Administration), and since 1934 Commissar for Internal Affairs. His fall was followed by the disgrace and punishment of the former dictator of Soviet literature (1929–32), Averbach, and of the latter's numerous following in the literary world and on its fringes. Among the persons affected were the very ones who in February 1937 had been most active in denouncing their literary rivals as "enemies of the people." Even writers who had opposed Averbach did not escape the purge. The case of Bezymenskii can be taken as more or less typical.

At the plenary session of February 1937, Bezymenskii was in the front line of the denouncers; he attacked

[5] "*Plenum pravleniia soiuza pisatelei,*" ibid., No. 56 (Feb. 26, 1937), p. 6.

[6] "*Sobranie moskovskikh pisatelei,*" ibid., No. 93 (Apr. 4, 1937), p. 6.

Radek, Bukharin, and Sel'vinskii, and defended "political poetry."[7] At that time he headed the list of "political poets" selected for highest praise by *Pravda.* The June number of the literary journal *Krasnaia Nov'* contained a satirical poem by Bezymenskii, "How Fame Is Made." The poem was an attack on Kirshon and Afinogenov, just previously deposed from their pedestals as the two outstanding Soviet dramatists. In a footnote Bezymenskii described how the poem had been composed in 1934, but had been rejected by several editors at that time. On June 12, 1937, *Pravda* published a poem by Bezymenskii glorifying the execution of Tukhachevskii and seven other military leaders.[8] On the very next day the party group of the administration of the Writers' Union devoted a session to Bezymenskii. The chief concrete accusation was based on his having allowed several "politically harmful" poems to be reprinted between 1925 and 1934. Bezymenskii's claim that this had happened "automatically" and "without his knowledge" was rejected with scorn. Comrade Iudin, now one of the chief defenders of the new party line, emphasized that there "was no real difference between the creative slogans of the Averbach group and those of the Literary Front" (led by Bezymenskii prior to its absorption in the Writers' Union in 1932): "Both of them were directed against Soviet literature."[9]

The final attack on Bezymenskii was launched by *Komsomol'skaia Pravda,* the influential daily of the Young Communist League, or rather of its Secretary-General, Comrade Kosarev. "Bezymenskii's silence was the more intolerable since among the people who had given him unstinted praise were the most evil enemies of the people, Lelevich, Gorbachev, Vardin, led by the

[7] *"Plenum pravleniia soiuza pisatelei,"* ibid., No. 57 (Feb. 27, 1937), p. 6.

[8] A. Bezymenskii: *"Kak delaetsia slava," Krasnaia Nov'* (June 1937), pp. 246–7; Bezymenskii: *"Zakon millionov," Pravda,* No. 160 (June 12, 1937), p. 5.

[9] *"V partgruppe pravleniia soiuza pisatelei,"* ibid., No. 163 (June 15, 1937), p. 6.

chief bandit, Trotskii. . . ." Bezymenskii replied: "Is not the main thing what I have written, not what they . . . have written about me?" Bezymenskii was finally driven to write a letter of repentence to the newspaper; the latter then demanded that the party group of the Writers' Union give the poet his due.[1] From the June to the July issue *Molodaia Gvardiia* removed Bezymenskii's name from the list of its editors. Finally his career as a "political poet" in the Soviet literary Olympus came to an end on August 11, with his expulsion from the Communist party, of which he had been a member since 1916.

The list of such dramatic reversals of fortune could be extended indefinitely. Their effect on the development of literature can scarcely be overestimated. It is sufficient to bear in mind that recognized writers are at the Soviet pinnacle of success; they receive the largest incomes in the country; they have the use of private homes in the city and country, sometimes a private automobile; they are sent abroad from time to time to attend congresses "against fascism and war." The position of a person expelled from the Communist party is usually of the very lowest; commonly he can find only the very humblest and worst-paid work, and that in some remote corner of the country. However, some of the writers recently expelled from the party and the union have probably no occasion to worry about their future occupations and living accommodations; the charges of espionage, treason, and Trotskyism, made so freely against them, would suggest that the Commissariat of Internal Affairs is taking charge of their "re-education as socially useful citizens."

A partial list of the proscribed authors of 1937 was to be compiled from the soviet literary journals. *Novyi Mir* for June 1937 listed sixty of them; one was reported as shot, six were described as "enemies of the people," two as fascist spies, one as a terrorist, one as an agent of the Gestapo, and forty-nine as Trotskyites. In the same

[1] *Komsomol'skaia Pravda*, June 27, 1937.

breath this journal denounced three leading editors, including its own, for their lack of "Bolshevist vigilance." For good measure, a cinema director and two "counterrevolutionary" painters were thrown in. Critics who made indecent haste to denounce the writers on whom they had only recently been lavishing praise were also given a sharp rap on the knuckles. *Molodaia Gvardiia* added six names to the list. It described in some detail how the now-fallen dictator of literature, Averbach, had utilized the writing of the colossal panegyric on the White Sea-Baltic Canal, and the several millions of rubles which Yagoda and the G.P.U. had spent for this shameless self-advertising, to add recruits to his personal following among the writers. Kirshon had been able to do the same through his control of the large funds of the dramatists' section of the Writers' Union. *Okt'iabr'* added eleven more names to the list.[2] The seventy-seven authors thus pilloried as "enemies" and "Trotskyites" in a period of only two months represented just over five per cent of the 1934 membership of the Writers' Union of the Russian Republic.[3]

The impetus to the widespread purge in music, painting, architecture, sculpture, and literature was given, it will be recalled, by the *Pravda* article of January 28, 1936, against Shostakovich. On the preceding day the same newspaper had set in motion a similar wave of housecleaning in the social sciences. It was inaugurated by the publication of a government decree calling for the creation of a new history textbook, and by the instructions for it, written in 1934 by Stalin, Kirov, and Zhdanov. The significance of the new line in history was elaborated at length by Bukharin and Radek; at

[2] "*Literatura i iskusstvo. Za bol'shevistskuiu bditel'nost' v literature,*" *Novyi Mir*, No. 6 (1937), pp. 194–209; "*Likvidirovat' politicheskuiu bespechnost' v literature,*" *Molodaia Gvardiia*, No. 6 (1937), pp. 199–205; "*Posledyshi Trotskogo,*" *Okt'iabr'*, No. 6 (1937), pp. 3–7; P. Iudin: "*Ob averbakhovshchine,*" ibid., pp. 8–18.

[3] 1535 for the R.S.F.S.R.; *Pervyi vsesoiuznyi s'ezd sovetskikh pisatelei, 1934. Stenograficheskii otchet* (Moscow: 1934), p. 663, report by P. Iudin.

that time official spokesmen on the "ideological front," the former has since been executed, the latter condemned to a long prison sentence, as counterrevolutionary traitors.[4] The essence of the new era in historical science lay in the elimination of the influence of the late M. N. Pokrovskii. An Old Bolshevik and a competent historian, Pokrovskii had, till his death in 1932, dominated the Institute of Red Professors, the historical section of the Communist Academy, and the various historical journals. His *Brief History of Russia*[5] was for fifteen years the official Soviet text. Between 1928 and 1931 Pokrovskii and his disciples removed from the universities and sent into exile, under various political accusations, many of the historians who did not belong to their particular school. The government and party decree of May 16, 1934, marked the first decline in the influence of the Pokrovskyites. Several non-Pokrovskyites were brought back from the provinces and from exile to teach history. Instead of such topics as the "class struggle," "imperialism and the colonial peoples," and "commercial capitalism," history was again to be taught along traditional divisions by periods and countries. But Pokrovskyite teachers and ideas still continued to exercise a strong influence.

The decree of January 1936 inaugurated a new wave of reaction against Pokrovskii's oversimplification of history. The reduction of history to a series of sociological formulas was now condemned as "antiscientific." *Pravda* urged greater attention to historical facts and personalities. On March 4, 1936, the papers announced the opening of a competition for the creation of the new

[4] "*Postanovlenie TsK VKP (b) i SNK SSSR, 26 ianv. 1936 g.,*" Pravda, No. 26 (Jan. 27, 1936), p. 2; "*Zamechaniia tt. Stalina, Kirova, Zhdanova, 8 i 9 VIII, 1934 g.,*" ibid., p. 2; "*Prepodavanie istorii v nashei shkole,*" ibid., p. 1; Karl Radek: "*Znachenie istorii dlia revoliutsionnogo proletariata,*" ibid., p. 3; "*Na fronte istoricheskoi nauki,*" *Izvestiia*, No. 23 (Jan. 27, 1936), p. 3; "*Istoricheskaia nauka i ee prepodavanie,*" ibid., p. 1; N. Bukharin: "*Nuzhna li nam marksistskaia istoricheskaia nauka? (O nekotorykh sushchestvenno vazhnykh, no nesostoiatel'nykh vzgliadakh tov. M. N. Pokrovskogo),*" ibid., pp. 3–4.

[5] In English. 2 vols. (New York: International Publishers; 1933).

history text. On August 22, 1937, the results of the competition were announced.[6] The new text was distinctly patriotic in tone. It described the adoption of Christianity by the Russians as progressive for that early period; it pictured St. Alexander Nevskii as Russia's defender against foreign intervention. It exposed the continual "treason" committed by Trotskii, Kamenev, and Zinoviev against the revolutionary cause from 1905 to 1937; among the leaders of the 1905 revolution it listed Voroshilov, Molotov, Kirov, and Kaganovich, then in their teens.[7]

Evidently, the historians paid too little attention to the danger signal of January 1936. In March 1937 *Pravda* returned to the attack. *Istorik-Marksist,* the leading historical journal, was accused of publicizing fascist ideas through its uncritical reports of historical studies in Germany. Five days later the party organ described as "vile enemies of the people, members of Trotskyite bandit gangs," historians Friedliand, Seidel', Dubyna, Vanag, Nevskii, Piontkovskii, Dalin, and others. In studying the French Revolution Friedliand "beyond a doubt was 'ideologically' serving the spying, diversionist, and wrecking activity of the Trotskyite-Fascist robber band. Significantly, his work was highly praised by the traitor Radek." In picturing prewar Russia as a feeble, will-less appendage of European imperialism, Vanag had been secretly supporting the Trotskyite thesis of the impossibility of building socialism in one country. Piontkovskii had "come out with every sort of nonsense of an obviously counterrevolutionary brand." Aside from a perfunctory attack on

[6] "*Ob organizatsii konkursa na luchshii uchebnik dlia nachal'noi shkoly po elementarnomu kursu istorii SSSR s kratkimi svedeniiami po vseobshchei istorii,*" *Izvestiia,* No. 54 (Mar. 4, 1936), p. 1; "*Postanovlenie zhiuri pravitel'stvennoi komissii po konkursu na luchshii uchebnik dlia 3 i 4 klassov srednei shkoly po istorii SSSR,*" *Pravda,* No. 231 (Aug. 22, 1937), p. 2; "*Znat' istoriiu narodov SSSR,*" ibid., p. 1.

[7] D. Osipov: "*Novyi uchebnik istorii SSSR,*" ibid., No. 234 (Aug. 25, 1937), pp. 2–3.

the "enemies of the people," the *Istorik-Marksist* had done nothing to unmask their machinations.[8]

A final article in *Pravda* listed the chief errors of Pokrovskii and his school of historians. He had substituted the history of Russia for that of the U.S.S.R.; he had called Russia "a nation of Oblomovs"; he had denied the superiority of Russian over Tartar culture, and had concealed the fact of the Russian struggle against the Tartar yoke; he had emphasized the anti-Moscovite tendencies in the history of the Ukraine, while ignoring its struggles against Polish domination. He had denied the progressive character of Peter's reforms, and exaggerated the aristocratic class-selfishness of the Decembrist revolutionaries of 1825; his followers had praised the Populists of the 1870's and their use of political terrorism. In the following issue of *Istorik-Marksist* its editor, Comrade Lukin, pleaded guilty to all the sins enumerated by *Pravda*, and promised to correct his mistakes.[9]

Perhaps in order to divert the fire of official disapproval, in the very same issue *Istorik-Marksist* embarked on a scathing exposure of the "enemies of the people" in archaeology and ethnography. Their leaders had wasted time on useless "disputes"; they had monopolized the control of expeditions and of publications. Like the Pokrovskyites in history, they had tried to "abolish" their science by cutting it up into artificial and unusable sociological segments. Prigozhin was "the leader of a terrorist band"; Zelenin had published a book in Germany (before 1933, be it noted); Bogaevsky had attributed class antagonisms to Cretan society, which Marxism classified as a pre-class society; Nikolskii, Tol-

[8] "*Ob idiotskoi bolezni—bespechnosti v zhurnale 'Istorik-Marksist,'* " ibid., No. 73 (Mar. 15, 1937), p. 4; I. Fedorov: "*Politicheskaia slepota i bespechnost'; zhurnal 'Istorik-Marksist' za* 1936 *god,*" ibid., No. 78 (Mar. 20, 1937), p. 3.

[9] P. Drozdov: " *'Istoricheskaia shkola' Pokrovskogo,*" ibid., No. 86 (Mar. 28, 1937), pp. 2–3; "*Ot redaktsii,*" *Istorik-Marksist*, No. 2 (1937), pp. 32–9.

stov, and Meshchaninov underestimated the duration of tribal society in the history of mankind. On May 20, 1937, the Permanent Secretary of the Academy of Sciences, Comrade N. P. Gorbunov, denounced ethnographers Motorin, Busygin, and others for attempting to "liquidate ethnography as a science."[1]

If the field of historical studies required three years or more for the eclipse of the Pokrovskii school, the Pashukanis school of law and political science far "surpassed" it in the speed of its "liquidation." Pashukanis and his followers had for many years monopolized the "commanding positions" in Soviet jurisprudence. Authoritative articles on Soviet law in the party organs, *Pravda* and *Bol'shevik*, were regularly signed by Pashukanis. In June 1936 he wrote on "Personal Property in the Socialist State"; in November, on "Soviet Socialist Law."[2] On December 21, 1936, *Izvestiia* printed a notable "Letter to the Editor," signed by none other than the redoubtable Commissar Krylenko; it wholeheartedly recommended Pashukanis for membership in the Academy of Sciences.[3] But the train was already laid which was to blow the "juridical front" sky high.

The first breach was made in 1935. Works on Soviet international law, by Kleist in Germany and Taracouzio in the United States, forced Professor Korovin to renounce several of his earlier views. He now denied the existence of a specifically "socialist" international law;

[1] A. Artsikhovskii, M. Voevodskii, S. Kiselev, and S. Tolstov: "*O metodakh vreditel'stva v arkheologii i etnografii*," ibid., No. 2 (1937), pp. 78–91; "*Obshchee sobranie Akademii Nauk SSSR*," *Izvestiia*, No. 118 (May 21, 1937), p. 4.

[2] E. Pashukanis: "*Sotsialisticheskoe gosudarstvo i ego konstitutsiia*," *Sovetskoe Stroitel'stvo*, No. 4 (Apr. 1936), pp. 5–12; Pashukanis: "*Vsenarodnoe obsuzhdenie stalinskoi konstitutsii*," ibid., No. 11 (Nov. 1936), pp. 19–28; Pashukanis: "*Stalinskaia konstitutsiia i sotsialisticheskaia zakonnost'*," *Sovetskoe Gosudarstvo*, No. 4 (1936), pp. 18–28; Pashukanis: "*Lichnaia sobstvennost' v sotsialisticheskom gosudarstve*," *Pravda*, No. 162 (June 14, 1936), p. 3; Pashukanis: "*Sovetskoe sotsialisticheskoe pravo*," *Bol'shevik*, No. 22 (Nov. 25, 1936), pp. 20–32.

[3] N. Krylenko: "*E. B. Pashukanis*," *Izvestiia*, No. 296 (Dec. 21, 1936), p. 4.

the assertion of its existence had been interpreted abroad as implying Soviet rejection of the validity of existing "bourgeois" international law. He rejected the substitution of the party for the state as the subject under international law; this substitution had lent countenance to those critics who identified the Soviet state with the Bolshevist party and the Communist International. He now denied the existence of a qualitative distinction between "European" and "colonial" culture—a distinction which could be twisted to justify imperialism.[4] Foreign attacks on Soviet international "morality," together with the Soviets' new responsibilities as a member of the League of Nations and the ally of European states, had thus led to a radical revision of earlier accepted concepts in one branch of jurisprudence.

A second and broader wave of attack was launched against a number of jurists for having published articles in German, Italian, and French journals; the fact that several of them had been published abroad after rejection by Soviet editors only made the offense more heinous. In November 1936 the line of fire crept nearer. The present war horse of Soviet orthodoxy, Comrade P. Iudin, led the attack against Pashukanis's journal, *Soviet State*, and against one of his pupils, Dotsenko, but without making a direct assault on Pashukanis's own position. On January 1, 1937, Pashukanis and Dotsenko were openly accused by *Bol'shevik*, the periodical organ of the Central Committee of the party, of distorting Marxism-Leninism and of bothering themselves too much with legal formalism; still the tone of the attack was mild, by Soviet standards.[5]

The grand offensive against Pashukanis was opened

[4] E. Korovin: "*Pis'mo v redaktsiiu*," *Sovetskoe Gosudarstvo*, No. 4 (1935), pp. 171–2.

[5] Alekseev: "*O sotrudnichestve v fashistskikh 'nauchnykh' zhurnalakh*," *Sovetskaia Iustitsiia*, No. 26 (Sept. 15, 1936), p. 21; P. Iudin: "*Sotsializm i gosudarstvo*," *Bol'shevik*, No. 21 (Nov. 1, 1936), pp. 26–38; S. Ingulov: "*Pomen'she putanitsy, pobol'she samokritiki*," ibid., No. 1 (Jan. 1, 1937), pp. 76–81.

by Iudin's article in *Pravda* on January 20, 1937. He quoted Pashukanis's earlier works as asserting that the Soviet government had begun to wither away at the moment of its origin, in 1917, that it must wither away completely by the end of the Second Five-Year Plan (December 31, 1937), and that government and law were bourgeois categories which could not be filled with a socialist content. Pashukanis's journal was condemned for having ignored the question of the constitution from February 1935 till June 1936. Iudin ended by denouncing Pashukanis as an anti-Leninist; "the journal must be directed to militant Marxist-Leninist positions." A month later *Pravda* extended the attack to Pashukanis's pupil, Grishin; the latter had declared that "labor law" applied only to the workers and employees, and had thus denied the socialist character of the collective farms, and spread "most repulsive Trotskyite slander." [6]

The attack was now taken up in full cry by the two more popular legal journals, *Sovetskaia Iustitsiia* and *Sovetskoe Stroitel'stvo*.[7] The final blast was delivered by Pashukanis's former journal, *Soviet State*; but the blast was slow in coming. The first issue for 1937 was not sent to press till August 3, 1937, almost eight months behind schedule—an eloquent testimony to the confusion created by the purge. Pages thirty-nine to ninety-eight were devoted to attacks on Pashukanis and his school. Thirteen of his followers, including Dotsenko, Grishin, and Korovin were denounced as "fascist agents on the juridical front." Even these attacks still seemed to the inexorable Iudin so superficial as to border on "sabotage"; he added Bukharin, A. Goikh-

[6] P. Iudin: "*Protiv putanitsy, poshlosti i revizionizma (zhurnal 'Sovetskoe Gosudarstvo' za 1936 god)*," Pravda, No. 20 (Jan. 20, 1937), p. 4; A. Leontiev: "*Ob odnoi vrednoi 'teorii,'* " ibid., No. 57 (Feb. 27, 1937), a review of Z. Grishin: *Sovetskoe trudovoe pravo*, 1936.

[7] E.g., V. Sakach: "*Protiv revizii marksizma-leninizma v oblasti gosudarstva i prava*," *Sovetskaia Iustitsiia*, No. 5 (Mar. 15, 1937), pp. 3–6; N. Aleksandrov: "*Protiv antimarksistskoi lzheuchenosti v teorii trudovogo prava*," ibid., No. 8 (Apr. 30, 1937), pp. 6–8, and many others; P. Lopukhov: "*O trotskistskoi kontrabande v voprosakh gosudarstva i prava*," *Sovetskoe Stroitel'stvo*, No. 4 (Apr. 1937), pp. 43–8.

bart, F. Wol'fson, and Krylenko himself to what *Bol'shevik* now described as "the vile Trotskyite-Bukharinist band of Pashukanis and the rest, faithful to its fascist masters. . . ." A later attack by the Soviet State's Attorney, Vyshinskii, added the names of Stuchka, Volkov, Ginzburg, Amfitcatrov, and Berman to the ranks of "anti-Marxist wreckers" in the field of jurisprudence.[8]

Shortly before his sudden downfall, Pashukanis had demanded that the historical comments of Stalin, Kirov, and Zhdanov be applied to political and legal science, and had called for a relentless struggle against "schematizing, naked sociologizing, and opportunism."[9] The same militant slogans were applied shortly thereafter to economics. Existing textbooks of political economy were roundly criticized for devoting too much space to the economics of capitalism and too little to those of socialism; economists were condemned for an anti-historical approach to their science. This general broadside was followed by concrete denunciations. Strumilin was raked over the coals for failing to distinguish state property in industrial enterprises from co-operative property in the collective farms, and for relegating the ruling party to the economic category of "unproductive social servicing."

Another economist, Kubanin, explained the growth of productivity in the collective farms by the improvement in their mechanical equipment; Stalin, on the other hand, had denied the importance of such "objective" conditions in determining productivity, and had stressed the "subjective" factor of enthusiasm, "socialist competition," and Stakhanovism, which Ku-

[8] *Sovetskoe Gosudarstvo*, No. 1–2 (1937); P. Iudin: "*Sotsializm i pravo*," *Bol'shevik*, No. 17 (Sept. 1, 1937), pp. 31–46; "*Leninskaia teoriia, preobrazuiushchaia mir*," ibid., pp. 1–8; A Vyshinskii: "*Marksistskoe uchenie o prave i gosudarstve*," ibid., No. 12 (June 15, 1938), pp. 11–34.

[9] E. Pashukanis: "*Neotlozhnye zadachi v nauchnoi i uchebnoi rabote po istorii gosudarstva i prava*," *Sovetskoe Gosudarstvo*, No. 2 (1936), pp. 103–14.

banin ignored. The latter also concealed the *leading* role of the party in promoting collective farming, and failed to mention its struggle against the Trotskyite and right-wing "restorers of capitalism."[1]

Laptev renewed the attack with a broadside against *Problems of Economics.* This journal had practically ignored the new constitution, as well as the struggle against the Trotskyites and Bukharinists; it had failed to expose Strumilin and Kubanin as anti-Leninists. Tsukernik had asserted that the productivity of Donbas miners declined after the age of forty; this was "slander against the working class of the U.S.S.R." The journal had also given a mild review of "Mercantilism," by I. Plotnikov, "now exposed as an enemy of the people."[2]

The history of psychology under the present regime has been marked by a life-and-death struggle among successive and competing schools. The idealist school of Chelpanov dominated the Central Institute of Psychology from 1917 to 1925. It gave way to "the most crude vulgarization of materialism" under Enchmen. The latter was replaced by Bekhterev's "reflexological theory"; the latter in turn was eliminated by Kornilov's "reactological school" and by the "Freudo-Marxism" of Zalkind, Sapir, and Lurie. Since the destruction of this last school, no new theory has appeared.[3] "Revolutionary pedology," as preached by Katsnel'son and Zeitlin, dominated child medicine for several years; it involved subjecting the child to all-round psycho-physical tests, lasting five or six hours, instead of making a single diagnosis and prescription for the young patient. This theory has now been

[1] B. Tal': "*O predmete politicheskoi ekonomii i ee prepodavanii,*" *Bol'shevik,* No. 22 (Nov. 25, 1936), pp. 33–41; I. Laptev: "*'Balans' grubeishikh oshibok,*" ibid., No. 7 (Apr. 1, 1937), pp. 89–96; A. Likomidov and G. Stukov: "*O knige M. Kubanina, 'Proizvodstvennye tipy kolkhozov,'*" ibid., No. 9 (May 1, 1937), pp. 108–12.

[2] I. Laptev: "*Zhurnal, stradaiushchii politicheskoi bespechnosti,*" ibid., No. 13 (July 5, 1937), pp. 87–91.

[3] *Za kommunisticheskoe prosveshchenie,* Sept. 28, 1936.

eliminated from Soviet science, especially since Zeitlin's teacher, Tscherni, was discovered to have the approval of German fascist educators.[4]

The high mortality of schools of psychology is paralleled by a similar process in the study of philosophy. After the revolution, idealists such as Losskii and Chelpanov continued to be regarded as authorities. They were then eliminated and Bukharin's "vulgar mechanism" came to dominate. It gave way in turn to Deborin's "petty school of Menshevist idealism," which, in co-operation with its pretended opponents, the Mechanists, undertook to revise dialectical materialism. In a recent article *Pravda* denounced ten philosophers as followers of Bukharin, Deborin, or Shabalkin; the detailed survey mentioned no philosopher of note in Soviet Russia today.[5] In another article Mitin applied Stalin's notes on history to the study of dialectical materialism. Bukharin was for him "a kulak ideologist and a restorer of capitalism"; Slepkov and others he denounced as followers of Bukharin. Tymianskii and Ral'tsevich were "enemies of the people"; a half-dozen other writers on dialectical materialism were thrown in for good measure.[6]

The attitude underlying these "philosophical" discussions is that the truth has already been established in the form of Marxism-Leninism-Stalinism; henceforth it can only be elucidated by commentary. Any divergence in the formulation of truth therefore fastens the charge of "wrecking" and "treason" upon predecessors or contemporaries who have the misfortune to visualize or formulate "the truth" in any other form than the official one of the moment. Under these conditions, the place of philosophical "doubt" as the motive which

[4] E. Strogova: "*Pedologi iz narkomzdrava*," *Izvestiia*, No. 226 (Sept. 28, 1936), p. 3.

[5] M. Mitin and P. Iudin: "*O filosofskom obrazovanii v SSSR*," *Pravda*, No. 55 (Feb. 25, 1937), pp. 2–3; A. Maksimov: "*Zavety Lenina i estestvoznanie*," ibid., No. 63 (Mar. 5, 1937), pp. 2–3.

[6] M. Mitin: "*Ob uchebnikakh po dialekticheskomu i istoricheskomu materializmu*," *Bol'shevik*, No. 12 (June 15, 1937), pp. 29–40.

provokes discussion is taken by political "suspicion" and denunciation.

If the arts and social sciences have been the chief sufferers from the purge of 1936 and 1937, the physical and biological sciences have not been entirely immune. The one worst hit has been genetics, the very field in which Soviet science has won world-wide recognition through its remarkable achievements in theory and practice. The struggle opened in June 1936, with a bitter attack on A. S. Serebrovskii by Lysenko and Prezent. It was followed by a fierce assault on S. G. Levit, head of the Medico-Genetical Institute, in November. The latter was accused of recognizing "the absolute significance of heredity in the origin of almost all diseases. . . ." A month later the attack was broadened to include Levit's pupils. Presniakov was accused of supporting racialist theories; Ignatiev's studies of inbreeding had led him "to counterrevolutionary conclusions"; Levit had signed an article defending "the Trotskyite-Zinovievist bandit Karev."[7] On December 14 *The New York Times* reported the cancellation of plans for the Moscow Genetics Congress announced for August 1937, and linked it with the reported arrest of a geneticist, Yagol', and the bitter attacks of a brilliant young scientist, Lysenko, on N. I. Vavilov, head of the All-Union Institute of Plant Industry and dean of Soviet geneticists.[8]

This report in the foreign press brought an immediate reaction. Vavilov sent a telegram to the *Times* praising Soviet encouragement of science, while *Izvestiia* confirmed the arrest of Yagol' as a "fascist agent."[9] The geneticists' discussion during the last ten

[7] T. Lysenko and I. Prezent: "*O 'logiiakh,' 'alogiiakh,' i deistvitel'noi nauke*," *Pravda*, No. 174 (June 26, 1936), p. 4; Bratia Tur: "*Kontramarka v Panteon*," *Izvestiia*, No. 265 (Nov. 16, 1936), p. 4; Tur: "*V pylu uvlecheniia*," ibid., No. 287 (Dec. 10, 1936), p. 3.

[8] "Moscow Cancels Genetics Parley," *The New York Times*, Dec. 14, 1936, p. 18.

[9] "*Telegramma akademika N. I. Vavilova v amerikanskuiu gazetu 'New-York Times,'*" *Izvestiia*, No. 297 (Dec. 22, 1936), p. 4.

days of December, however, seemed rather to confirm the report of a bitter political struggle going on in that field. Lysenko accused Vavilov and most Soviet geneticists of denying the direct inheritance of acquired characteristics; such a denial, he insinuated, implied their acceptance of the dominance of heredity over environment and even a leaning toward Nazi "racialist" concepts. Meister also accused Vavilov of anti-Darwinism. Serebrovskii made haste to denounce his own ideas of 1929 as "counterrevolutionary and unscientific"; at that time he had expressed approval of "human selection" and sterilization. In the concluding speech of the congress a mild reproof was administered to Lysenko and other hotheads. "Each one of us, including Comrade Lysenko, must keep in mind that each of our theoretical words reaches the masses very quickly, and hence one must be very exact and cautious in stating formulae on theoretical questions. . . ."[1]

This advice was evidently not to Lysenko's liking. With other geneticists he was invited to address a conference, early in January 1937, on the problem of raising agricultural productivity. In a rather demagogical speech he severely denounced the opponents of his own pet theories. Yakovlev, then Commissar of Agriculture, interrupted him: "Whom do you mean in particular? Why do you omit their names?" Lysenko then seized the opportunity to denounce Karpechenko, Lepin, Zhebrak, Vavilov, and "the majority of geneticists" in the presence of the highest government officials.[2] In October 1937, the "cleansing" of the "genetics front" was pursued further by *Bol'shevik* in reviewing the work of the *Journal of Biological Reference*. The theories of

[1] "*Diskussiia na sessii Akademii sel'skokhoziaistvennykh nauk imeni Lenina*," ibid., No. 299 (Dec. 24, 1936), p. 4; "*Zakrylas' sessiia Akademii s.-kh.nauk im. Lenina*," ibid., No. 302 (Dec. 28, 1936), p. 3; "*Diskussiia na sessii Akademii s.-kh.nauk im. Lenina, Rech' akademika G. K. Meistera*," ibid., No. 303 (Dec. 29, 1936), p. 4.

[2] "*Soveshchanie peredovikov urozhainosti po zernu, traktoristov, i mashinistov molotilok s rukovoditeliami partii i pravitel'stva*," ibid., No. 2 (Jan. 3, 1937), p. 2.

"creative evolution," "orthogenesis," and "aristogenesis" were rejected as anti-Darwinist and hence anti-Soviet. Until 1936 the journal had been edited by the "fascist agent in Soviet biology, M. Levin." The party journal concluded by declaring: "Soviet science has every reason to be the most progressive in the world; and we will make it progressive despite all underhanded attacks by our enemies and their agents." [3]

Other fields besides genetics have been carefully raked over in the search for counterrevolutionaries, Trotskyites, and Bukharinites. "Enemies" were uncovered at work in the Pulkovo Astronomical Observatory. The director of the Soil Institute, Polynov, proved to be a member of a counterrevolutionary organization. Luzin and his followers had been "wrecking" mathematics and the physical sciences. At the same time it was announced that the government had spent over eight million rubles in 1936 on equipment for the academy and its dependent institutions.[4]

Lumping together all these individual cases, one can see that the periodical process of "purging" Soviet intellectual and artistic life tends to follow a common pattern. The signal is first given by a denunciatory article in *Pravda*, less frequently in *Izvestiia*, *Komsomolskaia Pravda*, or *Bol'shevik*, which take their cue from the Central Committee of the Communist party. That is followed usually by the "elimination" of the persons attacked, with no opportunity for reply through any public organ. Then the special newspapers and journals follow up with many months of detailed denunciation and correction of the heresies noted, and with lavish promises of greater vigilance for the future.

At present the control of creative work rests with three bodies: the Secretariat of the Academy of Sciences, the Secretariat of the Writers' Union, and the

[3] Z. Beletskii: "*Rupor vrazhdebnykh idei v biologii,*" *Bol'shevik*, No. 19 (Oct. 1, 1937), pp. 91–6.

[4] "*Obshchee sobranie Akademii Nauk SSSR,*" *Izvestiia*, No. 118 (May 21, 1937), p. 4.

Committee for the Affairs of the Arts. Each of them is headed by a secretary who is held responsible for the political "soundness" of his "front": Comrade Gorbunov for science, Comrade Stavskii for literature, and Comrade Kerzhentsev for the arts. Each of these secretaries exercises what is in practice of monopoly right of patronage over his respective field. Comrade Gorbunov has to give his imprimatur before any publication can be issued by any one of the numerous institutes grouped under the Academy of Sciences. For the appearance of any literary work, the approval of Comrade Stavskii is as essential as the consent of the censors of Glavlit (the bureau of literary censorship); Stavskii is at the same time a member of the editorial board of several of the literary journals. Comrade Kerzhentsev and his staff must accept any new play, opera, or ballet, and also each individual staging of it, before it may be shown to the public. Comrade Kerzhentsev also controls the selection and purchase of paintings and sculpture for exhibition and acquisition by the museums. Such absolute power enables these "leading comrades," through material and political pressure, to lend unlimited support to certain creative workers and to force others to abandon forever their chosen field of activity. In addition to these three secretaries, there are a few powerful publicists, like Comrade Iudin, backed by *Pravda*, the central organ of the party. On the authority of the Central Committee of the party, they exercise a roving commission to purge any field of work—yesterday jurisprudence, today philosophy, tomorrow literature—until they, too, are "eliminated" in turn.

This system naturally leads creative workers to seek the "protection" of some "leading comrade." Such protection brings with it material support from the organs of the state, through favorable consideration of requests for funds, as well as comparative immunity from sudden denunciation and "liquidation." As an uncritical English observer writes, "a Communist administrative director with moderate intellectual powers may be able to help an institute much by merely securing the attention of influential persons, who happen to be old friends, for its problems."[5] These advantages have concomitant dangers. The downfall of a Bukharin, a Radek, or a Yagoda is likely to destroy the groups which he has "protected." Similarly, attacks on a "protected" institute may contribute to the downfall of the "protector," as in the cases of Bubnov, for many years Commissar of Education, and of Krylenko, who was compromised by his glowing endorsement of Pashukanis and the latter's school of jurisprudence.[6]

One universal characteristic of creative work in the Soviet Union is its "politicization." There is no sphere of intellectual or artistic endeavor that is not immediately or potentially charged with political passion, even if that political fervor has to be injected into it by the party against the passive resistance of its own practitioners. The hasty "getting in step" with the party line reduces to a minimum the scientific or artistic self-respect of the "creative worker." Until he unfolds his *Pravda* in the morning, he never knows but that today may bring an urgent and inescapable command to change his fundamental conceptions of scientific and artistic truth. When that command comes, even silence is no longer a way out. Under such conditions, the more flexible characters survive; men with convictions which cannot be changed at the word of command may overnight become "enemies of the people." There is no room for the slow development and gradual discarding of underlying concepts. In fact, there is no room for the growth of such concepts, since they are held to be present, ready-made, in the doctrines of Marxism-Leninism-Stalinism, and need only to be applied through opportune exegesis. Since the line

[5] J. G. Crowther: *Soviet Science* (London: 1936, p. 79; Dutton; 1936).

[6] "*Pis'mo v redaktsiiu. Kak gotoviatsia kadry istorikov,*" *Pravda,* No. 157 (June 9, 1937), p. 4.

has been subject to frequent and violent change over the past twenty years, individuals ought perhaps to be pardoned if they view its day-to-day claim to universal validity with a certain skepticism. But such skepticism is in itself criminal under the Soviet system, and in turn provokes fresh violence from above. The one unvarying characteristic of the ever-shifting line is the urge to create conformity at whatever cost.

Each charge brings with it a serious wastage in personnel. This constant elimination of the individual bearers and creators of thought would be serious in any country and at any time. In the Soviet Union it is peculiarly serious because of the enormous expansion in the demands made upon intellectual and artistic personnel by a government engaged in carrying through the economic and cultural reconstruction of a vast country. Besides the measurable losses exacted by a rigid policy of conformity, there is the intangible loss which results from the restriction of individual thought through political pressure. Politicians, but slightly acquainted with the complex problems which are being worked out along the frontiers of knowledge, attempt crudely and arbitrarily to define the channels and goals of human thought. If scientists with a lifetime of work behind them are unable to define once and for all the interaction of heredity and environment in biological and social development, how can that problem be settled in an article by some political journalist with a smattering of knowledge? This method of arbitrarily pigeonholing creative workers in their specialized fields and forbidding them to tackle the larger problems of their discipline is, however, approved by one English observer, very sympathetic to the Soviet scientific setup.

> The scientific specialist is given the maximum scope in his own field, and on subjects in which he is not expert he must defer to those who are. In this way a social and intellectual structure is erected, in which every scientist knows his place and the degree of his dependence on others. He is unable to give

> harmful expression to illusory ideas of absolute freedom, or behave with social irresponsibility, or to use his authority as a specialist in one branch of science to urge the adoption of his views on other aspects of human activity.[7]

Soviet science cannot question the general concepts within which it works at any given moment. It is not allowed to treat its axioms as provisional hypotheses in the search for larger and more inclusive concepts. Such a hamstrung species of science is not likely to advance the frontiers of general knowledge very far. Over a short period of time, extreme specialization, based on intensive work and also on the general advances borrowed from countries with a relatively broad scientific freedom, may give striking and valuable results. In the long run, and especially if cut off from like activities in other countries by deliberate self-isolation, this policy is likely to result in intellectual sterility. Such restriction of freedom in abstract science will ultimately affect unfavorably the development of practical knowledge; there is no need here to labor the point of the interdependence of abstract and applied science for the progress of both.

The statement of the case for the freedom of the arts is somewhat more difficult. Theoretically speaking, an absolute political authority is forced to regulate the arts with minute care for the sake of perpetuating its own power. Yet, in the long run, artistic and literary talent, even if it is perhaps present in roughly equal quantities at all times and among all peoples, is closely dependent upon intelligent understanding and patronage for its fullest development and prosperity. The Soviet system of monopolistic patronage, exercised through the party-state, imposes a constantly changing standard of conformity upon its creative workers. The standard varies; the insistence upon conformity is constant. Those who have conformed to some earlier and

[7] J. G. Crowther: op. cit., p. 9.

now discarded standard set by the line are in danger of artistic and even personal elimination; those who conform to the present line will be exposed to the same danger whenever the line shifts in the future. The state enforces conformity by an unhealthy oversatiation with power and material rewards, and punishes real or imagined deviation from it by professional and even personal annihilation. Such a form of patronage can scarcely be described as intelligent. Its operation is destructive of artistic independence and personality. Its rewards and punishments are too extreme and sporadic to evoke a steady, confident, creative effort on the part of the artist-thinker. If Goethe had been "eliminated" for writing *Iphigenie*, he could scarcely have composed the Second Part of *Faust*; it is equally absurd to imagine a Boswell in the role of an agent of the G.P.U.

* * *

After this survey of the condition of artistic creation and intellectual inquiry under the first Marxist state at its twentieth birthday, it is encouraging to turn to a profound, if not entirely original, analysis of the nature of scientific thought, given by the co-founder of Marxist philosophy, Friedrich Engels, in his *Anti-Dühring*.

> The perception that all the phenomena of Nature are systematically interconnected drives science on to prove this systematic interconnection throughout, both in general and in detail. But an adequate, exhaustive scientific statement of this interconnection, the formulation in thought of an exact picture of the world system in which we live, is impossible for us, and will always remain impossible. . . . Mankind therefore finds itself faced with a contradiction: on the one hand, it has to gain an exhaustive knowledge of the world system in all its interrelations; and on the other hand, because of the nature both of man and of the world system, this task can never be completely fulfilled. But this contradiction lies not only in the nature of the two factors—the world, and man—it is

> also the main lever of all intellectual advance, and finds its solution continuously, day by day, in the endless progressive evolution of humanity. . . .[8]

Apparently, Engels's keen perception of the nature of intellectual activity has not been fully assimilated by those who control scientific and artistic expression today in the Soviet Union.

[8] Friedrich Engels: *Herr Eugen Dühring's Revolution in Science* (*Anti-Dühring*) (New York: International Publishers; no date), p. 46.

PART II

Uneasy Alliance and Abortive Peace: Soviet Foreign Policy, 1941–1949

:5:

DISMEMBERMENT OF GERMANY: THE ALLIED NEGOTIATIONS FROM YALTA TO POTSDAM[1]

[*February 1950*]

INTRODUCTORY NOTE · A totalitarian regime can enforce for a long time, perhaps indefinitely, policies which are deeply repugnant to the basic sentiments of the people it controls. It may even hope that prolonged submission and adaptation will lead to acceptance. Relying on a disciplined apparatus of rule, it can pursue almost any policy of its choosing so long as it preserves the integrity and striking power of that instrument. A democracy which aspires to cherish and promote compatible habits of self-rule among other peoples cannot afford such policies, however immediately plausible and tempting they may seem. Its goals must be in harmony with its own habits of mind if it is to persist in them with inner comfort of conviction.

"Dismemberment," the "Morgenthau plan," and similar wartime fevers had no firm footing in the American psychology. It was unpopular but reasonable in 1943 or 1945 to predict that the imposing of very harsh policies on Germany would result, sooner rather than later, in a

[1] *Foreign Affairs*, Vol. xxviii, No. 3 (April 1950), pp. 487–98. Copyright 1950 by the Council on Foreign Relations, Inc.

strong revulsion against them. Did the shift in American policy from punishment to co-operation and alliance arise from a desire to align Germany (or West Germany) with the democracies? Or from a desire to make western Europe secure against Soviet threats? Between May 1945 and June 1948 American policy shifted steadily toward helping Germany find a reasonably comfortable status within the democratic West, without, at first, any thought of restoring its military strength. Above all, the Soviet blockade of Berlin, sprung in June 1948, convinced the West of West Germany's essential strategic role.

Will an again powerful Germany accept indefinitely the partition of its people between two incompatible systems? In the long run the most unfortunate consequence of the "dismemberment" imbroglio of 1945 may have been that it contributed to dissipating whatever limited time or modest opportunity there may have been for planning, before the end of hostilities, a minimum of agreed Allied policies for the joint administration of an undivided Germany. Perhaps the result would have been the same, but of this we cannot be certain; witness the different pattern and the opposite outcome in the fate of Austria.

*

DURING World War II, the idea of punishing Germany for obeying Hitler to the end and supporting the Nazi bid for world domination found strong backing. Many influential Allied leaders felt that the most telling reprisal could be inflicted on her by decreeing her dismemberment. This feeling reached its high point at the Yalta Conference. There a provision for dismemberment was added to the surrender instrument previously prepared for German signature, and a secret committee was established to study and report on the steps necessary for carrying the plan into execution. Three weeks after V-E Day, however, Marshal Stalin complained to the late Harry Hopkins that Foreign

Secretary Eden and the American Ambassador to Britain, the late John G. Winant, had rejected dismemberment.[2] In the absence of other evidence it might be assumed that Stalin's complaint gave a full account of the fate of the Yalta decision on German dismemberment. Actually, this is not the case. As we shall see, it was Stalin's own decision which put an end to effective discussion of this issue; and on May 8, 1945, he publicly renounced dismemberment as a Soviet aim. In the meantime, however, the action at Yalta looking toward dismemberment had gravely compromised the arrangements which had been agreed upon for recording Germany's unconditional surrender.

The idea of keeping Germany divided into several or many independent and rival states has had a long history. It was a prominent objective of French policy, from Richelieu to Napoleon III and Clemenceau. The hope and desire for the partition of Germany haunted Allied policy makers during World War II, and played an important part in delaying and confusing the efforts to achieve, before Germany's surrender, a consistent and effective Allied policy for the postwar treatment of defeated Germany. One of the main difficulties was that the proponents of dismemberment never made clear exactly what it really implied. Was Germany to be divided into several completely independent states? Was partition to be welcomed and encouraged if it emerged spontaneously after defeat? Or was it to be imposed and maintained by force? Did dismemberment mean the destruction of Prussian preponderance within the Reich and the strengthening of the historic smaller states within a loose confederation? These questions remained unanswered throughout the Allied discussions.

Apparently the first official discussions took place during Eden's visit to Washington in March 1943.

[2] Robert E. Sherwood: *Roosevelt and Hopkins, an Intimate History* (New York: Harper; 1948), p. 904. The full report of the Yalta discussions regarding dismemberment has been given by the late Edward R. Stettinius, Jr., in *Roosevelt and the Russians: The Yalta Conference* (Garden City, N. Y.: Doubleday; 1949).

Eden raised with President Roosevelt the question of whether the Allies were going to deal with Germany as a unit after the war, or whether they "were going to insist that it be broken up into several independent states." Mr. Roosevelt "hoped we would not use the methods discussed at Versailles and also promoted by Clemenceau to arbitrarily divide Germany, but thought that we should encourage the differences and ambitions that will spring up within Germany for a Separatists Movement and, in effect, approve of a division which represents German public opinion." ". . . Both the President and Eden agreed that, under any circumstances, Germany must be divided into several states, one of which must, over all circumstances, be Prussia." [3] This rather obscure reference to Prussia meant, presumably, that Prussia should be divided into several smaller states in order to destroy its ability to dominate Germany. In a memorandum of March 16 Hopkins reported that Litvinov thought Russia would want to see Germany partitioned, while Eden reported that Ambassador Maiskii in London believed it should be either partitioned or decentralized. Eden had reported to Roosevelt, however, that he believed Stalin "will insist that Germany be broken up into a number of states." [4]

But these formal discussions which Eden inaugurated in the spring of 1943 did not, as a matter of fact, mark the start of American studies on this important question. There are some grounds for believing that Churchill may have suggested the possible dismemberment of Germany at the time of his first visit to Roosevelt in December 1941. At any rate, Roosevelt seems to have had the possibility in mind early in 1942 and to have brought it to the attention of Under Secretary

[3] Sherwood: op. cit., p. 711; Hopkins's memorandum of March 15, 1943.

[4] Ibid., pp. 713, 711. Presumably Eden had in mind his conversations of December 1941 with Stalin, reported by Churchill in his memoirs, *The New York Times*, February 24, 1950, p. 25.

Sumner Welles as deserving of study in the Department of State.

However this may have been, the pros and cons of dismembering Germany received careful discussion in the State Department beginning early in 1942. Under Secretary Sumner Welles referred the problem for study to the Advisory Committee on Postwar Problems, which had been appointed by President Roosevelt in January 1942 and which consisted of a number of outstanding public persons possessed of wide experience in world affairs. It was one of the principal questions to which this committee gave prolonged consideration. Detailed statements of the arguments for and against partition were also prepared by a staff of research workers recruited by the State Department. Projects for the partition of postwar Germany into three, five, and seven separate states were drawn up, and analyses were made of the political, economic, and demographic problems involved.

Certain members of the advisory committee and the expert staff itself were skeptical of the effectiveness of dismemberment as a means of preventing future German aggression and believed that the United States would not be willing, in the long run, to impose and maintain it by force. They also pointed out that dismemberment would prepare the ground for rallying all Germans against the victorious powers, would discredit all attempts to develop a democratic regime and spirit in Germany, and would render the economic problem of German livelihood absolutely unmanageable. They foresaw that the Germans would strive in every way to undo partition through playing off the victorious powers against each other, and would thus increase greatly the dangers of a postwar falling-out among the victors.

During April, May, and June 1942, the advisory committee carefully weighed these and other considerations and also reviewed the question from time to time during the next year and a half. Its majority conclusion was a strong rejection of dismemberment and the recommendation of a vigorous long-range policy for preventing German rearmament, promoting democratic institutions, and reducing or controlling Germany's economic preponderance in Europe. This view, stated effectively by Hamilton Fish Armstrong and the late Isaiah Bowman, left Welles unconvinced. His proposal, published in 1944, was for the division of Germany into three states. Roosevelt, to whom the advisory committee's views were doubtless transmitted by Welles, maintained his position. The President's suggestion, made at Teheran, was for the partition of Germany into five autonomous states and two internationally controlled areas.[5]

Partition was discussed briefly at Quebec, in August 1943, by Hull and Eden. Eden felt that some members of the British government favored partition, but expressed strong skepticism of its practicability. Hull also elaborated on the difficulties and dangers which it involved.[6] On October 5, however, President Roosevelt stated to Hull, on the eve of the latter's departure for the first three-power conference at Moscow, that he strongly favored the partition of Germany into three or more states, joined only by economic arrangements. Later in the same discussion, however, Roosevelt expressed less assurance of the workability of partition.[7]

At the Moscow Conference of October 1943 preliminary discussion of postwar policy toward Germany was based upon two papers submitted by the United States delegation. These memoranda, submitted "as a basis for discussion," called for the joint occupation and control of Germany by the three powers and for the elaboration, during the war, of an agreed Allied policy

[5] Sumner Welles: *The Time for Decision* (New York: Harper; 1944), pp. 336–64 and map opposite p. 342; Sherwood: op. cit., pp. 797–8.

[6] *The Memoirs of Cordell Hull* (New York: Macmillan; 1948), Vol. II, pp. 1233–34.

[7] Ibid., Vol. II, pp. 1265–6.

toward Germany. This policy was to be based upon the destruction of Germany's war-making ability and of Nazism, upon the maintenance of economic unity, and the promotion of a democratic regime of freedom for democratic parties and freedom of opinion, association, and elections. Germany was to contribute to the reparation of the damage she had inflicted but was to be allowed to provide for her own sustenance.

Dismemberment was discussed briefly at the session of October 25. Mr. Hull noted that it had found favor in "high quarters" in the United States government, but that the experts on German matters were extremely skeptical of its practicability or long-range utility.[8] The writer, who was present at this session, recalls that both Eden and Molotov stated that the same situation prevailed in their own governments, with the same divergence of opinion between the "top-level" and the experts. The American papers on Germany were referred to the European Advisory Commission (the E.A.C.), which was established by the Moscow Conference to "study and make recommendations to the three governments upon European questions connected with the termination of hostilities . . ."

The question of dismemberment was taken up in a different spirit at the Teheran Conference, only a few weeks later. During its last session, when the Big Three were already poised for flight, President Roosevelt submitted a plan for the division of Germany into five autonomous states and two other areas to be under United Nations control. Churchill expressed a preference for a two-way division, joining Bavaria to Austria to form a South German state. According to Hopkins's notes, "Stalin was not enthusiastic about either proposal . . . and saw little difference between the people of one part of Germany and another" . . . "there would always be a strong urge on the part of the Ger-

[8] Ibid., Vol. II, p. 1287.

mans to unite. . . ." After this brief and inconclusive exchange the question was referred to the E.A.C. which was about to begin its work in London.[9]

As the E.A.C. set about its task of negotiating Allied agreements concerning the surrender of Germany and its postwar occupation and control, the urgency of arriving at a definite United States policy on dismemberment became apparent, since so many other questions depended on it. In the Department of State during the autumn and winter of 1943–4 an interdivisional committee made an intensive study of postwar policy toward Germany. Its conclusions and recommendations were then discussed at three long meetings, in early May 1944, of the Department's Postwar Programs Committee, composed of the highest officers of the State Department and presided over by Under Secretary Stettinius. The resulting basic memorandum on Germany, contained in some fifteen pages, was approved by Secretary Hull in July.

This statement of Department policy again reviewed the arguments for and against dismemberment. While it welcomed every move toward strengthening the federal character of the German state and reducing centralized control wherever possible, especially in education and police, it expressed complete doubt of the spontaneous emergence among the Germans of support for partition. It went on to point out that the forcible imposition and maintenance of dismemberment would rule out any future development of democratic institutions, since any governments representative of the popular will would, it predicted, strive to restore German national unity. The problem of enforcing and maintaining disarmament and demilitarization for a long period would be complicated rather than facilitated by imposed partition. Finally, a dismembered Germany could not become economically viable. If each separate German state had to develop its economic resources to the full, the total economic equip-

[9] Sherwood: op. cit., pp. 797–8.

ment of Germany would be increased; on the day when the separate states recombined Germany's economic strength would be greater than before.

The State Department's memorandum further predicted that partition would lead to the separate states falling under the influence or control of outside great powers, while the latter would find themselves bidding for German support by promising to work for the reunification of Germany, thus eventually allowing German nationalism to play upon the resulting rivalry among the victors. Since it had already been decided in principle that Germany was to be divided into three zones of occupation, there was a real danger that this would lead to a *de facto* partition, unless the Allies could agree during the war upon a joint policy for the treatment of defeated Germany. It was in the American interest, therefore, to make every effort to work out an agreed Allied policy toward Germany by completing the negotiations for the establishment of an Allied Control Council for Germany and by giving this council a firm basis of directives to be enforced as uniformly as possible throughout Germany. Basically, this was the function which had been entrusted to the E.A.C. at Moscow and Teheran, and this was the purpose to which Winant devoted a major effort between December 1943 and July 1945.

The memorandum summarized above was the policy only of the Department of State, not of the United States government. As events turned out, it ran head-on into the Morgenthau Plan for the de-industrialization, "pastoralization," and partition of Germany, which took form during the summer of 1944. The Morgenthau plan included a provision for dismemberment, suggesting that responsibility for the continued enforcement of dismemberment be left to Germany's neighbors. The memorandum of Harry D. White of September 2, 1944, which advocated partition, thus clashed directly with a State Department memorandum of September 1. At a meeting of the new Cabinet Committee on Germany, on September 5, Hopkins apparently supported the antipartition view strongly pressed by Secretary of War Stimson and seconded by Secretary Hull.

After Roosevelt and Churchill had approved the Morgenthau plan at the second Quebec Conference, Roosevelt's enthusiasm for it declined. The best the State Department could achieve, however, was a decision to postpone any decision concerning partition. Hull urged this course in his memorandum of September 29. In approving it on October 20, President Roosevelt said: "I dislike making detailed plans for a country which we do not occupy." By the same token, however, he put an effective stop for over four critical months to the process of formulating a consistent American policy toward Germany.[1] During these months of "no policy" Winant was unable to press for Allied agreement on a broad range of agreed policy in preparation for the surrender of Germany, because he had no backing from Washington for this effort.

While there was a further exchange of views on the problem of partition, in October 1944, during the Churchill and Eden visit to Moscow,[2] the crucial discussion took place at Yalta. There, at the February 5 meeting of the three Foreign Ministers, Eden stated that the British War Cabinet had not discussed partition, though studies had been made at the expert level. Molotov felt that the Americans and British were ahead of the Soviet government in their study of German problems. In effect, he invited his partners to commit themselves on partition, while withholding a Soviet decision for later.

On the same afternoon, at the second plenary session, the issue was thrown open by Marshal Stalin's proposal that the conference now reach a decision on dismem-

[1] Hull: op. cit., Vol. II, pp. 1604–8, 1619, 1621–2; Henry L. Stimson and McGeorge Bundy: *On Active Service in Peace and War* (New York: Harper; 1947), p. 572; Henry Morgenthau, Jr.: *Germany Is Our Problem* (New York: Harper; 1945), *passim.*

[2] Stettinius: op. cit., p. 122.

berment. Churchill proposed referring the question to a special committee for study. Stalin suggested including in the surrender instrument a mention of the intention of the Allies to dismember Germany. Roosevelt proposed to dismember Germany and meanwhile to empower the Foreign Ministers to develop concrete plans to give effect to the decision. On this the Big Three agreed.

On February 6 the Foreign Ministers discussed insertion of "dismemberment" in the surrender instrument. The Soviet version committed the three Allies to dismemberment, while the American and British drafts constituted a less binding approval of this policy. At the plenary session that afternoon Molotov withdrew his draft in favor of the American text. The three heads of government were now in agreement that the relevant article (Article 12a) drafted by the E.A.C., should provide that, in the exercise of supreme authority with respect to Germany, the three governments "will take such steps, including the complete disarmament, demilitarization and the dismemberment of Germany as they deem requisite for future peace and security." [8]

At the February 7 meeting of the Foreign Ministers, Molotov proposed that a commission consisting of Eden, Winant, and Gusev be established in London "to study the procedure for the dismemberment of Germany." To the concern expressed by Eden and Stettinius at the exclusion of France from these discussions, Molotov suggested that the question of French participation be decided by the commission itself. Eden asked what terms of reference were to be given to the commission, but no definite instructions were given. The final protocol merely provided: "The study of the procedure for the dismemberment of Germany was referred to a Committee, consisting of Mr. Eden (Chairman), Mr. Winant and Mr. Gusev. This

[8] Ibid., pp. 119, 121–6, 138, 344.

body would consider the desirability of associating with it a French representative."[4]

The Moscow and Teheran Conferences of 1943 had foreshadowed a keen interest of the Big Three in the dismemberment of Germany. Yalta turned this interest into an intention. Yet at Yalta the problem was not once discussed in concrete form. The Yalta agreement merely provided that the three powers would announce to Germany, at the time of surrender, that they were entitled to "take such steps, including the complete disarmament, demilitarization and the dismemberment of Germany as they deem requisite for future peace and security." In this nebulous form the entire question was referred to a committee, the members of which could, of course, negotiate only under instructions from their governments. The theory that they could or would "decide" these questions in a vacuum was only a pretense.

The failure of the Yalta Conference to include France in the new committee was consistent with Soviet and (until lately) American policy, but it became the source of much new confusion. France had been admitted in November 1944 to membership in the E.A.C., which could act only by unanimous decision. On February 7, when it was decided to appoint the committee of three on dismemberment, Stalin had not yet agreed to admit France to share in the occupation and control of Germany. When he agreed, on February 10, that France would participate in the control of Germany, there was no move to include France in the Committee on Dismemberment. The new and secret committee, without the French, overlapped in membership the E.A.C., in which the French were equal members.

The first meeting of the Committee on Dismemberment, held at the Foreign Office on March 7, 1945, with Eden, Winant, and Gusev present, was devoted

[4] Ibid., pp. 162–3, 344.

to a discussion of the committee's mandate.[5] Asked at the end of the meeting to put into writing the understanding of the three representatives, Sir William Strang prepared and circulated to them on March 9 a draft memorandum, in two parts. Part One provided that, in studying the procedure for effecting dismemberment, the committee would undertake its work with certain considerations in mind. (A) The primary purpose of the Allies in their treatment of Germany after surrender or termination of hostilities was to prevent any renewal of aggression by Germany in the future. (B) In studying how this purpose could best be achieved, one question to consider was whether it could be accomplished by such measures as destruction and control of industry, supplementing measures of demilitarization and disarmament, or whether it would also be essential to divide up Germany. (C) If, in order to achieve this basic purpose, it should be found essential to partition Germany, the committee should inquire into the following problems: (1) in what manner Germany should be divided, into what parts, with what boundaries for each part, and with what interrelationship among the various parts; (2) at what time division should be carried out; and (3) what steps the Allies should undertake in order to carry out and enforce dismemberment. Part Two provided that the committee's investigations of the concrete measures set forth under "C" would be carried out in the light of their discussions of the problems set forth under "A" and "B." The memorandum of understanding clearly subordinated concrete decisions concerning dismemberment to a prior discussion of the broader problems of what military and economic measures

[5] The author is grateful to the Department of State for having permitted him to refresh his memory concerning the records of the Committee on Dismemberment. He participated closely in the negotiations as political adviser to Mr. Winant on the European Advisory Commission (June 1944–August 1945) and assistant to Mr. Winant for the Committee on Dismemberment.

should be taken to insure against a renewal of German aggression in future.

The Strang memorandum, which presumably had been approved by Eden, was circulated to Winant and Gusev. Winant felt that the term "destruction and control of German industry" was more sweeping than was justified under the committee's terms of reference. He proposed to Strang and Gusev that this expression be replaced by the words "elimination or control of all German industry that could be used for military production" (borrowed, at the writer's suggestion, from the communiqué of the Yalta Conference). Strang agreed to this modification in his draft, and Gusev stated that he had no objection to it. Thereupon, Winant addressed a letter to Eden, saying that, with this change included, he was willing to accept Sir William Strang's draft as a statement of the committee's mandate.

On March 26, presumably after receiving his instructions from Moscow, Gusev also replied to Eden, first showing his reply informally to Winant. In it he stated that he had no objection to the formula set forth in the Strang draft with the Winant revision, as the understanding of the committee's mandate. His letter added, significantly, that the Soviet government understood that the Yalta decision regarding the dismemberment of Germany was not an obligatory plan for partition but a possibility for exercising pressure upon Germany for the purpose of rendering it harmless if other means proved insufficient.

In a secret report to the Secretary of State on March 29, Winant stressed the significance of Gusev's reply. The Soviet note meant that the committee was intended to consider not merely matters of "procedure" for the purpose of effecting dismemberment, but should, in the first place, consider the substantive question of the desirability and feasibility of partition. Thus far he had found no indication of a firm Soviet view concerning partition. Gusev's letter made it plain that at this stage the Soviet government was not committed in principle to a program of partition. In a private conversation the writer had also asked the Soviet representative whether his information led him to believe that any strong movements for separation would appear in Germany as a consequence of defeat and whether he believed that the Germans would strive for or support dismemberment. To both queries the answer given was an unhesitating "No."

Winant's report on the work of the committee was referred to President Roosevelt, and his instructions were forwarded to Winant on April 10. They were: "I think our attitude should be one of study and postponement of final decision" [concerning dismemberment]. The State Department asked Winant to be guided by this instruction in future discussions.

In all, the Committee on Dismemberment held only two formal meetings, aside from a number of informal conversations. The committee never discussed the substantive questions. Being without instructions from their governments, the members had no proposals to discuss. As the tumultuous events of the German debacle unfolded, all the Allied leaders were straining their efforts to cope with day-to-day problems. Dismemberment, which had seemed so attractive a goal at Yalta, remained among the topics which had least urgency.

Meanwhile, however, the Yalta decision to insert the word "dismemberment" in the surrender instrument had already given rise to complications both real and prospective. As early as February 22, Winant had called the State Department's attention to the problems which arose from the failure of the governments to authorize the members of the committee of three to inform the French of this addition, and the present writer reviewed this question briefly with higher officers of the State Department during a hasty visit to Washington in March.

In effect there were now two versions of the instrument of unconditional surrender. There was the version agreed upon in the E.A.C. on July 25, 1944. In November 1944 this version had been communicated to the French delegation, which in January submitted to the E.A.C. a draft protocol for the inclusion of France as a signatory to the surrender instrument, without any changes of substance. (The E.A.C. signed a protocol to this effect on May 1, 1945.) Since Yalta, however, there was a second version of the surrender instrument, revised to include the word "dismemberment," but this version was known to and approved by only three powers. In order for France to accept this addition, her government must first be informed of its existence; once informed of the Yalta addition, France would logically have to be admitted to membership in the Committee on Dismemberment.

The State Department informed Winant (through this writer) that it had no objection to including a French representative in the committee; this meant that Paris would be informed of the word added at Yalta and would be invited to approve the surrender instrument with this modification. On March 29 Winant confirmed receipt of these instructions, and reported that he and Eden had not brought up the question in the committee in order to avoid confusing the simultaneous discussions among the three governments over the question of including the French in the Reparations Commission which was expected to meet shortly in Moscow. Meanwhile the French representative on the E.A.C. had again pressed, on March 28, for the formal admission of France as a signatory of the surrender instrument. Winant's message went on to hint that it would be better for the three governments to clarify their own positions concerning partition before inviting the French government to join in the discussions.

On April 3, however, the State Department urged that the Yalta modification of the surrender instrument be communicated promptly to the French government and that arrangements be made for formal adherence by France. Referring to the Yalta decision that the committee consider the desirability of adding a French member, the State Department instructed Winant to give active support to the inclusion of France in the committee. On April 5 Winant raised with Eden the question of inviting France to join the committee, and Eden agreed to call the committee together for this purpose. At the meeting, on April 11, Winant made a forceful plea to his colleagues in favor of informing France of the addition of "dismemberment" to the instrument and inviting her to adhere to this decision and to join the committee. Eden and Gusev promised to consult their governments, and Eden expressed assurance that his government would approve this proposal. No answer was ever received from Moscow to this proposal, and therefore France never joined the committee.

Meanwhile, on April 11, the French government learned unofficially of the existence of the added word and of the committee. The State Department's instruction of April 3 had been repeated to the United States Embassy in Paris, for information, and in his reply of April 5, also repeated to the Embassy in Paris, Winant expressed his hope that no action would be taken by the Embassy there until he could secure Soviet and British agreement to approach the French. On April 12, however, the writer was requested to call on the French representative to the E.A.C. On the previous evening the American Embassy in Paris had informed the French Foreign Ministry of the existence of the secret committee, and France was deeply hurt at its exclusion from a subject in which it had many interests. This writer was able to point out that the American government was strongly urging the inclusion of France in the committee, that Soviet consent to this step would be jeopardized by any French protests or leaks to the press, and that Paris should await the result of Winant's new proposal. At the close of this interview feeling was considerably better than at the beginning.

Late that evening a message was prepared for transmission to the State Department and to the Paris Embassy, pointing out the disagreeable consequences which might follow from this unauthorized communication. At midnight, London time, as the text of the telegram was about to be reviewed with Winant, the news came of the death of President Roosevelt. In the light of this blow, the telegram was of course put aside and never sent.

By the first week of May, Germany was clearly on the verge of surrender or complete collapse. Still there was no clarification concerning the final text of the surrender instrument, although on May 1 the E.A.C. signed the protocol making the textual changes necessary to include France among the future signatories. But which document would be used—the one with "dismemberment" or the one without? Repeated visits to the Soviet delegation brought no answer. Meanwhile, on the basis of the agreed English, Russian, and French texts of the instrument, and the agreed German translation, the writer had had prepared sets of signature copies in both variants and held them ready in the office of the E.A.C. delegation in London for immediate use.

On Friday, May 4, Winant discussed the question of the surrender instrument by telephone with Lt. Gen. Walter Bedell Smith, at SHAEF (Supreme Headquarters Allied Expeditionary Force). He reminded General Smith of the E.A.C. instrument of July 25, 1944. In guarded terms Winant informed General Smith of the word which had been added at Yalta, explained the difficulty which had arisen over the two variants, and reported the efforts which he was making to secure a clarification from the Soviet delegation. He also informed General Smith that he had available for the use of SHAEF the two sets of signature copies, together with two mimeographed sets of the approved German translation.[6] General Smith stated that he was familiar with the E.A.C. surrender instrument; however, an authoritative text of the instrument had not been transmitted to SHAEF by the Combined Chiefs of Staff, in Washington, nor had authority to sign the E.A.C. instrument been delegated to SHAEF by the four governments. On that same evening, which was midday, Washington time, Winant talked with the State Department by telephone, informing it of the status of the surrender instrument in the eyes of SHAEF and urging it to arrange at once with the Secretary of War and the Combined Chiefs of Staff for the necessary authorization to be wired to SHAEF.

On Saturday, May 5, Winant saw Gusev before the meeting of the E.A.C. The latter telegraphed his government, at Winant's request, asking again for permission to inform the French of the addition of "dismemberment" to the surrender instrument. A quick approval from Moscow, after waiting since April 11 for a reply, even now would clear the way for the E.A.C. surrender instrument to be used, in its Yalta variant.

On that same afternoon Sir William Strang was called away from the E.A.C. meeting to discuss with Churchill the instrument of unconditional surrender. Winant assumed that Churchill was trying to clarify the question of which variant of the text was to be used in the impending surrender. Later in the evening, however, he learned that SHAEF was discussing with Churchill, in repeated telephone calls, the substitution of an entirely new text for the E.A.C. instrument. The new text provided only for a military surrender in the field, and omitted all mention of the assumption by the four Allies of supreme power over Germany.

[6] This account differs substantially from the brief account given by General Smith in *My Three Years in Moscow* (Philadelphia and New York: Lippincott; 1950), p. 20. The discrepancy is no doubt due to the difficulty of exact recollection after nearly five years, and the writer intends no reflection upon General Smith's sincerity.

The principal motive behind the action of SHAEF was, apparently, the belief that surrender could be secured from the German representatives with least dispute and delay through presenting a brief and simple instrument of military surrender. Apparently, SHAEF assumed that the Germans would argue over the more detailed provisions of the E.A.C. document or might even refuse to sign it. A short document would, in their opinion, save lives, through hastening the German signature and ending German resistance by German military order.

These military factors were important. However, they ignored two important political considerations. By allowing the German High Command to sign a purely military surrender in the field the Allies would forfeit the opportunity to secure a German acknowledgment of unconditional *political* surrender. This failure would place in question the supreme authority which the Allies had agreed to exercise over Germany. For example, a purely military surrender would leave in force, for an indefinite future, the provisions of the Geneva and Hague Conventions; this would, legally, require the Allies to maintain the laws and institutions of the Nazi regime, would prevent them from trying and punishing political war criminals, and, in general, would deprive them of the right to exercise full control over Germany. A purely military surrender was adequate to cover the capitulation of separate armies, as in the surrender of Kesselring's army. It was quite inadequate as an instrument of final and unconditional surrender on the part of the German government and High Command.

There was another danger in the adoption of the SHAEF proposal. The E.A.C. surrender instrument was, at the same time, an agreement among the four Allied governments. Its provisions were to be binding on the Allies in their dealings with each other, as well as upon the Germans. It was risky to inaugurate the postwar co-operation of the Allies by scrapping a basic document of Allied agreement and substituting for the instrument agreed to by the four governments a new instrument, whose very existence and contents were unknown to several of them.

Having discovered, late on Saturday, that a new surrender instrument was being drawn up, Winant was able to present these dangers personally to Churchill and by telephone to General Smith. As he reported to the State Department in a later message, Winant wished to make sure that the degree of agreement which had been reached by the four powers after long and painful negotiations would be fully safeguarded in the act of surrender. Through his personal insistence a new article, Article 4, was included in the surrender instrument, which was then signed at Rheims on May 7.[7] This article was worded as a general enabling clause, leaving the way open for imposing on Germany the additional military and political conditions which had been embodied in the E.A.C. instrument. Article 4 became the basis on which the four powers issued the Declaration on Germany of June 5, 1945, and assumed supreme authority to control and administer Germany.

On Sunday, May 6, assuming that SHAEF had cleared its brief draft with the Combined Chiefs of Staff and with the War Department in Washington, Winant wired the State Department reassuringly, that there had been full co-ordination and agreement in London on surrender terms. On May 9, however, the State Department wired Winant for more detailed information, asking what arrangements were envisaged for utilizing the E.A.C. surrender instrument. It re-

[7] Article 4: "This act of military surrender is without prejudice to, and will be superseded by any general instrument of surrender imposed by, or on behalf of the United Nations and applicable to Germany and the German armed forces as a whole." Act of Military Surrender, Rheims, May 7, and Berlin, May 8, 1945. *Surrender by Germany*, Department of State Publication 2515 (Washington, D. C.; 1946), pp. 1, 4.

ported that the War Department also had no news on the origin of the brief instrument of surrender or on the reasons why the E.A.C. instrument had not been presented for signature at Rheims or Berlin.

Thus, during April 1945 the presence of "dismemberment" in one version of the surrender instrument and its absence in the other version had been a source of great prospective difficulty. In May the very existence of an agreed surrender instrument was brushed aside by SHAEF, although it had had many printed copies of the instrument of July 25, 1944, and its representatives had discussed with Winant the details concerning the arrangements for the signature copies of the instrument and for the authorized German translation. The leaders of SHAEF were, apparently, indifferent to the fact that the E.A.C. instrument had been approved by four governments, and that the inclusion in it of "dismemberment" had been the subject of much discussion at Yalta.

Naturally, the brief military instrument contained no reference to "dismemberment." And reference to dismemberment was also omitted, by agreement, from the Declaration on Germany, which was later issued in Berlin by the four Commanders in Chief on June 5. Discussions of a draft declaration had begun with the circulation of a British draft, on March 30. At this time it appeared likely that no German authority, military or civil, would be available to sign a formal surrender and that the victors would have to resort to another procedure, that of proclaiming the complete defeat of Germany and assuming supreme power over it. Accordingly, in April the E.A.C. had been reworking the surrender instrument of July 25, 1944, into a declaration to be issued by the four Commanders in Chief. The Declaration proclaimed the right of the victors to determine the future status of any and all parts of Germany, and it therefore appeared unnecessary to include a specific mention of "dismemberment."

In addition, the Soviet government, without consulting its Allies, had now taken an official stand in opposition to dismemberment. In his "Proclamation to the People" of May 8, Marshal Stalin declared that "the Soviet Union . . . does not intend to dismember or destroy Germany."[8] On May 10 Winant confirmed to the State Department that the British and Soviet governments concurred in the view that the word "dismemberment" should not appear in the Declaration. After May 8 the draft declaration was revised to take account of Article 4 of the brief surrender instrument, signed at Rheims and Berlin, and the text was completed and approved by the E.A.C. on May 12. Thus the term "dismemberment" disappeared both from the military instrument and from the Declaration which was issued on June 5.

Meanwhile, the partition of Germany was actually taking place. As the victorious armies advanced into Germany, they had set up SHAEF and Soviet military government regimes in the occupied territories. The *de facto* division of Germany which followed had not been forestalled by the preparatory efforts of the E.A.C., and it was not overcome by the Potsdam agreement for the unified treatment of Germany. By midsummer 1945, Germany was, in fact, dismembered into four zones of occupation, plus Berlin as a fifth zone under four-power control. As General Clay reported to Secretary Byrnes in May 1946: "After one year of occupation, zones represent air-tight territories with almost no free exchange of commodities, persons and ideas; Germany now consists of four small economic units which can deal with each other only through treaties . . ."[9] The gloomiest predictions of the State Department memorandum of May 1944 concerning

[8] "*Obrashchenie tov. I. V. Stalina k narodu*," *Pravda*, No. 3 (May 10, 1945), p. 1.

[9] General Lucius D. Clay: *Decision in Germany* (Garden City, N. Y.: Doubleday; 1950), p. 73.

the consequences of the failure to lay down during the war a consistent and agreed Allied policy toward Germany had been more than fulfilled.

Allied pursuit of the mirage of dismemberment—in which the United States participated conspicuously—had contributed substantially to this failure.

:6:

THE OCCUPATION OF GERMANY: NEW LIGHT ON HOW THE ZONES WERE DRAWN[1]

[*April 1950*]

INTRODUCTORY NOTE · If there was a real chance, during World War II, to lay a basis for some enduring measure of postwar co-operation among the three major Allies—Britain, the Soviet Union, and the United States—it could only have been on the question of Germany and the precautions to be taken against a revival of German militarism. Germany, it was agreed by late 1943, would be occupied and administered jointly by the three (later, four) powers. If they could co-operate in this enterprise, they might possibly come to workable compromises on several other questions; for example, on a wide measure of internal independence for the East European nations. If they failed this crucial test of their wisdom and moderation, Germany as well as Europe would be split down the middle, and a new contest for supremacy would begin immediately, with new contestants and even higher stakes.

In hindsight it is easy to say that the attempt was hopeless and not worth making because the Soviet leadership

[1] *Foreign Affairs*, Vol. XXVIII, No. 4 (July 1950), pp. 580–604. Copyright 1950 by the Council on Foreign Relations, Inc.

would never abate its claims to reshape the world in its own image or forgo any immediate and material advantage for the sake of retaining the good will of what it regarded as temporary allies. Still, it is to the credit of Western statesmen that they made many efforts to offer postwar co-operation among equals in the hope that Stalin would grant this breathing spell to the sorely tried people of the Soviet Union. To make the co-operation stick, much more should have been done to assure him of assistance in rebuilding the Soviet economy; as it turned out, Stalin and the Soviet people soon felt that their vast sacrifices were forgotten by less war-damaged Allies as soon as the fighting was over. That and other policies would have required a much more integrated policy than American policy seemed capable of achieving during World War II.

Among the best accounts of wartime negotiations are: John R. Deane, *The Strange Alliance; the Story of Our Efforts at Wartime Cooperation with Russia* (New York: Viking Press; 1947); and *Negotiating with the Russians*, edited by Raymond Dennett and Joseph E. Johnson (Boston: World Peace Foundation; 1951). Two excellent later studies are: William H. McNeill, *America, Britain and Russia, Their Cooperation and Conflict, 1941–1946*, edited by Arnold Toynbee, *Survey of International Affairs, 1939–1946*, Volume III (London: Oxford University Press for the Royal Institute of International Affairs; 1953); and Herbert Feis, *Churchill, Roosevelt, Stalin; the War They Waged and the Peace They Sought* (Princeton: Princeton University Press; 1957).

*

THE first steps toward three-power planning for the occupation and control of Germany after her eventual defeat were taken at the Moscow Conference of Foreign Ministers in October 1943. In those days the Red army was continuing its powerful advance against the German armies (Kiev was liberated during the conference), and the forces of the Western Allies were preparing their tremendous attack upon Hitler's "Fortress Europe." The need for co-ordinating the political planning of the major Allies thus became more and more obvious and acute. During Mr. Eden's visit to Washington the previous March, Harry Hopkins had noted the necessity of reaching an understanding "as to which armies would be where and what kind of administration should be developed." [2] A few days later President Roosevelt instructed Secretary Hull to explore, first with the British and then with the Russians, "the question of what our plan is to be in Germany and Italy during the first months after Germany's collapse." [3] Even so, the Italian surrender caught the Allies politically unprepared. The cross-purposes and frictions revealed during the negotiations over Italy showed how urgent it was to begin co-ordinating Allied purposes and arrangements for the surrender of Germany, and to do so well before the event. In September 1943 it was decided to arrange a first meeting of the three Foreign Ministers in preparation for a first conference of the three heads of government.

At the Moscow Conference, Mr. Hull presented to Mr. Eden and Mr. Molotov the American view of postwar policy toward Germany.[4] Although this memorandum was received favorably, no attempt was made to reach concrete decisions concerning Germany, and the problem was referred to a new body, the European Advisory Commission (the E.A.C.), which was to have its seat in London and carry on its work continuously. The memorandum recommended that an inter-Allied control commission be set up to enforce upon Germany

[2] Robert E. Sherwood: *Roosevelt and Hopkins, an Intimate History* (New York: Harper; 1948), p. 714.

[3] *The Memoirs of Cordell Hull* (New York: Macmillan; 1948), Vol. II, pp. 1284–5.

[4] Summarized in Hull, ibid., Vol. II, pp. 1285–7. The memorandum was drafted during the conference by two members of the delegation, including the present writer, mainly on the basis of studies and recommendations approved by the Interdivisional Committee on Germany, in the Department of State, and of studies prepared by the War and Peace Studies Project of the Council on Foreign Relations, New York.

the terms of surrender and the policies of the Allies, and that Germany should be occupied by British, Soviet, and American forces. Thus the principle of joint responsibility in German policy and of joint occupation of Germany was accepted tacitly in October 1943 as a basis of future planning.

The terms of reference of the E.A.C., as established in the Moscow protocol of November 1, 1943, reflected a sharp divergence between British and American views. The Foreign Office wanted the E.A.C. to receive a broad mandate to settle promptly, during the war, many questions concerning both the enemy and the smaller Allied states in Europe. In this view, the E.A.C. should have competence in such matters as the future regimes to be established in France, Poland, Yugoslavia, and elsewhere, and also be authorized to settle minority and boundary disputes. It can be assumed that the British leaders hoped to settle as many of these questions as possible during the war, while the major Allies were compelled by necessity to act together to a considerable degree and while the United States had powerful forces in Europe. A British government has excellent facilities for studying matters of this sort and deciding on definite policy objectives; and the existence of a wartime coalition cabinet provided an even better opportunity than usual for the formulation of a final British view.

The dominant official view in the United States was that it would be unwise to attempt to solve postwar problems while hostilities were continuing, except for achieving the establishment of a United Nations organization. There was doubt as to the authority of the executive to commit the United States on matters which are usually settled in treaties of peace. There was uncertainty regarding the degree to which American opinion would, after the war, maintain a detailed interest in and responsibility for specifically European problems. There were fears that groups of American citizens of foreign origin would be distracted from the unified war effort—and, incidentally, from support of the administration—if attempts were made during the war to settle concrete boundary and other issues. These lines of thought led the United States government to favor limiting the mandate of the E.A.C. primarily to working out arrangements for the surrender of the Axis states in Europe. While the American delegation at Moscow accepted the broad wording of Article 1 of the terms of reference, it laid emphasis upon the limiting provision that questions could be referred to the E.A.C. only by unanimous consent of the three governments, and it actually regarded Article 2 as the only real mandate of the new body.[5] Preparations for beginning the formal negotiations concerning Germany were advanced during the Teheran Conference when the three heads of government appointed their representatives to the E.A.C.—Sir William Strang for the United Kingdom, Fedor T. Gusev for the Soviet Union, and the late John G. Winant for the United States.

Thus the Moscow and Teheran Conferences committed the three major Allies to proceeding promptly to the elaboration of joint arrangements for the postwar occupation and control of Germany. In the view of those at the "working level" within the State Department, and in Mr. Winant's view, the task was one of great and immediate urgency. If the Allies could agree on a detailed program of postwar co-operation with regard to Germany, other European problems might prove much more manageable and there would be far stronger hope for some measure of continuing

[5] The principal terms of reference of the E.A.C. were: (1) "The Commission will study and make recommendations to the three Governments upon European questions connected with the termination of hostilities which the three Governments may consider appropriate to refer to it . . . ;" (2) "As one of the Commission's first tasks the three Governments desire that it shall, as soon as possible, make detailed recommendations to them upon the terms of surrender to be imposed upon each of the European States with which any of the three Powers are at war, and upon the machinery required to ensure the fulfillment of those terms. . . ."

co-operation in a United Nations organization. No one assumed that co-operation would be easy. But there was hope that the great damages which German aggression had inflicted on the world might have created such a shared sense of urgency among the Allies that they would be able to plan a common Allied policy for dealing with Germany in a manner to prevent the recurrence of the danger.

The E.A.C. held an informal organizing meeting on December 15, 1943, and began its formal meetings on January 14, 1944.[6] Naturally, it could work effectively only when all three representatives had full instructions from their governments. The E.A.C. was not, in fact, able to "study and make recommendations to the three Governments" on its own initiative. From the beginning it was a negotiating body, and the twelve agreements which it succeeded in reaching had to be approved in advance, down to the last detail and word, by the three (later four) governments before they could be presented as "recommendations" to those governments. Only then would such recommendations receive formal "approval." In matters of such profound concern as those which were referred to the E.A.C. each of the national representatives could speak and act only upon detailed instructions.

In this respect the British representative was fortunately situated. As the seat of the commission was London, he had direct personal access to the final political authority in his government and so was able to receive clear guidance rather promptly. Interdepartmental conflicts could be resolved with reasonable expedition through joint committees (in which the primary responsibility of the Foreign Office in matters of foreign policy was recognized), through the ad-

[6] In all, the E.A.C. held 20 formal and 97 informal meetings between January 14, 1944, and August 1945, in addition to frequent private consultations among the delegations. It concluded 12 agreements dealing with German, Austrian, and Bulgarian affairs. The armistices with Rumania, Hungary, and Finland were not referred to it for negotiation.

mirable functioning of the Cabinet Secretariat, and, if necessary, through reference to the War Cabinet. The American representative on E.A.C. was less fortunate. Until December 1943 there was no established procedure through which he could receive the instructions of his government. Clearly, postwar policy toward Germany transcended the competence of either the Department of State or the War Department.

In order to meet this lack and to provide the American representative in London with instructions based upon the combined views of the departments concerned, there was established in December 1943, under the camouflage name of the Working Security Committee (the W.S.C.), an interdepartmental committee, consisting of officers of State, War, and Navy Departments. The W.S.C. was designed to co-ordinate the views of the three departments and, on this basis, to transmit agreed instructions to Mr. Winant in London. The instructions might be draft documents to be circulated and negotiated in the E.A.C.; or detailed statements of American policies and objectives for his guidance in negotiation, whether formal or informal; or comments on reports of E.A.C. discussions and on proposals submitted by other delegations; or, finally, comments on suggestions and recommendations worked out by the United States delegation in London.[7] Formally, the Department of State provided the channel for transmission of instructions to Mr. Winant. But in practice it could forward only instructions and drafts which had been approved by the W.S.C., or rather by each of the departmental components of the W.S.C. In theory, the officers of the three departments concerned with German policy were supposed to work out agreed recommendations in the W.S.C. and then to "clear" the draft instructions with the superior officers

[7] A brief and formal account of the composition of the Working Security Committee is presented in Harley A. Notter: *Postwar Foreign Policy Preparation, 1939–1945*, Department of State Publication 3580 (Washington, D. C.: 1949, released in 1950), pp. 225, 228–9, 271, 368.

within each department; when notified of such multiple clearance, the chairman of the W.S.C. could then transmit the approved telegram or dispatch to London. In practice, each departmental component within the W.S.C. could exercise a "veto" over any proposed instruction.[8]

The Department of State was represented on the W.S.C. by officers of the Division of European (later Central European) Affairs and the Division of Political (later Territorial) Studies. In presenting recommendations to the W.S.C., the State Department component could draw upon a large number of background and policy studies which had been reviewed by the President's Advisory Committee on Postwar Foreign Policy since January 1942, and upon the continuing and intensive work of the departmental Interdivisional Committee on Germany.[9] The War Department component was to be provided by the Civil Affairs Division, which had been established in the spring of 1943.[1] If the Civil Affairs Division had made studies of future policy toward Germany in the intervening period, this fact did not become evident in the discussions of the W.S.C.

Although the establishment of the W.S.C. had been

[8] The interdepartmental basis of American policy making was reflected in the composition of the United States delegation to the E.A.C. Mr. Winant was assisted by a political adviser designated by the Department of State (Mr. George F. Kennan, January to April 1944; the present writer, June 1944 to August 1945), and one or two political officers; a military adviser, with staff; a naval adviser, with staff; and later an air adviser, with staff. The service advisers communicated directly with their superiors in Washington through their own channels.

[9] Regarding the Advisory Committee, see H. A. Notter: op. cit.; see above, Five, "Dismemberment of Germany." For a brief account of the Interdivisional Committee, see Notter: op. cit., p. 177. The present writer served as chairman of this committee in its initial stages, and continued as a member until June 1944; he served continuously as a member of the W.S.C., occasionally as acting chairman, from December 1943 to June 1944. David Harris, professor of history at Stanford University, became chairman of the Interdivisional Committee in October 1943 and a member of the W.S.C. in June 1944.

[1] Henry L. Stimson and McGeorge Bundy: *On Active Service in Peace and War* (New York: Harper; 1947), p. 559.

agreed to early in December by the three departments "at the Assistant Secretary level," it could not begin to function at once because the Civil Affairs Division of the War Department refused at first to take part. For a fortnight the representatives of this division maintained that the surrender and occupation of Germany were purely a military matter which would have to be decided "at the military level"; and that therefore there was no need for the W.S.C., or, for that matter, for the E.A.C. In rejoinder, it was pointed out that the President, who was also Commander in Chief, had joined with the heads of two other governments in creating the E.A.C. and in expressing the intention to work out Allied agreements on postwar Germany. According to the Civil Affairs Division, military government was a purely military matter; when the time came, the necessary orders would be issued by the Combined Chiefs of Staff, and that was all. This view ignored the fact that the Combined Chiefs of Staff would probably not be allowed to determine American *postwar* policy, that there was no Soviet representation on it, that the President was committed to seeking postwar agreement on Germany with both the Soviet and British governments, and that meanwhile the American representative on the E.A.C. was completely without instructions. This deadlock, which threatened to postpone indefinitely the establishment of the W.S.C. was finally broken by intervention from above, and on December 21, 1943, officers of the Civil Affairs Division met for the first time in the W.S.C. It should be pointed out that the Civil Affairs Division was staffed largely with civilians who had recently gone into uniform. Some of them who had been lawyers in civilian life seemed to regard the jurisdiction and prestige of the military service as they might the interests of a client, to be defended by every device of argument, delay, obstruction, and veto against an "adversary," in this case the State Department.

Thus although the W.S.C. began its meetings, it

made little progress on the co-ordination of policy. The Civil Affairs Division representatives who attended were of relatively junior rank. They had been given strict instructions to agree to nothing, or almost nothing, and could only report the discussions back to their superiors. This system of negotiating at arm's length, under rigid instructions and with the exercise of the "veto," resembled the procedures of Soviet negotiators in their more intransigeant moods. Under such conditions the pace of work in the W.S.C. was, of necessity, determined primarily by the outlook of the Civil Affairs Division.

This explanation of the procedure by which American policy was formulated in Washington for presentation in the E.A.C. in London has been necessary, since it had a great deal to do with the determination of the American position regarding the future zones of occupation in Germany.

While the W.S.C. was struggling to be born, the Interdivisional Committee on Germany in the Department of State had been giving active consideration to the problems which should be dealt with by the E.A.C. Upon returning from the Moscow Conference, I had outlined to the committee three matters of immediate concern—the formulation of an instrument of unconditional surrender, the definition of zones of occupation, and the establishment of Allied control machinery for the joint administration of Germany—and urged that the American proposals be formulated as promptly as possible and circulated in the E.A.C. Experience had shown that it was advantageous to have American proposals available to the Russians before they drew up their own recommendations. Moreover, the negotiator who put his proposals in first could frequently get his drafts accepted as a basis of discussion. At this stage of the war, too, American negotiators were often in a "middle position" between Soviet and British views, and therefore it was important to enable the American member of E.A.C. to take the lead in submitting proposals. The hope that this might be done in the present case faded rapidly. While the Civil Affairs Division wrangled over jurisdiction in the W.S.C., Mr. Winant was left without instructions. He could not even discuss the British and Soviet proposals presented in E.A.C., much less present any American proposals. On occasion, when he wired urgently asking why he had received no replies to his requests for comment and instructions, the Civil Affairs Division representatives even vetoed draft messages informing him that he should not expect an early reply.

Despite the deadlock over the question of zones, the W.S.C. did make some progress on the formulation of a draft instrument of German unconditional surrender. The American draft, which was circulated in the E.A.C. on March 6, 1944, became the basis of the E.A.C. protocol of July 25, 1944, setting forth the agreed terms of German surrender.

Already our office had been making a study of possible and desirable zones of occupation, and by mid-December 1943 a tentative proposal was ready for submission to the W.S.C., together with demographic and economic studies of the suggested zones and the necessary maps. In preparing this proposal we had to assume either that there would or would not be a German central administration in operation at the time of surrender. In the former case, the Allied authorities could work through it, though of course drastically changing its composition and policies. Berlin then would be the logical seat of the joint Allied authority. If there were no German administration in being, it would still be necessary to use the German staffs and records, and Berlin again would be the natural center. A further factor favorable to making Berlin the seat of Allied authority was that any proposal to create a new capital, especially one situated in a western zone, seemed bound to meet with unrelenting Soviet opposition. It seemed unwise to begin negotiation for an agreed Allied policy by presenting a proposal which could only lead at once to deadlock, thus sacrificing larger interests of Allied co-operation to a contingent advantage which might or might not be of practical importance.

More significant, I believe, was the proposal that a corridor should be established connecting the prospective western areas of occupation with Berlin, this to be accomplished by joining certain intervening districts of Saxony-Anhalt and Brandenburg to the western zones. This proposal, for which I was responsible, ran counter to the principle of retaining the administrative boundaries of the existing *Länder* and provinces; but it was consistent with the proposal to break up Prussia and thus to destroy its preponderance within postwar Germany. Since it was assumed that for most purposes Germany would be treated as a political and economic entity, the economic disruption caused by creating this corridor for purposes only of occupation and enforcement of Allied authority would be negligible. I realized that such a proposal by the United States would probably meet with Soviet objections, but I believed that if it could be presented first, with impressive firmness, it might be taken into account by the Soviet government in framing its own proposals. I believed that in order to safeguard the dignity and security of the American authorities in Berlin provision should be made in advance for free and direct territorial access to Berlin from the West.

This proposal was never acted upon in the W.S.C. in Washington and was therefore never presented to the E.A.C. in London. The position of the Civil Affairs Division of the War Department was that the determination of the future zones of occupation was no concern of the W.S.C. or of the E.A.C. It was a "military matter" which would be decided "at the proper time" and "at the military level." [2] The Civil Affairs Division

[2] Admiral Leahy reports that in November 1943 the Joint Chiefs of Staff considered the question of future zones of occupation. (See William D. Leahy: *I Was There; The Personal Story of the Chief of*

even denied for many weeks the "right" of the E.A.C. to negotiate an agreement on zones. It argued that zones of occupation would be determined by the location of troops at the time of Germany's surrender or collapse. This, the State Department members felt, was to rely on an extremely risky expedient. If there were no Allied agreement on postwar zones, there would be constant suspicions between the Allies. The Germans could fan these fears by hints of a separate understanding with East or West. In the closing phase of the war, strategy and tactics might be determined by the desire to occupy the largest possible area of Germany rather than by the aim to defeat Germany as quickly as possible.

In their reply, the representatives of the War Department indicated that they expected all of Germany up to the Rhine to be in Soviet control upon Germany's defeat, and that therefore it was useless to expect the Soviet government to carry out any agreement regarding the division of Germany which might have been reached in advance, since this would be to its disadvantage. To this the answer was obvious. If the prospects were so gloomy, all the more reason to seek early agreement on future arrangements for Germany, since clearly it was not in the interest of European stability and of American security that all or nearly all of Germany should pass under sole Soviet control. As for the doubt concerning the Soviet government's fulfilment of its agreement, no American government could afford to report to its people and its Allies that it had refused to negotiate a postwar agreement on this ground. Nothing would be lost by assuming that agreements would be kept. If they were made with good faith on the American side, and were later broken by other governments, the situation would be far clearer for all

Staff to Presidents Roosevelt and Truman. Based on His Notes and Diaries Made at the Time. [New York: Whittlesey; 1950], p. 197). I have no knowledge of the conclusions of the Joint Chiefs of Staff, if any were reached.

the world, the American people included, to judge. After many days of argument and counterargument, the Civil Affairs Division exercised its right of veto in early January 1944. W.S.C. was debarred from providing Mr. Winant with proposals concerning the future zones of occupation.

It has sometimes been suggested that it was a basic error to divide Germany into zones of occupation; and that it would have been better to station Allied forces in dispersed or interlarded fashion and thus avoid the creation of separate zones. A tentative proposal to this effect was put forward informally in late December 1943 by a member of the British Foreign Office during a reconnaissance visit to Washington.[3] If this proposal had been adopted, the establishment of zones and the *de facto* partition of Germany might conceivably have been avoided. It was rejected by the Civil Affairs Division. There were indeed strong arguments against it. Interlarding of forces under different commands would have created serious problems of supply and communications for the very large forces which would be on German territory at the time of defeat. It would be difficult for regional and local commanders to deal with German administrative authorities only through Berlin. Conflicts and misunderstandings might arise between troops of different language and background. The State Department planning group gave the suggestion careful consideration but felt that it could not support it in opposition to the unanimous military opinion. It was assumed also that the Soviet government would wish to concentrate its forces in a compact territory and would not want its troops to have the wide and free contact with other Allied forces which

[3] (Author's note, 1959) A proposal of this kind had been discussed in July and August 1943 by the British Post-Hostilities Planning Subcommittee and by the Chief of Staff to the Supreme Allied Commander (COSSAC), an Anglo-American military planning group. See Sir Frederick Morgan: *Overture to Overlord* (Garden City, N. Y.: Doubleday; 1950), p. 117. I first learned of this background to the proposal in 1951.

would be inevitable if Soviet forces were interlarded with British and American troops all over Germany.

The Foreign Office representative who visited Washington in December 1943 and January 1944 also wished to find out whether the United States was preparing to take the initiative in presenting proposals to the E.A.C. We may assume that his report made it clear that no rapid formulation of agreed American views was to be relied upon. In January, therefore, the Foreign Office took the initiative. At the first meeting of the E.A.C. the British representative presented a draft surrender instrument and a draft agreement on zones of occupation (circulated January 15, 1944). The latter provided for the division of Germany, within its 1937 boundaries, into three zones. The area which it proposed for Soviet occupation was the one which was accepted later by all three powers. Mecklenburg-Pomerania, Brandenburg, Saxony-Anhalt, Thuringia, and the areas to the eastward were to come under Soviet occupation, except for Greater Berlin, which was to be under joint occupation.[4] As a division of Germany, it was equitable. The Soviet zone, it was estimated, would contain forty per cent of the territory, thirty-six per cent of the population, and thirty three per cent of the productive resources of the pre-1937 country. In terms of war effort and of war-inflicted sufferings, the Soviet Union might have claimed a larger share.

The British proposal would have placed all of northwestern Germany, including Brunswick, Hesse-Nassau, the Rhine Provinces, and the areas north of them, under British occupation. The zone proposed for American occupation included the Saar and the Bavarian Palatinate west of the Rhine, together with Hesse-Darmstadt,

[4] (Author's note, 1959) I later learned from Sir Frederick Morgan's *Overture to Overlord* (pp. 113–7, 247) that the British proposal on zones and Berlin had "received general approval," presumably from the Foreign Office and the British Chiefs of Staff, in August 1943. In the Department of State I knew nothing of this, although COSSAC included a U. S. military contingent.

Württemberg, Baden, and Bavaria. This arrangement, if approved, would have placed the greatest industrial areas under British control. Only the United States zone would have bordered on France, and if a zone were later allotted to French occupation, most of the French zone would have to be detached from the American-controlled area. On the other hand, if the United States withdrew from the occupation of Germany, the American zone could be taken over more conveniently by French forces. London presumably did not overlook the fact that the proposed British zone would give Britain a major voice in control over her greatest industrial and commercial competitor in Europe.

For these reasons the proposed allocation of the two western zones was rejected by the American military authorities and by President Roosevelt. The President insisted that the redeployment of major American forces from Germany to the Far East required United States control of the ports of northwestern Germany. Furthermore, occupation of the southwestern zone would necessitate using French lines of communication and transportation, and American-French military relations were not cordial. The British argued that redeployment of American forces to the northwestern zone and of British forces to the southwestern zone would create great confusion, since Montgomery's forces were to advance through the Low Countries into northern Germany, while American forces were to enter central and southern Germany. The American rejoinder was that this problem would diminish rapidly in volume as combat forces were transferred to the Far East and forces in Germany were placed on a garrison-and-security footing. The President urged instead that the British plan to occupy both the southern zone in Germany and all of Austria. This dispute over the allocation of the two western zones was to be settled only seven months later, at the Quebec Conference of September 1944.

On February 18, 1944, a Soviet proposal concerning

zones was also circulated in the E.A.C. It accepted the eastern zone as suggested by the British proposal, together with the designation of Greater Berlin as a separate zone of joint Allied occupation. The Soviet acceptance, without bargaining, of a zone of slightly more than one third of Germany, appeared a sign of a moderate and conciliatory approach to the problem of how to deal with postwar Germany. The Soviet representative implied clearly that the question of just how western Germany would be divided into separate British and American zones was not of particular concern to his government. However, he hoped for an early settlement of the dispute and hence for a prompt conclusion of a three-power agreement. At this time the Civil Affairs Division representatives on the W.S.C. were still maintaining that the E.A.C. was not entitled to negotiate concerning the future zones. Consequently no American proposals or instructions could be sent to Mr. Winant. He made urgent and repeated pleas for them, but to no avail.

At the end of February the Civil Affairs Division suddenly changed its position. It brought into the W.S.C. a small-scale map of Germany, on which pencilled lines radiating north, west, and south from Berlin had been sketched, explaining that this division represented President Roosevelt's instructions. I do not know who received this "instruction" from the President, or how much information had been presented to him concerning the British and Soviet proposals. This proposed division had the advantage of placing Berlin at the meeting point of the three zones. On the other hand, the proposed Soviet zone represented only about twenty-two per cent of the area, population, and productive resources of prewar Germany, and was therefore certain to be rejected by the Soviet and British governments. The hastily pencilled lines also cut across many lines of administration and communication. The Civil Affairs Division insisted that this proposal be communicated as it stood to the E.A.C. and that Mr.

Winant demand its acceptance. When it was asked to prepare a background memorandum for the negotiator's guidance in presenting this proposal, it declined to do so. After ten days of discussion, the W.S.C. agreed to transmit this bare proposal to London as it stood. The State Department component realized that Mr. Winant would undoubtedly ask for fuller instructions, and hoped thus to bring the Civil Affairs Division to a more realistic consideration of the character and difficulties of the proposal it was making. Frantic queries from London followed promptly. The War Department representatives could not be budged. The deadlock continued until the first week of April. The E.A.C. delegation in London insisted that it must be given fuller instructions both for presenting the proposal and concerning the attitude it should adopt if the British and Soviet governments joined in rejecting it. In the W.S.C. the Civil Affairs Division refused all further elucidations and contingent instructions.

In mid-March the wheels of the E.A.C., which had been barely turning, ground to a complete stop. The Soviet and American delegations were deeply perturbed by "informed comments" in the British press concerning matters in dispute, especially as one of the disputes dealt with the question of whether the German forces, after the final surrender, would or would not be treated as prisoners-of-war. Unauthorized disclosures of these discussions provided Goebbels with effective means of stimulating German resistance. This gave rise to considerable American and Soviet indignation. After a month, during which the work of the E.A.C. was suspended, Mr. Winant was able, by bringing to bear all his influence, to restore Soviet confidence in the future secrecy of E.A.C. discussions. The E.A.C.'s work was resumed.

In the meantime, Mr. Winant's Political Adviser, George F. Kennan, returned to Washington to try to make clear the difficult situation in which the E.A.C. delegation found itself and to clarify the issues which were before it. In the first week of April he was able to present the entire range of E.A.C. issues to President Roosevelt. The President thereupon reconsidered the arrangements for the future zones and authorized his representative in London to approve the proposed Soviet zone. He continued, however, to insist on American occupation of the northwestern zone. Mr. Winant now informed his colleagues orally of this new position, and the American acceptance of the Soviet zone undoubtedly contributed to the renewal of the work of the E.A.C. and to a strengthening of confidence in its ability to build a basis of postwar co-operation among the Allies. Mr. Winant continued to advocate vigorously that the northwestern zone be assigned for American occupation. From April to November, however, the dispute continued.

In May 1944 Mr. Winant paid a short visit to Washington to clarify a large number of issues concerning both the E.A.C. negotiations and numerous other matters. Mr. Roosevelt again affirmed to him his strong view concerning American occupation of northwestern Germany. In his discussions in the War Department, Mr. Winant raised with the Civil Affairs Division the question of access to Berlin from the western zones. He offered to propose detailed provisions safeguarding American access by highway, railroad, and air. Since the Soviet representative had repeatedly insisted that there would be no difficulty in arranging for transit through the Soviet zone to Berlin, and that the presence of American and British forces in Berlin "of course" carried with it all necessary facilities of access, Mr. Winant was confident that concrete provisions could be negotiated in the E.A.C. without great difficulty. Although the President had given new instructions early in April, as noted above, Mr. Winant so far had refrained from presenting the American position in writing, since he assumed that Washington would want to see some arrangements concerning access to Berlin included. At this time, of course, it was felt that such provisions would relate only to the personnel and matériel of the armed forces, since planning was proceeding on the assumption that Germany herself would be treated as a political and economic unit and therefore no special provisions would be needed to regulate the economic relations between Berlin and any of the zones.

The Civil Affairs Division opposed the insertion of a specific provision concerning access to Berlin. It felt that it was impossible to foresee, in May 1944, in advance of D-Day, what railroads and highways would be needed for use by the Allied forces. If specific roads and rail routes were assigned, they might be in a state of complete destruction when the time came to enter Berlin, and then it would be difficult to arrange for alternative facilities. They insisted that this was a purely "military matter" which would be taken care of "at the military level" when the time came. Mr. Winant felt that he could not further challenge this authoritative military view. When he returned to London he at last circulated to the E.A.C., on June 12, the American proposal concerning zones of occupation in Germany.

During July the E.A.C. negotiated actively for an agreement on zones and for the division of Berlin into three sectors. Maps were prepared showing the zones in Germany and the sectors in Berlin. The draft agreement specified that "Germany, within the frontiers as they were on the 31st December 1937, will, for the purposes of occupation, be divided into three zones, one of which will be allotted to each of the three Powers, and a special Berlin area, which will be under joint occupation by the three Powers." Article 2 gave a description of the western boundary of the zone which ". . . will be occupied by the armed forces of the Union of Soviet Socialist Republics, with the exception of the Berlin area, for which a special system of occupation is provided below." It also provided that "The Berlin area (by which expression is understood the territory of 'Greater Berlin' as defined by the Law of the 27th April, 1920) will be jointly occupied by armed forces of the United Kingdom, the United States of America and the Union of Soviet Socialist Republics assigned by the respective Commanders-in-Chief." In the meticulous drafting practiced by the E.A.C. it was provided that the boundaries of *Länder* and provinces would be "those which existed after the coming into effect of the decree of 25th June, 1941 (published in the *Reichsgesetzblatt*, Part I, No. 72, the 3rd July, 1941)," and that boundaries of districts within Greater Berlin would be "those which existed after the coming into effect of the decree published on the 27th March, 1938 (*Amtsblatt der Reichshauptstadt Berlin*, No. 13 of the 27th March, 1938, page 215)." The clear provisions of the E.A.C. protocol leave no basis whatever for the Soviet assertion, advanced in 1948 during the Berlin crisis, that "Berlin . . . is a part of that [the Soviet] zone."[5] I had been assigned to London to serve as political adviser to Mr. Winant late in June, succeeding Mr. Kennan, and I took an active part in these and subsequent negotiations, until August 1945.

By late July the draft protocol on zones was complete, except for the important question of the assignment of the two western zones, which was obviously beyond the competence of the E.A.C. and a matter which could be decided only between the President and the Prime Minister.[6] By mid-August, when plans

[5] Soviet note of July 14, 1948, addressed to the United States and United Kingdom governments, *Germany, 1947–1949, the Story in Documents*, Department of State Publication 3556 (Washington, D. C.: 1950) p. 208.

[6] The circumstances which affected the progress of the E.A.C. make it hard to understand the petulant comment of Robert E. Sherwood (op. cit., p. 818): "It will be remembered that when the question of the future treatment of Germany had come up for discussion among the Big Three at Teheran, agreement had not been reached or very nearly approached. It had been decided to refer this explosive subject to the Russian-British-American Advisory Committee in London and there it had remained through many long months of inconclusive conversations and 'exchanges of view' on all manner of subjects, beginning with the primary one as to which nation would occupy which zone."

were being made for the second Quebec Conference, it was clear that the decision regarding the British and American zones could not be delayed any further. At this time Mr. Winant was arguing vigorously in London for American occupation of the northwestern zone, although Mr. Stimson, Mr. McCloy, and Mr. Stettinius felt that this zone should be allotted to British occupation.[7]

In mid-August, in a telegram of some seven thousand words, Mr. Winant set before the President the position which had been reached in attempts to settle policy toward Germany. He pointed out that the E.A.C. had reached agreement on the terms of German unconditional surrender,[8] that it could complete the agreement on zones as soon as the assignment of the two western zones was decided, and that there was good prospect that it could shortly complete an agreement concerning the future machinery of Allied control. These three agreements, he emphasized, would provide the framework for dealing with Germany but would not supply the content of future policy toward Germany. He urged that every effort be made on the American side to go forward to negotiate the widest possible measure of agreed policies to be enforced jointly by the future occupying powers. It was not enough to set up the machinery of joint Allied administration; every effort should be made to work out agreed Allied policies which this machinery should carry into effect.

Mr. Winant went on to point out that the Russian need for material aid in repairing the vast destruction in the Soviet Union was bound to make the Soviet government particularly eager to receive reparations deliveries from Germany on a large scale. Since the major part of German industry was located in the west-

[7] Stimson and Bundy: op. cit., pp. 568–9.

[8] The American draft of the instrument of German surrender was circulated in the E.A.C. on March 6, 1944, and became the basis of the E.A.C. protocol of July 25, 1944.

ern zones, the Allies must try to work out, in advance, a reparations policy which would satisfy a part of the Soviet demands without involving an undue burden for the United States. He urged that Washington hasten the formulation of a reparations policy and then bend every effort toward reaching the earliest possible agreement with its Allies while the war was still in progress. He warned that it would be almost impossible to achieve such an agreement after the close of hostilities and that if no agreement had been reached on reparation the proposed system for the joint control in Germany would break down. Rivalry for control over Germany, he said, would rapidly follow. He urged that the United States consider ways of helping the recovery of the Soviet economy, such assistance to be linked to the achievement of a satisfactory settlement of the problem of German reparations and of the most important political issues between the two governments.

Instead of pursuing this farsighted program, the United States, in September 1944, dashed off after the will-o'-the-wisp of the Morgenthau "plan." For six months it indulged in a policy of "no policy" toward Germany. On October 20 Mr. Roosevelt wrote to Mr. Hull: "I dislike making detailed plans for a country which we do not yet occupy."[9] And five days later an F.D.R. memorandum, elicited by the Civil Affairs Division, put a complete stop to postwar planning for Germany and even placed in question the U.S. draft directives which had already been cleared in Washington and circulated to the E.A.C. Although Mr. Winant was in America in late October, he apparently was told nothing of this decision, which cut the ground completely from under the E.A.C. and from under the policy which he had advocated so forcefully on every possible occasion and particularly in his long telegram of mid-August to the President. The momentum which the E.A.C. had been building up was halted. Progress was not resumed until the beginning

[9] Hull: op. cit., Vol. II, p. 1621.

of April 1945, when time was already running out.

Mr. Winant wished to place not only his analysis of the chief postwar problems before the Quebec Conference, but also the E.A.C. draft protocol on zones. On September 12 the E.A.C. signed the protocol for transmission to the three governments. As outlined above, it defined the three zones of occupation in Germany and the three sectors of occupation in Berlin. It assigned the eastern zone and the eastern sector to Soviet occupation, and simply left blank the spaces for inserting mention of the two western occupying powers. The division of the western territory into two zones was that which had been advanced by the British on January 15 and approved by the American delegation on June 12. This division was satisfactory to each of the two governments—provided it was to receive the valuable northwestern zone!

At Quebec, President Roosevelt agreed to accept the southern zone, without Austria. Two further changes were made. The region of the Saar and the Palatinate, to the west of the Rhine, was transferred to the British zone, and Hesse-Cassel and Hesse-Nassau were shifted to the American zone. In addition, to meet the American demand for a German port for purposes of redeployment, it was agreed that (1) control of the ports of Bremen and Bremerhaven and the necessary staging areas in that immediate vicinity would be vested in the commander of the American zone; and (2) there would be access to the American zone through the western and northwestern ports and passage through the British-controlled area.[1]

When the Quebec decision was referred to the E.A.C. for incorporation into the protocol on zones it was found that American and British military views of its meaning were far apart. The American military position, transmitted to Mr. Winant by the State Department, was that "control" of the two ports meant that *Land* Bremen should form a special enclave under

[1] Leahy: op. cit., pp. 262–3; Stimson and Bundy: op. cit., p. 576.

direct American military administration, and that "access" through the British zone meant that certain railroads and highways must be placed under sole American control and occupation. The British War Office contested this interpretation and went on to point out that military government of Bremen was quite different from control of the ports; that creation of this enclave would seriously disrupt the administrative cohesion of the British zone; that "access" by road and rail meant that the American forces would receive, through agreement with the British commander, all necessary facilities for transportation and communications but would not actually run the railroads and monopolize any given highways. The new deadlock continued for many weeks, while the American military fought for their definition.

Meanwhile, it was becoming urgent to complete the revised agreement on zones. During the Churchill-Eden visit to Moscow in mid-October it had been agreed that the new French provisional government should be invited to join the E.A.C., and it was decided to extend the joint three-power invitation on November 11—Armistice Day of World War I—a day especially significant to the newly liberated French. Now the E.A.C. could operate only under the rule of unanimity. The admission of France prior to the completion of the two pending agreements on zones and on control machinery would thus mean that everything that had been agreed upon tentatively to date would be cancelled out, months of slow progress would be lost, and all the work would, in effect, have to begin over again. In Mr. Winant's absence in Washington, I found it necessary to try to complete the two agreements before the French joined the E.A.C. Personally, I assumed that France would eventually share in the occupation and control of Germany, although both the American and Soviet governments continued to oppose that proposal. But I felt that the major Allies and France both would be in a stronger position to reach solid agreements on the key problems of postwar Europe if the E.A.C. agreements which were so close to achievement after so many laborious months of progress were confirmed first.

During the first days of November I worked day and night to bring the British and American military views together. I urged that the private dispute be postponed until a later time, since the arrangements for access and transit did not interest the Soviet government, and that meanwhile the agreement be completed. After numerous sharp exchanges, in which I was the innocent go-between, the differences were narrowed down. The War Department wanted the American Commander in Chief to exercise such control of the ports and enjoy such transit facilities through the British zone as he might "deem necessary." The War Office, on the other hand, wanted him to exercise such control and enjoy such facilities "as may be agreed hereafter by the United Kingdom and United States military authorities to be necessary to meet his requirements."

The American wording would have allowed the United States commander to issue orders and would have bound the British commander to comply with his orders. The British wording, in effect, left the arrangements to be worked out later by mutual agreement. With the two drafts so close, I worked the wires and the transatlantic telephone several times daily. Finally, on the understanding that the American Joint Chiefs of Staff would have another opportunity to spell out in detail the meaning of "control of ports" and "access" through the British zone after the E.A.C. protocol was submitted to Washington for confirmation, the War Department reluctantly accepted the British wording, and the second protocol on zones was signed in the E.A.C. on November 14, 1944.[2] France joined the E.A.C. on November 27.

[2] The protocol on control machinery in Germany was signed on the same day.

This protocol on zones was in the form of a series of amendments to the protocol of September 12. Articles 1 and 2 inserted the detailed descriptions of the two western zones, as modified at Quebec, while Article 3 set forth the arrangements, outlined above, concerning American access to the ports and American transit rights across the British zone. Because of resentment felt in the War Department against the "mutual agreement" wording described above, approval of the protocol of November 14, as well as that of September 12, was withheld for many weeks. British approval was given on December 5. Soviet approval of E.A.C. agreements usually came only after that of both Britain and the United States had been given. Of course, until the two protocols had been approved by all three governments they were not legally binding.

Mr. Winant was greatly disturbed by the failure to give legal finality to the agreement on zones. When Harry Hopkins passed through London late in January 1945 on his way to the Yalta Conference, Mr. Winant urged upon him, as he had done in telegrams to Washington, the importance of confirming the protocol. Our failure to do so would place an unnecessary burden of doubt and suspicion on the work of the conference. At Malta, Hopkins reported to Stettinius, on January 31, that "Winant feared . . . that the Russians might reach the border of their zone and then keep on going" unless there was a firm prior commitment concerning the future zones of occupation.[3] Curiously enough, the decision to give United States approval to the protocol appears to have been taken by the Combined (U.S.-U.K.) Chiefs of Staff, rather than by the Joint (U.S.) Chiefs of Staff.[4] In any case, the American approval of the protocol was forwarded from Malta on February 1 to Mr. Winant in London

[3] Edward R. Stettinius, Jr.: *Roosevelt and the Russians: the Yalta Conference*, edited by Walter Johnson (Garden City, N. Y.: Doubleday; 1949), p. 56.

[4] Ibid., pp. 63, 69.

and was reported by him to his British and Soviet colleagues on February 2. Soviet approval followed, on February 6. The three-power agreement on zones of occupation was now in force.

Confirmation of the three-power agreement having been completed, there remained only two further aspects relating to the zones of occupation which concerned the E.A.C. These were the definition of the French zone of occupation and the preparations for the negotiations of June 1945 concerning access to Berlin. By the time of the Yalta Conference, President Roosevelt had abandoned his earlier opposition to French participation in the occupation of Germany, and he now joined with Prime Minister Churchill in securing Marshal Stalin's assent to this course. This was given on the condition that the French zone be formed out of the British and American zones, leaving the Soviet zone unchanged.[5] After Yalta, negotiation of the detailed agreement was turned over to the E.A.C. The French and British delegations agreed, after some haggling, on the transfer from Britain to France of the occupation of the Saar, the Palatinate, and a large part of the Rhine Province. In opening negotiations with the American delegation, the French representatives asked for Baden and Württemberg, as well as Hesse-Cassel and Hesse-Nassau. They pointed out that this would give them direct access to the Soviet zone. On the other hand, it would have cut off the United States zone from the British zone and further complicated the problem of access to the North German seaports.

The American counterproposal was based on strictly logistical conceptions. The boundary between the French and American zones was to be drawn so as to leave in the American zone the main highway, or *Autobahn*, through Ulm-Stuttgart-Karlsruhe, as well as the trunk railroad. Administrative and traditional divisions were disregarded completely. The sole con-

[5] Ibid., pp. 89, 126–9, 139, 163–4, 298–9, 344–5.

cern was to assure access under American control to the Middle Rhine region and the seaports. On two occasions Mr. Winant and I wired strong protests to Washington against the breaking up of both Baden and Württemberg. We pointed out that if it was the American intention to revive and strengthen the federal states in Germany as a possible safeguard against excessive centralization of power, it was hardly logical to begin the reconstruction of Germany by breaking up two of the *Länder* possessing a strong sense of regional identity and a certain attachment to democratic self-government. We suggested that some other device be sought for assuring freedom of movement over the highways and railways.[6] Renewed instructions from Washington to insist on the War Department's proposal finally ended in the French acquiescing. The only concessions were the addition of Baden-Baden to the French zone and a provision for French access to Baden administrative records located at Karlsruhe, in addition to written French assurance that United States forces would enjoy freedom of passage across and above all parts of the French zone.

By early June 1945 these aspects of the determination of the French zone had been completed in the bilateral Franco-British and Franco-American negotiations. The Soviet representative had meanwhile been inquiring somewhat impatiently when the agreement would be ready to sign in the E.A.C. Now, however, a new problem, and a new source of delay, arose when the third protocol on zones was put before the E.A.C. The American and British military authorities now insisted that the assignment of a sector to French occupation in Berlin required a partial readjustment of the sectors assigned earlier to the three other powers. They proposed that, in order to provide three *Bezirke* for the French sector, each of the three powers should give up

[6] Ambassador Murphy joined in support of Mr. Winant's second telegram of protest (Lucius D. Clay: *Decision in Germany* [Garden City, N. Y.: Doubleday; 1950], p. 13.)

one *Bezirk* from its own sector; then, by a little rearrangement, the French could be given three contiguous *Bezirke.* The Soviet delegation reacted violently to this proposal, insisting that the Yalta agreement admitting France to a share in the occupation had been conditioned on no change being made in the Soviet zone of occupation. Personally, I felt that the Soviet position was based on a valid analogy, but of course I argued strenuously on the basis of the instructions of my government. When the Potsdam Conference assembled, the E.A.C. was still deadlocked on the question of the French sector in Berlin, although the E.A.C. protocol, signed on May 1, 1945, had provided for full French participation in the control machinery in Germany and in Berlin.

On arriving at Potsdam I found that the representatives of the War Department "at the working level" were adamant on the question of detaching one *Bezirk* from the Soviet sector in Berlin. Two days later, however, this point of view was reversed. It was now clear that joint occupation of Berlin would mean joint participation in providing food and fuel for its inhabitants, since General Zhukov had declined, on July 7, to continue supplying all of Berlin from the Soviet zone.[7] At this time the western commanders had urged the Russians to meet the economic needs of Berlin. If their proposal had been accepted this would have resulted in the economic amalgamation of Berlin with the Soviet zone. It was Soviet insistence, in July 1945, which established Berlin as a separate economic area in addition to being a separate area of Allied occupation. American supplies clearly would be required to feed the British and French as well as the American zones and sectors, and it now seemed undesirable to reduce the size of the Soviet sector. The War Department representatives therefore abandoned their insistence on subtracting one *Bezirk* from the Soviet sector.

The British and American commanders were not

[7] Ibid., pp. 27–30.

yet in agreement, however, concerning which *Bezirke* of their sectors would be taken to form the French sector. Finally, new instructions were sent from Potsdam to the American and British representatives on the E.A.C., and on July 26, 1945, the E.A.C. signed a third protocol on zones. By it the French zone in Germany was defined, and the descriptions of the boundaries of the British and American zones were modified accordingly. The report transmitting the protocol to the four governments stated:

> In view of the physical conditions prevailing in the area of "Greater Berlin," the Commission in the drafting of Article 7 of the present Agreement did not attempt to delineate the area in "Greater Berlin" to be occupied by the armed forces of the French Republic. The Commission recommends that the question of the delimitation of the French area in "Greater Berlin," which will have to be allotted from the American and British areas of "Greater Berlin" as a consequence of the greater destruction in the Soviet area of the City, should be referred to the Control Council in Berlin for consideration.

Three weeks before the surrender of Germany a proposal to change the agreed zones of occupation had been presented in an unexpected quarter. According to Admiral Leahy's account, Prime Minister Churchill proposed to President Truman, some days prior to April 21, that the British and American forces remain, at least for the time being, on the lines to which they had advanced, far within the future Soviet zone, and that the two governments should use this unexpected bargaining advantage to bring about a clarification of Soviet policy toward Germany, and, in particular, to secure Soviet agreement to supply food from the eastern zone for a part of the needs of the food-deficient western zones. Mr. Winant reacted strongly to this proposal, regarding it, if adopted, as a fatal blow to inter-Allied confidence, and to prospects of any measure of Allied co-operation in Germany as well as on other matters. His reasoning, set forth in telegrams to the President as well as in direct conversations with British leaders, was fully upheld in President Truman's reply of April 21 to the Prime Minister. Mr. Churchill continued to defend his proposal until June 13.[8] Shortly after, on June 24, orders were issued to dissolve the Anglo-American SHAEF (Supreme Headquarters Allied Expeditionary Force) headquarters and armies by July 1, into their separate American and British components, and to prepare to withdraw American forces to the United States zone and to occupy the assigned sector in Berlin.

One further question concerned the E.A.C. only indirectly: the provision of access to Berlin. Ever since Mr. Winant's failure to secure the consent of the Civil Affairs Division of the War Department to the negotiation of guarantees, this matter had been on his mind. With his approval I had prepared a memorandum and a detailed draft agreement, remembering particularly the difficulties and chicaneries which the Russians had inflicted on American military missions in the countries of eastern Europe since August 1944. About one week after V-E Day a representative of the "American side" of SHAEF came to London, and for two days we discussed in detail the contents, background, and implications of the E.A.C. agreements. In reply to his inquiry concerning a guarantee of access to Berlin, I explained how it happened that this matter had not been dealt with and handed him my memorandum and draft agreement on the subject. Among other things, this draft agreement provided that the American Commander in Chief should choose any two railroads and any two main highways for use by his troops, one each westward to the British zone and one each southwestward to the American zone. It authorized him to carry out any repairs to railroads, roads, signal

[8] Leahy: op. cit., pp. 349–50, 382; Walter Bedell Smith: *My Three Years in Moscow* (Philadelphia and New York: Lippincott; 1950), pp. 21–2.

systems, and bridges which he might deem necessary, and to maintain gasoline pumps, repair patrols, rest stations, and communications points along these facilities. If any of the assigned railways or highways were unusable for any cause, the Soviet commander was to be obligated to make alternative equivalent facilities available at once. It seemed to me that these provisions would afford clear and necessary safeguards for free access to Berlin. I pointed out that the withdrawal of American forces to the assigned zone and the movement of American forces into Berlin were part of one and the same agreement and must be fulfilled conjointly. I noted that the American position in negotiations "at the military level" for guarantees of access to Berlin was very strong, for the Soviet forces had their eyes on the Zeiss and other important plants of Thuringia and western Saxony. The representative of SHAEF took this advice and my draft documents with him.

On June 13, in reporting to the President, the Secretary of State, and the Secretary of War that the British government had now agreed to an early withdrawal into the assigned zones, Mr. Winant again stressed the importance of linking up this movement with the entry of the Allied garrisons into Greater Berlin and "with the provision of free access" to Berlin.[9] He was anxious that every precaution be taken, now that the moment had arrived to negotiate at the military level, to assure freedom of access to the future seat of the Allied control machinery. So far as I am aware, neither Mr. Winant nor his staff received, at any time, any information concerning the exchange of telegrams between President Truman and Marshal Stalin on June 14 and 16, or concerning the subsequent negotiations of the American military authorities in Berlin on this subject.[1]

[9] Leahy: op. cit., p. 382, cites a part of this telegram.

[1] Clay: op. cit., pp. 24–6; Smith: op. cit., p. 234; identic note of July 6, 1948, addressed by the governments of the United States, the United Kingdom, and France to the government of the U.S.S.R., cited from *Germany, 1947–1949*, op. cit., p. 205, with Soviet reply, p. 207–8.

It has been hinted that the failure to make specific provision for the access of the Western Allies to Berlin was due to Mr. Winant's reluctance to appear to question Soviet good faith by insisting on detailed arrangements for this purpose. It has even been alleged that his sad and untimely end was, in some way, due to "remorse" over a failure to provide, in 1944, against the danger of a Soviet blockade of Berlin in 1948. The details of the E.A.C. negotiations given here should dispose of these legends.

A review of the record shows that during the time when the E.A.C. was striving to prepare the ground work for postwar Allied co-operation in Germany the problem of making sure that the Western Allies would be able to reach Berlin freely through the Russian zone was not a matter in which the American military authorities showed any particular interest. They did, however, show deep concern to secure free lines of communication across the British and French zones. At the insistence of the War Department, the duty of reaching Allied agreements which would provide for adequate access to Berlin was left for direct negotiation among the military commanders in Germany. The omission of any such provision was a decision of the military staff which assumed final responsibility for planning the occupation of Germany.

:7:

HOPES AND FAILURES: AMERICAN POLICY TOWARD EAST CENTRAL EUROPE, 1941–1947[1]

[February 1955]

INTRODUCTORY NOTE · Only slightly less vehemently than the bankruptcy of its hopes for a strong and democratic postwar China, the failure of the United States' aspirations in East Central Europe has given rise to bitter charges of blindness and even "treason." Both the failure and the emotions it has aroused have a complex background.

After World War I the simultaneous weakening of Germany and Russia, and the disappearance of the Hapsburg and Ottoman Empires, opened the way, for the first time since the Battle of Waterloo, or even earlier, for the peoples of East Central Europe to reassert their full claims to national statehood. For different and conflicting reasons they were aided in this by the helping hands of France, Britain, and the United States. To most

[1] *The Fate of East Central Europe; Hopes and Failures of American Foreign Policy*, edited by Stephen D. Kertesz (Notre Dame: University of Notre Dame Press; 1956), pp. 51–74. Copyright 1956 by the University of Notre Dame Press.

Americans, Wilsonian idealism seemed to have been fulfilled, even if imperfectly, in the burgeoning of the new or restored states.

In World War II American opinion and policy making were slow to recognize that the reappearance of a powerful and victorious Soviet Union was bound to lead to entirely new relations of power and to brand new problems. In this situation, idealistic pronouncements and hoping against hope for postwar co-operation among the victors served mainly to postpone the taking of decision and effective action. This study (delivered in February 1955 at a symposium organized by the Committee on International Relations at the University of Notre Dame) is an attempt to clarify the basic strategic assumptions and decisions which set pathetically narrow limits to American action.

For a more detailed examination of these problems, the following studies are especially helpful: *The Fate of East Central Europe; Hopes and Failures of American Foreign Policy,* edited by Stephen D. Kertesz (Notre Dame: University of Notre Dame Press; 1956); Robert Lee Wolff; *The Balkans in Our Time* (Cambridge: Harvard University Press; 1956); Stephen D. Kertesz: *Diplomacy in a Whirlpool; Hungary Between Nazi Germany and Soviet Russia* (Notre Dame: University of Notre Dame Press; 1953); and Hugh Seton-Watson: *The East European Revolution,* 3rd edition (New York: Praeger; 1956).

*

WHEN the attack on Pearl Harbor plunged the United States into its second world war, the immediate concern of political leaders and public opinion alike was to train its manpower and to mobilize its industrial resources as the first step in the long up-hill climb from initial defeat to decisive victory, first against Germany, then against Japan. Its prime political aim was to forge and maintain an effective working alliance with its major allies, Britain and the Soviet Union. If either faltered or failed in the joint effort, the road to victory and postwar security would stretch out beyond the horizon. After almost two decades of self-imposed isolation, American power was now to be concerned intimately with decisions, taken or not taken, which would in turn affect all parts of the world.

Of sympathy for the peoples of East Central Europe there was no lack, at least among the informed minority which took an active interest in what was happening abroad. There was no acceptance of the Nazi *Grossraum* theories, with their specious parallel to the Monroe Doctrine. Whatever division of opinion there had been over the absorption of Austria disappeared with Hitler's march into Prague. American critics had been prompt to condemn the British and French "appeasers" at Munich, but even very few of the critics assumed that the United States had any power to exert in Europe or any responsibilities to shoulder. During the events which completely shattered the prewar structure of East Central Europe, the United States, prior to December 1941, had alternately exhorted and condemned. It had not acted. It had no policy, in any effective sense of the word.

After the United States had entered the war, the Roosevelt administration adopted the basic position that the nation's first aim was to win the war as quickly as possible and to do so without making specific commitments on "local" questions of postwar settlement. All particular questions, especially territorial claims, were to be held open for decision in the peace conference. This decision, it was hoped, would avoid a repetition of some of the mistakes which had been made during World War I. Makers and students of American policy had heard over and again of the bad effects of the secret treaties of 1914–18 on the peace settlement which followed. Temporary strategic necessities had led the European powers to give and receive promissory notes which prejudiced many important issues, particularly the promises made to Japan, Italy, and Rumania. Policy makers were also hopeful that even the defeated nations might receive a fairer hearing than in 1919, in order to lay a firm basis for a genuine pacification of Europe.

After the fighting was over, exile governments, serving as trustees for the interests of their nations, could be replaced by freely elected and genuinely representative regimes, qualified to approve territorial adjustments and to enter into long-range commitments in support of general and regional security arrangements. Meanwhile, it was doubtful whether they could, constitutionally or conscientiously, make basic decisions affecting their nations' postwar futures. While exile governments were happy to claim additional advantages through wartime negotiations, they were prompt to retreat behind constitutional barriers when they were called on to pay part of the cost.[2] It also seemed impossible to satisfy, during the war, any one set of national claims without settling all of them, and since many of the claims, even among allies, were incompatible, there was a real danger that the main purpose of the war would be lost sight of. From the point of view of American constitutional procedure, the executive could not commit the government as a whole on the terms of peace, and therefore, even if the United States government had been willing to hold a whole series of detailed peace-aims negotiations during the war, it was doubtful just how effective that effort, if made, would have been.

For long anxious months there was a genuine uncertainty about the outcome of the war. If the Soviet Union collapsed, and if Hitler were then free both to intensify the sea and air blockade of Great Britain and to resume his drive through the Middle East and India to link up with the advancing Japanese forces,

[2] For example, the Arciszewski government in London, formed in late November 1944, declared itself incompetent to agree to the detachment of any part of Poland's pre-1939 territory until the Polish state had been restored within its prewar boundaries and the people could be consulted under constitutional processes.

of what use would be detailed and specific commitments on the peace terms of victory unfulfilled? While Stalin and Molotov argued vehemently for a postwar guarantee of the Soviet boundaries of 1941—a guarantee which the British leaders were willing to give—Roosevelt and Hull held out against it. Even during the critical German advance of 1942 into Russia, the United States clung firmly to the principle of "no predetermination," and, under American insistence, the territorial guarantee was omitted from the Anglo-Soviet twenty-year treaty of May 1942. The American logic was that, if one set of territorial claims received such powerful confirmation during the war, then all territorial claims could be pushed with equal right and soon the Allies would be squabbling over a division of the spoils instead of pushing on to victory. Since the United States had no territorial claims, except perhaps for the Japanese mandated islands, its government was naturally reluctant to allow its energies and those of its Allies to be dissipated in this way.

The reluctance of the American government, during hostilities, to discuss the "details" was reinforced by an awareness of its unfavorable military posture. By the time of Pearl Harbor the United States had mobilized only a modest part of its resources in preparation for war, and after Pearl Harbor it had to train and equip tremendous forces, on land, on sea, and in the air, as well as provide a large part of the needs of its Allies. All this took time and tremendous exertions. While the Soviet Union, fighting on its own territory and suffering tremendous losses, was carrying, as Churchill said, "the main burden" of the war, the United States was not in a good position, it seemed, to bargain hard with it over the "details" of a postwar settlement. Would the Soviet leaders, if threatened with the only bargaining counter available—a cutting back of lend-lease—feel any compunction later about repudiating promises wrung from them in time of mortal danger? Or would they not satisfy their own claims and then make a separate peace with Hitler, thus enabling him to thwart the cross-Channel liberation of western Europe? On the other hand, the successful invasion of western Europe would greatly raise the power and the prestige of Britain and America, which, on Germany's defeat, would be at the peak of their power. This military prospect, which promised a far stronger voice at the end of the war for American purposes, reinforced the political arguments, both international and domestic, for avoiding wartime commitments which would prejudge and preshape the postwar settlement. That the principle of "no predetermination" was partially abandoned later, during 1944 and 1945, did not make it any less attractive during 1942 and 1943 to hard-pressed war leaders. Once the Soviet Union, after Stalingrad, had begun to display an increasingly clear policy of subjugating the peoples of East Central Europe, it was difficult to meet its pressures with a deliberate policy of "no policy."

Finally, there was strong doubt as to the extent to which, after the war, American opinion would be willing for its government to remain involved in the problems of Europe or to commit its power to the enforcement of specific settlements. President Roosevelt was ever mindful of the way in which American sentiment had turned against the Versailles peace, and, if anything, he leaned over backward to avoid committing his country to continued participation in the postwar problems of Europe. Roosevelt had continually on his mind the necessity for bringing the armies home just as rapidly as possible after the defeat of Germany, and the prospect that a weakened Britain would stand alone, facing the huge Soviet forces, caused great anxiety to Churchill.[3]

[3] On November 18, 1944, Roosevelt to Churchill: "You know, of course, that after Germany's collapse I must bring American troops home as rapidly as transportation problems will permit. . . ." November 19, 1944, Churchill to Roosevelt: "Para two of your 649 causes me alarm. If after Germany's collapse you 'must bring the American troops home as rapidly as transportation problems will permit' and if the

On the assumption that Britain would emerge from the war weakened and overcommitted, and that America would shortly withdraw from any military commitments in Europe, the dangers of the entire continent coming under Soviet domination were great. As Admiral Leahy wrote Secretary Hull on May 16, 1944:

> . . . It is apparent that any future world conflict in the foreseeable future will find Britain and Russia in opposite camps. . . . In a conflict between these two powers the disparity in the military strengths that they could dispose upon that continent would, under present conditions, be far too great to be overcome by our intervention on the side of Britain. Having due regard to the military factors involved—resources, manpower, geography and particularly our ability to project our strength across the ocean and exert it decisively upon the continent—we might be able to successfully defend Britain, but we could not, under existing conditions, defeat Russia. In other words, we would find ourselves engaged in a war which we could not win even though the United States would be in no danger of defeat and occupation.[4]

If the ablest military leaders were so pessimistic about the postwar capability of Britain and the United States to defend the highly industrial and strategic area of western Europe, they were even more skeptical of American ability to influence effectively postwar developments in East Central Europe, which lay in the path of the Soviet advance against the Nazi citadel.

The logical conclusion from these premises, and from the assumption that Soviet-American interests were less in conflict than Anglo-Soviet ones, was that

French are to have no equipped post-war army or time to make one, or to give it battle experience, how will it be possible to hold down western Germany beyond the present Russian occupied line? We certainly could not undertake the task without your aid and that of the French. All would therefore rapidly disintegrate as it did last time. I hope, however, that my fears are groundless. I put my faith in you." *The Conferences at Malta and Yalta, 1945* Department of State Publication 6199 (Washington, D. C.: 1955), pp. 286–7.

[4] Ibid., pp. 107–8.

the United States should exploit its middleman position to bind the three major powers together, so as to hold postwar conflicts within manageable bounds. And this was the conclusion which Admiral Leahy drew.

> It is apparent that the United States should, now and in the future, exert its utmost efforts and utilize all its influence to prevent such a situation arising and to promote a spirit of mutual cooperation between Britain, Russia and ourselves. So long as Britain and Russia cooperate and collaborate in the interests of peace, there can be no great war in the foreseeable future. . . . From the broader view of national and world-wide security, . . . the United States should not support any such British proposals [concerning disposition of Italian overseas possessions] prior to ascertaining Russian views, lest post-war disunity of the three great powers be thereby fostered with all the possibility of ultimate impact upon the military position of the United States which such a disaster would entail.[5]

From these assumptions it logically followed, during hostilities against Germany, that British views concerning what could or could not be achieved on behalf of the peoples of East Central Europe carried a special weight. These views often counterbalanced traditional American aspirations, because the responsibility for maintaining whatever postwar adjustment could be reached in Europe between British and Soviet power would have to be enforced by Britain, feebly seconded by an absent America and a weakened France.

Despite its definite commitment against undertaking specific political and military obligations in postwar Europe, the United States government could and did take the lead in stating in universal terms the war aims of the coalition. There is no need to review the specific words of the Atlantic Charter or the Declaration of the United Nations, both of which received the ad-

[5] Ibid., p. 108, and n. 4, pp. 106–7.

herence of the Soviet government, or of the Moscow Declaration of November 1, 1943, the first statement of purposes which was actually negotiated among the three great powers. In addition, particular declarations and appeals, addressed jointly by the Big Three to the occupied nations and to members of the Axis, were also supposedly expressions of Soviet as well as American and British intentions.

The "futility" of these and similar general declarations has often been denounced in later years, and the United States has often been condemned for its "failure" to enforce the fulfillment of these promises. Two factors are often forgotten. First, the United States did not promise and could not have promised to use its military forces, which, incidentally, it no longer possessed shortly after V-J Day, to compel the execution of these promises by a hostile major power. Second, the fact that the United States strove conscientiously to fulfill the aspirations to which it had given expression does not make it responsible for the contrary conduct of the Soviet government, over which it had no power of control or compulsion.

One possible way to protect the future of Europe against overweening power from the East was to build up regional organs by which continental Europe could cope with its immediate problems of reconstruction. Through promoting the establishment and work of the Emergency Economic Commission for Europe, the Emergency Inland Transport Organization, the Emergency Coal Organization, and the United Nations Relief and Rehabilitation Administration, as well as the more broadly based Bretton Woods agreements and the Interim Commission on Food and Agriculture, the United States hoped to foster the ability of all Europe to revive its shattered economy and thus to avoid a prolonged period of economic and social disorder, such as had followed World War I.[6] Soviet

[6] E. F. Penrose: *Post-War Economic Planning* (Princeton: Princeton University Press; 1953).

policy makers, on the other hand, were deeply suspicious of all "European" projects and effectively cut off Soviet-dominated Europe from participation in all except UNRRA. The administrative arrangements of UNRRA, which placed Soviet representatives at the head of several of its missions in East Central Europe, unwisely gave recognition, at least symbolically, to the pre-eminent role of the Soviet Union in that region.

One further duty of the United States government, during the war, was to define its postwar aims in clear and detailed terms, even if their implementation was to be held in suspense during hostilities. Between January 1942 and July 1943, a series of advisory committees, which included high officials of the Department of State, carried through a detailed review of the problems which would confront the United States in making peace.[7] The deliberations of the committees laid the foundation for the Charter of the United Nations. In considering the specific problems of peace settlements the advisory committees were uncertain, in that period, of the degree of power which the Soviet Union would exert and were inclined to visualize a grand and concentrated process of peace making, on the pattern of the Paris peace conference of 1919. By mid-1943, however, a more realistic picture of Soviet intentions began to emerge. As the actual documents of the period become available, it will become clear that, whatever attitudes the urgencies of coalition warfare imposed upon the top leadership, there was, among the experts and diplomats, who had more time for reflection and prognostication in a period of "technological unemployment" imposed on them in time of war, no wish to escape into rosy dreams of a conflictless world. The studies prepared by the Country and Area Committees within the Department of State during 1943 and 1944 will show, when published, that there was a keen awareness of the menace of Soviet domina-

[7] Harley A. Notter: *Postwar Foreign Policy Preparation, 1939–1945*, Department of State Publication 3580 (Washington, D. C.: 1949).

tion over East Central Europe and an equally keen desire to ward off this menace. And both this awareness and this desire were fully shared by the Department's Committee on Postwar Programs.

Because Roosevelt and Truman realized that Allied unity, maintained precariously during a war for survival, would be gravely jeopardized after the defeat of the common enemy, they pressed on, even under the stress of war, to establish the United Nations before the close of hostilities. For the United States, certain of its need and hope for world-wide peace and doubtful of its ability or willingness to undertake specific commitments as, for example, in East Central Europe, "universal" obligations—shared in words with its major Allies—were easier to contemplate than particular and local responsibilities. One of its hopes was to prevent the division of the globe into spheres of influence.

In November 1943 in his address to Congress reporting on the Moscow Conference, Secretary Hull proclaimed as its greatest achievement the abandonment of "spheres of influence."

> As the provisions of the Four-Nation Declaration are carried into effect, there will no longer be need for spheres of influence, for alliances, for balance of power, or any other of the special arrangements through which, in the unhappy past, the nations strove to safeguard their security or to promote their interests.[8]

Hull's optimism found some outward support in the discussions of the three Foreign Ministers at Moscow, for, when prodded by Hull, both Molotov and Eden had hastened to disclaim any interest in "separate zones or spheres of influence." Molotov could even "guarantee that there was no disposition on the part of his government to divide Europe into such separate

[8] *The Memoirs of Cordell Hull* (New York: Macmillan; 1948), Vol. II, pp. 1314–5.

zones."[9] Fourteen months later, the briefing papers prepared by the State Department for the Yalta Conference gave a fairly clear analysis of the growing tendency for zones of wartime military responsibility to harden into postwar spheres of influence, as well as a prescient forecast of the dangers which this presented to the peoples of East Central Europe and to their ability to shape their postwar futures.[1] Meanwhile, military events and actions had been giving shape to the very spheres of influence which Secretary Hull and his department strove to avert. In any spheres-of-influence arrangement East Central Europe would fare badly. While American military leaders concentrated all effort on winning the war as quickly and as painlessly as possible, the Soviet leaders were not likely, after "the ball game was over," "to shake hands and go home."

Even as Hull spoke, military necessities had already created spheres of responsibility, precursors of the postwar spheres of influence. Of course, the Eastern front was the primary sphere of Soviet action, which gradually expanded westward from Stalingrad to the Elbe as the Soviet armies fought on to victory. The Soviet sphere, by the agreement of 1941 with the British, included northern Iran. At Yalta, Manchuria and the Kuriles were assigned to the Soviet sphere, and, by a last-minute decision in August 1945, Korea north of the 38th parallel.

While the other fronts were, in concept, Anglo-American in direction, the spheres-of-responsibility principle was also applied to them. On March 8, 1942, Roosevelt proposed that ". . . the British alone should assume the responsibility for the Middle East, the Americans the responsibility for the Pacific, while both nations jointly should operate in the critical Atlantic theater."[2] In general, by the end of 1943

[9] Ibid., Vol. II, p. 1298.

[1] *The Conferences at Malta and Yalta, 1945*, pp. 103–6.

[2] Henry L. Stimson and McGeorge Bundy: *On Active Service in War and Peace* (New York: Harper; 1948), p. 416.

the Mediterranean area, including Italy, Greece, and Turkey, was regarded primarily as a British, not an American, responsibility. When Greek leaders, worried at the prospect that only British troops would take part in the liberation of their country, requested some American troops, the request was turned down.[3] According to Admiral Leahy, at Casablanca Roosevelt had accepted Churchill's view that Turkey was within the British sphere.[4] The same source also notes, almost casually, that ". . . we recognized Italy as being primarily in the British sphere of influence . . ."[5] As Churchill cabled Halifax in December 1944 after the British veto on the nomination of Count Sforza as Foreign Minister of Italy: ". . . we have been accorded command in the Mediterranean, as the Americans have command in France, and therefore we have a certain special position and responsibility."[6]

Similarly, the war in the Pacific was conducted primarily by the American Joint Chiefs of Staff, with only a limited co-ordination with the Anglo-American Combined Chiefs of Staff. This special responsibility, is was assumed by Secretary of the Navy Forrestal, was to continue into an indefinite future.

> I take it as a premise about all discussions of world peace that the United States is to have the major responsibility for the Pacific Ocean security, and if this premise is accepted there flows from it the acceptance of the fact that the United States must have the means with which to implement its responsibility . . .[7]

The "special responsibility" of the military commander covered the entire range of political and economic activity in "his" theater: from public order,

[3] William D. Leahy: *I Was There* (New York: Whittlesey House; 1950), p. 181 (early September 1943).
[4] Ibid., p. 173.
[5] Ibid., p. 264.
[6] *The Conferences at Malta and Yalta, 1945,* p. 267.
[7] *The Forrestal Diaries,* edited by Walter Millis (New York: Viking Press; 1951), entry for April 17, 1945; dots as in original.

justice, punishment of war criminals, labor regulation, supply of food, fuel, and raw materials, and use of property, up to the appointment or removal of high officials. American commanders might be fully, and British commands largely, committed to exercise their proconsular powers primarily to meet immediate military needs, and might be prepared to give them up as soon as possible, but this abnegation could hardly be expected of Soviet representatives in the countries overrun by the Red Army. Nor could even the most "unpolitical" commander remain aloof from civil strife; during the autumn of 1944 the Anglo-American SHAEF (Supreme Headquarters Allied Expeditionary Force) gave frequent and anxious thought to what the role of their forces should be in case the widespread turbulence within France boiled over into civil war.

While both the British and Soviet commanders in various theaters received their political instructions from a well co-ordinated political-cum-military leadership and therefore operated under unified policy direction, there was no similar degree of unity within American policy making because of the serious cleavages among the President's various military and political advisers. In a belated effort to overcome the separation between diplomatic and military policy making, the SWNCC (State-War-Navy Co-ordinating Committee) was established at the end of 1944. One reason for the gap in policy making was that the President, as Commander in Chief, could make many decisions in wartime which would not have been feasible for a civilian authority. Another was the widespread and generally unwarranted fear of the War Department, from the landings in North Africa in 1942, that control of civil affairs might be transferred from it to the State Department.[8]

One result of the lack of systematic co-ordination was that many important decisions were taken on an *ad hoc* basis, without adequate consideration of their

[8] Stimson and Bundy: op. cit., p. 559.

implications. For example, the terms of the Italian armistice were negotiated between London, Washington, and SACMED (Supreme Allied Commander, Mediterranean) without consideration of the Russian claim to participate. For some days there was no thought even of inviting a Soviet signature to the armistice or of providing for Soviet representation in any part of the Allied control machinery, on the ground that Italy was not a "Soviet theater." State Department officers, learning accidentally of the proposed arrangements, protested strongly, pointing out that this precedent would allow the Soviet government in its turn to exclude the United States and Britain from any participation in the armistices with Hungary, Rumania, Bulgaria, and Finland. Only then was provision made for token participation by Soviet representatives in the Italian surrender and later in a powerless advisory council. As a matter of fact, the Western Allies took a far more active part in negotiating the armistice terms for the ex-Axis satellites and in the operations of the Allied Control Commissions. The difference in the outcome within the two areas was due, not to the negotiated arrangements, but to the Soviet ability to operate at all levels, through the political police, the Communist party and Communist-dominated trade unions in each country, and also through massive terror against the local population. The experience of World War II suggests that the only way in which the United States could have exercised a determining influence on the postwar status of East Central Europe was to appear there with large military forces.

In recent years it has often been argued that, if the American leadership had accepted the Churchill-sponsored project for an invasion of the Balkans in 1943, the later fate of East Central Europe might have been a very different one, for the need and opportunity for Soviet-style "liberation" would have been averted. The plans for a Balkan approach have remained obscure, as to forces proposed and limits of advance and schedule, but there has been no indication that they called for more than an advance northward to the Danube-Sava line. If carried out, this plan would presumably have brought Bulgaria within the British safety zone for the Mediterranean, but it is probable that Yugoslavia would have remained under the control of Tito's forces. In any case, Poland and Czechoslovakia, Hungary and Rumania would have remained within the Soviet military theater, with all the consequences deriving therefrom. In addition, the SHAEF invasion of western Europe could not have been carried out during 1944. It is possible that not only all of Germany, but also Denmark, the Netherlands, Belgium, and perhaps France would have experienced Soviet-style "liberation."

There was much more to be said in favor of Churchill's proposals, in the summer of 1944, that the Anglo-American forces should advance through the Ljubljana Gap into Austria and perhaps into western Hungary, but the American Joint Chiefs of Staff also overruled this proposal in favor of the invasion of southern France. By that time Hitler could no longer afford to withdraw forces from Western Europe to reinforce his hold on the Danube area, and Soviet forces were at the outskirts of Warsaw and on the eastern frontier of Hungary. An alternative campaign, discussed to some extent at the time, called for the use of Allied forces in Bulgaria and Albania, but this diversion of forces was also opposed by the American Chiefs. It is easy, in retrospect, to say that the landing in southern France in August 1944 was unnecessary and that this force should have been directed against the Balkan or Danubian area. But who can blame a commander for making assurance doubly sure at a time when the decisive campaign in Normandy hung in the balance?

Churchill's persistent advocacy of a Balkan campaign had one unfortunate repercussion on American planning for the postwar status of East Central Europe.

After the great debates of 1943 over strategy and the postponement of the Normandy invasion to May 1944, the American Joint Chiefs of Staff ruled, in the autumn of 1943, that the United States should take no responsibilities "in the area of the Balkans including Austria." It was many months before this veto against American participation in Austrian affairs was lifted. In May 1944 Ambassador John G. Winant, United States representative on the European Advisory Commission, took occasion to explain in person to President Roosevelt how serious it would be for the United States to refuse to participate in the re-establishment of an independent Austria. American abstention would leave Russia and Britain face to face as occupying or liberating powers and would result in the partitioning of Austria into two zones, thus nullifying the assurances which the three powers had given in their Declaration on Austria, of November 1, 1943. As a result, the Joint Chiefs of Staff agreed in June 1944 that the United States could participate in the central control machinery for Austria, but maintained their refusal to consider accepting an American zone of occupation.

At the end of December 1944 as the time for negotiating concrete arrangements for Austria was drawing near, Winant reopened directly with Roosevelt the question of policy toward Austria. In a series of strong messages Winant explained that, if the United States was to have an effective voice in Austrian affairs, it must also have a zone to administer. At the end of December 1944, the Joint Chiefs of Staff reluctantly agreed that the United States would administer a zone in Austria; since the United States had agreed in September 1944 to occupy the southern zone in Germany, bordering on its proposed zone in Austria, there was no longer any logistical reason for refusing to participate in the re-establishment of the Austrian state.

However, if Austria seemed to the military leadership to be a part of the Balkans, and was thereby excluded for so long from political as well as military planning, how much prospect was there that any of the countries of East Central Europe would fall within the sphere of effective American action? Echoes of this persistent military position were heard at the crucial White House conference of April 23, 1945, called by President Truman to discuss the American attitude toward the flagrant Soviet violations of the Yalta agreements. At this conference Secretary Stimson argued that "the Balkans and their troubles were beyond the sphere of proper United States action"; he urged caution in opposing the Soviet flouting of the Yalta agreement on Poland and the Yugoslav seizure of Trieste.[9]

The opposition of the military to the American acceptance of responsibilities in spheres lying outside their own theaters of command was reflected in political planning and action. Because of the reluctance of the President and the military to make political commitments regarding areas outside American direct control, the State Department was left adrift, to "make do" the best it could by means of notes and exhortations. One result was that, just as the Mediterranean was regarded as a wartime and postwar British sphere, East Central Europe, until Yalta and Potsdam, was also treated by the British and Americans, as primarily a British concern. The location of the governments in exile in London, and their partial financial dependence on the British government, made it plausible for many people in Washington to regard both the governments and their countries' problems as peculiarly a British concern. Suggestions that they would like to move to Washington were firmly rebuffed.

At both the Moscow and Teheran Conferences, in late 1943, the American assumption was that the first and most important step was to secure Soviet support for certain basic policies, such as an agreed policy

[9] Stimson and Bundy: op. cit., p. 609 and n. 6.

toward Germany and the establishment of the United Nations. Once the central problems of security were resolved to the mutual satisfaction of the Big Three, "minor" problems such as the future boundaries of Poland or the postwar regime of Yugoslavia, would, it was hoped, lose much of their urgency in Soviet eyes and could then be resolved in some way compatible with the internal independence of the East Central European nations.

At the Moscow Conference of October 1943, the British raised the questions of restoring Soviet relations with the Polish government in London, of resolving the Tito-Mihajlović clash in Yugoslavia, and of promoting the creation of a Danubian confederation which might help the peoples of the area to defend themselves against a resurgent Germany.[1] Molotov promptly accused Eden of wanting to rebuild a *cordon sanitaire* against Russia, and after long discussion, the British agreed to drop this item from the agenda. Obviously, any idea of federation or confederation in East Central Europe was anathema to the Soviet leaders.

The more real issue of the Soviet-Czechoslovak twenty-year treaty of mutual defense, whose signature had been held up for many months by British objections, also caused sharp discussions at the Moscow Conference. After urging that this and similar postwar commitments should be deferred until the exile governments had returned to their homelands and had been confirmed as representing their people and until the question of the compatibility of separate alliances with the future United Nations could be studied, the British again gave in, and it was agreed that the Beneš government would sign the alliance, as it did in December 1943.

When the character of the postwar Polish and Yugoslav regimes came up for discussion, the British again bore the brunt of the argument. Mr. Hull,

[1] An incomplete account in Hull: op. cit., Vol. II, pp. 1298–9.

pressed for his opinion, said that he hoped his British and Soviet colleagues would talk it over and come to a meeting of minds. Molotov, quick as a rapier, then pressed to know if the United States would accept whatever the British and Soviet delegations agreed on. Hull, of course, evaded this invitation to "bow out" from the entire complex of East Central European problems, but he made it equally clear that the United States government was not really concerned about this area of Europe, at least in comparison with the "big" issues. Certainly, this must have been the Soviet impression of the American position.

A similar tactic of playing down the American concern about the postwar prospects of East Central Europe was followed by President Roosevelt at the Teheran Conference, although he did not follow Churchill in endorsing the claim of the Soviet government to recover the boundary of June 22, 1941. Again, he left it to the British representatives, despite their acceptance of the Curzon line as Poland's eastern boundary, to uphold the interest of the West in the postwar status of the peoples of East Central Europe.

If the most influential American leader was uncertain whether his country would be willing to guarantee any specific postwar settlements even in western Europe, the pressure on Britain to accept Soviet-imposed decisions in the area of the Red Army's advance and thereby to gain some bargaining advantage for British interests elsewhere became almost irresistible. If no outside force could deter or dissuade the Soviet leaders from having their way in areas under their military control, then it was important for the British to accept the inevitable as early and as gracefully as possible and thereby to gain some counterpart, for example, through Soviet recognition of Britain's paramount interests in the countries bordering on the Mediterranean. If the Soviet government was determined on building its own sphere in East

Central Europe, then London must secure in advance a Soviet promise to respect the British life line to the East.

This question became especially acute with the Soviet entry into Rumanian territory in April 1944, and in May the British government proposed, first to Moscow and then to Washington, that Russia have a controlling influence in Rumania and Britain in Greece. Shortly after, Churchill also proposed assigning Bulgaria to Russian control and Yugoslavia to British. Following strong protests by Secretary Hull, Roosevelt cabled Churchill that he preferred to see consultative machinery for the Balkans set up to resolve misunderstandings and to prevent the development of exclusive zones of influence. However, two days later Roosevelt yielded to Churchill's pressure and agreed that the proposed division of responsibility would receive a three months' trial, after which it would be reviewed by the three governments.[2]

Four months later, in October 1944, an even more elaborate Anglo-Soviet agreement was negotiated by Churchill and Eden at Moscow. According to one version, it assigned to Russia 75/25 or 80/20 preponderance in Bulgaria, Rumania, and Hungary, while in Yugoslavia Russia was to share influence with Britain 50/50.[3] When, at Yalta, American influence began to be exerted more positively in favor of the national independence of the peoples of East Central Europe, this shift occurred against a long record of general declarations seasoned with inaction and with a weather-eye cocked to detect Soviet reactions. The

[2] Hull: op. cit., Vol. II, pp. 1451–9.

[3] Ibid., Vol. II, p. 1458. According to an unpublished official record, the ratio was stated to be 60/40 or 70/30 with respect to "predominance" in Hungary. In Churchill's version (Winston S. Churchill: *Triumph and Tragedy* [Cambridge: Houghton Mifflin; 1953], p. 277), the ratios he proposed were: Rumania 90/10 and Bulgaria 75/25 in favor of Russia, Greece 90/10 in favor of Britain, Yugoslavia 50/50, and Hungary 50/50. The discrepancies in the various percentages reported cannot be fully clarified on the basis of present evidence.

question always asked was whether it was worth while to risk a separate Soviet peace with Germany, and later a Soviet abstention from entering the war against Japan, in order to protest against Soviet actions which the United States was powerless to prevent. Perhaps the final outcome would have been the same, but those who were charged with negotiating were never given any valuable counters to use; they were left with the frustrating invitation to win over the Soviet government to American views by means of words alone. When at Yalta the United States began shifting from passivity to active interest, its British partner was too far committed to a division-of-spheres policy to render strong support.

For East Central Europe the crucial year was 1944 which saw the conclusion of several armistices and the installation of massive Soviet power, backed by Communist parties and the Soviet secret police, in most of the area. Unlike the Soviet role in determining surrender terms for Italy, the Western powers negotiated actively, if ineffectively, on the terms of the armistices. In the long negotiations on the Bulgarian armistice, for example, the author proposed that the Allied Control Commission operate under the "general direction" of the Soviet commander only during the period of hostilities against Germany. Several weeks of close negotiation in London, in the European Advisory Commission, ended in a draw; during the Churchill-Eden visit to Moscow in October 1944, the British representatives agreed to abandon the provision for tri-partite and equal control in the post-hostilities period. As a result, both the Bulgarian armistice of October 28, 1944, and, after it, the Hungarian armistice of January 20, 1945, provided that

> During the period between the coming into force of the armistice and the conclusion of hostilities against Germany the Allied Control Commission will be under the general direction of the Allied (Soviet) High Command.

But they made no corresponding provision for the period between the surrender of Germany and the coming into force of the peace treaty.[4]

During the period between the armistices of 1944 and the Yalta Conference of February 1945, it had become clear that the wartime policy of postponing to a peace conference the settlement of the specific issues of East Central Europe was no longer tenable. Reflecting both hope and alarm, the State Department staff, in preparation for Yalta, made detailed studies and recommendations in support of a positive United States policy designed to safeguard the internal independence of the one hundred million people of this area. In addition to specific recommendations for strengthening the American role in each of the countries, the State Department also prepared a draft Declaration on Liberated Europe and a detailed plan for creating a four power Emergency High Commission for Liberated Europe, empowered to carry out the lofty intentions of the Declaration.[5]

At Yalta Roosevelt put forward the draft Declaration, which, after a relatively brief discussion, was approved with minor changes. He decided not to present the proposal for establishing an Emergency High Commission. Why? On this the record is obscure. Perhaps he was fearful of jeopardizing Soviet participation in the war against Japan.[6] Perhaps he disliked the inclusion of the French provisional government in the proposed four-power commission. In any event, the opportunity, perhaps the last during the war, to assure

[4] For terms of armistice with Bulgaria, see Executive Agreement Series 437 (Washington, D. C.: 1945); with Hungary, same series, 456 (Washington, D. C.: 1945); with Rumania, same series, 490 (Washington, D. C.: 1946).

[5] *The Conferences at Malta and Yalta, 1945*, pp. 97–103; concurring the attitude of President Roosevelt to the proposed commission, see Edward R. Stettinius, Jr.: *Roosevelt and the Russians; the Yalta Conference*, edited by Walter Johnson (Garden City, N. Y.: Doubleday; 1949), pp. 36–7, 85, 88–9.

[6] For the basic Joint Chiefs of Staff recommendation on the necessity of Soviet co-operation in the defeat of Japan, January 23, 1945, see *The Conferences at Malta and Yalta, 1945*, pp. 396–400.

a more active and perhaps more effective participation by the United States in the wartime and postwar reshaping of East Central Europe was lost. The signing of the Declaration on Liberated Europe was, in itself, not enough to convince the Soviet leaders of the new and serious interest which the United States was now prepared to assert in the affairs of that region. Nor did the Yalta agreements on the affairs of Poland and Yugoslavia resolve the basic contradictions between the Soviet and American aims.

Between Yalta and Potsdam the cleavage between Soviet and Western aims in East Central Europe grew ever wider. In violation of the Yalta agreement on Poland in April, the Soviet government recognized unilaterally the unreconstructed Lublin regime. In violation of the Agreement on Zones of Occupation in Germany, in June it transferred a major part of the Soviet zone to Polish possession. The United States withstood the Soviet pressure to admit the Lublin government to the San Francisco Conference, but by the June 1945 compromise, itself a compromise within the Yalta compromise, the Soviet leaders secured the substance of power within Poland for their puppet regime by giving only token representation to the parties and leaders which represented the great majority of the Polish people. Within Yugoslavia Soviet encouragement to the Tito regime blithely ignored both the substance of the Yalta agreement and the Anglo-Soviet agreement for a 50/50 sharing of influence, as the Yugoslav Communists zealously consolidated their undivided control. At the end of February, in disregard of the Yalta Declaration and of strong American protests, Vyshinskii dismissed the Radescu government in Rumania and imposed the Communist-dominated Groza regime. Roosevelt's pleas and protests over Soviet actions in Poland and Rumania were dismissed abruptly by Stalin. By the time of Roosevelt's death the cleavage between Soviet actions and American hopes was complete.

Molotov's visit to Washington, on his way to the San Francisco Conference, gave occasion for the new President to review the Yalta agreements on East Central Europe and to consider what could be done to secure their fulfillment. At an important White House meeting on April 23, 1945, Truman received contradictory advice. Stettinius, Harriman, and Forrestal urged a strong stand, meeting the issue head-on. Leahy urged accommodation and Stimson argued that "the Balkans and their troubles were beyond the sphere of proper United States action," while Marshall warned that a break with Moscow might destroy the hope "for Soviet participation in the war against Japan at a time when it would be useful to us." President Truman felt that "our agreements with the Soviet Union so far had been a one-way street and that he could not continue."[7] His firmer stand succeeded in some details but was to fail in its broader purpose. By June, through the Hopkins mission to Moscow, the outward form of agreement on the new Polish government was all that could be salvaged.[8]

By the time of the Potsdam Conference the Truman administration was no longer shackled by the gnawing fear that through a "strong" policy on East Central Europe it might forfeit Soviet participation in the war against Japan, but the urgency of reaching agreement on post-hostilities policy toward Germany and a multitude of other pressing issues limited severely the pressure which could be exerted on behalf of the freedom and independence of the peoples of East Central Europe. Despite strong misgivings over placing so much German territory under Polish administration, the best that could be done was to leave open the final decision on the new western boundary. Even

[7] An incomplete account of the April 23, 1945, conference, Forrestal: op. cit., pp. 48–51; also, Stimson and Bundy: op. cit., p. 609 and n. 6. Cf. Harry S. Truman: *Memoirs*, Vol. I, *Year of Decisions* (Garden City, N. Y.: Doubleday; 1955), pp 77–8.

[8] Robert E. Sherwood: *Roosevelt and Hopkins, an Intimate History* (New York: Harper; 1948), pp. 883–917.

this agreement was promptly repudiated a few days later by the Soviet government which, in August 1945, guaranteed to Poland the annexation of the German territories which had been placed under its "provisional administration."

Despite State Department hopes that the Allied Control Commissions in Hungary, Rumania, and Bulgaria, would henceforth be placed under three-power direction, the most that could be accomplished was an agreement that directives would now be issued by the Soviet chairmen only after "co-ordination" with their British and American colleagues. Even this concession was promptly vitiated by Soviet action; side-stepping the commissions, henceforth the Soviet commanders issued their orders, as military commanders, directly to the Communist members of the puppet regimes. Stalin also agreed to freedom of movement and reporting for Western correspondents, but he firmly rejected plans for "internationalizing" the Danube and Rhine rivers.

The basic Soviet demand at Potsdam was for the immediate and unconditional recognition of the Soviet-dominated regimes in Hungary, Rumania, and Bulgaria. Obviously, if accepted, this meant abandoning all the Yalta promises of free elections and representative governments, and Truman and Byrnes insisted again and again that they would not recognize governments in these countries until they had a "free government established by themselves without pressure from beyond their borders."[9] Stalin made the Soviet position clear when he stated that "any freely elected government would be anti-Soviet and that we cannot permit."

After the vigorous assertion of the American policy of promoting free and representative governments in East Central Europe, Stalin and Molotov must have been somewhat confused by Secretary Byrnes's sudden

[9] Leahy: op. cit., pp. 405–6; James F. Byrnes, *Speaking Frankly* (New York: Harper; 1947), pp. 73–6, 79–81.

suggestion that "the United States would approve of any arrangement that was accepted by the United Kingdom and the Soviet government" concerning the recognition of the three satellite regimes.[1] This was a last echo of the wartime assumption that East Central Europe was more a British than an American area of concern. After Potsdam it was clear that whatever pressure Britain and America could muster in support of the Yalta Declaration would be determined primarily by American determination and political skill.

The new and stubborn American stand at Potsdam had some significant repercussions within East Central Europe. In Rumania King Michael refused to sign the decrees of the illegal Groza government. In Bulgaria the elections, which were being "prepared" by the Communists with great ruthlessness, were postponed at the last moment. In Hungary the non-Communist parties rejected the Soviet demand for a single-list election, though they agreed to continue the coalition with the Communists regardless of the outcome of the election. Thus, Potsdam encouraged a courageous posture by the non-Communist political forces, while the postponement of the evacuation of American forces from western Czechoslovakia enabled the coalition government to negotiate the simultaneous withdrawal of the Soviet forces. Potsdam also ratified a major reshuffling of ethnic distributions, through its approval of removing the German populations not only from Poland, Czechoslovakia, and Hungary, but also from the "Polish-administered" areas east of the Oder-Neisse line.

The first meeting of the Council of Foreign Ministers, held at London in September 1945, made clear the deadlock which had developed between Soviet and American aims in East Central Europe. Molotov made it plain that his government insisted on having its way in the settlements with Hungary, Rumania, and

[1] Leahy: op. cit., p. 421.

Bulgaria, and in support of Yugoslav claims against Italy. He insisted over and over on immediate and unconditional recognition of the Soviet-dominated regimes in the satellites. As at Potsdam, he denounced Secretary Byrnes's insistence on free elections as a desire to establish "anti-Soviet regimes" in these countries and to recreate the *cordon sanitaire* against the Soviet Union. To illustrate the absence of hostile intention on the American side and to make clear the American definition of free elections, Byrnes offered then and there to extend recognition to the Hungarian government, provided it assured a relatively free and unimpeded vote. Following a complete deadlock between the two positions, on September 22 Molotov injected the Soviet demand for equal participation in the control of Japan, and when the American representatives were unwilling even to discuss this Soviet incursion into an American "sphere of responsibility," Molotov broke up the conference.

The strong American stand at Potsdam and London in favor of free elections in East Central Europe threw a few handfuls of grit into the grinding wheels of the Soviet power machine, but it could not stop their turning. Meanwhile, a similar tug of war, this time in favor of the American position, was taking place between Moscow and Washington over the postwar control of Japan. At the Moscow Conference of Foreign Ministers in December 1945, the United States received Soviet acquiescence in the substance of its claims to sole control over occupied Japan, and the Soviet government gained the substance of American acquiescence in the policies which it was following in East Central Europe, making only a few concessions of form by allowing Western-nominated ministers to sit in the Rumanian cabinet. A similar Soviet promise to "suggest" to the Bulgarian government the inclusion of Western-recommended ministers was promptly vitiated in Sofia by Vyshinskii's "suggesting" the opposite. The defeat of the American effort to assure to the nations of East Central Europe the enjoyment, in some degree, of the right of self-determination—an effort begun belatedly at Yalta—was sealed within the same year at Moscow.

What could American policy do henceforth to help the peoples of East Central Europe to escape the yoke which was being pressed down upon their shoulders? One hope was to use the offer of American economic aid to strengthen their ties with the West. Through the sale of surplus supplies and the timing of the restitution of stolen property and shipping, some efforts were made in this direction, but there was no consistent plan and no popular understanding of the need for one. Another and somewhat contradictory line of action was to press for the protection of American property rights. This was a feeble and two-edged sword, for it fed the Communist propaganda against the "imperialists" at the same time that the United States was committed in principle to accepting the nationalization of foreign-owned properties provided the principles of nondiscrimination and compensation were observed.

A more substantial hope was that the speedy conclusion of the peace treaties and the withdrawal of Soviet troops would allow the non-Communist forces to recover control of their national destinies. To hasten the conclusion of the treaties the American government accepted many unfavorable provisions, including those for establishing the Free Territory of Trieste and for submitting the future status of the Danube to decision by a Soviet-packed conference. The Soviet negotiators made haste slowly. Agreed to in December 1946, the treaties were signed in February and entered into force in September 1947. In Hungary complete Communist domination had been established in May 1947, the Communist grip on Bulgaria and Rumania was unshakable, and the Polish "elections" of January 1947 set the seal on Communist control. In all these countries, except Albania, Soviet-dominated regimes had received American recognition, despite flagrant violations of the Yalta agreements. Soviet forces also remained stationed in Hungary, Rumania, and Poland.

March 1947 saw a major extension of American responsibilities. Greece and Turkey, which had been within the British sphere since 1942, were transferred to American protection by the adoption of the Truman Doctrine. By the Marshall Plan, proposed in June 1947, the United States abandoned its previous assumption that Europe could see to its own economic reconstruction and promised large-scale and continuing American assistance. In June 1948 it took on an added responsibility for assuring the construction of Western Germany.

Just how far the Marshall Plan was predicated upon co-operation with the Soviet Union and the Soviet-dominated countries of East Central Europe remains obscure. In any case Moscow chose to attack the plan as an "imperialist plot" to destroy its domination in East Central Europe, and in July 1947, it ordered the Czechoslovak coalition government to withdraw its tentative agreement to attend the Marshall Plan conference. With the founding of the Cominform, in September-October 1947, the Soviet leaders openly proclaimed their determination to exert a monopoly of decision making in East Central Europe, while continuing their probing of the vulnerabilities of Greece and Turkey. Soviet domination of East Central Europe, tentatively outlined as early as 1942, pursued relentlessly from 1944, and acquiesced in reluctantly by the West in 1946, was an accomplished fact except where, as in Yugoslavia, strong local forces later proved able to defend their own Communist-oriented independence.

During the war of 1941–5 the United States moved from a parochially continental concept of its responsibilities to the exercise of leadership over the more productive half of Europe and over Japan, and to the development of new policies toward the British Commonwealth and the Middle East. The two areas where its new concept of responsibilities failed were China and East Central Europe. The expansion of American interests and responsibilities had been unforeseen and unplanned. As late as 1946 American policy making assumed that, having defeated the aggressors, the United States would be free, once again, to limit drastically its commitments in other continents, leaving the United Nations to take care of what minor troubles and conflicts might arise.

Between 1941 and 1947 American hopes for a democratic and liberal future for the one hundred million people of East Central Europe rose and fell. Hopes were high so long as American opinion failed to realize that in East Central Europe, Soviet aims and American aspirations ran directly counter to each other. Here two separate wars were being waged, but Washington failed during the war to assure power positions from which it could achieve its hopes after the war. The location of forces at the close of hostilities was to be, more than was realized at the time, the decisive factor in the divergent fates of East Central and western Europe. Wartime strategy, in the event, determined the shape of postwar diplomacy. The strategy of coalition called for the assignment of military "spheres of responsibility," and these, as the Cassandras of the State Department warned over and over, were likely to harden into postwar "spheres of influence" and into competition and conflict between them.

Despite gnawing doubts as to how far the administration in power could commit the United States to the enforcement of specific postwar settlements anywhere in Europe, Roosevelt and Truman found strong support at home for the hopes which were expressed in the Yalta Declaration on Liberated Europe. But the new and active course was begun with a whole necklace of incubuses hung around its neck. Not least of these was the continuing failure to co-ordinate the use of political, military, and economic power within American policy making. By the end of 1946, against unyielding Soviet insistence on transforming East Central Europe into a closed preserve, the American government had a heap of broken Soviet promises to point to as a reminder that hope, divorced from power, is not a policy.

:8:

SOVIET POLICY AND NATIONALITY CONFLICTS IN EAST CENTRAL EUROPE[1]

[February 1950]

INTRODUCTORY NOTE · The principal instruments by which Moscow consolidated its domination over most of East Central Europe between April 1944 and February 1948 were Soviet military might, the Soviet-dominated (except in Yugoslavia) Communist parties, and, when less direct means of manipulation or intimidation failed, the intervention of the Soviet secret police. But the Soviet leadership did not neglect other and more traditional tools of imperialism. The tactic of the direct or indirect seizure of many "commanding positions" in the economies of the satellites, borrowed in part from Hitler's technicians, was carried to a high point through the confiscation of real and alleged German assets, the extraction of unilaterally defined restitution and reparation, the setting up of joint-stock companies, and the manipulation of the terms of trade. An additional wedge for Soviet and Communist penetration was pro-

[1] *The Soviet Union: Background, Ideology, Reality*, edited by Waldemar Gurian (Notre Dame: University of Notre Dame Press; 1951,) pp. 67–84; presented in February 1950 at a Symposium of the Committee on International Relations at the University of Notre Dame. Copyright 1951 by the University of Notre Dame Press.

vided by the many conflicting national claims and rivalries.

Naturally, the last thing the Soviet leaders wanted was any sort of East Central or Danubian federation or confederation, which might have overcome these national rivalries from within but which might also have stiffened their resistance to Soviet encroachments. (See above, Seven, "Hopes and Failures: American Policy Toward East Central Europe.") What was more surprising was the Soviet rejection of the idea of a Balkan federation of Communist states, a perennial plan of the Comintern ever since 1924. When subjected to the pragmatic test of Soviet power interests, this time-honored—and attractive—ideological promise was scuttled almost overnight. Stalin was not eager to see Tito's unexpected resistance to Soviet infiltration of his party, secret police, and military apparatus extended to Bulgaria, and perhaps to Rumania and Hungary, or even prospectively to Greece. After all, any social group which resists Moscow's whims may have the label of "bourgeois nationalists" pinned to it, whereas "internationalists" are those who eagerly carry out its every behest.

*

THE course of the war against Hitler, the massive power of the victorious Soviet armies, the success with which Soviet leadership manipulated separately and in combination an extensive armory of military, political, and ideological weapons, placed most of the smaller nations of East Central Europe, after the war, within an expanded Soviet sphere of domination. Always exposed to great-power pressures and released only recently from the rule of four great military empires—German, Russian, Austrian, and Ottoman—the smaller states, despite their long historical traditions and their great cultural contributions to European civilization, had enjoyed genuine independence for about two decades, only as long as the western nations, and particularly France, were able and willing to offer an ever-ready offset to the reviving power of Germany and Russia. The surrender of these countries to Nazi domination, or their defeat, was followed, without transition, by the encroachment of Soviet power.

What was new and unexpected to the peoples of the area was the degree of intensity and ruthlessness with which the newly dominant great power set about reshaping the entire social structure and the cultures of the region. In strengthening its control over East Central Europe the Soviet leadership, like previous conquerors, has made the most of the national disputes which divide its peoples, giving and withholding its support of national and territorial claims in a manner best suited to enhance its own power. The extension of Soviet control in depth was facilitated by the adoption of extreme nationalist claims by the various local Communist parties. After 1944 Communist propaganda also made full play of the compelling idea that only "loyal" obedience to the Soviet Union would win Soviet support of national claims to acquire or retain this or that disputed territory.

The Soviet system strives to substitute an integral political conformity for genuine and action-oriented national attachments. A culture "national in form, socialist in content," can afford to organize displays of "national dances," provided all permitted content of thought and all training of the younger generation are directed toward strengthening a single overriding political and nonnational loyalty. Whether the artificial separation and rejoining of "form" and "content" are feasible and lasting is open to serious dispute, even as applied within the Soviet Union. If it has succeeded to the degree claimed by Soviet spokesmen, it is difficult to understand why several of the Soviet nationalities were "liquidated" outright during the war—to mention only the Chechen-Ingush, the Kalmyks, the Crimean Tartars, and the Germans of the Volga—or why severe and wasteful purges have repeatedly eliminated large numbers of the local national intelligentsia, including a large proportion of Communists, supposedly educated completely in a Stalinist understanding of the role of national cultures within the "Soviet friendship of nations." [2]

In advancing the Soviet frontiers westward between 1939 and 1945 the Soviet regime made full utilization of claims based upon nationality, and the strength of the new frontiers has been solidified by large-scale and compulsory transfers of population. In other important instances, such as the conquest of the Baltic republics and East Prussia, Soviet leadership has conveniently ignored the factor of nationality, appealing instead to arguments based upon history and strategy, and relying above all on the *ultima ratio*, power. In the territory ceded by Finland to the Soviet Union, the withdrawal of the native population opened the way for Russian settlement, and the Karelian Union Republic probably contains a minority of Finnish-speaking inhabitants.[3] While the Soviet half of East Prussia (Kaliningrad *oblast'*) apparently has some German population and some German-language schools, it has a Russian majority and, like the Crimean *oblast'*, is attached to the Great Russian republic, despite the absence of territorial contiguity.[4]

The persistence of ancient patterns of culture is illustrated in the fact that in enforcing the removal of the large Polish minority from former eastern Poland membership in the Catholic faith was adopted generally as the test of nationality. Like the similar action of Nicholas I in the 1830's, the ruthless destruction of

[2] (Author's note, 1959) According to Khrushchev's speech of February 1956 against Stalin, the latter also wanted to "liquidate" the Ukrainian people, but found it too numerous.

[3] (Author's note, 1959) This estimate was confirmed by the Soviet government in July 1956, when it abolished the Karelo-Finnish Union Republic.

[4] (Author's note, 1959) The Crimean Autonomous Republic was transferred from the Russian to the Ukrainian Republic in February 1954.

the Greek Catholic or Uniat Church, with all its cultural and religious institutions, in Eastern Galicia and Carpathian Ukraine (or Ruthenia) by the Soviet regime has been designed to break the spiritual and cultural bonds which have long linked the newly annexed Ukrainian lands with the west. In the case of Bessarabia no large-scale transfers were undertaken, and the Moldavian Union Republic includes those areas where the Rumanian census of 1930 showed Rumanian majorities. However, the "Moldavians" are having it drummed into them that they are a people distinct from the Rumanians, from whose rule they have been "liberated," and the "Moldavian" language is now written and printed, with considerable inconvenience, in Russian characters.

Until the final stages of the war Soviet policy regarding Carpathian (now "Trans-Carpathian") Ukraine was cloaked in mystery. According to one well-informed source, while in Moscow for the signature of the Czechoslovak-Soviet alliance in December 1943, the late President Beneš "without his government's knowledge suggested to Stalin that Carpathian Ruthenia might find its new destiny within the Soviet Ukraine," but "Stalin emphatically refused Beneš's suggestion."[5] Vojta Beneš has reported, however, that when Dr. Beneš returned to London on January 6, 1944, a Soviet envoy handed him a letter from Stalin commanding him to transfer Carpathian Ukraine to the Soviet Union, and he calls this "the heaviest blow suffered by Dr. Beneš since Munich."[6] According to Dr. Němec, who had been sent to Carpathian Ukraine in October 1944 as the official delegate of the Czechoslovak government, not only Czechoslovak officials like himself but also the Czech and Sub-Carpathian leaders of the Communist party of Czechoslovakia assumed,

[5] Ivo Ducháček: *The Strategy of Communist Infiltration: The Case of Czechoslovakia* (New Haven: The Institute of International Studies; 1949), p. 10.

[6] Vojta Beneš: "Dr. Edvard Beneš As He Was" (in Czech), *New-Yorské Listy*, October 6, 1949.

until October 28, 1944, that this region would remain a part of postwar Czechoslovakia.[7] As late as his March 1945 visit to Moscow, Beneš expressed to Molotov his uneasiness over the reaction of his people to the cession of Ruthenia and asked him in return to "assure" the Czechoslovak boundaries with Poland, Hungary, and Germany.[8] To this request Molotov turned a deaf ear. The transfer, which had been in effect since early November 1944, was officially sanctioned in the Czechoslovak-Soviet treaty of June 29, 1945.

The westward advance of the Soviet boundary has been paralleled by the removal to the west of the boundary of German ethnic settlement, roughly to the line where it had stood early in the twelfth century. The removal of the German population from the area assigned to Polish administration and of the *Volksdeutsche* from prewar Poland, Czechoslovakia, Hungary, and Yugoslavia (large numbers of the *Volksdeutsche* in Transylvania had been removed to the Soviet Union in January and February 1945) has created a clear-cut ethnic situation in East Central Europe for the first time in many centuries. No one can even estimate the mass of human suffering which has been engendered by the massive "liquidations" and migrations inflicted successively by Nazi and Soviet power politics.

Fear of German revenge and of renewed German ambitions has served Soviet interests by binding the smaller nations to Soviet policy. The Workers (Communist) party in Poland has continually reiterated its claim that only unswerving "co-operation" with the Soviet Union on Soviet terms will assure permanent possession of the "recovered lands" which were assigned to provisional Polish administration at Potsdam. Although the Soviet government had joined with the

[7] Frantisek Němec: "The Betrayal of October 28, 1944" (in Czech), *New-Yorské Listy*, October 28, 1949.

[8] Zdeněk Fierlinger: *Ve Sluzbách ČSR; Pamětí z druhého zahraničního odboje*, Vol. II (Prague: Nakladatelství Svoboda v Praze; [1948]), p. 596.

United States and British governments in stating that the final disposition of this territory would await the conclusion of a treaty of peace with Germany in August 1945, only a fortnight after Potsdam, it unilaterally guaranteed possession of it to Poland. On September 19 of that year, while the Council of Foreign Ministers was meeting in London, Marshal Zhukov notified the Poles, again unilaterally, that several hundred additional square miles of territory west of Stettin were to be transferred at once to Polish control.

During these same months the German Communists were busily propagating by word of mouth the idea that only by "loyal co-operation" with the Soviet Union through its chosen instrument, the Communist (later, the Socialist Unity) party, could defeated Germany hope to bring about a revision of the Oder-Neisse boundary in its favor. In September 1946 the Soviet government was compelled by Secretary Byrnes's Stuttgart speech to undercut this powerful line of propaganda within Germany, by reaffirming its support of the Polish claims. Mr. Byrnes was on firm legal ground in asserting that the United States was free to support a more easterly boundary in the drafting of the final peace treaty with Germany, but the American position is decidedly weakened by the agreement, in which it joined at Potsdam, for removing the German population from the Polish-administered area. More recently, in June 1950, a major step toward integrating the Soviet-controlled East German Republic into the Soviet bloc was taken through the signature by it of an agreement with Poland confirming "forever" its acceptance of the "provisional" German-Polish boundary of 1945.

At the close of the war the Czechoslovak Communists were the most relentless proponents of the removal of all Germans, even of German Communists, from their country. During the coalition regime of 1945–8 their word-of-mouth agitation presented the

Soviet alliance as the strongest guarantee against an eventual return of the evicted Sudeten Germans and spread rumors that the United States was planning to return the "expellees" by force. In the case of the Germans of Hungary, the Budapest government was taken aback by the Soviet-sponsored Potsdam decision that the German population of Hungary must be removed to Germany. Again, the Hungarian Communists supported extreme nationalistic and even racialist measures. Simultaneously the Communists were pressing the Hungarian government to co-operate in resettling the Magyar minority of Slovakia, and they insisted that expulsion of the Germans would make room for accommodating the Magyars expelled from Slovak territory. Whether the two "counterbalancing" migrations were conceived as complementary at the time of Potsdam, or whether the original connection between them rested on coincidence, is not clear. In January and February 1945 the non-Communist Rumanian government headed by General Radescu had also opposed the forcible removal of a major part of its German-speaking citizens to the Soviet Union, demanding that punishment be visited upon guilty individuals and not upon an entire ethnic group. Resistance to this Soviet demand was one of the factors which led to Vyshinskii's abrupt dismissal of the Radescu government in late February of that year, and to the imposition of the subservient Groza cabinet.

In Austria the Soviet government did not support the somewhat tentative claims raised by Czechoslovakia in the region of Znaim and by Hungary in the Burgenland, but until its about-face in June 1949 it gave strong support to Yugoslav claims in Carinthia. The Soviet government's Austrian policy seems to have wavered between the idea of making the country as weak as possible, through opposing its claims in the South Tyrol and in Carinthia, and of securing internal strong points which might enable it to dominate the Austrian economy. How far the abandonment of the

Yugoslav claim was motivated by a desire to punish Marshal Tito for his display of independence within "the family of the people's democracies," and how far by the wish to hasten the withdrawal of American forces and perhaps of American economic support from Austria, is a matter of conjecture.

Against Italy Soviet policy at first supported Yugoslav claims to the full, short of a direct risk of war. In 1945 the Communist party of Italy at first urged the transfer of Trieste and Venezia Giulia to Yugoslavia as a gesture of "magnanimity" and a step toward strengthening the "forces of democracy." This position, logical enough from a Soviet and Communist viewpoint, raised an immediate threat to the popularity and unity of the party and had to be dropped very quickly. A new line was hastily adopted, stating that "Trieste is Italian" by omitting to say whether it should remain Italian or not. The true Soviet intention was better illustrated by its actions in placing Trieste under the jurisdiction of a separate "Giulian" Communist party, which operated from Ljubljana during 1945–8, and in forbidding the Italian party to operate in Trieste throughout those critical years and until some months after the Tito-Cominform rupture.

When all-out Soviet support of the Yugoslav claims came up against a strong Western insistence on a division of the area along roughly ethnic lines and, particularly, against Anglo-American occupation of an important part of Venezia Giulia, Soviet diplomacy made a partial retreat to the compromise position represented by the proposal to create a "Free Territory" of Trieste. During and after the conclusion of the treaty of peace with Italy, Soviet policy strove in every way to weaken the role of the proposed governor-general and of the Security Council and to leave the way open for a Yugoslav and Communist seizure of power from within. During the first half of 1950 the Soviet government again pressed for the establishment, long postponed because of great-power disagreements, of the Free Territory. Now, however, the Soviet aim was, as a minimum, to compel Marshal Tito to give up control of the Yugoslav-administered part of the Free Territory ("Zone B") and, as a maximum, to create a Free Territory regime dominated by Stalinist and anti-Tito Communists. Soviet policy has thus swung from promoting Yugoslav national claims in Venezia Giulia to opposing them sharply, utilizing the Trieste compromise of 1946 for each purpose successively.

Against Greece Soviet leadership has also been able to utilize the national claims of its northern neighbors —Albania, Yugoslavia, Bulgaria. In September 1944, during the negotiations over the terms of the Allied armistice with Bulgaria, the Soviet delegation to the European Advisory Commission tried very hard to leave Bulgarian forces in control of Western Thrace, claiming that since Bulgaria was now aiding the Soviet armies it was "not possible" to ask them to withdraw from Greek territory. Speaking for the United States in these meetings, the author rejected out-of-hand this Soviet claim to reward Bulgaria at the expense of Greece; he realized that a peace treaty with Bulgaria might be long delayed and that meanwhile the Bulgars would use every means of oppression to prepare the way for an eastern-type plebiscite as a step toward retaining permanent possession of the disputed area. Meeting strong resistance, the Soviet delegation withdrew its demand. In 1946, when Foreign Secretary Bevin and the United States Senate gave support to Greek "strategic" claims against Albania and Bulgaria, the Soviet government again gave its backing for some time to Bulgaria's claim to Western Thrace.

In the Greek civil war, which flared up with new strength in mid-1946, territorial claims early played a significant part in the assistance furnished to General Markos Vafiades's forces by Greece's northern neighbors. Whether or not Markos actually agreed to transfer Western Thrace to Bulgaria and "Aegean Macedonia" to Yugoslavia is not very important. After bringing Greece within the Soviet orbit Markos would hardly have been able to resist "comradely demands of gratitude," the military preponderance and the political pressures of his Communist "brothers-in-arms." Whether Moscow was committed to satisfy Yugoslav, Bulgar, and perhaps Albanian demands at Greek expense, or whether, at the decisive moment, the Soviet leadership would have taken Greek territorial integrity under its direct protection in return for receiving control of "joint" Soviet-Greek bases in mainland Greece and the Dodecanese, remains a matter of speculation.[9]

It is probable that the Yugoslav-Bulgarian agreements signed at Bled on August 1, 1947, had some reference to the future disposition of Greek territory. It is not likely that the Bulgars would have agreed to turn over Pirin Macedonia to Yugoslavia, as provided in a secret annex, unless they were promised Western Thrace with its outlet to the Aegean. Shortly afterwards the Communist leader of Yugoslav Macedonia, Vlakhov, speaking in Bulgarian Macedonia, referred openly to the role of the Bled agreements "in the liberation of Aegean Macedonia."[1] Once Greek Macedonia were annexed to Yugoslav Macedonia, Western Thrace, cut off from the rest of Greece, would naturally fall to Bulgaria, which had already tried to digest it during 1941–4. After the Soviet-Yugoslav rupture the Greek Communists, who had received their principal support from Yugoslavia, attempted to remain neutral. However, at the end of 1948 the Stalinist elements took control of the Greek Communist forces, dismissed

[9] (Author's note, 1959) In March or April 1946 the Soviet ambassador to Athens reportedly requested "joint" Greek-Soviet bases in the Dodecanese Islands in return for agreeing to their transfer to Greek sovereignty under the peace treaty with Italy.

[1] Dimiter Vlakhov, President of the Macedonian People's Republic, Vice-President of the Yugoslav Republic, speech at Razlog, October 28, 1947, summarized in *Christian Science Monitor* (Boston), December 1, 1947.

Markos and drove out the pro-Yugoslav and Slav-speaking Communists as "usurpers" and "annexationists." With the collapse of the Communist military movement the pressure from the Soviet sphere against Greece was greatly relaxed.

Within the Soviet sphere Moscow has had full opportunity and full responsibility for resolving and reconciling national and territorial claims among its satellites. As far as possible outside great powers were excluded from any consideration of intraregional disputes. The Soviet insistence upon a unilateral right of decision can be illustrated from the handling of the problem of Rumanian and Hungarian claims to Transylvania.

When the Allied armistice with Rumania was being hastily negotiated at Moscow in August 1944, Molotov was determined to return Transylvania in its entirety to Rumanian possession. This was to be a reward to Rumania for its valuable co-operation in expelling the German forces from its territory and a boost for the uncertain popularity of the Rumanian Communists, who were then few in number and extremely weak. In addition, the Soviet government had to decide whether to leave northern Transylvania, reannexed by Hungary in 1940, under Hungarian rule or whether to reinstate the Rumanian administration. From the British and American viewpoint, however, permanent decisions of this kind should belong in a treaty of peace, not in a purely military instrument, and the United States government in particular wished to leave the territorial issue open for more considered decision. After all, in 1919 the United States and Great Britain had opposed placing the Rumanian frontier as far to the west, at Hungary's expense, as was done in the treaty of Trianon. In August 1944 the formula of compromise as finally adopted stated that "all or the greater part" of Transylvania should go to Rumania. For many months the Soviet authorities rejected all requests of the coalition government in Bucharest for the return of northern Transylvania to Rumanian administration. The transfer of control was carried out with great pomp as soon as the Soviet-chosen Groza government had been installed in March 1945.

In September 1945, when the Council of Foreign Ministers began its negotiations on the peace treaties, the Soviet delegation seemed surprised to learn that there were any Magyars in Transylvania. Throughout the later negotiations it refused steadfastly to discuss the problem of Transylvania. When the United States delegation urged in March 1946 that the council either make a direct investigation of the problem or request the Rumanian and Hungarian governments to discuss the dispute directly, the Soviet representatives again refused all discussion. In May 1946, in an effort to reduce to a few clear issues the wide range of outstanding conflicts over the peace treaties, Secretary Byrnes abandoned the attempt, which had been entirely fruitless, to discuss the Rumanian-Hungarian boundary and agreed to restore the pre-1939 settlement. During the Paris Conference of 1946 the United States upheld this agreement, and the efforts of Mr. Evatt and the Australian delegation to raise the issue on its merits failed.

Meanwhile, the Hungarian delegation had come to Paris, assuming that the territorial issue was open for negotiation. Within Hungary the Communist party had been busily spreading the rumor that by "loyal co-operation" with Soviet demands Hungary could secure Soviet support for the revision of the frontier with Rumania, and its agitators pointed to the "loyal" attitude of the Groza government as explaining why Moscow had so far favored the Rumanian claim. After the close of the Paris Conference the Hungarian government again requested the four major powers to arrange direct Hungarian-Rumanian conversations concerning the status of the large Magyar minority in

Transylvania. Moscow again turned a deaf ear to this proposal.[2] No satellite which understood its proper place in the Soviet sphere should have addressed its appeal to any outside powers.

Within the Soviet sphere only one territorial conflict has been fully settled—the Rumanian-Bulgarian dispute over southern Dobruja. In this case, however, the direct pressure upon Rumania to return most of the territory annexed in 1913 had come from Germany, in August and September 1940, and the settlement of Craiova had been explicitly approved at the time by the Soviet, British, and American governments. During the negotiations of the Council of Foreign Ministers the Soviet delegation at first, from September 1945 to May 1946, opposed including in the peace treaties with the Balkan satellites any description of the Rumanian-Bulgarian boundary, as well as of all postwar boundaries, an attitude which ran counter to well-established international practice. Under force of Western arguments and in the realization that international recognition of certain of the new Soviet boundaries was bound up with the insertion of descriptions of the postwar boundaries, the Soviet delegation finally consented to their inclusion. By these provisions the United States and Great Britain also took part in determining the legal status of southern Dobruja.

On the other hand, the question of Teschen (Těšín, Cieszyn) has remained open between Poland and Czechoslovakia. By 1944 military and political factors made the role of the Soviet Union of prime importance in the solution of this dispute. In October 1944 even the Soviet-supported Lublin government was unwilling to discuss the restoration of the disputed area to Czechoslovakia, from which the Beck government had seized it in October 1938, with Nazi complicity. At this time Fierlinger, Czechoslovak Ambassador in Moscow, was content to remind the Beneš government

[2] Hungarian note of November 9, 1946, as reported in *The New York Times*, November 10, 1946.

in London that "it was clear that our old boundaries would be held inviolate" (the *de facto* annexation of Carpathian Ukraine was only one week away), although he himself seemed not unreconciled to discussing with the Lublin Poles "if not a minor boundary correction, then at least a partial exchange of population" in Teschen.[3]

In March 1945, during conferences between Molotov and Beneš, the latter reported that the British government favored the immediate restoration of Czechoslovak administration in Teschen and final recognition of the prewar boundary in the peace treaty. Molotov took no definite stand in the matter, according to Fierlinger's detailed report. Similarly, he evaded giving any reply to Beneš's proposal that the cession of Carpathian Ukraine be coupled with a Soviet guarantee of the prewar Czechoslovak boundaries with Germany, Poland, and Hungary.[4] It would have been an easy matter for the Soviet government to require the new Polish government to renounce the gains of the Beck government in Teschen, for only one week previously it had promised to it vast territorial gains at Germany's expense, in violation of the Yalta agreement that the three major powers would act together in determining Poland's new western boundary. Moscow's refusal to protect the Czechoslovak claim in Teschen can hardly have been due to oversight, for in 1938 the Soviet government had taken a strong stand against Beck's policy of joining Hitler in partitioning Czechoslovakia.

Despite the leading role of the Communists in it, the new Czechoslovak government did not realize at first that it was to have no share in the partition of German territory. On April 27, 1946, the then Foreign Minister, the late Jan Masaryk, despatched notes to the four major powers asking them to cede German territory to Czechoslovakia in four areas—Kosel (Kozle), Ratibor (Raciborz), Glatz (Kladsko), and

[3] Fierlinger: op. cit., Vol. II, p. 381.
[4] Ibid., Vol. II, pp. 595–6; conference of March 21, 1945.

Waldenberg (Walbrzych). Transfer of these areas to Czechoslovakia now meant separating them from the extensive areas placed under provisional Polish administration at Potsdam, and the Polish government denounced the Prague note as "an unfriendly act."[5] The Czechs' major mistake, it must be assumed, lay in addressing their request to all four powers, rather than to Moscow alone. While the Czechs gave full support, in principle, to Poland's new western boundary, and the Poles regarded this gain of territory as insufficient to offset the loss of more extensive but less valuable areas to the Soviet Union, the Polish claim to Teschen and the Czech claim to parts of former German Silesia remained unresolved.

On March 10, 1947, on the eve of the Moscow Council of Foreign Ministers, which was to come to grips with the problem of the peace treaty for Germany, the Czechoslovak and Polish governments concluded a Pact of Friendship and Mutual Assistance. Strengthening further their alignment with Soviet policy, the two governments undertook "to apply by mutual consent all means at their disposal to render impossible any new attempt of aggression on the part of Germany or any other country which would unite with Germany for this purpose, directly or indirectly." In an annex Prague and Warsaw recognized by implication their inability thus far to resolve their territorial disputes and agreed ". . . to decide by mutual agreement, not later than two years from the signing of the Pact of Friendship and Mutual Assistance, all territorial disputes pending between the two countries," and ". . . to guarantee to the Poles residing in Czechoslovakia and to the Czechs and Slovaks residing in Poland . . . the possibilities of national, political, cultural and economic development. . . ."[6] Foreign commentaries assumed that by this agreement Czech-

[5] *The New York Times*, May 3, 1946.

[6] Full texts in Polish Ministry of Foreign Affairs, *Information on Poland*, Dx 53–6.

oslovakia gave up its claims to German Upper Silesia. This interpretation did not necessarily follow from the use of the plural "disputes," although this usage might refer to minor Polish claims to Špís and Orava as well as to Teschen. The official communiqué issued on the following day made no mention of the question of the boundary disputes.[7]

On the occasion of a return visit by the Polish cabinet to Prague, in July 1947, the communiqué stressed "the need for carrying out in full and in the shortest time the additional protocol" assuring full rights to the respective minorities, and again it made no mention of the territorial disputes or of progress in settling them.[8] The two-year time limit passed in 1949, and there have been no reports of a settlement of the Polish-Czechoslovak dispute. In 1949 there were recurrent reports of a proposed three-way exchange, by which Poland would receive a part of the Teschen area, ceding Glatz to Czechoslovakia and part of Lower Silesia to the East German Republic.[9] It is hard to see how any part of Teschen could be yielded to the Czechs without cutting a vital east-west railroad connection. According to all indications the dispute is inactive. It may remain in abeyance indefinitely as a result of Polish-Czechoslovak arrangements for the co-operative development of the Upper Silesian navigation and power system.

A much larger area, with a Magyar minority of at least one-half million, and one dogged by an active tradition of inter-group hostility, has been involved in the Czechoslovak-Hungarian dispute. After the end of the war Slovak Communists outdid nationalists in demanding not only the restoration of the pre-1938 frontier, which at all points favored Czechoslovakia on economic and strategic grounds, but also the expulsion of the Magyars regardless of their individual conduct or attitude. During the autumn of 1945 the

[7] Ibid., Dx 56–7.
[8] Moscow *Izvestiia*, No. 159 (July 9, 1947).
[9] For example, *The New York Times*, April 16, 1949.

process of expulsion was put in swing, and all expellees were described by the Slovak press as "war criminals." The Hungarian government, in response to its appeals, received platonic assurances of American opposition to the unilateral transfer of the Magyar minority.[1] The Soviet representatives at Budapest were silent.

The announced policy of Czechoslovakia, on which the Communists were especially insistent, called for the exchange of 100,000 Magyars from Slovakia against a like number of "ethnic Slovaks" from Hungary, for deporting another 200,000 Magyars to Hungary without exchange, and for allowing some 200,000 to 300,000 Magyars to be "re-Slovakized" by declaring them to be of Slovak descent and depriving them of all use of the Magyar language in schools, administration, and cultural life. The first part of this program was implemented through a Slovak-Hungarian agreement of February 27, 1946, providing for the exchange of 100,000 ethnic nationals in each direction.

No agreement could be reached concerning the even more drastic features of the program, and the issue was brought before the Paris Conference of July-October 1946. Prague and Bratislava failed to receive international sanction for the policy of expulsion, and Article 5 of the peace treaty with Hungary merely provided for direct Czechoslovak-Hungarian negotiations on this problem.[2] During the winter of 1946–7 the Czechoslovak authorities proceeded rapidly to "solve" the problem of the Magyar minority through internal

[1] Department of State Bulletin, Vol. XIII, p. 937 (December 9, 1945). For a detailed account of Hungary's diplomatic efforts see Hungarian Ministry for Foreign Affairs, *Hungary and the Conference of Paris;* Vol. II, *Hungary's International Relations before the Conference of Paris;* Vol. IV, *Hungary and the Conference of Paris* (Budapest: both 1947). The three volumes published out of the five volumes planned for this series were initiated and executed under the direction of Dr. Stephen D. Kertesz, then Secretary-General of the Ministry of Foreign Affairs, prior to the Communist seizure of power.

[2] (Author's note, 1959) For a detailed account of this problem see Stephen D. Kertesz: *Diplomacy in a Whirlpool: Hungary Between Nazi Germany and Soviet Russia* (Notre Dame: University of Notre Dame Press; 1953), pp. 163–88.

measures. In Prague's view these steps could not be delayed because the precedent of expulsion had already been set through the removal of the Sudeten Germans and because of the still unsettled relationship between Czechs and Slovaks in the new republic. Some 200,000 Magyars of claimed Slovak ancestry were allowed to apply to be "re-Slovakized." The balance were to be removed to the western parts of the republic, where they would be resettled in dispersed groups among Czech and Slovak colonists, under provisions of the law for compulsory labor. Within Hungary Communist propaganda attributed Soviet silence concerning the fate of this large Magyar minority to the failure of the coalition government to give "full and spontaneous co-operation" to the Soviet "protector," while within Slovakia the Communists outbid more moderate groups in demanding "Slovakia for the Slovaks."

After the complete "co-ordination" of Czechoslovakia into the Soviet sphere in February 1948, with the establishment of a Communist monopoly of power, the Magyar issue lost its urgency for the new regime. On October 25, 1948, the Czechoslovak parliament restored Czechoslovak citizenship to Magyars who had been domiciled in the republic on November 1, 1938, and who had not been convicted of crime. In December the cabinet announced that Magyars deported to the western regions would now be permitted to return to Slovakia and would receive "the same or better" holdings of land. An Hungarian-language Communist weekly was established, but it is not clear whether the use of Magyar was restored in the elementary schools.

Aside from its general slogans ascribing all national conflicts to "bourgeois," "capitalist," and "reactionary" influences, prewar Soviet ideology had not elaborated comprehensive published programs for the nationality disputes in East Central Europe, with one major exception. That exception was Stalin's speech of 1924 to the Yugoslav Communists, calling for the development of federal autonomy on the Soviet pattern, as the proper solution to the nationality problems of their country. "Balkan Federation," a long-honored slogan of Balkan socialists and agrarians, also held a central place in the prewar Communist program for southeastern Europe. However, once the Soviet Union had acquired a dominant position in the Balkans, except in Greece and Turkey, the problem of applying these slogans proved to be far from simple and straightforward.

After Rumania and Bulgaria had swung into the Soviet orbit in August and September 1944, Soviet leadership apparently considered making Bulgaria the pivot of its Balkan policies. In line with this, Soviet diplomacy strove to leave the Bulgars in control of Greek Western Thrace, to relieve Bulgaria of all reparations to Greece and Yugoslavia, and to place no armistice limitations on its armed forces. Moscow also envisaged Bulgaria as the central factor in a South Slav federation, and between October 1944 and January 1945 it was actively considering what form to give to the future federation.

This was a difficult question. Supported by Dimitrov's extensive connections in Moscow, the Bulgarian Communists urged that Bulgaria as a unit should be joined with Yugoslavia as a unit. This would give the Bulgarian Communists one half of the responsible posts in the joint central agencies, although Yugoslavia is almost twice as populous and had a much larger number of Communists experienced in military and civil administration. Whether Moscow regarded a federation of this dual type as a step toward curbing any latent Yugoslav trend towards independence is a matter of conjecture. The Yugoslav position was that Bulgaria should become the seventh, or (with the expected incorporation of Trieste) the eighth, republic in the South Slav federation, side by side with Slovenia, Croatia, Serbia, Macedonia, Montenegro, and Bosnia-Herzegovina. Under this variant Bulgarian claims to coequal leadership would be minimized, and the argument for making Belgrade the federal capital would be irresistible.

In January 1945 Yugoslav leaders, on visit to Moscow, were dismayed to discover that Stalin appeared committed to the Bulgarian variant. They rallied to present their own views forcefully, and apparently Stalin swung over to the Yugoslav view. On the eve of the Yalta Conference the entire question was shelved, however, when the British government protested against the idea of allowing Bulgaria to escape the obligations incumbent upon it as an ex-enemy state through federating with Yugoslavia, a member of the United Nations coalition. Perhaps the British note gave Moscow a convenient escape, at least temporarily, from the dilemma posed by the conflicting Yugoslav and Bulgarian claims.

After the conclusion of the Bled agreements of August 1, 1947, both Yugoslav and Bulgarian leaders denied any urgent interest in creating a South Slav federation.[3] Yet the provisions of Bled, as since revealed, can hardly be understood except as preparation for creating a federation. Bulgaria agreed to transfer the substantial area and population of Bulgarian or Pirin Macedonia to the Yugoslav Macedonian republic. This promise represented a major abandonment of Bulgarian claims to a decisive voice in the future of Macedonia. In September and October 1944 the Bulgarian Communists had attempted to retain control over the Communist movement of Macedonia, only to be overruled by Moscow in favor of the Yugoslav Communist party, whereas in 1947 they agreed to the unification of Macedonia on Yugoslav terms. In return Bulgaria was to receive back three small border areas which had been annexed by Yugoslavia in 1920. In 1945, when Mr. Byrnes had proposed that the status of these three border strips be considered, Mr. Molotov had rejected the proposal, denying even the existence

[3] E.g. Georgi Dimitrov, press conference, August 2, 1947; as reported in *The New York Times*, August 4, 1947.

of any dispute over them. It must be assumed that in agreeing to transfer Pirin Macedonia to Yugoslavia the Bulgarian leaders looked to their compensation, not in the three small border strips, but in the acquisition of Greek Western Thrace with its valuable tobacco industry and an outlet to the Aegean.

At Bled tentative plans were presumably made also for establishing a South Slav and perhaps a wider Balkan federation. The timetable for the execution of these projects was upset by the failure of the Greek Communists to win out speedily in the civil war and by the presumed decision of Moscow to give only its political and propagandist blessing, while withholding any direct military assistance from General Markos's forces.

The cooling off of the Soviet leadership to the various projects for a Balkan federation was indicated in an *Izvestiia* article of late January 1948. In a press conference at Bucharest the late Georgi Dimitrov had made certain rather vague and innocuous references—a small change of good will rather common among Balkan politicians—to an eventual federation. The sharp denunciation by Moscow, out of all proportion to Dimitrov's own statement, meant that the Soviet leadership was following the concrete behind-the-scenes preparation of the federation and now felt that its realization would not serve the interests of Soviet hegemony, perhaps because of the growing difficulties of "managing" Tito and of infiltrating the Yugoslav regime with Soviet agents.[4]

After the Yugoslav-Soviet rupture of June 1948 Soviet policy mobilized a multiplicity of national and territorial claims directed against the unity and territorial integrity of Yugoslavia. The Yugoslav ambition to incorporate Pirin Macedonia was denounced as

[4] (Author's note, 1959) Additional though far from complete light has been thrown on the question of the Yugoslav-Bulgarian federation, 1944–8. See Vladimir Dedijer: *Tito* (New York: Simon-Schuster; 1953).

"Fascist imperialism," and the Cominform demand for the "liberation" of Yugoslav Macedonia reached a strident pitch. Albania was swiftly "emancipated" from Yugoslav tutelage and brought under direct Soviet domination, and its claims to "liberate" the Albanians of Metohija-Kosovo were supported vehemently in the Cominform press. The pro-Yugoslav Giulian Communist party in Trieste was stripped of its role, which was transferred to pro-Stalinist and anti-Tito party elements. Hungary and Rumania raised vigorous protests against the alleged persecution of their conationals in Yugoslavia. Insofar as political and propagandist pressure could do so, Soviet-directed policy organized a menacing ring of national claims around Yugoslavia.

One of the ideological claims advanced by the Soviet regime—one which has won it widespread sympathy and active support in many countries where national and racial discrimination and oppression contradict the powerful idea of human equality and fraternity—is that it has eliminated within its own borders conflicts based on national differences and that only a Communist regime can solve this and related problems elsewhere. Proponents of this claim usually fail to explain that within the Soviet Union, cultures are permitted to differ only in form, or rather in language. Uniformity of ideological purpose and even of content is enforced from above. The present and future "content" of each national culture is determined, not by spontaneous development from below, but by governmental and party decisions. In the absence of genuine self-expression it is hard to judge from a distance how far the basic problem of enabling peoples of different traditions both to develop their own cultures and to live constructively with other groups has, in fact, been resolved, and how far it has merely been adjusted to the demands of a monolithic system of control. Certainly, the periodic purges of "nationalists" within the

Soviet republics, the wartime uprooting of several of the Soviet nationalities, and the large proportion of non-Russians among the Soviet nonreturners are factors which require much more careful analysis than they have yet received.

Beyond its own borders and within its self-arrogated sphere of domination the Soviet government and the local Communist parties have not hesitated to appeal to rival national and territorial claims in order to strengthen their control. Of course, this policy has been merely an additional tool supplementing the basic factors of control: the presence (except in Yugoslavia) of Soviet armies after the close of the war, ruthless promotion of Communist parties as chosen instruments of rule, step-by-step weakening and suppression of rival parties, social forces, and institutions. Each satellite country, through its ruling party, has been forced to look to Moscow as the supreme and, increasingly, the sole arbiter of its national and territorial ambitions. "Loyal service" to Soviet interests has become the sole path to national self-enhancement and self-preservation. Under the decisive criterion of Soviet interest, some nationality claims have been pressed with violence, others have been placed on ice, while claims now latent may be revived at a wave of the Soviet wand. The advance of Soviet power across most of East Central Europe found many long-standing national disputes and a patchwork of conflicting national claims in being; it did not invent them. Neither can it claim to have solved them in any basic and enduring sense. Rather, it has manipulated them ruthlessly to enhance its own monolithic control and to strengthen its chosen instruments of local rule.

In a single decade two tidal waves of great-power expansion have swept over the hundred million people of East Central Europe. "Small-power imperialism," which exerted its blight on their development and on their inadequate efforts at regional co-operation between the two wars, has been an accessory rather than a prime cause of the resulting catastrophic interruption of their national and cultural advance. As one consequence of Nazi and Soviet exploitation of them, the excesses of local nationalisms may well have surrendered permanently their compelling attraction for the sorely oppressed peoples of Inner Europe.

:9:

PEACEMAKING, 1946[1]

[*January 1947*]

INTRODUCTORY NOTE · When the wartime alliance had sealed its victory over Germany in May 1945, it seemed logical and feasible to begin the peacemaking, even before the defeat of Japan, by drawing up treaties with Italy, a cobelligerent on the side of the Allies for almost two years, and with the former Axis satellites. The issues to be settled, while numerous and complicated, seemed not intractable to good will and compromise. The Western powers were also eager to get ahead with a state treaty with Austria (see below, Ten, "The Treaty with Austria"), which had been promised its independence and which had already established a freely elected government; repeatedly Molotov turned this proposal down flat.

The stubbornness with which the Soviet leadership used questions of procedure to press its demands on its recent allies was first displayed publicly in these sixteen months of negotiation. "Peacemaking, 1946" is a review of the procedures of negotiation, not of the substance of the issues. The latter can be followed vividly in James F. Byrnes, *Speaking Frankly* (New York: Harper; 1947), and, more historically, in *The Search for Peace Settlements* by Redvers Opie, Joseph W. Ballantine, Paul Birdsall, Jeannette E. Muther, and Clarence E. Thurber (Washington, D. C.: The Brookings Institution; 1951).

[1] *International Organization*, Vol. I, No. 1 (February 1947), pp. 22–32.

When the thunderclaps of charges and countercharges had faded, and the snowfall of drafts and counterdrafts had been swept away, the Western powers had gained a few concessions in the treaties with the East European satellites. But Soviet pressure had won the reality of power throughout that part of Europe by actions taken far from the green tables in Lancaster House and the Palais du Luxembourg. Similarly, the Italian treaty gave a few sops to Soviet intransigence, but denied it the stranglehold it had sought. By the time the treaties were ready to be signed they merely registered the partition of Europe which had been shaped by the strategy of World War II.

*

THE first days of December 1946 saw the completion of the first round of the peace treaties. Except for the verification of the texts and the final arrangements for signature, the treaties with Italy, Rumania, Bulgaria, Hungary, and Finland were now ready, after fifteen months of backbreaking and often heartbreaking effort. The initial installment of peacemaking had, in fact, taken more than fifteen months, for several of the thorniest questions—notably, the disposition of the Italian colonies, freedom of commercial navigation on the Danube, and Italian reparation—had received their preliminary going over at Potsdam. And at least one question, the disposition of the Italian colonies, had been postponed for later settlement.

The period of negotiation saw four lengthy sessions of the Council of Foreign Ministers, at London in September–October 1945, at Paris in April–May and June–July 1946, and at New York in November–December 1946. The procedure of peacemaking was also one of the principal topics at the conference of the three Foreign Ministers at Moscow in December 1945. In addition, the deputies of the Foreign Ministers had been at work almost continuously since mid-January

1946, and numerous committees of the council had held hundreds of meetings on special aspects of the treaties. Finally, a conference of twenty-one Allied states, meeting in Paris from July 29 to October 15, had reviewed the draft treaties and presented its recommendations in great detail.

At the end of this wearisome process, relief at the thought that the first round of peacemaking had actually been completed prevailed over disappointment at the amount of time it had consumed and the tensions it had brought to light. But there was no room for complacency when it was realized that the settlements with Germany and Japan and the establishment of Austrian and Korean independence were still to be worked out.

The comparisons which have usually been drawn between the present process of treaty making and that of 1919 have not been to the advantage of the statesmen of the present. It is easy to point out that the treaty of Versailles was drafted and imposed upon Germany in a matter of some five months. It is usually forgotten that an Allied decision on German reparations was reached only in 1921 and that a temporarily workable arrangement was negotiated in 1924. Similarly, the settlement with Turkey which became a reality in 1923 was very different from the terms which had originally been laid down in Paris. Of course, any such comparisons have meaning only if they take into consideration the contribution made by the peacemaking process to a lasting peace between victors and defeated and among the victors.

The Paris Conference of 1919, which began as a conference of all the victor states, conducted its real work in private meetings of the Big Five, later the Big Four, and for a time the Big Three, for the great powers had to make peace with each other before they could impose it on the defeated countries. Unlike the general conference of 1919, which had mainly a ceremonial role, the Paris Conference of 1946 worked for long hours and with grim seriousness.

In the peacemaking of 1945–6 it was recognized from the outset that in the absence of prior agreements among the principal victors it was necessary for them first to harmonize their views on the main lines of the settlements. The Potsdam arrangements provided for the drafting of the treaties by a council of foreign ministers of the five principal victors. The expectation was that the ministers, at a first meeting, would block in the broad outlines of the settlements, leaving it to their deputies and staffs to fill in the detailed provisions of the treaties. At a second meeting the ministers would review the work of the deputies and decide any outstanding questions. The draft treaties would then be examined in a general conference of the Allied states, and the recommendations of the conference would be studied by the council in preparing the final drafts.

The treaty-making arrangements contained one further provision of great importance. It was agreed at Potsdam that in the drafting of the five treaties decisions would be taken by the powers which had been signatory to the surrender terms, except that for the drafting of the Italian treaty France would be considered a signatory to the armistice. This meant that within the Council of Five, four governments would be responsible for drafting the treaty with Italy, three for the treaties with Rumania, Bulgaria, and Hungary, and two for the treaty with Finland. This flexible and apparently expeditious program, to which France and China gave their concurrence, soon ran into unforeseen difficulties.

At the opening meeting of its first session in London, on September 11, 1945, the council agreed unanimously that all five Foreign Ministers would be present at, and participate in, the discussions of all the treaties, while decisions would be adopted on the basis of the "four-three-two" formula. After nine days of discussion, during which the outlines of the Italian and Rumanian settlements were reviewed inconclusively and a beginning was made on a review of those with Hungary and Bulgaria, Mr. Molotov suddenly demanded that the council reverse its previous decision on procedure. He now insisted that the council's decision of September 11 had been "illegal" and that it was "a violation of the Potsdam decisions" for the French and Chinese representatives to attend discussions of treaties on which they did not have deciding votes. From then on, for nearly two weeks, the Soviet delegation pressed, with all five Ministers present, for the complete exclusion of the Chinese and the partial exclusion of the French Foreign Minister. It must be said in passing that there had been nothing in the conduct of the two Ministers to justify this abrupt change in the Soviet attitude. The Chinese had been largely silent although they had submitted written drafts of treaties, and the French had played a similarly cooperative role.

During the remaining days of the London session little headway was made on questions of substance. The council meetings were largely devoted, on Soviet insistence, to discussions of procedure, in which vehement and endlessly reiterated accusations of "destroying Allied unity" took the place of any reasoned consideration of the question on its merits. The search for a reasonable compromise was pressed by the other Ministers, especially by Mr. Byrnes, but no suggestions found favor with Mr. Molotov. It can be assumed, however, that, if far-reaching concessions of substance had been made at once to the various Soviet demands, the procedural roadblock would have been removed just as suddenly as it had appeared.

After several days of discussion and of searching for a compromise which would have met the Soviet demand at least halfway without compounding the indignity inflicted on the representatives of France and China, Mr. Byrnes and Mr. Bevin agreed, with obvious reluctance and solely in order to get on with the work at hand, to accept Mr. Molotov's demand, subject to one condition, and they secured the consent of the French and Chinese representatives to this unwelcome change. The only condition which Mr. Byrnes advanced was that, in order to avoid a repetition of this "misunderstanding" at a later stage, the council should agree on a somewhat fuller statement of the arrangements for the future peace conference at the same time that it accepted the new Soviet interpretation of the Potsdam formula.

Having come so close to winning its contention, the Soviet delegation now presented an even more extreme demand. Mr. Molotov insisted that the record of the council's decision of September 11 must be revised by deleting the decision of that date on the procedure of the council and substituting for it the new Soviet text, which would then appear in the final record of the session as having been accepted on the date of September 11! All entries in the agreed records subsequent to that date were also to be revised to eliminate all references to the "illegal" participation of the French and Chinese Ministers in the work of the council and to make it appear that the new Soviet version of the "four-three-two" formula had been applied from the first meeting of the council. It is hardly necessary to recall that the council had issued numerous communiqués which had reported the French and Chinese Ministers present and in the chair, and that both of them continued to be present and to occupy the chair by rotation throughout the debates over the Soviet proposal for their exclusion! This most unusual proposal was rejected, as the Soviet representative no doubt intended it to be, and the council adjourned its London session *sine die* and without approving a final record of its decisions or issuing a communiqué.

In retrospect, as at the time, it can only be assumed that Mr. Molotov was so dissatisfied with the course of the first days' discussions, particularly with the poor welcome received by his proposals to transfer Trieste outright to Yugoslavia, to establish a Soviet trusteeship over Tripolitania, and, in effect, to repeal the Yalta Declaration insofar as it made provision for the establishment of representative regimes in Rumania and Bulgaria, that he made up his mind to suspend the Potsdam agreement to expedite the five treaties and embarked on a campaign to test the nerves and the degree of determination of the other four governments. It is interesting to note, however, that although the London session failed to agree on a final protocol, the substantive decisions of that session, few though they were, actually formed the basis of the work of the deputies when they finally began their labors in January 1946.

During the discussions of the Soviet reinterpretation of the "four-three-two" formula Secretary Byrnes had urged the council also to clarify the arrangements for the peace conference, but the Soviet Foreign Minister refused even to discuss this question until the council adopted without condition his own proposals on procedure. Three months later this intransigence was somewhat relaxed. In December 1945 at Moscow the compromise proposal which Mr. Byrnes had advanced at London was adopted with minor modifications, thus enabling the council to resume its work. The role of the peace conference was further clarified in January 1946 through an exchange of letters between M. Bidault and Mr. Byrnes, the latter acting for the three Ministers who had participated in the Moscow Conference. With this clarification, which emphasized the right of the future peace conference to examine all aspects of the draft treaties, the French government accepted the Moscow formula. The Chinese government also gave its concurrence, while reserving its rights with respect to the settlements with Germany and Japan.

The Moscow protocol contained one provision which

was dubious in language and in law. It stated that "the peace treaties will come into force immediately after they have been ratified by the Allied states signatory to the respective armistices. . . ." This unfortunate departure from customary international practice would have allowed any Allied state except the Big Four to claim the benefits of the Italian treaty without accepting any obligations on its own part. The *lapsus* was pointed out at the Paris Conference, which, by a simple majority, recommended adoption of a new article that "the provisions of the present treaty shall not confer any rights or benefits on any State named in the Preamble . . . unless such State becomes a party to the treaty by deposit of its instrument of ratification." This necessary correction of the Moscow protocol was inserted into the Italian draft treaty by the Council of Ministers in December 1946. Without this safeguarding clause the Yugoslav government, which had withdrawn in protest from the final plenary session of the Paris Conference and had announced that it would not sign the treaty with Italy unless it conformed more closely to Yugoslav demands, would have received the territorial and other benefits of the treaty without undertaking any obligations on its part toward Italy or the Free Territory of Trieste.

The Moscow reinterpretation of the "four-three-two" formula was applied in the work of the Council of Deputies, which began in London in mid-January 1946. The French deputy took part only in drafting the Italian treaty, while the Finnish treaty was considered only by the Soviet and British deputies. Since one of the delegations was not empowered to change by one iota the positions previously adopted by its minister, the deputies' range of effective negotiation was narrowly circumscribed. However, their intensive study of the treaty problems resulted in the first detailed examination of the numerous treaty proposals, in clarifying a large number of technical and legal points, and in clearing the ground for the major decisions, which, under the circumstances, could only be taken by the Foreign Ministers in person.

When the Ministers resumed their meetings at Paris in late April, it was uncertain whether the Soviet delegation would again insist on the strict application of the "four-three-two" formula. At the first meeting, however, Mr. Molotov brushed aside this question, over which he had broken off the London session, by moving that all four Ministers participate in all meetings of the council. M. Bidault was, of course, in the chair at the first meeting; the Paris press had shown some sensitiveness on this question; a constitutional referendum and an election were approaching. In practice the French representative took almost no part in the discussion of the treaties with the four satellites, while the American delegation, which continued to abstain from the discussion of the Finnish treaty, was subsequently free to offer from the floor of the conference certain recommendations on that treaty.

In the work of the Council of Foreign Ministers the governments of the smaller Allies had no direct part, while on the other hand Italy received a much fairer hearing than Germany had been granted in 1919. At its London session the council had invited the various Allied governments to submit their suggestions and recommendations in writing. Most of the governments presented memoranda, usually dealing with their direct claims and interests. In addition, Australia, New Zealand, and the Union of South Africa had requested, and received at that session, an opportunity to present their views orally to the council on the Yugoslav-Italian boundary. On this occasion Mr. Evatt of Australia advanced the claim of the smaller Allied states to participate fully in the deliberations of the council. His proposal, if adopted, would have meant entrusting the drafting of the treaties to a general conference as in 1919. It is doubtful whether such a procedure would have had much effect on the actual process of treaty drafting, or whether most of the Allied states would have relished this enlargement of their political role. When they were eventually confronted at Paris with the full range of problems over which the Big Four had tussled for nearly a year, many of the Allied delegations were none too happy over their added responsibilities.

On a few matters, mainly territorial in character, the council heard, at a formative stage, the views of an ex-enemy state, long since accepted, it is true, as a cobelligerent on the Allied side. On the future boundary between Yugoslavia and Italy the views of the two governments were heard four times in the council. On the Italo-Austrian boundary both governments presented detailed memoranda and were heard both by the deputies and by the conference. The Italian government also presented its views in detail on the Franco-Italian boundary, on reparations and war damages, and on many other problems. In addition, special commissions of the council carried out on-the-spot investigations of the Yugoslav-Italian and Franco-Italian boundary questions. Proposals for similar consultations with representatives of the four Eastern satellites were turned aside by the Soviet delegation. Finally, each of the five governments presented its case at length in full sessions of the conference and, by invitation, before various of its commissions. At Paris their delegations had full freedom of personal access to the various Allied delegations, unlike the situation of the German delegation in 1919. Full hearings naturally did not lighten the burdens imposed on them by many of the provisions of the treaties, and several of the ex-enemy delegations showed great diffidence in pressing their views, presumably because of the limited degree of independence exercised by their governments within their countries. Only Bulgaria proved able and willing to present far-reaching claims of its own.

As the Council of Ministers progressed haltingly through its agenda at the two Paris sessions, between April and July, the question of the future peace conference came to occupy an important place in its discussions. For a long time the Soviet representative maintained that the date for the conference could be set only when the draft treaties had been agreed down to the last detail. Since several score of major and minor matters were still in dispute, it sometimes seemed as if the conference could never be called. Secretary Byrnes maintained that the Potsdam and Moscow agreements merely called for the great powers doing all they could to advance the drafting of the treaties, and that these agreements had been intended to facilitate the calling of the conference, not to prevent the other Allies from having their say on the treaties.

Meanwhile, the council had agreed to postpone the disposition of the Italian colonies for consideration during the year following the coming into force of the treaty with Italy, and had accepted the international status for Trieste as a way out of another deadlock. In early July two decisions were taken in a single meeting of the council, which prepared the way for the calling of the conference. An agreement was reached on Italy's reparation deliveries to the Soviet Union only a few hours after it had been agreed to set the opening of the conference for July 29, without waiting for a complete agreement to be reached on all provisions of the treaties.

This decision automatically gave a far wider range of effective deliberation to the conference than could have been foreseen at Potsdam almost one year before. The conference, as it turned out, had before it two main groups of issues, some on which the council had reached agreement and others on which separate and unagreed drafts were submitted. In addition, the conference was able to assert its right to present recommendations of its own on subjects which had not been covered in the drafts submitted to it.

The decision to call the conference, itself the result of long negotiation, was only a prelude to further disputes. After the decision had been taken the actual dispatch of invitations was held up for several days, during which the Soviet delegation fought hard to secure the adoption by the council of its proposed draft rules of procedure to govern the work of the conference. In the arguments which followed the Soviet delegation implied more than once that the acceptance of these rules should be regarded as a condition for the issuance of the invitations and for the admission of the Allied governments to the conference. Mr. Byrnes defended the traditional right of a conference to determine its own rules of procedure, but he was willing to meet Mr. Molotov more than halfway by agreeing on draft rules which would then be circulated to the participating governments as a suggestion, and by promising to vote for the adoption of the agreed draft in the conference.

Concurrently, a further controversy developed over the organization of the conference. The Soviet draft rules provided, in effect, for the plenary conference to assemble only in the opening and closing sessions, and for the real work of the conference to be carried on in five commissions, one for each treaty, each commission to be composed of those states which were recognized by the council as having "actively waged war" against the respective ex-enemy state. This arrangement, if adopted, would have had some curious consequences. Belorussia and Ukraine, for instance, would have had full memberships on each of the five commissions, while France would have been a member only of the Italian commission, and Norway of none. It was pointed out repeatedly that these narrow limitations on the organization of the conference were not in harmony with the provisions of the Moscow protocol of December 1945, or of the Byrnes-Bidault exchange of letters of January 1946.

It was finally agreed to abandon the idea of having a separate commission for each treaty and to adopt a somewhat more functional arrangement. The council agreed to recommend the establishment of five political commissions, one for each treaty, two economic commissions, one each for the Italian treaty and for the Balkan and Finnish treaties, a military commission, and a legal and drafting commission. In the upshot France was represented on all the commissions, while a Norwegian delegate served on the legal and drafting commission. There were also discussions as to whether recommendations could be voted only by the commissions with, in the case of the two Balkan commissions, their more limited membership, or also by the plenary conference. In the end it was agreed that both the commissions and the conference would be able to vote on recommendations.

As soon as the conference had met and had passed to the working stage, the Soviet delegation again pressed for the adoption of the more restrictive rules which it had advocated and then abandoned in the Council of Ministers. Many days were consumed in controversy, and at times it seemed as if the conference would not be able to complete its organization, much less proceed to the work at hand. The Soviet representatives again accused other members of the council of having violated agreements, despite the clear record of the council's decisions. After the smoke and fury had cleared away, the rules adopted were substantially those which had been proposed by the council in July. In the course of the debates over procedure Mr. Byrnes had gone beyond the other Big Four delegations in asserting his desire to strengthen the role of the conference; he stated that, in the later deliberations of the Ministers, he would support recommendations made by a two-thirds majority of the conference even if they ran counter to the vote of the American delegation in the conference.

The conference served the purpose for which it had been planned. It gave recognition to the views of the Allies upon the making of the treaties. Its role was, of course, limited from the outset by the fact that the

Big Four entered it pledged to vote for the decisions which they had already arrived at. Such questions as Italy's boundaries with Yugoslavia, Austria, and France, the surrender of the Italian colonies, and the reparation deliveries to the Soviet Union by Italy, Hungary, Rumania, and Finland, could not have been effectively modified by the conference. On the other hand, the conference made important recommendations on Italian reparation deliveries to other Allied countries, on compensation for Allied properties in ex-enemy countries, on freedom of commercial navigation on the Danube, on the cession to Czechoslovakia of the bridgehead opposite Bratislava, on the Trieste statute, and on numerous economic and legal provisions. During the conference the Italian and Austrian governments also arrived at an agreement on the status of the German-speaking population of the South Tyrol, or upper Adige, which the Council of Ministers, in December, agreed to mention in the Italian treaty.

The obligation of the Big Four to "support" the council's decisions in the discussions of the conference was interpreted by the Soviet delegation to mean that the other three delegations were under obligation to exert all their influence to win the votes of other delegations for the support of agreed decisions. The Soviet-led "Slav bloc," which emerged as a striking feature of the conference, showed good teamwork and careful timing. Other great-power delegations interpreted the pledge of "support" to mean that they would cast their votes for the agreed decisions but that they were under no obligation to "strong-arm" other Allied delegations into voting in the same way. Many of the Allied delegations, in fact, cast their votes in a manner intended to demonstrate their independence from domination by any great power. This circumstance did not prevent the Soviet delegation and press from asserting that other members of the Big Four were exerting all kinds of improper pressure on other delegations and were using other delegates as "stooges" to raise obstacles to the acceptance by the conference of the agreed decisions of the council. In this respect Soviet resentment appears to have been directed particularly against Mr. Evatt, who, taking the council's invitation literally, had presented a large number of draft amendments to the treaties.[2]

At its close the conference referred back to the Foreign Ministers a long series of recommendations, some supported by a two-thirds vote, others by a simple majority. Many of the recommendations represented real improvements of substance or language over the previous work of the council, in which there had developed a reluctance to bring up suggestions for technical or textual improvements in view of the slight chance of their being considered by all four delegations on their merits.

For a time it was hoped that during the latter part of the conference its recommendations could be considered at once by the Council of Ministers, which could then incorporate those which it adopted into the final texts of the treaties, the latter then to be signed before the conference disbanded. For political and technical reasons this schedule proved to be impossible to follow, and instead it was agreed to hold a further meeting of the council on November 4 in New York. When the Foreign Ministers resumed their labors they were again confronted by most of the same questions which had been before them so often before. It was anyone's guess whether the council could complete the drafts of the treaties at that session or at any later one. After three weeks of zestless leafing through of old controversies it at last became evident that the Soviet delegation was now prepared to make certain concessions in order to conclude the treaties. It is a fair comment to say that if the same compromises could have been reached during the first three or six months

[2] E.g. V. Borisov: "*O pozitsii avstraliiskoi delegatsii v Parizhe*" (Concerning the Australian Delegation's Position at Paris), *Novoe Vremia*, No. 19) (Moscow: October 1, 1946), pp. 30–1.

after Potsdam, a great contribution would have been made to inter-Allied unity and to the feeling of confidence throughout the United Nations. As it was, the completion of the treaties was received, if not with indifference, at least without any noticeable upsurge of enthusiasm.

Could the procedural difficulties which were so conspicuous in the treaty-making process have been foreseen and avoided? It seems fair to conclude that if the original arrangements had been interpreted in a reasonable and conciliatory spirit they would have been adequate to the purpose. Likewise, once the initial obstacles raised by Molotov at London had been by-passed at Moscow, much more progress could have been made if the Soviet delegation to the meetings of the deputies had been empowered to advance, or even to consider, possible adjustments and compromises. Unfortunately, in a negotiation of this kind the most reluctant government determines the maximum rate of progress. In the work of the Council of Foreign Ministers the search for a basis of settlement could begin only after the Soviet delegation had become convinced that further delay was no longer working to the advantage of Soviet interests.

Since the Soviet method of negotiation, illustrated in the history of the Council of Foreign Ministers, is based on an assumption that relations between states are regulated by the rivalry of competing systems, their negotiators tend to turn every decision, whether vital or trifling, into a test of endurance and will power. One by-product of this approach is ordinarily to confine negotiation to formal across-the-table debate and to rule out the less formal methods which might assist in reaching an understanding.

At the end of the first fifteen months of treaty making the advantages to the Soviet Union of further delays tended to be outweighed by growing disadvantages. In the intervening period the balance of political forces in western Europe and Italy had been tested in free elections, while Soviet predominance in the countries of Eastern Europe had been heavily reinforced by many forms of political and economic action. The peace treaties contained no provisions which would admit of a challenge to the predominant control of the Soviet Union over the affairs of the four Eastern satellites, but the Italian treaty had not added greatly to the pressures which the Soviet Union could bring to bear on Italy. In many respects the treaties simply registered the consequences of a new division of power which had come into being in Europe during the final stages of the war. The implications of this new division of power were of a nature to discourage those who feel that exclusive spheres of power, whether they be regarded as offensive or defensive in the motivations alleged to justify them, must be held to a minimum through co-operative action of the great powers if the general structure of international co-operation and security is to function effectively in the postwar world.

:10:

THE TREATY WITH AUSTRIA[1]

[*April 1950*]

INTRODUCTORY NOTE · The situation of sheer Soviet inaction, which I described in April 1950, persisted even longer than I foresaw at that time. During his three last years Stalin refused to come to an agreement on the few unresolved issues of the Austrian state treaty. Perhaps his annoyance at seeing Austria slip through his fingers constituted a minor resentment, compared with his smouldering anger over the defeat of his blockade of Berlin, the growth of the North Atlantic Treaty Organization, the successful defiance of his thunderbolts by Yugoslavia, and, above all, the failure of Communist aggression in Korea. Or perhaps he cannily preferred to retain even a weakened grip on eastern Austria just in case something turned up to give him control of the entire country.

Meanwhile, whenever the Soviet government accused the Western powers of not wanting to "reduce tension," they could and did point to Soviet stubbornness in refusing to sign an Austrian treaty even on terms to which it had already agreed. And when the post-Stalin leadership decided to re-enter the arena of negotiation, the long overdue conclusion of the Austrian treaty—against Molotov's strong resistance, as we have learned from Khrushchev's attacks on him—offered an inexpensive price of admission. However, since 1950 the Soviet position in

[1] *International Organization*, Vol. IV, No. 2 (May 1950), pp. 219–35. Copyright 1950 by the World Peace Foundation.

Austria had become much weaker. Participating in the general upsurge of the European economy, Austria was becoming less vulnerable to Soviet economic pressures, and the Austrian Communists had lost their last seats in parliament.

In March 1955 the Soviet government proposed the completion of the Austrian treaty, and, with relatively minor changes from the terms which had been hammered out by late 1949, the treaty was signed on May 15, 1955, and the last of the Soviet and Western troops left Austrian soil on October 14, 1955. The Austrian treaty is one of the relatively few success stories in Western dealings with Soviet ambitions. Here the West also had a number of trumps, of which the most valuable was the unshaken determination of the Austrians to regain their freedom.

*

BY THE Moscow Declaration of 1943 the Soviet, British, and United States governments pledged their efforts to re-establish a "free and independent Austria" after the defeat of Germany. In the spring of 1950, five years after the liberation of Austria from German forces and Nazi rule, this pledge, like many other wartime declarations of aims, remained unfulfilled and the Austrians were still asking, as a Viennese witticism put it, when they would be "liberated from their liberators."

During 1946 the Soviet negotiators successfully blocked all Western efforts to begin negotiations for a four-power treaty on the Austrian settlement. Active discussions carried on throughout 1947 gave no grounds for hope that agreement could be reached then or ever, but at least they clarified the wide divergence in views between East and West and measured the degree of determination on both sides. Real progress was made in the first half of 1948, only to be cancelled out in the second half of the year, while the Soviet blockade of Berlin tested the willingness and ability of the Western powers to stand their ground. A slight shift in the position of the Soviet government, opening the way for a partial relaxation of East-West tension in Europe, was foreshadowed by the renewal of the Austrian negotiations in February 1949, and a major step towards a settlement in Austria was taken in June of that year, at the Paris meeting of the Council of Foreign Ministers. From this impetus the deputies for the Austrian treaty proceeded to close many of the remaining gaps, and the last months of 1949 brought close a definite prospect of an early settlement.

In the first weeks of 1950, however, the progress of the treaty came to a full stop. Meeting, and as regularly adjourning, the deputies could agree on March 1 only to meet again on April 26. Was the Soviet government clinging to the unresolved clauses of the draft treaty out of resentment at its failure, in 1949, to prevent the strengthening of the new regime in Western Germany? Or was it keeping alive the remaining points of disagreement in Austria to use as bargaining counters, in case the much discussed proposal for a Truman-Stalin meeting became a reality? Or was it merely reluctant to see Austria relieved of the presence and pressure of its forces of occupation?

The treaty with Austria is not a treaty of peace. The special status of Austria dates from the Moscow Declaration on Austria, of November 1, 1943. By it the United States, British, and Soviet governments declared null and void the *Anschluss* of March 15, 1938, and agreed that Austria "shall be liberated from German domination." They expressed their desire "to see re-established a free and independent Austria." [2] The treaty with Austria is, therefore, to be a "state treaty" which, according to its draft preamble, re-establishes Austria "as a free, independent and democratic state."

[2] "Declaration on Austria," Department of State Bulletin, Vol. IX, p. 310. The French provisional government concurred in this statement of policy by a declaration of November 16, 1943.

It could be argued that no treaty with Austria was needed. Once Austria had been restored within its frontiers and a freely elected government had been recognized, the four occupying powers could, theoretically, have settled their various questions through negotiation with that government and then have withdrawn their forces at an agreed date. In actuality, the "liberating" powers have needed to come to an agreement with each other even more than with the Austrian government. The questions which have divided them, especially those relating to Yugoslav territorial claims and to the disposition of German assets in eastern Austria, are crucial to the future independence and stability of Austria. Decided in accordance with the original Soviet demands, they would have handed over a helpless and hopeless Austria to Soviet domination; on the basis of Western proposals, Austria would at least be master in its own home and would have a full opportunity to seek economic ties of its own choosing.

Even in planning for the occupation of Austria an effort was made to differentiate the function of the Allied forces from that which they were expected to fulfill in Germany. The four-power agreement on zones of occupation provided, for example, for the joint occupation of the *Innere Stadt*, the central district of Vienna containing the principal administrative, economic, and cultural institutions. In the negotiations of the European Advisory Commission this key district had been claimed during many weeks for occupation by Soviet forces alone. It was finally placed under four-power control through the stubborn insistence of the American delegation. The agreement on control arrangements established "an Allied Commission to exercise supreme authority until the establishment of a freely elected Austrian government recognized by the four powers."[3] Thus, in contrast to the parallel

[3] Agreement on Zones of Occupation in Austria and the Administration of the City of Vienna, signed July 9, 1945, in the European

agreement for control in Germany, the agreement for Austria foresaw the early emergence of a self-governing regime.

An even greater contrast to Germany is found in the fact that an Austrian government was in actual operation in eastern Austria and was attempting to re-establish the political and economic unity of the country long before the Allied Commission began its work. A coalition cabinet, headed by the veteran socialist leader, Karl Renner, had been established in Vienna on April 25, 1945, and had received unilateral Soviet recognition. After the establishment of the Allied Commission and after the impenetrable lines of military demarcation gave way to the more porous zonal boundaries, the provisional Renner government was promptly broadened in September to include representative figures from the western *Länder* and on October 20 received four-power recognition. After the free elections of December 1945 the government was reorganized as a coalition of the People's Party and the Socialists, and the Communists, who received only five per cent of the votes (four seats out of one hundred sixty-five in the *Nationalrat*), were excluded. The new government was in turn recognized by the Allied Council. In the election of October 9, 1949, the Communist party again polled five per cent of the votes, and the same coalition has continued to govern. The leaders of postwar Austria have shown political skill, patriotism, and a real attachment to political democracy. The disputes between urban and rural parties, between socialists and clericals, which had wracked interwar Austria, have been subordinated to the need for presenting a united front to the occupying powers

Advisory Commission; Agreement on Control Machinery in Austria, signed July 4, 1945, in the European Advisory Commission. The author of this article conducted these negotiations, under the authority of the late John G. Winant, the United States representative on the E.A.C. The term "Allied Commission" was chosen instead of "Allied Control Commission" in order to emphasize the difference between the status of Austria and that of Germany.

and for finding the means for political and economic survival.

As the occupying powers began to show signs of seeking the Austrians' good will, the Austrian government was increasingly alert to add to its powers. In January 1946 when the Allied Council approved in principle the free movement of surplus goods among the zones, the way was opened to restore gradually the economic unity of Austria. In March 1946 Austria was permitted to exchange diplomatic representatives with all countries except Germany and Japan.

The most important step in relaxing Allied control was the adoption of a new control plan on June 28, 1946. From then on all laws enacted by the Austrian government, with the exception of constitutional provisions and international agreements, were to enter into force after thirty-one days unless unanimously disapproved by the Allied Council. Thus in Austria the principle of the great-power veto worked in reverse, to enlarge the authority of the Figl government. The provision for unanimous approval of international agreements was not too serious a limitation, for agreements with any of the occupying powers were exempt from control by the Allied Council. In December 1946, the Austrian government received blanket authority to conclude trade agreements with foreign countries. Shortly thereafter it rejected a Soviet proposal for setting up a series of Soviet-Austrian companies, on the "fifty-fifty" basis which has been one of the chief Soviet instruments for control of the economies of Hungary and Rumania. In 1948 Austria was thus able to join the Organization for European Economic Cooperation and to benefit substantially from the Marshall Plan, despite loud Soviet outcries against its "enslavement to American capitalism." By the spring of 1947 the Allied Commission mainly exercised functions of supervision and advice.

Economic recovery, which had proceeded only haltingly for two years, took a marked upturn in the spring of 1947, with the allocation of $100 million in American aid, followed by Economic Co-operation Administration (E.C.A.) assistance. Thanks to its wider freedom of action, the Figl government was able, in 1947, to carry through an effective currency reform. Soviet acquiescence in it was obtained only after great delay and after granting special concessions for the conversion of large Soviet-held stocks of Austrian currency acquired as loot or under guise of "occupation costs." Even this inequitable demand could not vitiate the process of economic recovery.

When Byrnes's direct appeals in 1946, for a reduction in the numbers of occupying troops, and hence in the burden of occupation costs, fell on barren ground, Marshall forced the pace by renouncing all Austrian payment of United States occupation costs, beginning July 1, 1947. The Soviet government, which had previously exacted the lion's share in these costs, more than the three other powers together, gradually reduced its demands thereafter. Although it has never renounced them entirely, Soviet occupation costs were brought down within reason, and the number of Soviet troops, no longer able to live off the land so freely as before, was cut to garrison size. Potentially, the Austrian economy was better equipped to stand on its own feet than before the war, because of the expansion in industrial plants and in hydroelectric power during the Nazi period. But all these advantages were only potential until the Austrians could recover full control of their own country.

As early as January 1946 American officials concerned with Austrian affairs were pointing out to Washington that the conclusion of an Austrian treaty should be disentangled from the problems of Germany and should be taken up with the negotiation of the peace treaties for Italy and the Soviet satellites.[4] The State

[4] A recommendation to this effect was presented by John S. Erhardt, United States Minister. A similar recommendation was submitted to the Department of State by the author of this article, in January 1946, after a brief mission to Vienna.

Department, in consultation with other executive agencies, now began the preparation of a draft treaty, and at the second session of the Council of Foreign Ministers (Paris, April–May 1946) Secretary Byrnes made strenuous efforts to include the Austrian treaty in the agenda. When Molotov objected to this, alleging that no concrete proposals had been presented, Byrnes hastened, at the beginning of June, to circulate the draft of a treaty with Austria.

In the second part of the Paris session (June–July 1946) Byrnes pressed hard, but without success, for discussion of the Austrian treaty and for an agreement limiting the number of occupation troops stationed in Austria as well as in Italy and the Danubian satellites. Continuing his tactic of stalling, Molotov blandly asserted, six weeks after the United States draft had been circulated, that he had had no time to study it. In the meantime the Foreign Ministers had agreed, in June, that the treaties of peace with Hungary and Rumania would provide for stationing Soviet "lines of communication" troops there until Soviet troops were withdrawn from Austria. In 1946 the Soviet government was in no hurry, by completing the Austrian treaty, to abandon the legal basis for maintaining Soviet forces in Hungary and Rumania.

Upon completion of the Italian and satellite treaties in December 1946 Molotov at last agreed that the Austrian and German treaties would be the next items on the Foreign Ministers' agenda, and their deputies began discussion of the Austrian treaty on January 14, 1947, in London. From these meetings the Austrian question passed to the Moscow session of the Foreign Ministers (March 10 to April 24, 1947). As East-West conflicts over Germany deepened, wide divergencies were also recorded on Austrian questions, and only a few minor points were resolved.

At Moscow, the Soviet government agreed in principle, though not in practice, to exempt from its claim for "German assets" Jewish-owned properties which had been confiscated after 1938, and to allow Austrian legislation to apply within certain limits to Soviet-owned properties. But it still insisted that the definition of the Soviet-owned "German assets" was a matter to be decided solely between itself and the Austrian government, and it gave all-out support to the Yugoslav claims to territory and reparations. The full range of Soviet demands, if accepted, would have bound Austria hand-and-foot through Soviet ownership of numerous industries operated on a basis of extraterritoriality. The Soviet industries within Austria would have been a lusty parasite preying upon the rest of the economy, depriving the country of any opportunity to become self-supporting, and reducing its political independence to a mere fiction. The Western powers, who were trying to help the Austrians become masters in their own house, and thus keep Austria from being absorbed into the Soviet orbit, could not accept these demands, and decided to sit them out. Austrians began to wonder whether the Russians were not aiming at incorporating eastern Austria, at least, into their sphere, leaving the rest of the country to fend for itself as best it might.

On the last day of the Moscow session the foreign ministers had agreed to continue the discussion of the Austrian problems through a Treaty Commission. Joseph M. Dodge, of Detroit, now replaced General Mark W. Clark as chief United States delegate, and K. N. Novikov took the place of Fedor T. Gusev, promoted to be Deputy Minister of Foreign Affairs. During eighty-five meetings between May 12 and October 11, 1947, no signs of agreement emerged, but after many procedural halts the commission succeeded in reviewing fully the legal and economic aspects of the problem of "German assets." Moving to London, the commission continued its meetings, before and during the fifth session of the Foreign Ministers (November 25 to December 15, 1947). A turning point was reached when the French delegate proposed, on November 28, that the commission give up the attempt to arrive at a mutually acceptable juridical definition of "German assets" and concentrate, instead, on determining which specific assets would be retained by the Soviet government and which would revert to Austrian ownership. Two days after the London session of the Foreign Ministers had broken up in ever more complete disagreement over Germany, the new Soviet deputy for the Austrian treaty, K. V. Koktomov, announced that he was willing to discuss this new approach, which had actually been suggested to the French delegation by the American negotiators.

On February 20, 1948, the deputies resumed their discussions with Samuel Reber replacing Dodge as the United States representative. Very important progress was made in reconciling conflicting views concerning German assets, but on May 25 the deputies were forced to break off their work because of the complete deadlock which had developed out of Soviet support for Yugoslav claims to Austrian territory and to reparations. Since the preceding March the Soviet government had been increasing its pressure on the Western position in Berlin, and the imposition of the Soviet blockade, in late June, left the Austrian negotiations in complete suspense. In Vienna, where the Western powers held a similarly isolated foothold, surrounded by Soviet-occupied territory, there were numerous pinpricks and incidents, but there was no parallel to the Soviet blockade of Berlin. After an interval of eight months, marked by the tense conflict between the Soviet blockade of Berlin and the Western airlift, the deputies resumed their task on February 9, 1949, with Ambassador Zarubin as the new Soviet deputy, only to suspend their meetings again on May 6 to await the outcome of the impending sixth session of the Council of Foreign Ministers, which was to meet as a condition of the Soviet government's abandonment of its ten-month-long blockade of Berlin.

Though barren of agreement concerning Germany, the Paris session of the Foreign Ministers (May 23 to

June 20, 1949) marked an important advance toward completion of the Austrian treaty. In a dramatic reversal Andrei Vyshinskii abandoned most of the Yugoslav claims, withdrawing the demand for cession of Austrian territory in return for minority guarantees protecting the Slovene and Croat minorities, and giving Yugoslavia the Austrian properties there, long since nationalized in any case, as a sop for the dropping of the Yugoslav claim for $150 million in reparations. In return the Soviet Union received a number of concessions which bolstered its economic interests in Austria. The deputies were also instructed to reach agreement on the treaty by September 1. When this date passed without agreement the four governments directed them to resume their work on September 22 in New York. During the General Assembly of the United Nations, the four Foreign Ministers also met informally, on September 26 and 28 and again on October 5, and settled some of the points still in dispute.

By mid-December the completion of the treaty was at last in sight, and only five relatively less important questions remained in dispute. At this point, however, the negotiations came to a standstill. The Soviet representative introduced a new and unforeseen obstacle. He declared that no further progress could be made until agreement was reached directly between the Soviet and Austrian governments on reimbursement to Moscow for certain supplies and technical services rendered by the Soviet occupation authorities. Article 48b of the draft treaty provides that Austria shall acknowledge and pay compensation for such claims of the occupying powers, although the United States, Britain, and France have announced that they will waive their own claims under this article. Reportedly, the full Soviet claims total about $6 million. The claims include food stocks and equipment seized by the Soviet forces in Austria and then turned over to the Austrian authorities, and are offset, in large part, by Austrian counterclaims for compensation for use of buildings, houses, grounds, and labor furnished by Austria to the Soviet forces. Since the Soviet-Austrian negotiations began in late September 1949, the Austrian government has given every indication of its desire to meet the Soviet claims more than halfway, while Moscow has delayed even replying to the Austrian proposals.

When the deputies resumed their talks at London, on January 9, 1950, the Soviet representative was still without instructions which would enable him to proceed to settle the few unresolved points, even on the terms previously stated by him. On January 18 the United States, British, and French Ambassadors at Moscow expressed to Deputy Foreign Minister Gromyko the deep concern of their governments and asked for assurances, which were not forthcoming, that the negotiations could be resumed shortly. At successive meetings held on January 24, February 15, and March 1 (followed by adjournment to April 26), Soviet deputy Zarubin gave no indication of how the Soviet-Austrian negotiation on compensation for occupation costs was progressing or when he would be willing to join with the other three deputies in a discussion of the remaining articles of the draft treaty.

From January 1947 until June 1949 one of the most bitterly contested questions concerning the Austrian treaty was whether southern Carinthia would be ceded to Yugoslavia or retained by Austria. Following the 1920 plebiscite, which has been generally regarded as well organized in procedure and equitable in its outcome, Carinthia south of the Karawanken mountains had been assigned to Yugoslavia, but Slovene nationalists were vociferous in denouncing the plebiscite and in demanding annexation of the Drau (Drava) valley, north of the mountain chain. In March 1945, after a much publicized visit to Moscow, Marshal Tito again raised an emphatic demand for the acquisition of southern Carinthia.

In a memorandum presented to the Council of Foreign Ministers on January 22, 1947, Yugoslavia formally advanced its claim to one third of Carinthia, an area of about 1,100 square miles. It can be estimated that the area contained about 80,000 Slovene-speaking and 100,000 German-speaking inhabitants, but most of the Slovene peasants, attached to their religion and to their homesteads, gave no support to the pro-Yugoslav agitation. On April 28, 1948, the Yugoslav government restated its claim, reducing it to an area of about 788 square miles, but including Villach and Klagenfurt, the principal cities and key junctions on the railway and highway routes between Vienna and northern Italy. Throughout these months of negotiation the Yugoslav claim received full Soviet backing, and Soviet support continued for many months after the estrangement between the two *Politburos* had become public knowledge in June 1948. After December 1948, however, Austrian sources gave out hints of a Soviet willingness to abandon the Yugoslav claim, provided further concessions were made in the question of the "German assets."

Finally, in June 1949 Foreign Minister Vyshinskii abandoned the Yugoslav claim to Austrian territory and agreed to the restoration of Austria's 1937 boundaries, on the basis of a compromise proposal which had been advanced by Reber on March 3, 1949. In the following months the deputies elaborated detailed guarantees to safeguard the rights of the Slav-speaking groups to form their own associations and to use their own languages locally for administrative purposes, in the press, and in elementary and secondary education. The Yugoslav demand for separate political and administrative autonomy for the Slav-speaking or bilingual region was rejected. The Carinthian Slovenes have traditionally lived on good terms with the Austrians, and their national-cultural identity should be adequately protected by these new safeguards against any revival of the oppressive measures which were practiced against them under the Nazi regime between 1938 and 1945.

The Soviet attempt to extract reparations from Austria has a long history, beginning with the Moscow Conference of 1943. In October 1943, while Soviet forces were about to liberate Kiev, Soviet diplomacy was already attempting to impose upon Austria an undefined and unlimited burden of reparations. At one of their first sessions Hull, Eden, and Molotov agreed that a declaration on Austria should be issued, encouraging the Austrians to "work their passage home" and promising independence. A draft declaration, introduced by Eden, was referred to the Drafting Commission, consisting of James C. Dunn, Sir William Strang, and Andrei Vyshinskii.[5] During several long sessions of the drafting commission Vyshinskii made one of his most determined and eloquent efforts, this time to insert a statement that "Austria bears full political and material responsibility for the war."

To this wording and its implications, strenuous objection was raised by the American and British delegates, who pointed out that, having ceased in 1938 to exist as a state, Austria could hardly bear "political responsibility" for the war, while "material responsibility" implied the exaction of unstated amounts of reparation. It was pointed out to Vyshinskii that the words "material responsibility for the war" could mean, in legal terms, that Austria would be obligated to make good all the damage inflicted upon all the United Nations during the course of hostilities, and that all Austrian property would cover only a small part of

[5] This account of the origins of the Declaration on Austria supplements substantially the brief report given in *The Memoirs of Cordell Hull*, Vol. II, p. 1297 (New York: Macmillan; 1948). As a member of the United States delegation, the author of this article participated in all the sessions of the Drafting Commission and attended most of the plenary sessions of the conference. Drafts of a declaration had been prepared independently, in Washington and London; upon comparing them in Moscow, members of the British delegation preferred the American version, which was then "loaned" to them and was submitted by Eden to the Conference.

these losses. On the other hand, if the three powers wished to see Austria re-established as an independent state, they should not begin by placing this vast burden on Austria. After long arguments the text of the declaration was watered down to read, somewhat cryptically, that "Austria is reminded . . . that she has a responsibility which she cannot evade for participation in the war on the side of Hitlerite Germany. . . ."

The demand for reparation, parried at Moscow in 1943, was strongly pressed at London in the negotiations of the European Advisory Commission (April–July 1945). The Soviet member pressed strongly, against American and British objections, for including in the control machinery a reparations division. After many weeks of controversy, and after a number of Soviet concessions had been secured in return, it was agreed to insert this provision. However, after prior notification to the Soviet delegate, the author of this article, as the American alternate representative, made an oral statement, circulated simultaneously in writing, that his government considered that the inclusion of a reparation division did not prejudge the question of whether or not Austria could or should pay reparations. Similar written reservations on this question were subsequently circulated by the British and French representatives.

Early in the Potsdam Conference (July–August 1945) the Soviet delegation presented its demands for reparations from Austria and Italy, as well as from Germany. In the Economic Commission, I. M. Maiskii pressed vigorously for $250 million in Austrian reparations.[6] Confronted with strong arguments concerning Austria's inability to provide reparations and the in-

[6] The author attended many sessions of the plenary conference, of the Foreign Ministers and the Economic Commission, as a member of the United States delegation. Because of another meeting he was absent from the plenary session at which the decision on "German assets" was adopted, and learned of the decision that evening. Cf. James F. Byrnes, *Speaking Frankly* (New York; 1947), pp. 161–3.

compatibility of such exactions with the Allies' declared intention of re-establishing Austria as an independent and presumably self-sustaining state, and desiring no doubt to concentrate its efforts on its vastly more important demands for German reparations, the Soviet delegation after several days withdrew its demand against Austria. The renunciation was not published, however, since it formed only one part of a later settlement with Austria. Indeed, under Article 34 of the draft treaty the four principal powers renounce reparations claims against Austria.

On the last day of the Potsdam Conference the effect of the Soviet renunciation was more than cancelled out by the ill-considered acceptance of a provision allocating to the Soviet government all "German assets" located in eastern Austria. The source of this provision may be found in the great divergence between Soviet and Western concepts of "war booty" and in the division, agreed on at Potsdam, of Germany's external assets.

In general, the Anglo-American definition of "booty" limited it to war materials which could not be adapted to peaceful uses. Staff cars, blankets, medical equipment, and army boots, for example, could be put to civilian use and were not classified as war booty. The Soviet definition included all materials which had been or could have been used to support the war effort of the enemy, including raw materials and factory equipment; a factory which produced footwear for workers to wear while producing for the war effort was therefore classified as "war booty." When pressed, Maiskii admitted that the Soviet definition covered any form of property which could be transported to the Soviet Union. Soviet negotiators brushed aside all questions of what would be left for reparation if everything except the soil itself was eligible for transfer as booty. In addition, simply by looking about in Potsdam and Berlin, members of the United States delegation could observe all forms of goods, from carefully greased and packed machinery to grotesquely rusted bathtubs and broken-down sofas, piled on barges and quais, on flatcars and loading platforms, ready to be moved eastward. It was hopeless to expect an accounting or an appraisal of the value of the war booty. The same frantic and wasteful process of collecting booty was going on in Austria. It could not be stopped. Refusal to concede Soviet ownership of German assets in eastern Austria would not change the *de facto* situation, or so it must have seemed to the American representatives, worn out by Soviet methods of negotiation and eager to come to an agreement. Thus, when, at the last minute, Marshal Stalin casually proposed adding to the Soviet share the German assets in eastern Austria, the chief American negotiators were preconditioned to concede this request as a matter which was in any case beyond their control, and accepted it without consulting their technical advisers.

At Potsdam, the division of Germany's external assets among the Allies was a part of the desperate attempt to achieve a compromise between widely divergent conceptions of the capacity of Germany to provide reparations. In a final, feverish compromise the Soviet Union renounced its claims to Germany's gold; the United States and Great Britain acquired, on behalf of the reparations claimants except the Soviet Union and Poland, all German assets located in neutral countries (German assets in Spain, Switzerland, and Sweden were of special importance). In turn the Soviet Union acquired German assets located in Hungary, Rumania, Bulgaria, and Finland. It should be noted that in these four countries enemy assets had, by the armistices, been placed under the Allied Control Commissions which were under Soviet "direction." When on the last day, as the heads of governments were poised for flight, Marshal Stalin asked that the Soviet share include the "German assets" in eastern Austria, as well as in the four satellites, President Truman asked only a few questions and gave his consent;

with more hesitation Attlee and Bevin followed suit.

This part of the Potsdam agreement became a major obstacle to reaching a settlement in Austria and to Austria's recovery. The provision was bad enough in itself, and, on a cautious estimate, it will result in the Soviet government receiving at least $600 million instead of the $250 million which it renounced at Potsdam. What made it worse was that no conditions or definitions were attached to it. If "German assets" had been defined as German properties owned in eastern Austria prior to the *Anschluss* of 1938, there would still have been many complicated problems to resolve in disentangling the assets from the rest of the Austrian economy, because of mixed ownership of factories and banks. For example, were oil-exploration rights, partly owned by Socony-Vacuum prior to 1938 and later forcibly absorbed by a German company without compensation to the American holders, to be treated as "German assets"? As interpreted by the Soviet negotiators in the absence of any agreed definition, "German assets" included Austrian properties which had been confiscated after 1938 for the benefit of the Nazi state or of individual Germans, Austrian banks and businesses which had been forced under the control of German banks and corporations, and properties which had been built by the German state or by private German or Austrian capital in Austria after 1938. It can be estimated that the total of "German assets" claimed by the Soviet government in eastern Austria represented almost half of the industrial equipment of the entire country. In addition, serious disputes arose over the question whether Vienna was included in "eastern Austria" for this purpose and whether "German assets" included bonds, stocks, debts, and mortgages, or only physical assets. Generals Mark Clark and Keyes fought a long and, on the whole, successful fight for restrictive answers to these questions.

If the "German assets" were removed, Austria would be bled to death. If they were left in Austria under

Soviet ownership, Austria as a whole would be completely mortgaged to the Soviet Union and its daily bread would depend on obeying Soviet demands. In addition, since the hastily drawn Potsdam agreement made no arrangements for four-power determination of what constituted German assets, the Soviet government insisted for many months that this question should be left to direct negotiation between itself and the Austrian government.

There was a potentially important limitation on the definition of German assets, contained in the London Declaration of January 5, 1943. By this declaration the United Nations, including the Soviet Union, denounced the Nazi seizures of property throughout Europe and declared them null and void. At Potsdam, when the author of this article called Vyshinskii's attention to the London Declaration and showed him a copy of it, he seemed quite unaware of its existence. At Moscow, in April 1947, Gusev stated specifically that, according to the Soviet view, the London Declaration did not apply to Austria. And there is a certain legal basis for the Soviet view; the only way to counter it would have been to extend the effect of the London Declaration to Austria at Potsdam, *before* assigning the "German assets" to Soviet ownership. But this was not done. Potsdam did not define the "German assets" and entirely irreconcilable definitions could be and were advanced.

After many months spent in debates on the meaning of "German," "assets," "force" and "duress," the deputies were able in February 1948 to turn to a concrete examination of Soviet claims to property in Austria. A French proposal of November 28, 1947, was taken as a starting point. According to this proposal, the Soviet government would take one half of the existing oil-producing areas and one third of the registered areas of oil exploration located in its zone, together with a corresponding volume of the oil-refining capacity, and would accept $100 million in cash as compensation for all other German assets which had not been removed to the Soviet Union and which would be returned to Austrian ownership.

The question of the German assets now entered the phase of actual bargaining. The Soviet claim was high. The Soviet delegate asked for two thirds of the 1947 oil-production level (564,000 tons out of an extraction of 846,000 tons, in 1947) and two thirds of the areas designated for exploration (2,317,000 acres out of 3,460,000), under concessions to be held for fifty years. He also wanted a 25 per cent interest in the property of the Danube Shipping Company throughout Austria. And he asked for $200 million, to be paid within two years, in compensation for other claims to German assets. From these claims, estimated to be worth at least $800 million, and later whittled down to some $600 million, it is easy to see how the Potsdam concession of the "German assets" had fortified the position of the Soviet government, which had originally asked for a mere $250 million in reparation. And these final claims were in addition to the gains which the Soviet government had already secured through removals of "war booty" and "German assets," through large purchases financed by funds exacted in the guise of "occupation costs," and through various black-market enterprises.

By early April 1948, after relentless haggling on both sides, the Soviet demand for cash had been reduced to $150 million, payable in equal installments over a six-year period, instead of two. Meanwhile, the United States and British delegations raised from 50 to 53 and then 58 per cent the proposed Soviet share of existing oil production, as of 1947, in the Soviet zone, while the Soviet negotiator gradually reduced his demand to 60 per cent. The Western delegates raised their offer of oil-exploration concessions from 40 to 47 per cent, while the Soviet representative pared his claim from two thirds to 60 per cent and reduced the term of the proposed concessions from fifty to twenty-five years. The Soviet delegation also dropped its demand for extraterritorial status for Soviet enterprises in Austria, but still insisted on full freedom to export their profits in easily convertible currency. The Soviet demand for oil refineries with a capacity of 564,000 tons of crude oil was gradually reduced to 450,000, then to 420,000 tons, while the United States raised its offer from 350,000 to 420,000 tons.

As this crucial phase of haggling came to a close, the Soviet government also agreed to abandon its claim to a 25 per cent interest in the Danube Shipping Company and, instead, to accept the physical assets of the company in eastern Austria, as well as in Hungary, Rumania, and Bulgaria, in full liquidation of its claim. Ever since 1945 successive Soviet negotiators had striven to secure control over the Austrian Danube Company, to add it to their control of shipping in Hungary, Yugoslavia (the Soviet-Yugoslav Danubian Shipping Company was dissolved in August 1949), Rumania, and Bulgaria. By yielding to Soviet ownership the physical assets of the company in its eastern zone, Austria will, at least, be free to build up its own national company within its boundaries, though it cannot expect to revive its former shipping activity beyond them. Transfer to Soviet control of the company's assets in the three satellites, particularly of the coal mines at Pecs, merely confirmed a Soviet claim which had been asserted in fact since 1945; these former Austrian assets, having become Soviet property, add further weight to the Soviet position in the economies of the satellites.

The months of strenuous arguments which had moved step by step towards a compromise, bore fruit at the June 1949 session of the Foreign Ministers. Here, in return for accepting detailed agreements concerning oil and shipping, the Soviet delegation gained two long-fought demands. The Austrian government was now deprived by treaty of the right to nationalize the Soviet properties without Soviet consent. The

Western governments had tried to protect Austria's presumptive right to nationalize property, on condition that foreign interests receive no worse than "national treatment," but the Soviet government regarded this as a loophole for terminating its property rights under an appearance of "equal treatment." In defending Austria's right to nationalize property, the American delegation was supporting the very same provision which it had proposed for the Italian, Rumanian, and other satellite treaties. In the end it accepted the Soviet demand for a specific exemption of its properties from this general rule.

A second demand, also accepted in June 1949, was that these properties should be transferred to Soviet ownership free of all charges of debt or taxes as of the date of transfer. It is customary for liabilities to be transferred together with assets, and the Soviet enterprises in Austria have regularly refused to pay taxes. However, this additional concession, freeing the ceded property of all charges, which thus fall on the Austrian state, was made in order to speed the conclusion of the treaty, which then seemed close at hand.

When the deputies set about translating the Paris agreement into a definite list of enterprises to be retained by the Soviet government, the Russian representative again bargained hard, but without success, to retain as much as 70 to 80 per cent of the 1947 level of production, instead of the 60 per cent as agreed at Paris. The deputies now reduced to textual exactness the agreement that Soviet properties in Austria, "shall remain under Austrian jurisdiction" and that "Austrian legislation shall apply to them," except with respect to nationalization. The Soviet companies are to be free to export their net profits (earlier, the Soviet negotiator had implied that "gross profits" were meant) in kind or in freely convertible currency. The Soviet government is to receive three refineries, with an annual capacity of 420,000 tons, together with the distributing facilities now controlled by it. The Soviet government is free, within a period of eight years, to conduct explorations in 1,800,000 acres (instead of 2,317,000 acres, as demanded in February 1948) designated for this purpose and to receive twenty-five year concessions for those areas which yield oil. Oil-exploration areas which have not been tapped within eight years of the coming into force of the treaty, revert to Austrian control at that time.

By December 1949, when the Soviet government ceased negotiating, only a few points separated the deputies from complete agreement. Should the eastern European refugees in Austria receive any assistance from the Austrian government, pending their transfer out of Austria, or should they be returned by force, as the Soviet delegation insisted, to their countries of prewar domicile? Both the occupying powers and the Austrians were eager to see Austria relieved of the problem of the displaced persons. Would Austria be allowed to employ foreign technicians? The Western governments wanted Austria free to do so, particularly for the development of its civil aviation, but the Soviet government was opposed. The five peace treaties of 1947 had provided that, if disputes arose over the interpretation or execution of the treaty and if the two governments could not agree within one month upon the appointment of a citizen of a third country as the third member of an arbitration commission, an arbitrator could be appointed by the Secretary-General of the United Nations. A similar provision, proposed for inclusion in the treaty with Austria, has not been accepted by the Soviet government.

Even if the relatively minor unagreed points can now be settled, further delays in concluding the treaty are always possible. In spite of careful drafting of individual agreed articles, new difficulties may be raised when the text undergoes a final review. After signature, ratification may be delayed. Periods of one to three months are provided for carrying out the relinquishment of German assets and the evacuation of the occupation forces. Still, the steady progress towards completion of the treaty remains as one of the few encouraging aspects of East-West relations in 1949.

One factor which has favored progress in this question has been the separation of the Austrian from the German treaty negotiation. In December 1946 Molotov appointed a single Soviet deputy for both treaties, but Byrnes and later Marshall wisely insisted on having separate American deputies for each. When it proved useless for the deputies on the German treaty to continue their work, the deputies for the Austrian treaty were still able to plow ahead, and the Soviet government has had a separate deputy for the Austrian negotiations since April 1947. If the Austrian treaty had remained linked to the German problem, there would have been constant Soviet efforts to secure concessions in German policy through pressure on Austria.

It is also important to note the extremely thorough preparation of the American staff under Dodge and Reber, their alertness to detect numerous Soviet "jokers" which would have vitiated the basic purpose of re-establishing the Austrian state, and their patience in arguing the case over and over again. It must be remembered that throughout the negotiation there have been strong cards in the hands of the Soviet government. It has had the vague wording of the Potsdam agreement. It could take actual possession of the industrial plants which it has agreed to return, almost in their entirety, to Austrian control. Simply by sitting tight and running their own zone as rigidly as they have done in eastern Germany, the Soviet authorities could have effectively prevented the restoration of Austria's political independence and economic viability, for the Soviet zone contains the best of Austrian industry as well as most of its food surpluses.

The Soviet adoption of a more conciliatory position in the Austrian problem must have been influenced by the grim attachment to the Western concept of democracy which has been displayed by the Austrian electorate and parties. The elections of 1949 must have confirmed their diagnosis of the inability of the Communist party to gain political control through serving as the chosen instrument of Soviet policy in Austria. Direct access by Austria to American aid and world markets has probably played a decisive role in strengthening its ability to resist absorption into the Soviet bloc.

The decision to return to Austria more than three hundred factories earlier claimed as "German assets" may be due to the difficulties involved in keeping these plants in production without large outlays for the provision of raw materials and of new equipment. In both respects Soviet-controlled plants in eastern Austria must be in competition with the needs of similar plants located in the Soviet Union and in the satellite areas. In the end the Soviet government may be better off with its concessions in oil and shipping, which can be operated with relatively little impingement upon the rest of Austrian economy.

The progress of the Austrian negotiation has, it is clear, been influenced at all stages by the general climate of East-West relations. The intransigent Soviet claims of 1947 were probably due, not only to the habit of staking out the widest possible claims, but also to a desire to test the firmness of American policy immediately following the announcement of an American concern for the independence of Greece and Turkey. On the other hand, the complete breakdown of negotiations over Germany, in December 1947, was followed at once by the first serious Soviet gesture toward compromise on the Austrian treaty. A new burst of compromise followed the sudden rise of tension caused by the Communist seizure of power in Czechoslovakia. Meanwhile the further presence of Soviet "line-of-communication" troops in Hungary and Rumania, which was legally dependent upon the continued occupation of Austria, became unnecessary as the consolidation of Communist rule reached its goal in both countries.

With the rise in tension over the Berlin blockade there came an eight-months suspension of the Austrian negotiations, which were renewed in February 1949, after the Western powers had, through the airlift, made good their right to remain in Berlin. Meanwhile, the Soviet government was discovering that it lacked the means short of military invasion, to bring the recalcitrant Yugoslav regime to heel. Both the German and Yugoslav factors played their part in the Soviet decision of June 1949 to clear away the principal remaining obstacles to a settlement.

The Soviet government has recognized the skillful and persistent resistance to its moves for integration of Austria into its sphere, and this has been reflected from time to time in minor concessions, particularly when East-West tension has reached a point reacting on the Soviet program in Germany or the satellite countries. It is notable, nevertheless, that in three years there have been few major changes in the positions of the various powers; it has been patient, day-to-day plodding which has at length brought working agreement despite continued differences of principle. The Austrian negotiations have been a study in the technique of exhaustion, and they represent the achievements possible when swift and spectacular results have proved unobtainable. The steady work of technical experts has brought near consensus through sheer attrition.

PART III

The Cold War

:11:

SOVIET POLICY IN A TWO-WORLD SYSTEM[1]

[*April 1948*]

INTRODUCTORY NOTE · Written in April 1948, "Soviet Policy in a Two-World System" is a brief explanation of why the wartime alliance had been replaced by an ever more menacing Soviet attitude of irreconcilable hostility. It traces the source of this hostility to Soviet ideology, to the way deeply indoctrinated Soviet leaders and spokesmen think and feel about "history" and their duty to shape that history to fit their doctrine. Much of this analysis has become commonplace since the spring of 1948. But that was not the case then. In the American elections of 1948, for example, the Soviet leaders hoped for a bursting forth of pro-Soviet feelings which would thrust aside the bipartisan "conspiracy" of "reactionary leading circles" and give them at little or no risk the new gains they sought.

One of those aims became clear just as this essay was published: the seizure of West Berlin. In the struggle to conquer two million free people through hunger, cold, and fear, Stalin sought revenge for his failure, between Potsdam and mid-1948, to secure a stranglehold on all of Germany. He hoped to destroy the new West German state in its

[1] *International Journal* (Toronto), Vol. III, No. 3 (Summer 1948), pp. 191–200. Copyright 1948 by the Canadian Institute of International Affairs.

cradle. And he sought, short of a direct clash of arms, to demonstrate the weaknesses of the West. Somehow, he did not foresee that the West would emerge stronger and more closely united from the trial of wills which he imposed on it. But ten years later, in 1958, this failure of Stalin's did not deter Khrushchev from again brandishing the same threat against West Berlin and the Atlantic alliance. And again the peoples of the free world debated anxiously how to cope with the threat of Soviet ambitions.

*

THE three years since the end of hostilities against the Axis have seen the emergence and widening of a division between the Soviet and non-Soviet worlds, a division which now dominates all considerations of policy. How did this division arise? What can be done to overcome its effects? Can the issues in dispute be made "manageable"? These are the questions which are being anxiously posed, and to which every variety of answer is offered.

Could the division have been avoided? Were Western statesmen negligent in failing to foresee it? As more of the important memoirs of the war period become available they will confirm the fact that the possibility or even probability of this split was foreseen during the war, even at the time when greatest emphasis was being placed on the hope for the continuance of close Allied co-operation into the postwar period. During hostilities Soviet policy followed a course which assured it of many concrete advantages but which was not entirely incompatible with a postwar policy of co-operation. The concrete advantages sought and conceded could be interpreted as the expression of a national policy of unilateral assurance of security; they could also be regarded as building a springboard for further extension of Soviet influence. The policy of Roosevelt and Churchill accepted Soviet "national" aims, which in any case could not have been denied to the victorious Soviet armies, in the hope that the postwar Soviet Union, as a "satisfied power" like Britain and the United States, would place its chief emphasis upon the maintenance of the new *status quo* in co-operation with the other great powers. Hence Roosevelt pressed on with the establishment of the United Nations without waiting for the final defeat of the Axis. Substantial progress was also made in planning for the postwar control of Germany, again on the assumption that a joint Allied policy to prevent the resurgence of Germany would help to bind the three great powers to further co-operation.

These fragile assumptions had broken down within a year after the defeat of the Axis. During those few months the Soviet government had brushed aside all limitations upon its control over eastern Europe. It had embarked upon a competition for control over Germany. It had established a tradition of treating each question within the United Nations as a struggle for political advantage rather than as a common responsibility of the great powers. The only conclusion to be drawn was that the Soviet government was not a supporter of the *status quo*, that its ambitions were not limited to those wartime aims which had been conceded by its Allies, and that a new period of great-power competition had begun almost before the struggle against the Axis was over.

There have been many precedents for the breakdown of wartime coalitions. The history of all great peacemakings, from Westphalia to Paris, is marked by the struggle for competitive advantage between the great-power participants. The present struggle is exacerbated, however, by the basic differences which shape outlooks and policies today. During the war Soviet propaganda stressed the differences between Western democracy and fascism; today it stresses their basic identity and presents itself as the only defender of "democracy." During the war it drew a sharp line between warlike and peace-loving nations, while now it claims a monopoly of the term "peace-loving." In the struggle against Axis domination it recognized the progressive character of its democratic Allies; now it reserves the term "progressive" for those regimes or groups which follow its own political line without the slightest independence of thought or expression.

The shift to the postwar party line was felt within the Soviet Union as early as November 1944. With increasing intensity Soviet propaganda abandoned the "national," patriotic slogans which had served so effectively during the harsh struggle for survival. Instead of the Soviet and Russian people being praised as the great force behind victory, it was the Communist party and its "wise leadership" which now received entire credit as the "organizer of victory." Admission to the party, which had been thrown open to hundreds of thousands of brave leaders and organizers, was again restricted, and new emphasis was placed upon the "acquisition of Marxist-Leninist hardening" by the great mass of new wartime members.

In the occupied areas Soviet "black propaganda" increasingly set forth the line that Allied co-operation was only a wartime expedient, that America and Britain must now be regarded as future enemies, and that all Soviet citizens and local Soviet adherents must therefore beware of "Western" propaganda and infiltration. The official seal was placed upon the revived policy of Soviet exclusivism by Marshal Stalin's speech of February 1946. He now proclaimed that there was an absolute difference of quality between the Soviet system and the Western powers and that conflict for predominance was inevitable between them. It was again proclaimed that the Soviet system would never be fully secure until it had turned the "capitalist encirclement" of the Soviet world into a "socialist encirclement" of the remaining capitalist states.

Public opinion in the Western countries, especially in Great Britain, Canada, and the United States, was reluctant to accept at its face value this reversion of Soviet policy to the pugnacious, "isolationist" philosophy of militant Communism. It was inclined to search its own conduct and conscience for causes of this change from its wartime hopes. It was slow to accept the reality of the new challenge. In their countries none of the responsible leaders, and few exponents of public opinion, wished to face the burden, or bear the onus, of forming a new power combination strong enough to confront the expanding ambitions and the multiple techniques of Soviet policy.

This lag in reaction and this reluctance to seek new policies left the initiative in Soviet hands until mid-1947. The slowness of outside reaction to their policies must have confirmed the Soviet leaders in their analysis of their own strength and the weakness and indecision of their potential opponents. As they looked over the world they could feel that the temporary economic weakness of the Soviet Union was compensated by its unity of action; inferior resources brought to bear by a single will are immediately more effective than much larger but dispersed aggregates of power.

The Soviet leaders saw no power or combination of power within Europe or Asia capable of opposing their pressure exerted both from without and from within each country. The United States, which had greater resources, might withdraw within the American continent, or might be weakened by a great economic crisis. During the war had not President Roosevelt himself insisted upon limiting American postwar commitments, emphasizing that he could not pledge his country to any but general obligations of international co-operation, in view of a possible reversion to isolation? Did not American spokesmen insist upon the imminence of a great postwar economic crisis, arguing only over differences of intensity and duration? United States power and intentions were an uncertain and puzzling factor in Soviet calculations, more difficult to estimate than those of countries nearer at hand, yet not sufficiently uncertain to cause the Soviet leaders to doubt the accuracy of their basic analysis.

It is difficult for people of the Western democracies to believe that the Soviet leadership actually builds its program of action upon a philosophy of power. We are accustomed to regard politics as a system of devices and habits by which individuals and groups achieve compromises, agreeing upon methods but not upon detailed programs of aims. The fact that the political struggle is carried on within the framework of a broad consensus of common ethical and social beliefs is often overlooked. This basic fact of democratic life becomes evident only in great crises; at other times reference to it is felt to be somewhat immodest.

This difference of psychology makes it hard for citizens of Great Britain, Canada, or the United States to understand the confidence of the Soviet leadership in the "correctness" of their analyses and prognostications, or their willingness to pursue, to the immediate disadvantage of their prestige and interests, policies which arouse the fear and the antagonism of peoples beyond the range of their system of thought control. "Compromise," which is the daily product of our political systems, is an evil word in Soviet vocabulary, the word "reasonable" has no real equivalent in Russian, and, more fundamentally, Soviet leadership feels that its moral right to rule rests on the "correctness" of its analyses and the "monolithic" unity of its action. Western democracy is flexible in its aims and rigid in its procedures; the Soviet power is rigid in its aims and flexible in its techniques.

Whatever misgivings the Soviet leaders may feel from time to time concerning their short-range policies, they profess complete assurance concerning the correctness of their long-range prophecy. Why should they come to a "compromise" on Germany which might place German resources and man power beyond their control for a long time to come, when their analysis tells them that American capitalism, unable to solve its own problems at home, is even less able to solve those of Germany? Why should they offer any political concessions, such as greater co-operation in the United Nations, in return for a reconstruction loan, when their analysis tells them that in a few months or a few years an economic crisis will send United States businessmen, and therefore the United States government, to Moscow to beg the Soviet government to accept a loan, or even a gift, in order to keep the capitalist industrial machine going and to avoid mass unemployment?

One problem which plagues foreigners attempting to decipher Soviet policy is whether the Communist program dictates to the Soviet leaders the use of Soviet power to extend their ideology, or whether the leaders are power-hungry men who use the ideology as one weapon among many for the extension of the power and influence of the Soviet state. A subsidiary question, which derives from it, is whether the Soviet leaders are primarily Communist ideologues in command of a powerful state, or power politicians exploiting the Communist philosophy to unite their friends and divide their enemies. In dealing with immediate problems and policies these questions are both unanswerable and not very important.

Of course the Soviet leaders act in accordance with the program which brought them to absolute power in Russia and which gives them the support of large bodies of devoted followers in other countries. They would be both foolish and derelict in their duty if they turned on their own instruments of power and destroyed them in order to win the passing favor of regimes which, in the Soviet analysis, are bound at some stage to seek actively the downfall of the Soviet regime. In addition, the Soviet leaders are not at all troubled by the fact that satellite regimes have been brought into power only in countries in which Soviet military and political power was dominant. Lenin and Stalin made it clear, even in the early years of the new regime, that the existence of a strong Soviet Russia would be an important factor in assisting Communist regimes into power in nearby countries. The fact that the new pro-Soviet regimes in eastern Europe have been imposed from above and without, through manipulation of the levers of power, through division and weakening of opposing forces, and under the protecting shield of Soviet power—through "cold" rather than "hot" or spontaneously generated revolution—is of no immediate concern to the Soviet leaders. But it must make clear to them, as well as to the outside world, that the extension or the containment of Soviet power is largely the result of an equation of power, and that the establishment of Communist-controlled states need not await the "ripening" of a revolutionary situation from within.

The difference between traditional calculations of force and Soviet political algebra is that Soviet calculations are based not only on estimates of military and industrial power and potential, but also on a fourth-dimensional element of will power. Soviet leaders, more than others, take account of the ability of other countries to direct their efforts to a consistent purpose. Where strong forces devoted to Soviet purposes operate openly or clandestinely within a country regarded as hostile, Soviet calculations take this into account. Thus they are less likely to regard the recent Communist setbacks in France and Italy as the turning points which they were made to seem by the press in the United States.

Does this attitude toward the world, based upon a sublimely confident assurance in a "correct" Leninist analysis, mean that the Soviet leaders are megalomaniacs who have lost touch with reality and who will push on unrelaxingly until "we" or "they" are destroyed in war? This assumption is almost as misleading as the opposite one, that the Soviet leaders are really kindhearted people who have been cheated and wronged so often that their confidence must now be won by giving in again and again to whatever demands they advance. Poorly or wrongly informed as they often appear to be, the Soviet leaders have not shown an inability to recognize basic facts of international life, grounded in realities of power. Admittedly, these "realities" omit many factors which are real and basic to us. That a nation may be possessed of great power and yet use it for generally shared purposes, that there may be a concept of the general good which is superior to special class interests, seems to them impossible. When we express in terms of general humanitarian ideals policies which are well suited to preserve the security and prosperity of our own countries this appears to Soviet analysts as proof that we are hypocritical in our thinking. That great nations can practice to some degree a policy of *noblesse oblige* seems incredible to them. That our practice falls short of the high ideals we profess is even clearer to Soviet commentators than to us. What is not so clear to them is that self-governing peoples inevitably carry over into their thinking about international affairs a large part of the ethos which has shaped their own political and social growth.

The Soviet leaders have shown time and again their ability to adjust the application of their basic idea to surrounding circumstances recognized as beyond their control. When the Soviet regime found itself contained within the new boundaries of 1921, it proclaimed that revolutions were not a commodity for export. When it claimed that it was being contained in the 1920's by a French-inspired *cordon sanitaire*, it concluded carefully phrased pacts of nonaggression with the very states which were, it alleged, preparing to attack and dismember Soviet territory. When its leaders felt that German and Japanese forces were planning to invade the Soviet Union, they abandoned the view that all "imperialists" were cut from one cloth, and entered into the "capitalist" League of Nations and into special alliances. When they felt that these alliances were inadequate to stop German expansion, the Soviet leaders entered into an agreement with Nazi Germany for the division of eastern Europe, and, as the German diplomats themselves stated, lived up to their agreements to the full. In dealing with a *raison d'état* which has shown so much flexibility in adapting its policies and methods to the real situations in the world around it, it is unwise to assume that it has now lost that ability and that it is committed to a program of unlimited conquest.

Unlike the Hitler conquest-mania, the Soviet urge to expand is not bound to any particular timetable. If pressure in one direction yields results, it will be exploited as far as appears safe; if it meets with resistance, it can be relaxed. If Iran or Turkey seek and receive United States support in opposing Soviet demands, the pressure can be turned off. At a later time, when other countries are involved in troubles elsewhere, the Soviet Union will still be a close neighbor of Turkey and Iran. In the Soviet conception it is conflict, and not war as such, which is basic in international relations. Conflict can be warlike or peaceful in form, but it is real and constant and cannot be wished away. Soviet analyses of foreign policy regularly include the two elements of conflict and coexistence. What is significant in each new statement is the overtone of emphasis, stressing conflict more at one time or coexistence at another.

Not much has been said in Soviet statements of recent months concerning "the second round of wars and revolutions," although this crucial theme was sounded repeatedly in the early months of the post-hostilities period. Lenin and Stalin agree with Clausewitz that war is a supreme test for any political or social order. They have gone beyond Clausewitz in emphasizing the revolutionizing effect of war. Does the shift of emphasis away from this theme mean that Soviet analysts may be discussing whether the advantages of the "second round" have now been exploited to the full?

Even though the Soviet economist, Eugene Varga,

has been denounced for asserting that underproduction in the rest of the capitalist world would offset, for a period of five to ten years, the effects of potential overproduction in the United States and Canada, and that therefore a general crisis of capitalism is not to be expected immediately, this does not necessarily mean that the Soviet leaders are prepared to reject the practical implications of his statements. It may mean merely that they consider it inopportune to present them to their supporters at home and abroad with the stamp of official approval. If Soviet leaders wish to relax the tension in Soviet-American relations they have merely to accept the view that the capitalist world is moving toward greater stabilization, that the opportunities offered by the "second round" have been exhausted, and that the Soviet interest now lies in stressing the coexistence of two worlds and in seeking, step by step, a settlement, or at least an alleviation, of the present conflicts.

This policy, from a Soviet viewpoint, offers long-run advantages. It means that attention and anxiety will be less exclusively centered on Soviet-American conflicts and that opposition in the United States to large outlays for national defense and for the economic defense of friendly nations will increase. In a period of relaxed tension the solidity of the Soviet bloc is not likely to be seriously weakened, while the unity of purpose of the larger and more heterogeneous non-Soviet groupings may well be weakened. Assuming, then, that the Soviet government has no desire to let present conflicts develop into outright war, at a time when Soviet economic strength is low, it would find many advantages in abating the tone of its attacks and in seeking through reciprocal concessions a solution of some of the points in dispute.

The two methods of settlement which are most commonly put forward are "great-power unity" and "division of spheres." By "great-power unity" Soviet spokesmen mean a return to the wartime system under which three powers, usually after sharp argument, adopted joint decisions, sometimes held secret for substantial periods of time, and then imposed those decisions upon weaker states and justified them to their own peoples. Under this procedure the democratic leaders were unable to inform their people until after a decision had been taken, or even carried out. This approach was, even in wartime, applied only in those questions in which the Soviet Union demanded and could impose an immediate solution.

To the Soviet leaders the pre-eminence of the Security Council within the United Nations, and the special position of the five great powers within the Security Council, seemed to offer a promise that this system, which had worked to their satisfaction in wartime councils, would continue to operate to their benefit in time of peace. In the American approach, the five great powers, having an overriding interest in the maintenance of peace, would, through the Security Council, co-ordinate their efforts, which could not be resisted by any lesser power. It is no longer possible, short of a direct threat of war by the Soviet Union, and probably not even then, for the United States to return to the Soviet and wartime concept of "great-power unity."

It has often been suggested that the alternative, based on a frank recognition of great-power disunity, is the division of the world into two exclusive spheres, Soviet and Anglo-American, with each power agreeing to refrain from "interference" in the sphere of the other. This alternative to constant bickering and conflict has attractive features. But is it realistic? To assume, for example, that the Soviet Union and the Communist program would cease to attract large and important groups of people in France and Italy is to deny the real forces which are commonly lumped together under the name of Communism. Would Germany, Austria, China, and Korea remain in a state of division, or be denied their urge to unification, because the great-power spheres cut through their territories? Would the Soviet Union be satisfied permanently with what is now regarded as its "sphere" in practice? In his reply of May 9, 1948, to Ambassador W. Bedell Smith, Mr. Molotov hinted that the Soviet government had no objection to the United States pursuing its interests in the two Americas. Could either the United States or the Soviet Union propose or voluntarily accept its own exclusion from a share of influence in Europe or in the Far East, without the risk of seeing populous and productive areas organized against it? To ask these questions is enough to illustrate the fallacy of assuming that Chinese walls can be erected today to close off one sphere or another. Neither Soviet power or ideology, nor the power and ideas for which the Western democracies stand, can be contained by accidental frontiers.

The third course, the only one which remains open, is to accept the Soviet analysis, to recognize that two great spheres based on competing interests and ideologies do in fact conflict and coexist, and to attempt to restrain the conflicts within manageable limits. This course requires the pursuit of unity and strength within the non-Soviet world. It also requires the avoidance of boasts and threats. It means that, being unable to persuade the Soviet leaders by arguments, the democratic nations must influence them by facts. The non-Soviet world lives under a pluralism of systems; Soviet monism can, in practice, be adjusted to admit the indefinite coexistence of differing regimes. Peace by mutual toleration may yet be achieved. Peace cannot be "proclaimed." It must be earned each day.

:12:

SOVIET-AMERICAN RELATIONS SINCE THE WAR[1]

[*April 1949*]

INTRODUCTORY NOTE • By early 1949 American opinion was adjusting, reluctantly, to a world of unremitting struggle, a struggle waged by force as well as by ideas. The stalwart defense of West Berlin against the Soviet blockade overshadowed in American minds the rapid advance of the Chinese Communists southward from Manchuria and Peking. Events were forcing a fresh evaluation of the meaning of words, and Moscow's upside-down definitions of "war" and "peace" were becoming familiar to Americans as, in prolonged debate, they made up their minds to support Europe's economic recovery and its strategic security through the Marshall Plan and NATO.

Despite a wider access to factual data about the United States, despite Khrushchev's extensive travels—unthinkable in Stalin's mode of rule—the present Soviet rulers preserve and propagate the same doctrine-warped and self-seeking picture of world politics. The attempt simultaneously to project outward the images of Soviet doctrine while regulating narrowly the admission of outside in-

[1] *Annals of the American Academy of Political and Social Science*, Vol. CCLXIII (May 1949), pp. 202–11. Copyright 1949 by the American Academy of Political and Social Science.

formation and ideas to Soviet minds continues unabated, though in more flexible forms.

Meanwhile, important changes have taken place in the Soviet power position. The rapid growth of the Soviet economy, predicted briefly in this essay of 1949, has given Soviet policy a new source of world-wide prestige. The United States, which was relatively impregnable to a direct Soviet attack in 1949, is now increasingly exposed to the risks of Soviet missile aggression. Even more than in 1949, an alert, active, farsighted foreign policy, backed by a spirit of sacrifice, has become essential to America's national survival.

*

THE problem which now dominates all aspects of postwar politics is that of the antagonism between American and Soviet politics. If there is a ballot on admitting new members to the United Nations, or a decision to be taken on reconstruction in Germany, it cannot be discussed on the merits of the case. Each position is taken with an eye to its effect upon the two contending greatest powers.

The extreme polarization of power is reflected along sensitive frontiers, as in Norway and Iran. It cuts across critical areas of homogeneous nationalities, as in the cases of Germany, Austria, and Korea. It is paralleled in dangerous fissures within many national communities and is reflected in the continuing unrest within Soviet satellites and in the struggles of the Communist parties in France and Italy, in Greece and China. The factors of conflict have been tumultuous and remain dangerous.

The dangers are increased by the fact that both Soviet and American centers of power are largely self-contained; the outlook and purposes of each of these powers are generated internally, are secreted from its own way of life. The intentional or unforeseen repercussions of their acts affect many other peoples in their most sensitive interests and aspirations. In addition, each of these two great powers finds it difficult to arrive at a coherent judgment of the power and intentions of the other.

When the Soviet leaders look at America, they think primarily of its great economic power. No doubt, they are rather well informed of its strength in specific skills and of its inventiveness. Their insistence upon the validity of a single philosophy prevents them from understanding the political and social experience and outlook which form the underpinning of American society. In applying with extreme rigor the system of piece-rate rewards and penalties to their own workers, they overlook the fact that in America differential incentives to workers rest on a high minimum standard of living. Admitting the technical superiority of American industry, always measuring their own achievements against American statistics, the Soviet leaders also believe unshakably that the American economy is certain to be pounded to pieces from within. And since the United States is now the only other great power, they wait impatiently for the time when that power will disintegate and American policy will be paralyzed by internal stresses.

The duality in the Soviet evaluation of American strength was clearly shown in the question of a postwar loan. The Soviet representatives were eager to secure a very large loan—figures of $6 to $10 billion were bandied about—and admitted freely that Soviet reconstruction would be immensely facilitated by the inflow of American equipment. On the other hand, they were absolutely convinced that this loan was not something for which they would have to make an effort, even an effort to maintain some degree of diplomatic decorum. They were certain that America would come hat in hand, begging them to accept a large loan, solely for the purpose of staving off a catastrophic depression at home. They felt they would be doing a favor to

American manufacturers by giving their rickety economic system a few years of grace. Holding these views, the Soviet leaders assumed that their own offensive against American interests and sentiments was in no way incompatible with the obtaining of a loan.

A similar opaqueness has shaped the Soviet leaders' understanding of American policies in the postwar world. They can recognize that Americans are basically oriented inwards and find it hard to be concerned steadily with world affairs. They know that the United States did not take the initiative in starting either of the world wars in this century. From the full and open discussion of policy which goes on in this country, they can see that most disputes revolve around the question of finding the best way to prevent a new war. Yet the Soviet leaders insist that America is the center of a new and active conspiracy to unleash a new world war.

Believing that the Soviet system alone has solved the inner contradictions of industrial society and that it is bound to expand into ever wider areas and some day to encompass the world, the Soviet leaders conclude that any forces which are outside Soviet control are, potentially or in reality, a menace to their ambition and to their regime. Professing to believe that the non-Soviet world envies the achievements of the Soviet Union and desires to destroy their system, they assume that the forces of the non-Soviet world are bound, sooner or later, to coalesce around the strongest non-Soviet power. Power beyond Soviet control and "anti-Soviet" power tend to become identified in their way of thinking.

In 1941 the Soviet leaders fully expected Britain and the United States to sit idly by while Hitler attempted to destroy the Soviet regime, or even to join with him. The prompt support which the Soviets received in a time of greatest danger, the great contributions of supplies, and the constant efforts to promote closer co-operation did not shake their faith in the dogma of "capitalist encirclement." In February 1946 this basic tenet was reaffirmed by Marshal Stalin as the central point in the postwar Soviet program.

The trouble about Soviet reasoning is not that it is illogical—it is usually too strictly logical—but that its premises ignore or distort simple facts which are readily discernible to minds which have not been subjected to the process of "Bolshevist hardening." If "lasting peace" is declared to be possible only under the Soviet system, then, logically, only the Soviet Union and its obedient satellites can be considered truly "peace-loving" countries. Whatever "subjective" horror of war may be expressed by "capitalist" leaders, their governments, "objectively" analyzed, are engaged in "war-mongering." Anyone who criticizes or opposes Soviet claims and actions is, of course, "spreading anti-Soviet slander," "undermining peace," "promoting fascism," or "destroying Allied unity." This syllogism rests in turn on an assumption, which cannot be questioned or criticized in areas under Soviet control, that a small group of leaders in command of the regime has, through self-appointed apostolic succession to Lenin, a monopoly of wisdom and virtue.

Of course, the faculty of reasoning logically from unprovable hypotheses to untenable conclusions is not confined to any one group of men, although it seems to appear most often under conditions of absolute power. Such a faculty is dangerous when its pronouncements monopolize access to men's minds, including the minds of those who direct or serve the dictatorship.

There is a continual danger in the Soviet leaders' habit of taking action upon a set of facts which appear as facts to them alone. An even more serious danger lies in the marshaling and interpreting of a commonly perceived body of facts in accordance with a rigidly enforced philosophy, adherence to which is the password to authority and responsibility within the Soviet system.

Most Americans cannot make up their minds as to

whether the Soviet Union is strong or weak. Because the Soviet war effort was greatly assisted through lend-lease, many Americans suppose that the Soviet Union cannot wage a major war on the basis of its own production. This assumption overlooks the fact that up to the turning of the tide at Stalingrad, the Soviet armies had received relatively small quantities of supplies from abroad. Throughout the war, the basic tools of war—artillery, tanks, planes—were almost entirely of Soviet manufacture. It would be shortsighted to suppose that Soviet capacity to wage war is far smaller, or is not actually substantially greater, than it was when the Soviet forces broke the German onslaught.

It is sometimes felt that a denial of technical equipment and knowledge derived from the West will slow down or even disrupt the development of Soviet industry. It must, however, be assumed that in the production of machine tools the Soviet Union is "over the hump" in the process of industrialization. Failure to obtain abroad certain specialized or more modern types of equipment may delay or hamper but cannot prevent the broad development of Soviet industry on the basis of skills already acquired. Finally, the ratio of total industrial power to war potential varies considerably under diverse systems. The Soviet system gives its leaders great leeway in deciding what proportion of industrial power shall be directed towards military needs.

A contrary notion is also advanced that the Soviet leaders may lightheartedly engage in a new trial of strength by war, as soon as they feel confident of thereby gaining some immediate and decisive advantage. Their real range of choice seems to lie somewhere between two extremes. It is unrealistic to suppose that they would make concessions from their basic program, either to secure economic aid or to win favor in the eyes of the non-Soviet world. It is also unreasonable to assume that the urge to extend their system to new areas will lead them into war without considering the effect of war upon the low Soviet standard of living or without reflecting on the possibly unpredictable outcome of a war against a powerful, highly ingenious, and relatively impregnable enemy.

If the Soviet leaders have, since 1945, steadily weighted their choice in favor of a relentless political offensive against the non-Soviet world, this may be due in large part to their habit of subordinating economic considerations to factors of power. It may be due to a short-run assumption that the economic advantages which might be gained immediately through a more conciliatory policy are of minor importance to them when compared with the great extension of political power on which they are gambling. It may also be credible that they have felt sure that a policy of strong pressure offered no risk to their basic security, since the American military machine was being dismantled with great haste and there was no other power to challenge their ambitions.

Because the Soviet government rules through a centralized dictatorship and severely limits the range of suggestion or criticism allowed to its citizens and to supporters abroad, an American readily concludes that the system is inherently weak, maintained only through the constant stimulation of fear. This impression of political instability has been enhanced by the sensational abandonment of Soviet allegiance by individual citizens and by the much less publicized refusal of several hundreds of thousands of its citizens to return to the Soviet Union. To people accustomed to a regime which periodically submits to the judgment of the voters, these facts suggest weakness, hence, a necessity for such a regime to avoid war at all cost.

This interpretation, natural in American eyes, overlooks many unfamiliar factors: a long tradition of rule by a strong and irresponsible power, the tradition of combining incessant persuasion with coercion, and absence of conscious formulation of alternative programs despite widespread discontent with privations and injustices. It would be shortsighted to disparage the substantial level of disciplined action achieved under Soviet rule or to assume that internal discontent would be an important factor, especially in a limited test of strength. In any major war, of course, a defeated and occupied country may undergo a change of government, and new currents may come to the surface. In Russia today, or anywhere in Europe, few of these currents would be tender of individual rights.

It is hard for Americans to realize that Communism meets with acceptance and even fanatical support in many segments of the population. Communism remains a powerful force in France and Italy, for American gifts and economic recovery do not reach far into the basic factors making for discontent. Backward countries may be attracted to the Soviet recipe of quick action through dictatorship, rather than to the American method of piecemeal improvement and changes brought about through consent. Where problems of overpopulation, absence of technical skills and capital, and age-old accumulations of social and national resentments set discouragingly high barriers to modernization, the appeal of Communism is bound to remain strong. There it is judged by its promises of "progress" —not by the as yet unknown effects which may follow from the quality and direction of the "progress" it offers. The Soviet leaders choose to regard American democracy as a "conspiracy." It would be equally dangerous for Americans to think that their own type of democracy is universally admired and desired, and that the strength of Communism resides only in a centralized conspiracy of force.

Since the Soviet leaders accept the duty of spreading their system and rejoice at the appearance of each new "people's democracy," it is easily and widely assumed that this political ambition motivates its leaders at all times with an unvarying emotional intensity. It is difficult to judge the emotional intensities within the Politburo, but it is clear from the record that the outward pressure of Soviet expansionism has fluctuated rather widely over the past thirty-one years. This intensity may vary in the future.

A relative relaxation of the outward thrust may come about in one of several ways. It may arise from a discouraged recognition of solid and impassable barriers erected in its path; or it may develop from the operation of internal factors. In the case of an ideology which offers the only "scientific" basis for prediction, repeated failures to predict accurately may result in the growth of skepticism towards the doctrine of infallibility itself. Or, when a militant ideology has outlived the generation which formulated it in the heat of revolutionary struggle, and becomes the property of a generation which docilely received the tradition ready-made, the fervor of the revolutionary "fathers" may not pass integrally into the postrevolutionary "sons."

The written word of revelation may remain sacrosanct, but if it is believed with, say, ten per cent less fervor by a new generation, the compulsion to act hazardously on behalf of the doctrine may slacken. As a dogma becomes more rigid, it may not evoke the same desire to act. Since about 1937, Soviet dogma has achieved a remarkable posture of rigidity, unnatural in a people of quick mind and ranging curiosity. Meanwhile, since no confident prediction of a slackening of the Soviet urge to messianic expansion can be made, it has become necessary to act on the assumption that this urge can be restrained only by constructing external barriers and setting clear warning signals.

While there was the stress of common danger a limited degree of co-operation was established between the Soviet Union and the United States, and a modest amount of combined planning for the postwar period was accomplished. During the war the American government made many efforts, not always well directed, to win the confidence of a very distrustful group of leaders and to lay the groundwork of a postwar community of interest. It was agreed to establish a new security organization, dominated by the great powers, and specific agreements were reached concerning the postwar occupation and control of Germany and Austria. Some limited successes were achieved, and it could not be said with finality that the Soviet leaders were determined to go their own way in the postwar world and to ignore completely their Allies' constant invitations to co-operative action. It can be said that in this phase the Soviet government insisted on safeguarding its own strength, security, secrecy, and independence of decision, yet was willing, when none of these factors was directly involved, to make limited commitments to joint action. This phase lasted through the Yalta Conference, which marked the high point in the prospects for closer understanding and cooperation.

A fortnight after Yalta there occurred a significant shift in the emphasis of Soviet policy. While the slogan of "Allied unity" continued to be chanted in every key by Soviet propagandists, there took place a rapid ebbing in any signs of Soviet consideration for the interests or hopes of the Western Allies. In direct violation of the recently signed Yalta agreements, the Soviet government proceeded to impose governments of its own choosing upon the smaller countries of eastern Europe. In violation of another part of the Yalta agreement it gave its full support to the minority Lublin regime in Poland, and signed with it a close alliance and a unilateral agreement defining Poland's western boundary, again in disregard of a specific agreement with its Allies. At this very time it also backed away, in a significant respect, from implementing the agreement to co-operate with its Allies in the postwar control of Germany.

After the signing, in November 1944, of the Allied agreement for establishing joint control over postwar Germany, the three governments of Great Britain, the Soviet Union, and the United States had agreed orally to set up immediately a nucleus of the future control machinery. The three, later four, nucleus control groups could thus, in advance, become accustomed to working together, could adjust their diverse administrative conceptions and establish their twelve working divisions, and would be ready to begin operations within a few days after the German surrender. The Soviet representative on the European Advisory Commission, in London, informed his colleagues that the Soviet nucleus group was being selected, that it was nearly complete, that it was almost ready to join the American and British groups. At Yalta Marshal Stalin agreed to expedite the arrival of the nucleus group, and about ten days later his representative in London informed his American colleague, with obvious satisfaction, that the Soviet group would arrive on a fixed day. Shortly after, the Soviet delegate sent a subordinate to inform the American delegation that the Soviet group was not coming at all. Viewed in retrospect, this reversal was merely one additional sign pointing to a strong trend towards unilateral Soviet policy everywhere in Europe.

There may be several partial explanations of this post-Yalta shift from limited co-operation to an attitude of sharp rivalry. As Soviet troops entered German territory, the dominant voice in Soviet policy may well have passed from the Foreign Ministry, which had until then been responsible for planning the occupation on the agreed basis of joint Allied action, into the hands of the powerful economic ministries, bent on squeezing every bit of economic relief out of Germany, and of the secret police, responsible directly to the Politburo for enforcing Soviet control in occupied areas. Another factor may have been the strong Soviet expectation of a rapid withdrawal of American forces from Europe.

At Yalta, American officials had insisted that the United States government could not commit its people to any specific and continuing responsibilities in Europe, and that American forces would be withdrawn across the ocean just as rapidly as the availability of shipping would permit. At that stage the Morgenthau plan, which dominated official thinking about the German problem, showed no trace of any concern for Germany's longer-range future. Turning Germany into a "pastoral" country would, of course, have left Communism as the sole hope for German survival. Knowing after Yalta that American power would be withdrawn with utmost speed from Europe, the Soviet leaders could also, and did, treat with contempt American protests, even President Roosevelt's personal appeals to Stalin, concerning the open and frequent violations of the Yalta agreements on eastern Europe.

The same factors must have encouraged the Soviet leaders, after digesting the experience of Yalta, to hope that France and Italy, where the native Communist parties were far stronger and better organized than in Poland, Hungary, or Rumania, would also come under Russian Communist domination. In addition, throughout 1944–6 one of the strongest arguments of Communist supporters in western Europe was that America, though it appeared strong and friendly, was an unreliable friend, that its armies were nonexistent in time of peace and its economic assistance would melt away in a postwar economic crisis of its own, while the Soviet Union would remain close at hand and would know how to reward its adherents and punish its opponents.

As the Moscow Politburo wrote to the obstreperous Belgrade Politburo in 1948, the way in which the war ended had, "unfortunately," made it impossible for the Soviet Union to establish "people's democracies" in Italy and France. But if they could not be established in western Germany, France, and Italy by the expeditious means of Soviet military assistance, the same goal might still be achieved through combined pressure from within and without, provided American support were withdrawn and American policy reverted to transoceanic isolationism.

The new phase of Soviet initiatives and intensive Soviet pressure, which began shortly after Yalta, continued into the spring of 1947. During this period Soviet policy was based on the assumption that France was beyond recovery, that Britain was done as a great power, and that the United States was about to isolate itself from European affairs or fall into economic impotence. At Potsdam there were still some slight traces of willingness on the part of Soviet leaders to give a hearing to the views of their Allies and to compromise in minor details. But it was at Potsdam that the Soviet leaders gave frank expression to a program of expansion which, if achieved, would have made their power supreme in Europe and in the eastern Mediterranean.

To list the Soviet demands, flatly presented or delicately adumbrated at Potsdam, is to outline the policy which the Soviet leaders have pursued since 1945 with remarkable persistence. In Germany they wanted to rewrite the Allied agreement on zones of occupation by setting up a separate Ruhr region under three-power control, with a veto assuring them of a high degree of bargaining power. They wanted to slap a ten-billion-dollar reparations mortgage on Germany, regardless of its effects on the survival of the German people or on the American taxpayer. A completely unmanageable mortgage of this kind would have given them unlimited opportunities to promote the Sovietization of all Germany through hunger blackmail. Marshal Stalin tried hard to secure a release from the Yalta agreements concerning eastern Europe and to secure a carte blanche for whatever he might do there. The Soviet delegation pressed for an immediate confirmation of the Polish-German boundary which the Soviet government had laid down; it reluctantly agreed to consider the boundary as provisional in return for Allied support of Soviet annexation of part of East Prussia.

The Soviet leaders also made it clear that they wanted control of the Straits of Constantinople, and expressed their "interest" in the Dodecanese Islands. They pressed for the immediate removal of British troops from Greece, and at the same time asked to be relieved of the obligation, signed in 1942, to remove their troops from northern Iran after the end of the war. Stalin did gain a definite advantage in this respect, for he now secured consent to keep his forces in Iran until six months after the end of the war against Japan —not against Germany as had been assumed until then. Stalin's main argument was that "it [Iran] is too near Baku." Marshal Stalin also said he was "definitely interested" in the Italian colonies, but postponed asking for a trusteeship over Tripolitania until six weeks later, at the London Council of Foreign Ministers. Shortly after Potsdam the Soviet government also demanded, without success, an equal share in the occupation of Japan.

The Potsdam demands were set forth in a matter-of-fact manner, without the propaganda orchestration which was applied after the going became rough. Nevertheless, they added up to a very substantial program: a stranglehold on the Ruhr and on the entire German economy; an uncontested domination of the one hundred million people of eastern Europe; domination of the eastern Mediterranean through control of Greece, Turkey, and Tripolitania; and domination of Iran.

To the great perplexity and anger of the Soviet leaders, this second phase, outlined at Potsdam, was successful only in those areas where Soviet forces were on the ground at the close of the war. Elsewhere the execution of the program was averted through delaying actions, improvisations, evasion, and by the growth of an awareness in western Europe and America that Soviet ambitions had grown far beyond the "natural" sphere of a concern for security.

In the beginning of the second phase, American opinion was extremely sensitive to any disparagement of Soviet actions or intentions. In the wave of sympathy for Soviet sacrifices in the war, of enthusiasm for Soviet courage, and in the passionate hope that a solid basis of Allied understanding had been found, American sentiment discredited or ignored many facts which, added together, suggested that the Soviet leaders saw no obstacles in the path of their ambition to extend and entrench their power in a world which had been devastated and hollowed out by Nazi brutality and by war. By the end of this phase, which was marked by the Truman Doctrine and the Marshall Plan, the pendulum had swung so far, under the hard impact of evidence of the Soviet challenge for power, that anyone who admitted the possibility of ever settling any dispute with the Soviet government was likely to fall under suspicion of favoring "appeasement."

In the third phase, the United States broke with ancient tradition to offer specific assistance and to furnish specific guarantees to countries which lay in the path of Soviet expansionism. Overcoming its scruples concerning the governments in Greece and Turkey, it came to their assistance. The alternative would have been acquiescence in the establishment of a Communist-dominated regime in Greece and the submission of Turkey to Soviet overlordship, either through Soviet control of the Straits of Constantinople and of the highlands of eastern Anatolia, or through the installing of a "friendly" regime, according to the Soviet definition. By this decision the United States undertook to deter the Soviet government from any sudden move to control the eastern Mediterranean.

The United States embarked on a far broader program of strengthening the economic and social structure of western Europe, although the program, announced tentatively in June 1947, went into effect only in 1948. Instead of joining the Committee of European Economic Co-operation and demanding a large share of American aid for itself and its satellites, the Soviet government mobilized its supporters in opposition. Its attacks were not fully consistent. It asserted, on one hand, that the program was only a bluff and was bound to fail, and in the same breath denounced it as the spearhead of military aggression directed against the Soviet Union. To offset the attractions of the Marshall Plan among its satellites, it established the Cominform in September 1947 and rounded out its control of the Soviet bloc by the Communist seizure of power in Czechoslovakia in February 1948, and by a pact of mutual assistance with Finland in April. The nervous insistence of the Soviet leaders on complete subservience of subsidiary Communist regimes, and their difficulties in securing a reliable picture of the true situation through their overindoctrinated agents, were high-lighted in the falling away, or rather the kicking away, of the Yugoslav member of the Soviet bloc in June. The Soviet correspondence with the Yugoslav Politburo has shown clearly that the only "nationalism" that can be tolerated within the Soviet orbit is Soviet nationalism.

The movement in western Europe for self-protection against Soviet pressure moved steadily forward in 1948 and 1949, from Bevin's speech in January 1948 to the Franco-British agreement for mutual assistance, to the five-power Brussels Pact, and to the signing of the twelve-power North Atlantic Treaty on April 4, 1949. In bolstering western Europe against the massive land power of the Soviet Union, the United States had to choose between two approaches. It could have encouraged the formation of a Western European Union, in the hope that over a period of years this advanced and populous region would become strong enough to be, in itself, a deterrent to a possible Soviet attack or threat of attack, without becoming too closely bound to American policy. Western Europe might, it was hoped, emerge as a "third force," standing between the Soviet and American centers of power and able to deal effectively with both.

In the short run, however, western Europe has proved too weak to make adequate provision for its own security. It requires American support if it is to constitute even a moderately powerful deterrent. Furthermore, western Europe is unable to cope with the economic and political rehabilitation of Western Germany except with American co-operation. In American policy the consolidation of western Europe and the recovery of Germany have become increasingly closely associated. To provide a firm barrier against Soviet domination of western Europe, it has become necessary to avert a Soviet domination of all Germany. To attract Western Germany to the side of the Atlantic powers, it is necessary to promote the emergence of an effective economic and political regime in Western Germany.

Since 1947 the Soviet Union has lost the momentum of military and ideological expansion in Europe, and political initiative has passed to western Europe and the United States. In China, on the other hand, the American effort to bring together Nationalist and Communist forces, to help in the strengthening of an effective central government, capable of active efforts at reform and of protecting China's national independence, was a failure. Parallel to the effort in Germany, there has been a shift in the occupation of Japan towards more strenuous promotion of economic recovery. The Soviet government has constantly denounced American policy in Germany and Japan as a plot to acquire additional allies for an attack on the Soviet Union. Since both occupied countries are completely disarmed, these accusations are somewhat wide of the mark. However, the question of how the security of these two countries may be assured poses a serious dilemma. Certainly, there are strong misgivings about permitting any form of rearmament, but it is doubtful if the United Nations, which they can enter only with Soviet approval, can offer sufficient assurance of their continued independence.

Looking back to Yalta and Potsdam, the Soviet leaders must realize that the successes which they anticipated have, in many instances, eluded their grasp. The hardening of American policy has been due to successive shocks administered by the Politburo. Their relative lack of success they owe, in large part, to their failure to understand the nature of the American polity and the underlying motives of American action abroad. They have underestimated the repugnance with which Americans view the destruction of the national independence of small but proud peoples. They have overestimated the elements of instability operating within the American economy. The mysterious workings of a democratic public opinion which first praises them to the skies and then turns on them, while they feel they have remained themselves throughout, they explain away by reference to a malevolent "conspiracy." Attributing to others their own habits of thought, they are certain that there is an American "Politburo" which secretly manipulates the press, the economy, and the government. The fact that the location, the membership, and the operations of this Politburo remain undiscoverable, they attribute to that well-known tradition of American ingenuity.

Beyond the building of adequate deterrents to Soviet expansion, American policy has another duty. It has a difficult path to walk in these next years, strengthening the supports of a tolerable democratic peace and at the same time avoiding provocative actions and gestures. There is no better gift to the Soviet propagandists than speculation in the press by an American officer on how many atomic bombs it would require to "eliminate" the Soviet capacity to make war. American policy makers must likewise be prepared to state the terms on which they would be willing to settle specific problems through negotiation. Such terms have been stated repeatedly with respect to Austria and Korea. When the western German state is a going concern, the United States and its allies must be prepared eventually to negotiate for a reunification of Germany on terms guaranteeing its independence, or else allow the eastern and western German states to work out terms for their own unification.

Even after the American people were pitchforked by Japanese and German aggression into a war for national survival, it was far from clear that they would accept, after the war, any continuing responsibilities beyond their ocean borders. In 1945 they assumed that the United Nations, if firmly supported, would suffice to keep the peace and that they, as a nation, need have no concern for developments abroad beyond some temporary assistance in economic recovery. If the Soviet leaders had curbed their own postwar ambitions, they would have profited by a great fund of good will in America. If, in 1945 and 1946, the Soviet leaders had been less cocksure of the validity of their "scientific" prognosis and had met American interests and sentiments a part of the way, a continuing basis for correct and fairly co-operative relations might have been laid. This did not occur. The philosophy of world-wide expansion, which the Soviet leaders had muted down during the co-operation with Hitler, was turned on full blast against their recent allies. In their gamble, the Soviet leaders threw into the discard those human *imponderabilia* which even Bismarck considered as important in the conduct of successful policy as the possession of great power.

:13:

SOVIET POLICY AND THE KOREAN WAR[1]

[*February 1952*]

INTRODUCTORY NOTE · One of Stalin's major miscalculations was the resort to armed conquest in Korea, launched in June 1950. Was his decision due to frustrated anger, to an urge to reverse the decision made almost casually in August 1945, to divide Korea "for purposes of liberation" at the 38th parallel, instead of establishing sole Soviet occupation? Or was it merely the first step in the program, loudly proclaimed by Soviet and Chinese Communist propaganda, to round out the new Communist empire in Asia by the conquest of Korea, Formosa, and Indochina?

Whatever the sources of Moscow's and Peking's decision, the results of the North Korean attack ran directly counter to their hopes. The Republic of Korea demonstrated a strong will to survive even in its exposed sector of the free world, and the Communist invaders found no support in the South, even in the periods of retreat. Japan's recovery of independence and its re-entry into the society of nations were accelerated. NATO, from being a concept and a promise, was transformed into an actual

[1] "Soviet Policy and the War," in "The Korean Experience," *Journal of International Affairs*, Vol. VI, No. 2 (Spring 1952), pp. 107–14. Copyright 1952 by the Board of Editors of the *Journal of International Affairs.*

strategic force. Within the Soviet bloc, the unexpected war led to a drastic stepping up of military production. The resulting distortions and strains within the economies of the European satellites intensified the bitterness of the subject peoples and helped pave the way for the dramatic events of 1956 in Poland and Hungary. The "Peace Movement," which had enlisted many millions of signatures, all but collapsed under the impact of the new evidence of Soviet aggressiveness. The political, strategic, and economic costs of Stalin's Korean adventure were high.

*

THE signal for the attack of the North Korean forces against South Korea was given by the Soviet leadership. The first effective proposal for the opening of negotiations for an armistice was made directly by a Soviet representative. A cease-fire will not be concluded until the Soviet Politburo is convinced that this is necessary or useful within the framework of its own larger purposes, in which Korea is an incidental and largely passive factor.

The invasion of June 25, 1950, was carefully prepared. In the light of easily accessible information concerning the numbers and armaments of the Republic of Korea forces, the North Korean forces had been well trained and equipped. They were prepared to overwhelm the forces available in South Korea, and they very nearly succeeded in doing so. It has since been revealed that it was a bluff which saved Pusan in mid-July and gave the several days needed to save the Republic of Korea-United Nations bridgehead. If the North Korean or Soviet strategists were nearly right in believing that a sweep through to victory was assured, their view was widely shared in Western military circles.

The North Korean army had been trained by a Soviet mission and has been led, in part, by Korean officers trained in Soviet and Chinese Communist armies. Its equipment, especially its armor, could have been provided only by the Soviet government. By withholding this equipment and its later replacements the Soviet government could have brought the war to a close. From the Soviet attitude towards Yugoslavia, as disclosed in the Soviet-Yugoslav correspondence,[2] it is clear that no such risk-fraught decision could, in the Soviet view of proper Communist conduct, have been taken by the North Korean Communists acting alone. Whether the Pyongyang regime urged on Moscow the necessity of a military campaign to unify Korea and received Soviet permission and aid, or whether the decision to bring into action a military plan for the unification of Korea under Soviet auspices was directly initiated by the Soviet government is relatively immaterial.

It is probable that the final preparations for the Korean campaign were decided on at Moscow, in January 1950, during Mao Tse-tung's extended conferences with the Soviet leaders. Prior to the conquest of the Chinese mainland, the Soviet government would presumably have hesitated to launch an attack on South Korea. Begun at a time when Nationalist Chinese forces still held substantial bridgeheads in the south, such an attack might have led to the abandonment of South Korea by the United States—and to a substantial reinforcement of the Nationalist armies which were resisting Mao Tse-tung's advance. In any case, after January 1950 the possibility of a direct American retaliation against Communist China for an attack on South Korea must have seemed a slight risk.

Having completed the conquest of the Chinese mainland, Mao Tse-tung was probably glad to learn of the Soviet decision to expel the "Western imperialists"

[2] *The Soviet-Yugoslav Dispute*, 1949, *passim*. The Soviet Politburo resented deeply the risk of being involved in war by the Yugoslav shooting down of American planes in August 1946.

from their last foothold on the mainland of northeast Asia. In this respect Soviet and Chinese Communist sentiments and interests are directly parallel, and it seems useless to try to discover some complicated anti-Soviet maneuver in the Chinese intervention into the Korean War. A clash of interests between them might conceivably arise after the completion of the conquest of Korea, but it is highly improbable, that Peking would even consider contesting the predominant strategic and economic interests of the Soviet Union in Korea. It is also quite possible that the Soviet promise, in January 1950, to withdraw from Dairen and Port Arthur and to return them to Chinese control was adopted on the assumption that the, to Russia, much more valuable and advanced naval and air facilities of the Korean peninsula would shortly be brought solidly under Soviet control, through the device of "joint" Soviet-Korean bases or of a Soviet-Korean treaty of mutual defense.

The Soviet-Chinese conferences at Moscow, which must have covered a wide range of common interests in Asia, coincided with a particularly uncertain phase of American policy. The attitude of the United States government at that time must have led the Soviet government to assume that America was unwilling and unprepared to use force to defend the Republic of (South) Korea. In an address to the National Press Club on January 12, 1950, Secretary of State Acheson defined the security interests of the United States in the western Pacific. His carefully worded address was the more impressive, as there had been heated discussions in the Congress and within the executive branch concerning the extent of American security interests and commitments in this area. Members of the Congress had been vocal in demanding a clear statement that the United States was not under any obligation to defend Korea. Leaders of the defense establishment had long regarded South Korea as militarily indefensible; its protection depended on political factors, in other words, on just how far the Soviet Union would wish to go in promoting or avoiding provocation of the United States.

In his address Mr. Acheson stated that ". . . there is no intention of any sort of abandoning or weakening the defenses of Japan. . . . This defensive perimeter runs along the Aleutians to Japan and then goes to the Ryukyus. . . . The defensive perimeter runs from the Ryukyus to the Philippine Islands." For the United States' relation to Korea the important part of the statement was the following:

> So far as the military security of other areas in the Pacific is concerned, it must be clear that no person can guarantee these areas against military attack. . . . Should such an attack occur . . . the initial reliance must be on the people attacked to resist it and then upon the commitments of the entire civilized world under the Charter of the United Nations . . .[3]

While Korea was not directly named in the passage relating to military security, it was obviously excluded from the "defensive perimeter" and from the benefit of any "guarantee" on the part of the United States.

That the Acheson speech was carefully studied in Moscow is suggested by the fact that Foreign Minister Vyshinskii replied to it directly in a statement issued by him on January 21, 1950.[4] Of course, this statement, designed to refute Mr. Acheson's charges of Soviet designs on Chinese territories, made no reference to Korea, though it described the American "defensive perimeter" as a "line of aggression."

The question of whether the United States would even continue to provide economic aid for South Korea was also placed in doubt at that very time. On January 19, the House of Representatives rejected, by 193–191,

[3] Department of State *Bulletin*, Vol. XXII, No. 551 (January 23, 1950), pp. 115–6.

[4] "*Zaiavlenie Minindel SSSR t. A.Ya. Vyshinskogo po povodu vystupleniia Gosudarstvennogo Sekretaria SShA g. Achesona,*" *Pravda* No. 21 (January 21, 1950), p. 2.

a bill to furnish $60 millions in economic aid to the Republic of Korea. While some votes were cast against the bill in protest against the Administration's decision not to support the Chinese Nationalist government in Formosa, others among the majority urged the House to stop "pouring money down the rathole" of Korea. If Korea had been deprived completely of economic aid, it is possible that the then existing government would have lost control of the situation, and that it might eventually have been overthrown by domestic forces which would have effected a fusion with the North Korean regime. Certainly, from a Soviet point of view, it would have been preferable for this course of events to develop, since no soldiers would have to cross the demarcation line to unite North and South, and the United States, having cut off even its modest economic aid, could not have complained of this outcome provided direct force was not used. The restoration of economic aid to Korea by the Congress must have convinced the Kremlin that South Korea could not be subverted from within in the near future and that the United States government would not go beyond offering economic aid and protests before the United Nations to keep the Republic of Korea in being. While the South Korean elections of May 30, 1950, threatened to unseat the Syngman Rhee government, they offered no encouragement to Soviet hopes for an early subversion of the Republic from within.

In view of the apparently slight risks involved in equipping and launching the North Korean forces, the potential gains to the Soviet Union were great. Once in possession of the Korean peninsula, the Soviet forces would be able to develop a well-rounded sea-and-air perimeter, one much nearer to Japan and much more threatening to United States bases there. At the same time, the defense of the thin and vulnerable railroad network in the Soviet Far East would be greatly strengthened; it would be difficult for unaccompanied bombers to reach them without great cost, and advanced fighter bases in Korea—otherwise potentially available to the United States—would then be in Soviet hands.

The political shock to Japan would be great. Instead of feeling greater readiness to entrust their defense in major part to the United States, the Japanese would be directly exposed to Soviet air attacks based on Korea and would doubt the ability of a distant America, strongly committed in Europe, to give adequate or timely protection. It was safe to predict a great upsurge of "neutralism" in Japan, certainly, a greater reluctance to conclude a separate treaty of peace without the Soviet Union and Communist China, and possibly a strong movement to reject all military entanglements with the United States as directly dangerous to its survival. Judging from the simultaneous concentration of Soviet and Chinese Communist propaganda upon Korea, Formosa, and Indochina (Vietnam) between January and June 1950, it is possible to hazard a guess that the Soviet Union was "looking after" Korea, while Mao Tse-tung would "take care" of Formosa and Indochina after waiting to see the reactions to the Communist seizure of South Korea.

If the need for reinforcing Japan and the Philippines drew United States equipment and man power from the build-up in Europe, that was an added but not decisive advantage. Potential gains were great, and probable risks seemed slight. Once again the Kremlin showed its inability to gauge public opinion in democratic countries and its probable reactions. Because the United States had stated, in effect, that Korea was not within its "defensive perimeter," the Kremlin concluded that it would not, under any circumstances, attempt to defend South Korea. Because it was not equipped or staffed, either in Korea or in Japan, to defend South Korea against the forces which the Soviet government had prepared, Moscow assumed that it would not, under any circumstances, attempt to do so, or, if it attempted, that it would fail.

In the light of these calculations it is still not clear why the Soviet government was unwilling to wait and see whether South Korea could not be undermined and annexed from within. Perhaps it was impressed by the fact that since 1945 nearly two million Koreans had moved from the North to the South, while only a few thousands had trekked in the opposite direction. Perhaps it is only a reflection of the general impression that during and since World War II the Soviet government has increasingly placed its primary reliance upon military force in being and available for use.

If the Soviet government wished to prevent the United Nations from taking action to resist an attack by North Korea, why did it absent itself from the meetings of the Security Council after January 13, 1950? One possible motive was to act in a way consistent with its unilateral assertion that the Security Council was not qualified to act in the absence of the representative of any permanent member-state. On later returning to the council, subsequent to the conquest of South Korea, it would be in a position to allow the council to disregard tacitly as null and void any resolution of protest adopted in its absence.

In line with this hypothesis the Soviet government may have calculated that it would be preferable to allow a resolution of censure against the North Korean government to be adopted in its own absence from the Security Council, on the assumption that no effective action would be taken by the United Nations. Once a unified government of Korea had been created, it would only be a matter of time, it could be assumed, before it could be admitted to the United Nations.

The political build-up for the attack of North Korea on the South was, at best, rather half-hearted. On June 7, 1950, the Central Committee of the United Democratic Fatherland Front of Korea, meeting at Pyongyang, issued an appeal to all Koreans to join in unifying the country prior to the fifth anniversary of the liberation from Japan, to hold a general election throughout Korea on August 5–8, and to call a meeting of the supreme legislative body of all Korea at Seoul on August 15. The appeal offered to co-operate with all political parties in South Korea except for those led by Syngman Rhee and Sonsu Kim, and appealed by name to a number of the parties which were opposed to the Rhee government. It also proposed the convocation of a political conference on June 15–17 at Haeju or Kaesong, near the 38th parallel, to work out the steps for unification. On June 10, an emissary of the United Democratic Fatherland Front crossed the frontier with the appeal, was arrested and protested the arrest.[5] The response in South Korea to this prelude of political warfare was negligible.

There has been much speculation over the Chinese Communist leadership in the second main phase of the Korean War, but reliable facts are few and far between. The victorious counteroffensive of the United Nations forces and their advance into North Korea were followed by the entry of Chinese "volunteers" into the war, while from September on there had been circumstantial reports of Chinese divisions being moved from the south of China to Manchuria and the Yalu. The first Soviet report of Chinese volunteers taking part in the fighting appeared in *Pravda* of November 11, and in the following days these reports became a regular feature.[6] Thus the participation of Chinese

[5] "Appeal of Central Committee of United Democratic Fatherland Front of Korea to Korean People," *Pravda*, June 10, p. 4; "For a United Korea," *Izvestiia*, June 10, p. 3; "Plenary Session of Central Committee of United Democratic Fatherland Front of Korea," *Pravda*, June 11, p. 3; "For Unity of Korea," *Izvestiia*, June 11, p. 3; "South Korean Troops Fire on Peaceful Emissaries," *Pravda*, June 13, p. 5; "Korean People Express Indignation at Barbarous Deeds of Syngman Rhee's Treacherous Clique," *Pravda*, June 14, p. 6; all cited from *Current Digest of the Soviet Press*, Vol. II, No. 24 (July 29, 1950), pp. 36–8.

[6] "Chinese Press on Struggle Against American Aggression and Aid to Korean People," *Pravda*, November 11, p. 4; "Chinese Volunteers on their Way to Korea," *Pravda*, November 13, p. 4; both cited from

forces was officially reported in the Soviet press a fortnight prior to the great Chinese counteroffensive. Whether or not the relatively poor initial armaments of the Chinese, especially in armor and aircraft, were due to a deliberate Soviet desire not to strengthen China, as some have asserted, remains doubtful. From the fact that up-to-date and highly effective air support was made available to the Chinese forces in 1951 and 1952, it is more reasonable to assume that the Chinese forces had to be thrown into combat without having time to be supplied with and to master more complex types of equipment, provided by Soviet industry.

The first direct indication that the Soviet-dominated bloc was prepared to negotiate the cease-fire and an armistice came from the startling official radio speech by Jacob Malik, on June 23, 1951. It is clear now that in June 1951 the Chinese Communist forces were in a very difficult situation. Surrenders had increased noticeably in the preceding weeks; supply had been disrupted by systematic air attacks; it was not clear that the Chinese Communist forces could rally on any predetermined line to check the United Nations-ROK forces in their advance. The first effect of the *de facto* cease-fire which followed the offer to negotiate was to relieve this pressure upon the Chinese Communist armies.

In retrospect it is probable that the Soviet government had been trying for a month to evoke from the opposing side a request for a cease-fire and that it took the direct initiative in proposing it only when its indirect approach to the problem failed. In May 1951 Senator Johnson of Colorado had presented to the Senate a resolution urging the proclamation of an armistice to take effect on June 25 and the withdrawal of both forces north and south of the 38th parallel.

Current *Digest of the Soviet Press*, Vol. II, No. 42 (December 2, 1950), p. 16.

This proposal was reproduced in full by *Pravda* and *Izvestiia* on May 19.[7] Such prominence is not "accidental" in Soviet practice. The *Daily Worker* at once undertook a full-fledged campaign to rouse public support for Senator Johnson's proposal. It may well be that the failure of this campaign to win public attention, together with the increasingly critical situation of the Chinese forces in North Korea, impelled the Soviet government to take the initiative, through Malik's speech, in a manner which would focus attention and hopes throughout the world on the early conclusion of an armistice and bring the United Nations advance to a halt.

Why has the Soviet government allowed the cease-fire negotiations to drag on since July 1951? Once the psychological atmosphere of a cease-fire had been created, the Soviet government and its allies at once acquired all the military advantages which they could expect to secure through an actual cease-fire. The North Koreans are "at home" and the Chinese Communist soldiers are under no pressure to return home. Since it is the United Nations forces who wish to return home, it is, from a Soviet point of view, up to the United Nations Command to make one concession after another to secure an armistice. If any particular concession is unwelcome to the Soviet side, it is prepared to let the Chinese Communist and North Korean representatives sit the negotiations out indefinitely. Aside from the military advantage of having a full opportunity to rebuild their forces and to replenish supplies and equipment, to a point where, in May 1952, the Communist forces were reported to be far stronger than at any previous time, what has been the Soviet political tactic?

If the military terms of the proposed cease-fire had

[7] "Resolution by Senator Johnson in U. S. Senate," *Pravda*, May 19, p. 4; *Izvestiia*, May 19, p. 4; both cited from *Current Digest of the Soviet Press*, Vol. III, No. 20 (June 30, 1951), p. 14.

been fully satisfactory to the Soviet-dominated side, it would have been logical for it to hasten the conclusion of the armistice and to try to speed the departure of the United Nations forces from Korea. Once international attention had shifted from Korea, the accumulated misery of destruction and reconstruction would have offered fertile ground for the growth of pro-Soviet forces even in the South. The South Koreans would now recognize that the unification of Korea through the United Nations had become impossible. Prior to June 25, 1950, the South Koreans could hope that unification, on Western terms, would some day be possible; now they would see that the maximum effort of the United Nations would not extend to the achievement of Korean reunification.

While Soviet plans are matured in secret and predictions concerning them are especially risky, it is probable that no Soviet decision concerning the final conclusion of a cease-fire in Korea will be made until after the national conventions in the United States, or possibly until after the presidential election. The comments of the Soviet press indicate that the Politburo believes that American attention, in an election year, will be distracted from affairs abroad and that there is also a deep cleavage between those "imperialists" who wish to maintain a wide front of anti-Soviet defense and other "imperialists" who believe that the United States has overextended its efforts and should cut its commitments.

The Soviet-led bloc is determined to outsit the American-led United Nations bloc in the Korean War. Meanwhile, it hopes to influence the political campaign in the United States by a combined policy of keeping up military pressure in Korea and of making "peace-like" gestures toward the revival of East-West trade and the unification of Germany. The deeper significance of the Soviet role in unleashing the war in Korea and in prolonging the Korean stalemate is that the Soviet leaders have been willing to run an appreciable risk of war in order to gain a goal which is, strategically and politically, not very urgent for them, and that by the, to them, unexpected counteraction of the United States and the United Nations they have so far been denied the easy prestige-success and strategic gains which they sought. Just what kind of long-range settlement in Korea can be satisfactory to the United Nations side has been obscure since June 25, 1950, and remains obscure today. Meanwhile, the timetable for expansion of Soviet power and influence in Asia has been seriously upset, without compensating gains to Soviet strength in Europe or the Middle East.

:14:

THE NINETEENTH PARTY CONGRESS[1]

[*November 1952*]

INTRODUCTORY NOTE · In retrospect, it is still not clear why Stalin summoned his last party congress in October 1952. It is not probable that he wished to consecrate a successor, and by 1957 the "top nine" in his new Presidium had shrunk to two: Khrushchev and the durable Mikoyan. Stalin's last Five-Year Plan, 1951–5, had to be revised substantially within a few months of his death. His advocacy of transforming the peasants of the collective farms into employees of state farms, with the consequent loss of their essential private holdings and private earnings, was also consigned to oblivion with his own demise, although Khrushchev is moving by more careful steps toward the same ultimate goal of creating a uniformly socialistic economy.

Perhaps the strongest effect of Stalin's pronouncements at the congress was in the field of foreign policy. He denied the "inevitability" or even the probability of a war between East and West, ordered the Communist parties abroad to shake off their passive waiting for a Soviet military victory and to seek new political allies by spearheading all forms of attack on American influence and by

[1] *Foreign Affairs*, Vol. XXXI, No. 2 (January 1953), pp. 238–56.

promoting dissension within the "capitalist" world. In his last months of rule Stalin's policy seemed to be balanced uncertainly somewhere between the tactical extremes of "we-or-they" intransigence and the more flexible and varied approaches of "coexistence."

*

A GAP OF thirteen and one-half years lay between the Eighteenth and Nineteenth Congresses of the Soviet Communist party instead of the three-year interval provided by the former party statutes. Although various references were made, from 1948 on, to plans for holding a new party congress, *Pravda*'s announcement, on August 20, 1952, of the date and the agenda came without forewarning. The assembling of the congress on October 5 was preceded by many and varied speculations concerning its significance. Its conclusion was followed by no less puzzlement as to why it had been held. The delay in the calling of a congress and its purely formal role once it had met emphasized the fact that in the Soviet party state the self-chosen and self-perpetuating party leadership has made the nominally ruling party a handmaiden of its own absolute control over the state apparatus. In this Siamese-twin relationship, the power of the state apparatus has flourished, and that of the theoretically all-powerful party has withered.

One formal purpose of calling the congress was to change the party name from "All-Union Communist Party (Bolsheviks)" to that of the "Communist Party of the Soviet Union." For this, was it necessary to call together 1,359 leading members? The official explanation is that the term "Bolsheviks" now has a purely historical significance, recalling the split of 1903 between Lenin's followers and the Mensheviks, who, after various maneuvers by Lenin, found themselves in a minority at the Second Congress of the Russian Social Democratic party. Perhaps another historic echo, better left unvoiced in view of the present Soviet dogma of the primacy of the Great Russian "elder brother" over the other Soviet peoples, was that the now discarded word "All-Union" recalls the period of 1922–4, when the Ukrainian, Belorussian, Georgian, and other parties were fused with their All-Russian counterpart into a single "All-Union" party on an allegedly equal and voluntary footing. The new terminology conforms to the fact of completely centralized control over the party, and eliminates any faint recollection of the time when the various non-Russian Communist parties believed that, at least for them, there would be some element of genuine federalism within both party and state in the Soviet Union.[2]

The newly-adopted party statutes record current practice, rather than change it. They emphasize even more clearly the principle of hierarchical subordination spelled out in the new rules. Until the exclusion of a party member from the party cell to which he belongs has been ratified by higher committees—provincial, regional, or Union Republic—he continues to take a full part in the work of the cell, including attendance at secret meetings. Obviously, the real right of expulsion is vested in the hierarchy of committees, and more specifically in their secretaries, who are appointed by the central secretariat in Moscow.

By contrast, the party *apparat*—the party committees at the county, city, district, provincial, regional, and Union Republic levels—is placed in a privileged position. The expulsion of these party leaders cannot even be considered by any lowly party cell; such a question can be decided only by a two-thirds majority of the plenary session of the party committee to which the

[2] Or perhaps, in dealing with nine ruling parties within the Soviet power-bloc, there is a convenience of terminology in referring to the Soviet party by a name which identifies its geographical and political status.

suspect belongs. Logically, therefore, the new statutes provide also that the exclusion of a member of the Central Committee is to be decided by a party congress, which is now scheduled once in four years, or, what is more important, by the Central Committee, meeting at intervals between congresses. These provisions help to safeguard the position of the hierarchy —the *apparat*—against possible control by the rank-and-file membership, and emphasize again the principle of hierarchical obedience within a monolith controlled and directed from the top.

The new statutes are, of course, silent on the question of limiting the power of the political police over party members. In its early decades the party assumed that the political police was intended to control the "enemies of the people," not to supervise and punish members of the party, which had its own Control Commission for this purpose. During Stalin's struggle for dominance and then for monopoly of power, the powers of the police not only over known oppositionists but also over all party members, expanded rapidly. However, efforts to uphold the tradition of party control over members—the best known efforts were associated with Satz and Akulov—persisted as late as 1934. Article 13 of the new statutes clearly reinforces rather than limits the complete ascendancy of the political police over the membership of the party. It provides that "in cases when a member of the party has committed misdeeds which are subject to punishment under judicial procedure, he is excluded from the party together with communication concerning the misdeed to the administrative and judicial authorities." Apparently, this clumsily worded provision refers only to "misdeeds" which have been discovered first by party organs and are then to be reported by them to the political police or the state's attorney. There is no reference to any action to be taken by the party committees in case a party member is accused or convicted of "misdeeds" under any of several public or secret procedures. The inference of the unchallenged supremacy of the political police over the "vanguard of the toiling people" is clear.

No little puzzlement has also arisen over the disappearance of the Politburo of the Central Committee, with, usually, nine members and two alternates, and its replacement by the Presidium, with its twenty-five members and eleven alternates. In an otherwise wordy report on the draft statutes, Khrushchev was a model of laconic brevity when it came to a discussion of this change. He stated in a single sentence that "such a reconstruction [Politburo into Presidium] is opportune because the term 'Presidium' corresponds better to the functions which are, in fact, being carried out at present by the Politburo." Obviously, the "functions" of the Politburo-Presidium were so clear to the party congress that no further explanation was appropriate, and the entire draft statute was "adopted unanimously."

The only way to guess at the difference between the old and the new organs of dictatorial rule is to examine the composition of each. The enlarged Presidium contains three elements. The most important part of its membership consists of Stalin and nine other members (Molotov, Malenkov, Voroshilov, Bulganin, Kaganovich, Mikoyan, Beria, Khrushchev, Shvernik), with long service on the Politburo. The portraits of these ten, and only of these ten, leaders were featured prominently in the November 7 celebrations at Moscow, in accordance with the Soviet principle of hierarchy. Aside from the disappearance of Andreyev, following Khrushchev's attack in 1950 on his methods of organizing collective farm work, this "leading cadre" has shown a remarkable stability for many years.

Among fifteen other less prominent members of the Presidium are four party leaders from three key regions: Andrianov from Leningrad, Aristov from Cheliabinsk, Korotchenko and Mel'nikov from the Ukrainian party. It is probable that Mel'nikov has the greater authority in the Ukrainian Communist party, but it would have been awkward not to include a representative, such as Korotchenko, with a Ukrainian family name. While another member, Otto Kuusinen, is nominally the head of the Karelo-Finnish Republic, a relatively unimportant region, it is more probable that he was included as an adviser on Communist parties abroad because of his many years' service as a high official of the Communist International prior to its formal dissolution in May 1943.

The third element in the Presidium consists of important central executives just below the top rank, such as Pervukhin, head of the Russian Republic, Kuznetsov, head of the trade-unions, Shkiriatov, chairman of the party Control Commission, and Saburov, chairman of the State Planning Office, while Mikhailov, Ponomarenko, and Suslov are members both of the Presidium and of the all-important secretariat of the Central Committee, which controls appointments, promotions, and demotions within the party *apparat* and participates in similar decisions affecting the higher ranks in the administrative, economic, and military bureaucracy. Among alternate members of the Presidium are other second-rank executives, such as Vyshinskii for foreign affairs, Zverev for finance, and Kosygin for light industry.

Saburov's new-found prominence deserves a special word. When he replaced Voznesensky in 1949 as chairman of Gosplan, he was referred to abroad as a "mere technician." In a sense all Soviet executives except Stalin are "technicians." As early as 1945, Saburov had emerged as the most important economic expert in Stalin's secretariat. In that year he was in command of the Soviet campaign to round up and ship to Russia all possible supplies and equipment found in eastern Germany. In this field his authority overrode that of the Soviet military command. American negotiators who dealt with Saburov at the Potsdam Conference and later in the Allied Council at Berlin found him incisive and efficient, extremely well-informed about economic and reparation problems, very direct and, in that sense, "unideological" in his approach to concrete problems. Incidentally, Saburov was reportedly one of some eighty young Soviet party specialists selected to study engineering and production methods in the United States between 1931 and 1933. He and Mikoyan are probably the only high Soviet leaders who have a first-hand acquaintance with America's industrial power. His speech to the congress, which supplemented and expanded Malenkov's treatment of economic issues, was forthright in treating both achievements and defects of Soviet production.

The most important and least known factor in the operations of the Politburo-Presidium is its system of committees. There are, it is believed, standing committees on foreign policy, on economic development, on military affairs, on ideological controls, on the direction of foreign Communist parties, and perhaps on other topics. For example, it is probable that Molotov, Voroshilov, Malenkov, and perhaps on occasion Mikoyan and Beria, form a committee on foreign policy, to which Vyshinskii and some other leading officials of the Ministry of Foreign Affairs report. Zverev may report on financial questions to a committee consisting perhaps of Molotov, Khrushchev, Kaganovich, and Saburov. A similar committee on Foreign Communist parties might consist of Molotov, Beria, Malenkov, and Kuusinen.

In the absence of permitted channels for freely expressed pressures and competing views, "cabinet committees" of this type, backed by careful staff papers, are essential if divergent demands and interests are to be taken into account in policy making. Given the almost complete continuity of persons and responsibilities from the Politburo to the Presidium, the committee system has presumably also continued its functions. The only slight change is that about ten responsible executives who were immediately below the Politburo in terms of their functions have received outward recognition through membership in the enlarged Presidium. Whether the Presidium will actually function or even meet as a body is a matter of sheer speculation.

A study of the hierarchical details of the congress confirms the impression that Malenkov, who was chosen, trained, and raised to power by Stalin, has emerged as a probable successor, after having outmaneuvered and outlived his rivals. Conceivably, a Khrushchev-Beria-Molotov combination might offer competition to his influence over general policy and over the power of appointment, but no such "combination" would be imaginable unless Stalin fostered it. At the same time there is no logical ground for assuming that Stalin would allow access to him to be centered in a single person, however much trusted, or that he will not continue to remain in close touch with important decisions through the committees and their agreed and unagreed recommendations to him.

Malenkov's deportment at the congress was well designed to mark him as the "modest second" reporting on behalf of the "incomparable" leader. While his very long report, dealing with the whole range of domestic and world policy, was referred to with approval by subsequent speakers, no "adjectives" similar to those inevitably coupled with Stalin's name were applied to Malenkov. By comparison, the background role assigned to Molotov was striking. The hierarchically planned proceedings strengthened the impression that active conduct of policy—"leadership" must remain unique—has been passing since the war into the hands of men of long administrative and party experience in their fifties, backed by administrators of substantial experience in their forties.

The congress itself reflected this important shift of executive responsibility to the postrevolutionary generations. Of 1,192 voting members, 61.1 per cent were between forty-one and fifty, 15.3 per cent over fifty,

17.7 per cent between thirty-five and forty, and 5.9 per cent were under thirty-five. This is a striking reversal in age-structure, compared with the 1920's and even the 1930's. In terms of length of party membership, 1.2 per cent were members before 1917, 6.2 per cent joined between 1917 and 1920, 36.4 per cent between 1921 and 1930, 36 per cent between 1931 and 1941, 16.1 per cent between 1941 and 1945, and 4.1 per cent since the war. The importance of advanced education for entry into the leading ranks of the party is indicated by the fact that of 1,192 delegates 709 had completed their higher education and 84 had received some higher education.

In effect, the Nineteenth Congress consolidated the fusion between party and state, ratifying the interdependence which had been clearly outlined by the mid-1930's, consolidated by the great purges of the late 1930's, and extended further by the mass inflow of military and civilian administrators during World War II. The power of direct appointment or of review of appointment, increasingly monopolized by the party secretariat from the mid-1930's on, would in itself have sufficed to consolidate the direct authority of the Politburo over all ranks of the party, administrative, economic, and military apparatus. There is evidence that the power of the secretariat over appointments in the party machine includes the posts of party committee secretaries down to the level of counties, cities, and important factories. All ministerial appointments in the central government and the Union Republic governments are believed to be similarly centralized, as well as the appointment of the principal administrators in the provinces. In the army, all appointments from the rank of colonel up are believed to be subject to review and ratification by the secretariat. Within the central government, the state and the vast economic machine, actual policy is made by the Politburo-Presidium of the party. Probably the unwieldy Council of Ministers never meets, and the ministries are grouped by subject matter under the direction of relevant committees of the Presidium. The original parallelism between state and party organs, expressed in the duality of the general secretary of the party and the chairman of the Council of People's Commissars, has been replaced by the direct rule of the party leadership which utilizes for its ends both state machinery and party apparatus.

For the rulers the party performs three principal functions: mass indoctrination, supervision of performance, and recruitment of personnel. While Khrushchev emphasized the role of the party as the bearer of doctrine, the Nineteenth Congress added nothing to the picture of this function beyond exhortations to improve its methods and to strengthen its propaganda efforts. The listing of the principal party schools, as given by Moskatov, chairman of the party's Central Review Commission, gave some insight into the organization of indoctrination. Among such schools he listed "one-year courses for the advanced training of first secretaries of provincial committees, of regional committees of the Soviet party and of the central committees of Communist parties of Union Republics, chairmen of provincial and regional executive committees, and of presidents of the councils of ministers of Union and Autonomous Republics." The fusion of party and state apparatus could not be better illustrated than by the picture of both party and state high officials, including presidents of Union Republics, attending the highest party school for a year, presumably to receive their final initiation into the arcana of Soviet rule.

Khrushchev's speech on the work of the party gave many illustrations of the failure of party organizations to exercise supervision over the quality of the work of its own members and of state officials, and emphasized the duty of party members to organize continuous criticism and review of the work of the entire apparatus. According to Malenkov, the basic duties of the party are: to develop "self-criticism" (officially sanctioned criticism), while punishing "slander"; to improve discipline of party members and of all organizations within the Soviet system; to select personnel for both party and state organizations; and to improve "ideological work" both within the party and within "the nonparty masses."

The exact relation of party to state apparatus has fluctuated greatly in the past. Until the mid-1930's the two were to a considerable extent distinct in personnel, and the authority of even low-level party groups or Komsomols to interfere with all levels of the state machinery in the name of "Bolshevist vigilance" constantly made itself felt. As the apparatus of state operation and economic management, of the military and of the secret police expanded during the 1930's, the filling of higher posts by Communists and the tendency to concentrate the best administrators on concrete tasks rather than on the more generalized functions of the party itself gave greater authority to the administrative corps. The purges accentuated the tendency of administrators to regard with distrust any overemphasis of the party's role as a nagging supervisor of their "practical" work. During the war, administrative talents were concentrated on the urgent concrete tasks of producing and fighting, and the ideological test for admission to the party was blurred at the edges by the emphasis upon the patriotic rather than the "ideological" character of the war. By the end of the war party officials were often merely "whippers-up" of sentiment, while power, prestige, and party-influence went to those who "did things."

The revival of emphasis upon party doctrine, upon the unique role of the party, and the concept of "party duty" as supplementary to administrative efficiency, had begun before the end of the war, and has been reinforced steadily, to be stressed again at the Nineteenth Congress. Criticism of the failure of party units to exercise ideological leadership and supervisory control over other apparatus suggests that within the party real power continues to be handled in the main by the managerial elite concerned with the manipulation of large units of power, and that purely party functionaries are often chary of challenging the power of industrial and political "magnates."

The fusion of party membership with operational responsibilities was illustrated by Marshal Vasilevskii's comment that 86 per cent of the generals and officers of the Soviet armed forces are members of the party or Young Communist League. He also added that since the war the principle of "single command" has been further strengthened. Before and at the beginning of World War II the position of "political advisers" or "commissars," party officers attached to the military commanders, had been reinforced; they were often able to veto operational orders of the commanders, whose authority over their men was seriously undermined. In the later course of the war the rôle of the commanders was greatly strengthened. Now, with most of the officers members of party cells, direct ideological supervision of the officers can be strengthened without lessening their outward role as "single commanders" over the troops.

In the past three years there has been a good deal of discussion of the nature of the projected "transition from Socialism to Communism." The party Congress referred frequently to the "preparation" for this transition, but failed to supply a concrete description of the road to be followed. The earlier assumption that the state would begin to "wither away" during the approach to "Communism" had already been rejected by Stalin. But some Soviet economists speculated that the establishment of Communism would be signalized by some dramatic changes in economic life, for example, that a basic commodity like bread would be distributed free to all. Without directly attacking this notion, Stalin chose this time to emphasize in his September article in *Bol'shevik* the idea of the continuity of the basic laws of the economy and to insist that economists should aim to discover basic laws inherent in its working and should cease "inventing" new laws.[3] If Stalin's article, his first major "ideological" work since his explosive article on Soviet linguistics, failed to define the steps for the achievement of "Communism" and in fact emphasized that the Soviet economy cannot "leap over" the basic laws of economic development, it would obviously be imprudent for lesser economic "geniuses" to speculate too far. Perhaps the task of defining "Communism" has been put off until the new party program can be unveiled.

Since the Eighteenth Party Congress, held in 1939, had appointed a special commission to prepare a new program to replace that of 1918, it had been suggested that the delay in calling a postwar congress was due to the difficulty of carrying through the postwar reconstruction of the country and at the same time devoting sufficient time to the major effort of "ideological reconstruction" which the drafting of a new program would entail. Perhaps, also, the new party program would find it embarrassing to reduce to exact definition the relation of the Soviet party to the Communist parties of the European satellites and of China, not to mention its relation to Communist parties in other countries, such as France and Italy, where the Communist leaders have pledged their followers to the active defense of the Soviet government. Any reasonably frank definition might make it difficult for that government to advertise its policy as one devoted to the joys of "coexistence" with the non-Soviet world and to the defense of "national sovereignty" and "peace" against the wicked "imperialists" and their "lackeys."

At the recent congress the problem of effecting a

[3] Joseph Stalin: "Economic Problems of Socialism in the U.S.S.R.," *Current Digest of the Soviet Press*, Special Supplement, October 18, 1952; also *Bol'shevik*, September 1952, pp. 1–50 (placed on sale October 3).

comprehensive restatement of the party program was again postponed, and a committee of eleven was appointed, without announcing a date for its report. Whether it will report to a plenary congress four years from now, or whether the party will simply have to make shift with the program of 1918, is anyone's guess. Since the transition from "Socialism" to "Communism" has already begun, the Soviet people may simply go on working their hides off as heretofore, only to be told some fine morning that they have already attained the stage of "Communism."

The party congress was at least told by Malenkov that "the Fifth Five-Year Plan marks a big new step forward on the road to our country's development from Socialism to Communism."[4] And the economic goals of the 1951–5 plan were set forth in more concrete terms than has been usual in recent years. Without going into detail on this aspect of the Malenkov and Saburov speeches, or the "debates" which followed them, one can say that there is nothing improbable in the Soviet claim that in 1952 the production of steel will reach 35 million metric tons, pig iron 25 million, rolled metal 27 million, coal 300 million, and petroleum 47 million tons. These figures are generally in line with the high tempo of recovery and development which has been shown by the Soviet economy since 1947 when it came out of its postwar slump, and with the high rate of investment and the relatively low rate of consumption, which has been held to levels lower than before the war. Experts estimate that the increase of steel production in 1951 over 1950 amounted to 12 per cent; therefore the goal of an annual average increase of 10.1 per cent in steel during the current Five-Year Plan appears a reasonable one.

A striking factor in the new Soviet plan is that annual percentage rates of increase, as illustrated in the plan for steel, are beginning to slacken off. This is a

[4] *Pravda*, October 6, 1952, p. 4, col. 3; available in *Current Digest of the Soviet Press*, November 1, 8, and 15, 1952.

natural phenomenon in a society which is attaining a fuller degree of industrialization, but a declining percentage of increase against a steadily expanding base means a continued rapid growth in quantitative terms. While United States steel production is estimated at 102 million metric tons for 1952, as compared with 31.4 million for 1951 in the Soviet Union, we must not forget that Hitler challenged the world with only 22.7 million tons (1938), and Japan with 6.9 million (1940). Marshal Bulganin also emphasized, in his speech of October 12, that the Soviet economy was unusually well prepared to shift to a war economy.

Whether the planned increase of 50 per cent in productivity per worker can be achieved depends not only on the proposed maintenance of high rates of investment and on better methods of organization, but on improved satisfaction of the consumption needs of the nonagricultural labor force, which was reported as totalling 40 million for 1951 and a planned 44 million in 1955. As usual, the planned rates of increase in the production of consumer goods are lower than those for extractive and heavy industries, and in the past achievement in this field has usually fallen short of planned goals.

Especial significance attaches to Saburov's statements concerning the continued rapid development of industry east of the Volga River. Here, he claimed, industrial output had been tripled between 1940 and 1952. In 1951, after the reconstruction of industry in European Russia and Ukraine, the eastern areas accounted for one half of the total production of steel and rolled metal, and one third of total industrial output. The gain, as against 1941, in relative strategic protection of vital industries represents a major shift.

Whether the new and, as usual, ambitious goals in agriculture, which have regularly failed of fulfilment in the past, will be achieved in this plan is more doubtful, especially since only 15 per cent of 1951–5 investment is slated to go into agriculture. There is a real possibility that Soviet industry now rests on an inadequate agricultural base, especially in terms of basic foodstuffs. Certainly the per capita availability of livestock and livestock products is well below what it was in 1928, at the beginning of the drive for intensive industrialization.

Malenkov summarized in a few lifeless bureaucratic sentences a profound revolution which has been carried out in the life of the Soviet village, when he stated that 254,000 collective farms have been consolidated into 97,000 amalgamated collectives since January 1950. Obviously, this has been intended as an important step in improving agricultural techniques and in strengthening the grip of the state upon the labor and life of the peasantry. Malenkov repeated earlier criticisms of the "bureaucratic" tendency to amalgamate villages "mechanically," by taking down and moving the buildings to a central settlement, while neglecting the more basic factors of improving farming techniques and organization.

On this subject, Stalin's article in *Bol'shevik* was more revealing than any of the speeches at the congress. Before the stage of "Communism" can be reached, according to Stalin, it will be necessary to do away with the present mixed system by which agricultural land and machines are the property of the state, while the produce is the "property" of the collective farm, and to reach a stage in which agricultural produce will also be the property of the state. In his newest ideological pronouncement, Stalin has thus returned to the idea that all agriculture must be operated by the state, with the peasants working, in effect, as hired laborers. Whether such crude "organizational" methods are best suited to raise the productivity of agriculture is more than doubtful, but it is significant that Stalin, and hence his followers, still see the means of solving the agricultural dilemma primarily in increasing the grip of state control and compulsion upon the peasantry.

As an important intermediate step toward securing complete control over the lagging agricultural sector, Stalin recommends the rapid extension of the system of "product-exchange." This arrangement, which has long been applied in the government's buying up of especially valuable crops like cotton, sugar beet, and tobacco, involves the deliveries of agreed amounts of consumer goods to the peasants at low prices, in return for fixed amounts of produce delivered by the collectives, also at low prices. In respect to other crops such as grain and livestock the collective makes some deliveries to the state at low prices, other deliveries in kind to the machine and tractor stations in payment for their services, and sets up reserves; it may then sell the balance to the government under a "product-exchange" contract, sell it in the open market, or divide it among its members, allowing them to sell their shares directly in the open market. Under the present system a considerable part of the crops escape the direct control of the state, and, as Stalin stated, a large part of exchanges between city and village is regulated by the market. What Stalin is proposing is that all deliveries by the collective farms should be channeled through government agencies, which will, in turn, meet the peasants' need for consumer goods by supplying them under contract at low prices.

This would, from the point of view of the operators of a planned economy, be a great improvement. What would be an even greater improvement, from the peasants' point of view, would be for the government to increase the output of consumer goods, to reduce both prices and the extortionate turnover taxes now levied, and to expand the retail trade network. These steps, which seem Utopian under the current plan, would stimulate farm production, lower prices of consumer goods and food, and economize a great deal of time now wasted by consumers in searching for scarce, shoddy, and high-priced goods. However, since Stalin's slightest "ideological word" is the law for his party, and since he has always set his face against "consumer psychology" in Soviet planning, we may expect to see a reinforced campaign to do away with the collective farm markets, which now supply the cities with about one third of their food, to put an end to free-market selling by the collectives or their members, and to make government agencies the sole "organized" channel for exchanges between agricultural and industrial sectors. While the Soviet apparatus is better equipped to monopolize trade than it was in 1918–21 and in 1930–3, when it was tried out with disastrous results, this step toward "Communism" is not likely to meet with co-operation among the peasants, including even peasant managers of collectives.

In his report, Mikoyan announced that Soviet foreign trade is now three times greater than in prewar years. This statement was not very enlightening, for he did not indicate, nor was he asked by his listeners, whether he was speaking of constant rubles, variable rubles, constant prices, or quantities. One can hope, for his sake, that he was not speaking in terms of dollars, constant or variable, since the ruble has been proclaimed the "most stable currency" in the world. That Mikoyan's failure to indicate the basis for his calculations was no oversight is indicated by his reference to Soviet trade with Finland, measured "in comparable prices." Mikoyan complained bitterly of the "boycott" of Soviet trade by the West, and in the same breath declared that it was of no importance to the Soviet economy. He went on to boast that dealings with the "people's democracies" represented 80 per cent of Soviet foreign trade in 1952. Trade within the Soviet bloc, by which he seems to mean trade among all members of the bloc and not merely their trade with the Soviet Union, had, he reported, increased more than three times over from 1948 to 1952, while the Soviet export of machinery to the members of the bloc had risen ten times over.

In what appears to be a curious lapse from Marxist

concepts, Stalin has now argued, in his *Bol'shevik* article, that the "people's democracies" are raising their production so rapidly that . . . "these countries will not only have no need to import goods from capitalist countries but will themselves experience the need to dispose of surplus products of their own production."[5] Presumably, under a planned economy the appearance of any such "surplus" represents a failure in planning, since "surpluses" should be used to raise consumption or increase investment. Perhaps Stalin suffered a Freudian lapse into wishful thinking. If the satellites no longer needed to import from, and hence to export to, capitalist countries, they would be even better able than at present to donate their "surplus products" to the glory of the "Socialist Motherland," the "citadel of progressive mankind."

When attacking with the customary battery of Soviet vituperations America's "enslaving 'aid'" to European and other nations, Mikoyan also outlined a Soviet policy of offering "unselfish" assistance to underdeveloped countries. This is a cold war weapon which may become of real importance over the next few years, witness the Soviet propaganda effort in India. Despite the urgent requirements for industrial expansion at home and in the satellites and China, Soviet industrial production is reaching a level at which it could, by a purposeful effort, establish economic bastions of its own in countries like Iran or Afghanistan. The possibility that Soviet economic conquest might precede rather than follow political conquest of weak neighbors cannot be ruled out, and this Soviet ambition should not be ignored in any appraisal of the purposes and scope of United Nations, American, and other programs of economic development.

Stalin's concluding speech of October 14 was devoted to the problem of co-operation between the Soviet Union and the "fraternal parties" abroad. His

[5] Joseph Stalin: op. cit., *Current Digest of the Soviet Press*, Special Supplement, October 18, 1952, p. 7.

words were heard by delegations representing forty-four "fraternal Communist and Workers' parties," while addresses of devotion and "loyalty" were received from several other parties, including the Communist party of the United States. Stalin and the congress singled out for special praise declarations by Thorez and Togliatti that "their peoples will not fight against the peoples of the Soviet Union." In turn Stalin pledged the support of the Soviet party to "the fraternal parties" and "their peoples" in "their struggle for liberation, in their struggle for the preservation of peace," adding, to "stormy applause," that, "as is well known, that is exactly what it [the Soviet party] is doing."

Stalin made it clear that this "fraternal" support from abroad, while not decisive, was extremely welcome, when he added:

> It would be a mistake to think that our party, having become a mighty force, is no longer in need of support. That is untrue. Our party and our country always have been and always will be in need of the trust, sympathy and support of fraternal peoples abroad.

Stalin went on in a fatherly and patronizing tone to assure the "fraternal parties" that, however difficult their struggle for power may seem to them, they must realize that "it is not as hard for them as it was for us Russian Communists in the period of tsarism." Stalin further asserted that "not a trace of liberalism" or of national independence now remains under "bourgeois" rule, and urged the parties abroad to pick up the abandoned banners of personal freedom and national sovereignty. "It is obvious," he concluded, "that all these circumstances should lighten the work of the Communist and democratic parties which have not yet come to power." [6]

[6] *Pravda*, October 15, 1952, p. 1, col. 2; *Current Digest of the Soviet Press*, November 1, 1952, p. 10.

Stalin's condescending attitude toward his foreign auxiliaries and their leaders was expressed even more plainly in his *Bol'shevik* article, whose starting point was the discussions of the plan for a new textbook on economics. The textbook, Stalin wrote, is "especially needed for the Communists of all countries . . . who want to know . . . how . . . our country, only recently poor and weak, has been transformed into a rich and powerful country . . . in order to learn from us and to use our experience in their own countries. . . . It will be a handbook of Marxist political economy, a fine gift for the young Communists of all countries. . . . In those countries such a textbook could also be of great benefit to veteran Communists who are no longer young."

Stalin's concluding speech, like all others at the congress, expressed without deviation the basic theme of his postwar foreign policy, first stated in detail by him in February 1946. The world is now divided into two blocs, one of "Socialism, peace, national independence, human liberty" led, needless to say, by the Soviet Union, and another of "capitalist chaos, warmongering, suppression of all national and human rights," which the United States is accused of organizing and bullying. Stalin's newest instructions repeat and summarize the present basic Communist line abroad, which calls for the defense of "freedom" and "independence" against non-Soviet governments and against American influence. This finds tactical expression in Communist support for forces hostile to or fearful of American policies.

However, it is not probable that Communist parties will attempt to seek direct organizational alliances in a new "Popular Front," as in the 1934–9 period. At that time Communist parties were directed to seek cooperation with politically adjacent Socialist and democratic groupings: today they seek temporary alliances with ultranationalist and semitotalitarian forces against the democratic center. In view of the enhanced power of the Soviet Union, it is more useful for it to maintain the Communist parties abroad as small, disciplined and highly maneuverable auxiliary legions rather than risk "confusing" their membership and even their leaders by close co-operation with parties which compete with them for the allegiance of the same social strata.

If foreign supporters of the Soviet-led "peace campaign" harbor illusions concerning Stalin's attitude toward their efforts, these should be removed by his frank words in *Bol'shevik:*

> The aim of the present movement for peace is to arouse the masses of the people for the struggle to preserve peace and to avert a new world war. . . . It is most probable that the present movement . . . will, should it be successful, result in prevention of a *given* war, in its postponement, a temporary preservation of a *given* peace, to the resignation of a belligerent government and its replacement by another government, ready to preserve peace for the time being. . . . With all these successes of the peace movement imperialism still remains and remains in power, and consequently the inevitability of wars also remains. . . . Under a certain confluence of circumstances, the struggle for peace may possibly develop in one place or another into a struggle for Socialism. This, however, will no longer be the present peace movement but a movement for the overthrow of capitalism.[7]

The place of the "peace campaign" in Soviet strategy is that of a tactic to be applied against governments which oppose or resist Soviet policy and are thereby guilty of "warmongering." The double equation—"Soviet policy equals peace, therefore opposition to Soviet aims equals warmongering"—remains in full force.

But is not this concept of Soviet policy, which stresses Soviet-American conflict as the determining

[7] Joseph Stalin: op. cit., p. 8; sequence of sentences has been modified.

factor of world politics, incompatible with Stalin's further statement, also set forth in his *Bol'shevik* article, that new wars are most likely to break out between capitalist countries, not between the "capitalist" world and the Soviet Union? Stalin nows calls upon his followers to reject the assumption, which his own actions and propaganda have created, that "the contradictions between the camp of Socialism and the camp of capitalism are greater than the contradictions among capitalist countries," although he admits that "theoretically, this is, of course, true." Stalin then goes on to explain why this "theoretically true" proposition not only need not be, but is not, "true" in practice. "First capitalist Britain and then capitalist France will ultimately be forced to . . . enter into conflict with the United States in order to assure themselves an independent position and, of course, high profits," while there is "no guarantee" that "Germany and Japan will not again rise to their feet, that they will not try to wrest themselves from American bondage. . . . It follows from this that the inevitability of wars among the capitalist countries remains."

From the illustrations which Stalin offers of the conflicts of economic and political interests which certainly exist within the non-Soviet world, it is not clear on what basis he assumes that these conflicts must take the form of "inevitable wars." If Stalin believes even one tenth of his own propaganda he must doubt the desire or the capacity of Britain or France, of Germany or Japan, to prepare and launch a war against the United States. Perhaps the "genius-teacher" also underestimates the degree to which the leading nations in the non-Soviet world have been made aware, through his own pedagogical efforts, of the fate which would overtake them if they fell to fighting among themselves. Why did Stalin adopt this ex-cathedra position, which, if accepted literally, undercuts the emotional force of his "hate-America" campaign? If he believes what he said, he would logically direct the

Soviet and foreign Communist propaganda machines to forget about Soviet-American conflicts and to give all stress to conflicts within the "capitalist" world. The Soviet government might even make a few minor gestures of conciliation, such as giving Austria back its freedom, to lend more plausibility to the new "line."

The apparent incompatibility is, however, an incompatibility in logic rather than in real politics. After Stalin's pronouncement as before, Soviet propaganda maintains that American "warmongers" are preparing to launch a war upon the Soviet Union. All that is new is Stalin's assurance that the "capitalist" world cannot be unified, and the instruction to go all out to promote disunity and even armed conflict within the non-Soviet world. A "good Bolshevik" does not rest on his oars when his leader tells him that a certain line of development is "inevitable" but is expected to work with redoubled zeal to hasten the "inevitable." Stalin's *Bol'shevik* article, which is addressed to the leaders rather than the masses, is not a scientific prediction, but an instruction to Communist parties abroad to do everything to intensify conflicts *within* the non-Soviet world, in the hope that this may even lead to that most desirable event, a war *within* the "capitalist" world, leaving the Soviet Union and its allies uninvolved and hence capable, in the predicted "third round of wars and revolutions," of establishing Soviet power throughout the world.

In his new statement Stalin is also attempting, for tactical reasons, to play down Soviet and foreign Communist fears of the "inevitability" of war between the Soviet Union and America. For one thing, Soviet propaganda is unable to convince all Communists and their sympathizers of the "inevitability" of a Soviet victory. Once the West has grown stronger in arms and in unity of action, as it has since 1948, the doctrine of an "inevitable" war causes discouragement, apathy and passivity among Communists outside the Soviet bloc, and also passivity, furtive hope and withdrawal from effort among non-Communists and pseudo-Communists within it. If Communists abroad accept the "inevitability" of an East-West war and also agree with Stalin that the decisive factor in it will be the Soviet Union, they are tempted to "disarm" and to rely on the "automatism" of history to make them into subtyrants exploiting their peoples for Soviet aims. Stalin's pronouncement is designed to reawaken them from daydreaming about an "inevitable" war between the Soviet Union and America, to indicate the urgency of intensifying all factors of disunity within the non-Soviet world, and to indicate his belief that in a prolonged and even indefinite period of "cold war" the Soviet regime can maneuver among "capitalist contradictions" so as to preserve its own power untouched by war.

This reassurance to the faithful, backed up by the continued Spartan enforcement of rapid industrialization and armament at home, is Stalin's reply to the secret fears of the "faithful" as they watch the steady though uneven growth in the power and determination of the free world to defend its future. Stalin's pronouncement is a call to his foreign legions to help him contain the reviving strength of the West until it can be dissolved, as his dialectic conveniently insists it must be, by its own "inner contradictions," without risking the survival of the Soviet system in an all-out war.

PART IV

Soviet Policy Since Stalin

:15:

THE KREMLIN'S FOREIGN POLICY SINCE STALIN[1]

[*August* 1953]

IN THE months since Stalin's death the new leadership in the Kremlin has made serious efforts to break out of the East-West stalemate and has displayed an unaccustomed flexibility in wielding the almost disused weapons of diplomacy. It has brought its opponents, some reluctantly, some enthusiastically, to agree to participate in two major conferences, on Germany and on Korea. In so doing, it has chosen the terrain and the weapons for wreaking maximum damage against the vulnerable joints of the alliances which the West has shored up since 1948 against Soviet acts and threats of violence. As in the fable, the Soviet sun has suddenly taken to shining warmly; and the free world wayfarer, having forgotten the north wind, is ready to throw away his cloak and bask in its rays.

Some of the first steps in carrying out the new Soviet line were little more than gestures. The decision to allow several Russian wives, married to American citizens, to leave Russia with their husbands makes no

[1] *Foreign Affairs*, Vol. XXXII, No. 1 (October 1953), pp. 20–33. Copyright 1953 by the Council on Foreign Relations, Inc.

change, of course, in the unique Soviet law which, passed since their marriages, forbids Soviet citizens to marry foreigners.[2] Except in the Kremlin, no one would consider this an act of grace. The Soviet "recommendation" to the Chinese Communist and North Korean governments to exchange seriously ill and disabled prisoners-of-war could be regarded as an act of great generosity only by people who have unconsciously accepted the Soviet assumption that not only its own people but captured prisoners are the property of the captor, who has both the right and the duty to enslave them to his ideology. Moscow's intercession to secure the release of United Nations civilians illegally detained in Korea for almost three years would have been a routine action on the part of any Western power. Yet each of these "gracious acts" held the headlines for many days, and, cumulatively, they have led many people to believe, as one analyst wrote recently, that the new Soviet leadership is "digging a tunnel of friendship to the West," and that the main obstacle to peace is that the West may not begin "digging from its end."

Some of the new Soviet gestures have simply meant the scrapping of a profitless obstinacy. For many months the Soviet position in the question of selecting a successor to Trygve Lie as Secretary-General of the United Nations had been a fruitless one even from the point of view of Soviet interests. Moscow's attitude did not halt the work of the United Nations and it served to focus the fears and resentments of the nations of the non-Soviet world. Acceptance of a new Secretary-General was a step to allay them.

Similarly, the recall of ambassadors from Belgrade and Athens had been acts of hostile pressure. Whatever internal tensions and divisions this Soviet gesture was expected to generate had long since been dis-

[2] (Author's note, 1959) This decree was repealed in November 1953, but it is still extremely rare for a Soviet wife to be allowed to accompany her alien husband to his country.

counted, and a renewed exchange of ambassadors removed a useless annoyance. Meanwhile, the propaganda warfare against the Tito regime, the frequent border incidents, and the building of satellite forces ringing Yugoslavia go on unchanged. Renewal of diplomatic relations with Israel likewise liquidated a fruitless effort to intimidate a small state. In his announcement of July 20 Molotov stressed particularly that the government of Israel had repeated its unilateral pledge not "to take part in any alliance or agreement pursuing aggressive aims against the Soviet Union."

In June Moscow dropped its postwar claims against Turkey's territory and sovereignty. By a note of May 30 it renounced its claims to Kars, Ardahan, and Artvin, purely Turkish territories which it had demanded since 1945 as a token of "friendship." At the same time it abandoned its demand for "joint" Soviet-Turkish control of sea and air bases in and around the Straits of Constantinople; if accepted, this demand would have gone far to make Turkey a Soviet satellite by depriving it of control over its most strategic territories, including its largest city. The Soviet note went on to state that "it is possible to insure the security of the U.S.S.R. in the matter of the Straits on conditions equally acceptable both to the U.S.S.R. and Turkey." Without stating what conditions would be acceptable, the Soviet government clearly implied that Turkey would be well advised to come to a direct agreement with Moscow in advance of 1956, the year in which signatories are free to withdraw from the Montreux Convention on the Straits. Two later Soviet notes complaining against United States and British naval visits to the Straits, rebuffed by Ankara, presumably serve to build up Soviet pressure to change the Montreux Convention before agreeing to its renewal.

The hardheaded Turks needed more than a note of this kind to believe in a Soviet change of heart, but this renunciation of a prize which the Soviet leadership could not seize without risk of a major war allowed Malenkov to proclaim to the Supreme Soviet that "the Soviet Union has no territorial claims against any state whatever, including any of the neighboring states." In his speech of August 8 Malenkov also stressed the Soviet desire to maintain good relations with Afghanistan and to settle pending financial and border questions with Iran. He made no mention of Iran's long-standing desire to eliminate from the Soviet-Iranian treaty of 1921 the clause which permits the Soviet Union to introduce its forces into Iranian territory in case its security is threatened by the forces of a third power stationed in other parts of Iran.

In its foreign trade negotiations the Kremlin has also displayed greater flexibility. It has recently concluded a whole series of new trade and clearing agreements without insisting on breaking down the U. S.-inspired restrictions on the export of strategic commodities to the Soviet bloc. Perhaps Moscow assumed that these controls would break down rapidly once the truce was completed in Korea. Soviet representatives made a striking gesture in the meetings of the Economic and Social Council. Muting their traditionally shrill attacks upon the United Nations' program of technical assistance to underdeveloped countries, they offered, for the first time, a Soviet contribution to the program, which has great prestige in the unindustrialized areas. In the trading sessions sponsored by the Economic Commission for Europe, the Soviet spokesmen have also shown recently a desire to talk business rather than mere propaganda.

The most striking shift in Soviet policy has been the conclusion of the Korean truce, the liquidation of one of Stalin's most glaring mistakes. From the moment the United Nations, and particularly the United States, struck back against the Soviet-inspired and -supported aggression of the North Korean regime, it has, on balance, been to Soviet advantage to end the conflict sooner, rather than later, and the dragging out of the negotiations for more than two years after Malik's offer, in June 1951, of a truce, has compounded the original error of judgment. During this long and bloody struggle the Soviet bloc has been forced to abandon its original goal: the immediate annexation of South Korea and the elimination of Western influence from a key area on the Asiatic mainland. Resistance to Soviet-instigated aggression has greatly improved the capacity of the United Nations to take collective action, and it has stimulated a rapid expansion of the war potential of the United States, a substantial strengthening of the North Atlantic Treaty Organization forces in Europe, and a firmer attachment of Japan to the free world. It has focussed the attention of the free world more clearly on the international implications of the struggle in Indochina. Since May 1951 it has resulted in a more effective enforcement of controls over the export of strategic goods to the Soviet bloc.

The only gains which the Soviet regime has made from prolonging the struggle have been primarily in the propaganda field, and that within the Soviet bloc or among Soviet-oriented segments of opinion elsewhere. It has developed to the full its accusations of "germ warfare," and has enabled the Chinese Communist forces to win local offensive actions in the closing weeks and thus to assert that they had "forced" the United States and its allies to accede to a truce. Not even this great fanfare can conceal from the peoples in the Soviet bloc the fact that large numbers of North Korean and Chinese prisoners have refused to return to their Communist-dominated homelands and that the United Nations bloc has defended their right to refuse repatriation.

The Soviets assume that in Marxism-Leninism-Stalinism they possess the only valid "science" of prediction, but since the MacArthur hearings made clear the United States' determination to wage a limited war, the Soviet leadership seems to have followed a Micawber-like policy of waiting for something better to turn up. This was made evident in a striking statement by *Pravda* in January 1952. In an election year, said *Pravda,* it is probable that the "extreme imperialists" in America, who want to "conquer the world," will encounter many surprises, especially from the "reasonable imperialists," who favor the retraction of American ambitions to the Western hemisphere and who are urging an unconditional withdrawal from Korea. Thus, throughout all of 1952 Moscow watched eagerly for America to withdraw from the Korean struggle, leaving the Soviet Union free to take over the entire peninsula. The outcome of the election, and the growing demand in American public opinion to find new ways to break out of the self-imposed military deadlock, must have tipped the scales in favor of permitting or directing the conclusion of the truce, as Stalin hinted broadly but vaguely in his Christmas Eve written interview. Such is the power of self-deluding dogma that it required costly sacrifices of lives, between June 1950 and July 1953, to convince the Kremlin that the "decadent imperialists" were determined to thwart its plans of conquest in Korea.

With the conclusion of the truce, Moscow has recovered a wider range of diplomatic maneuver. The calling of a political conference for October opens the way to probe the political defenses of the West at their most vulnerable points. All the issues which divide the major powers of the free world will come before the conference, whatever formal limitations of agenda may be sought. The allies of the Unted States are dubious of Syngman Rhee's willingness to be restrained from some new venture to force the unification of Korea and skeptical of the American ability to restrain him without weakening the precarious stability of South Korea. They are eager to seat Communist China in the United Nations, and to renew unrestricted trade with the Chinese mainland. They are doubtful of the value of maintaining indefinitely the Chinese Nationalist regime on Formosa. The allies, and especially the French, hope that by yielding to Peking in all other issues they may persuade Mao to refrain from reinforcing the Communist-led Vietminh with Chinese troops and even to cut off its sole and indispensable supply of equipment and munitions. The Western powers enter the political conference with a tacit commitment to avoid the threat and risk of a new war, and with rigid limits imposed on their field of maneuver by strongly held sentiments at home, sentiments which differ from country to country. Whatever the invisible strains behind the façade of the Soviet bloc, it derives immediate advantage from its monolithic freedom of maneuver in both policy and propaganda. The amazing thing is that the Soviet leadership held off the conclusion of the truce for two years, instead of attempting to exploit more actively the political divisions among the powers which had joined to resist its aggressive plans.

In Germany the open defiance of Soviet power by the workers and peasants of the Eastern zone has dealt a body blow to Soviet prestige and has hampered, for some time to come, Soviet freedom of action. Whatever doubt there was of the hatred of most East Germans for the Soviet regime and its puppets has been dissipated by the uprisings of June 17. The Soviet leadership, probably misled by the optimistic reports of its own agents and stooges, again misjudged the temper of its German subjects.

Any attempt to reconstruct the inner sequence of Soviet decisions is hazardous, but it seems clear that by May the new Kremlin leadership had reviewed the situation in Germany and had marked out a program designed, at best, to harness to its own purposes the desire of nearly all Germans for a reunited and independent country and, at the least, to turn the striving for unity against the Adenauer government in the September elections, and against the attachment of

Western Germany to the European Defense Community and the North Atlantic forces. To achieve this, the Soviet government needed to stop the decline in living standards in Eastern Germany, restore the workers' and peasants' willingness to produce, and therefore slacken somewhat the recently tightened labor controls and reassure the individual peasants, the mainstay of the supply of food and raw materials, that there was no immediate intention for forcing them into the collective farms. Consulted as to whether this temporary relaxation could be carried through without risk, Beria and Zaisser, the police head in the Eastern zone, asserted, presumably, that there was nothing to worry about. Instead, the rank and file in East Germany took the concessions as a sign of weakness and, in an unprecedented act of heroism, arose and destroyed all pretenses that the Pieck-Grotewohl regime had any popular support.

Back of the program of relaxation was probably a longer-range plan: by making the East German regime more tolerable to its own subjects, its chances of being accepted as a partner in any negotiations for the reunification of Germany would be improved. While the Soviet leadership continually talks of the primary responsibility of the four major powers for bringing about the reunification of Germany (as in its note of August 16), it must realize that, at least in the Bonn Republic, the decisive voice in this matter has passed from the Western Allies to the German people itself. In the long run the Western powers cannot resist a strongly-pressed demand within the West German Republic that "Germans sit down with Germans" to resolve the question of reunification. It is probable that the proposed program of relaxation in Eastern Germany was intended not only to relieve the Soviet economy of onerous contributions of food and other supplies, and to strengthen, over the longer run, the economic and political stability of the puppet regime, but also to make that regime more acceptable to many West

Germans as a negotiating partner and thus to facilitate the Communist campaign in favor of a direct arrangement between the two German republics.

The blow which the uprisings of June 17 inflicted on Soviet prestige has been a sharp reminder to the Kremlin that behind all its propaganda smoke screens its domination over East Germany rests on the presence of Soviet troops and tanks and on M.V.D. (Ministry of Internal Affairs) controls. Moscow cannot now rely on its German puppets to control even the East zone, much less to capture control of a united Germany. But the Soviet leaders have skillfully salvaged some advantage from this unforeseen blow. The East German uprisings have intensified the demand in West Germany for the earliest possible liberation of their brothers from Soviet domination and have raised, probably too high, their confidence that the puppet regime in the East can be thrust aside with ease. Thus, the June events in the East made the issue of unity the paramount one in the September elections in West Germany.

The Soviet note of August 16 and the Moscow communiqué of August 23 were cleverly calculated to draw advantage from this reaction, even though it is most unlikely that a victory of the Social Democrats over the Adenauer bloc would bring any gain to Soviet policy. "The incorporation of West Germany into a European army and into the North Atlantic bloc," the note stated flatly, "would render impossible the unification of West and East Germany in a united state." It went on to propose the conclusion of a peace treaty within six months and the cancellation of reparations and of postwar state debts, as of January 1, 1954.

The offer to cancel reparations was designed to remove the fear that a united Germany would be saddled with a crushing mortgage of reparation, which the Soviet Union would then use to force it into economic and political subjection. The Soviet communiqué of August 23 also promised the return to German ownership of thirty-three Soviet-seized enterprises, presumably leaving some fifty large plants in Soviet possession. These enterprises are controlled directly from Moscow, operate without paying taxes or customs duties, and also enable the Soviet Union to milk the East German economy on a huge scale. The offer to cancel the German indebtedness to the Allies touches an emotional rather than a practical matter, since outright gifts of American aid since 1945 have greatly exceeded loans. The offer to limit the occupation costs to five per cent of the budget in each of the two German Republics is bound to be popular. Since the East German budget is a highly centralized one and also covers a wide range of investment and other nonadministrative expenditures, the proposed limitation would cause a relatively slight loss to the Soviet treasury and a relatively severe one to the British and French governments.

One of the most striking features in Malenkov's speech of August 8 was the shifting of the Soviet appeal from the Germans to the French. In it he reverted to an earlier Soviet theme, that a united and independent Germany must provide solid guarantees to its neighbors in Europe against a revival of militarism and aggression. He expressed particular sympathy for French fears of a rearmed Germany, even reminding Paris of the Franco-Soviet pact of November 1944 directed against a revival of Germany. In May 1952 Moscow had urged that a united and independent Germany should have its own armed forces, but in August 1953 this ticklish subject was not mentioned by Malenkov or the Soviet notes on Germany. The Kremlin appears most worried over the prospect of a rearmed Germany integrated into the Western bloc, and since the blow of June 17 it counts on the fears, widely shared by nationalist and neutralist as well as Communist opinion in France, to block the ratification of the European Defense Community and the integration of a partially rearmed Germany into the defenses of the North Atlantic area.

The E.D.C. and NATO remain, as before, the greatest bugbears of Soviet policy makers. As Malenkov stated hopefully in his speech: "Aggressive circles also take into account that, if today, in conditions of tension in international relations, the North Atlantic bloc is rent by internal strife and contradictions, the lessening of this tension may lead to its disintegration." In concentrating its propaganda on German hopes of unity and on French fears of a reunited and revived Germany, the Kremlin aim is clear. It hopes, by outwardly conciliatory words, to bring to a halt and reverse the movement which has been provoked by its own actions and menaces since 1948, toward strengthening the defenses and the political and economic unity of Western Europe and the cohesion of the free world. The only unity of Europe which it can accept is a Soviet-imposed unity.

In the light of the Kremlin's skillful recovery from the June 17 fumble, it hardly seems necessary to discuss in detail the notion, assiduously propagated in some quarters, that the Soviet regime is weak, frightened, and confused and that it is so eager to "appease" the West that it may withdraw voluntarily from East Germany and even relax its grip on the satellites, and that Malenkov is pressing for a four-power meeting in order to lay down the Soviet conquests at the feet of the West. True, the Soviet leadership was at first taken aback by the events of June 17. In order to present the suppression of the uprisings of unarmed workers and peasants as a Soviet victory, Malenkov has been forced to ascribe far reaching aims to the West and to confess that the situation was a most difficult one for his government. "They intended to strangle the democratic forces of Germany, to destroy the German Democratic Republic, which is a stronghold of the peace-loving elements of the German people, to convert Germany into a militarist state and to re-establish a hotbed of war in the center of Europe. There is no doubt that, had the Soviet Union not shown steadfastness and firmness in the defense of the interests of peace, the Berlin adventure might have led to quite serious international consequences. This is why one can consider that the liquidation of the Berlin adventure represents an important victory for the cause of peace."

After some delay the Soviet press took the unusual step of admitting to its own people that widespread strikes and demonstrations had occurred thoughout East Berlin and the Soviet zone, that definite concessions, long since taboo in Russia herself, had been made to the German workers, that small private businesses are to be permitted and even encouraged, and that the German peasants are free to continue as individual farmers and to withdraw from the collective farms. These are not examples of "Bolshevist firmness" which the Kremlin relishes placing before its own people and those of the satellites.

In East Germany the Kremlin has recognized the special political and geographical situation, and has applied the classic Bolshevist tactic of "one step back, two steps forward." The absorption of the "Democratic Republic" into the pattern of "peace-loving nations" is obviously far behind schedule. However, none of the Soviet gestures of relaxation which preceded or followed the uprisings of June 17 suggests the abandonment of the basic controls exerted by the Soviet system over its most valuable and profitable puppet, much less a willingness to cut it loose and allow it to be attached to the West.

The basic question which has plagued Western opinion since Stalin's death is whether the Soviet regime has been seriously weakened. One school of thought maintains that the regime is on the verge of being torn to pieces by the struggle for power in the Kremlin, that it must seek a breathing spell while the inner-party struggle is played to the end, until a new absolute dictator is enthroned. Here this school divides. Some assert that this is the very time for the West to intensify its efforts, to gain the maximum of concessions and to limit Soviet power and potential permanently. Others, the great majority, react to the assertions of Soviet weakness in an opposite way. They assume that the Soviet purposes have been changed radically, that the new leadership seeks actively to "join the club," that the period of alarms and costly efforts is over, and that it is no longer urgent to strengthen the political and military defenses of the West. Perhaps it is time to take a cool look at this newly discovered "Soviet weakness" and attempt to see whether it is apparent or real.

It should be stated at the outset that there is no sign of a demobilization of the very large Soviet armed forces, which are maintained in a high state of readiness, or of a slackening in the forced growth of war industry. Military observers agree that Soviet aircraft and armored units are as good or better than any United States equipment now in use, and that Soviet electronics are surprisingly good. Western observers accept generally the Soviet claim to know the secret of the hydrogen bomb. The remarkable postwar upsurge of economic recovery and industrialization has continued without let-up.

The recent meeting of the Supreme Soviet and Malenkov's speech of August 8 devoted special attention to two of the weaker sectors of the economy: agriculture and living standards. Foreign analysts have maintained since the war that the failure of farm production, the main source of foodstuffs and raw materials, to develop equally with industrial output could, if not corrected, become a major bottleneck limiting future progress and the ability to wage a prolonged war. Malenkov and other speakers at the Supreme Soviet outlined detailed measures which, over several years, can be expected to level agriculture up, and if this program is tackled seriously, there is no inherent reason why it should not succeed.

Greater productivity in agriculture is a key to improved living standards, and Malenkov's speech laid special stress on the improvements which have been made since March, and which are projected, in the supply of consumer goods. There are no inherent reasons why the Soviet economy cannot support a continuing high level of investment and war preparation and at the same time undertake a gradual improvement in agriculture, transportation, and consumer standards. The material available since March suggests no faltering in the program of economic expansion; indeed, it suggests much closer attention to improving labor efficiency and consumer satisfaction through offering a wider range of incentives. In the field of international politics the brief review already given of Soviet actions since March indicates that the Kremlin is maneuvering with confidence, flexibility, and speed.

The concept of the new Soviet "weakness" is thus reduced to the assumption that the Soviet dictatorship and Stalin were so completely synonymous that his disappearance was bound to lead to confusion and disintegration, that a "new Stalin" could not emerge except after a long struggle, and that during this struggle the Kremlin's policy, including its foreign policy, would be uncertain and wavering. In my opinion, this analysis errs in overpersonalizing the nature of the Soviet system and in overlooking the ways in which the present system recognizes the tendencies which would cause it to break up, and counteracts them, as did the Ottoman system during several centuries.

One basic misconception is that the Soviet system rests upon several independent and competing power institutions—particularly the party, the political police, and the armed forces. If this were true, Beria would have controlled the appointment of all echelons of the police and enjoyed their direct loyalty, Bulganin would hold a similar position in respect to the armed forces, and Malenkov or Khrushchev in relation to the party. True, something resembling this "separation" of power did exist at the beginning of Stalin's struggle for absolute control. Lenin treated his Politburo as a continuing conference of deputy chiefs of staff; once a decision was made in the Politburo, each deputy was responsible for carrying out the common decision within his own institutional sphere. Each deputy, in turn, selected his subordinates and developed groups or coteries of loyal supporters. Thus, at the time of Lenin's death, Zinoviev was responsible for the Leningrad organization and the Comintern, Kamenev for the economic system, and Stalin for party organization, in the rather narrow sense of control over personnel rather than of ideology or policy.

The basic purpose and result of Stalin's ruthless reconstruction of the party was to destroy this habit of "pluralism" or "appanage-building" within the party, to eliminate actual or potential centers of authority which might compete with the domination increasingly exercised by him through the central secretariat of the party, and thus to establish a genuinely centralized and monolithic control from above. The "Old Bolsheviks" could not forgive Stalin for having become the "dictator over the party," and Stalin took his bloody revenge on them in the 1930's. The system of unified party control was Stalin's great "invention." Through it he drove the party and the country to tremendous exertions. Prior to Stalin's death, Malenkov had been, for fourteen years, Stalin's direct assistant and deputy in manipulating this ruthless mechanism of unlimited power. There is no evidence that he has dismantled it since March.

Much has been made of the relatively self-effacing role which Malenkov has been playing, particularly in comparison with the daily laudations of the living Stalin. However, if Malenkov has the reality of power, it is to his advantage not to imitate Stalin in this respect. If he is in control of the party machinery, it is more useful for him to act as the spokesman of a collective "will of the party." This technique was also applied by Stalin in the struggle to consolidate his power. He undermined, attacked, and eliminated one potential rival after another, always defending the "unity" of the party against "factionalism" and "splitting." It was not until the last rival power centers within the party had been eliminated that Stalin began the campaign of self-glorification as "the leader." The celebration of his fiftieth birthday in December 1929, after six years of struggle for monolithic control, was the first striking occasion of Stalin's personal glorification, with a great display of tributes and portraits.

Even if Malenkov is in undisputed control of the party machine, and hence of all other levers of power, it is to his advantage to stress the difference between his alleged service to the party as a whole and Stalin's highly personal, arbitrary, and unpredictable habits of rule. Stalin's death has been followed by a strong reaction against his "manner of work." Even the funeral orations showed a rapid discarding of the enforced deification of the "all-wise" leader. Malenkov's speech of August 8, similarly, contained only perfunctory references to Stalin, no longer "the Great."

Most significantly, the party declaration on the fiftieth anniversary of its founding, published in *Pravda* of July 26, gave only modest praise to Stalin's role. "Generalizing the wealth of experience in building Socialism in the U.S.S.R. and the experience of the modern international liberation movement, J. V. Stalin creatively developed the Marxist-Leninist doctrine in application to new historical conditions and enriched revolutionary theory with new theses on many questions." Cutting Stalin down to size makes the rule of his successor easier. Stalin's role is now pictured as subordinate to that of the party as a whole, and the party, like the entire power machine, has begun to breathe more freely since he has passed from the scene.

The need for "protection of the rights" of citizens and especially of officials is felt strongly in the Soviet structure; the higher the official, the more precarious his position and even his life. Malenkov, the man of the party machine, has made reassuring gestures to the "apparatus." His moves to increase the flow of consumption goods also reflect the aspirations of the bureaucracy. When he promises more private cars and television sets, better quality clothing and household equipment, he is appealing, not to ordinary citizens, but to the hierarchy, which alone can expect to achieve these benefits.

What are the devices through which the party leadership prevents the full-fledged development of competing institutions of power? First of all, party responsibility, on the one hand, and police, military, administrative, economic, and cultural responsibilities, on the other, have long since been fused. All activities of importance to the party are subjected to a system of multiple supervision, through the hierarchy of party cells, through the party Control Commission, through the central secretariat, and through the personal secretariat which Malenkov presumably inherited from Stalin. All appointments above a certain level are subject to active initiation, review or veto by the central secretariat; this includes military personnel from the rank of colonel up, directors of factories, all commissioned officers of the secret police, county and city party secretaries. The power of appointment, control, and removal is actively exercised in the central locus of power, the party secretariat.

Did Malenkov relinquish that central control when the office of Secretary-General was eliminated and Khrushchev was appointed First Secretary? The change in title may simply indicate that Khrushchev was not to have the direct powers which Stalin had possessed but was to act as an agent of the party Presidium, which Malenkov appears to dominate. Did the elimination of

Beria, announced in July, mean that Malenkov was weakened, or strengthened? The official statement on his arrest accused Beria of attempting to place the police above the party. Perhaps Beria aspired to restore the system of power sharing which had prevailed at Lenin's death, or perhaps Malenkov felt that Beria had been too long a competitor for the succession and was better out of the way.

Beria's downfall tends to confirm the picture of the supremacy of party controls over all competing controls. Did the army, which is dominated by party generals and is even easier to permeate with party controls than the secret police, take part in Beria's elimination? While reports speak of tanks rumbling through the streets of Moscow on June 27, there is no authentic information as to whether these were army tanks, or whether they belonged to the special M.V.D. army, controlled by Malenkov through Kruglov and used against its nominal chief, Beria.

In analyzing the structure of power in an on-going system, it is misleading to rely upon analogies with the past. In the system which Stalin had elaborated by 1929 and which he increasingly tightened in the following twenty years, strains of "separatist" institutional loyalty were recognized and deliberately contained. Under a system like this, individuals find it all but impossible to lay their hands on independent levels of power. What is important is not whether this or that prominent individual survives or is destroyed, but whether there is likely to develop a direct and mutually destructive clash between power instruments. Will the army destroy the secret police, or the secret police destroy the party? This is most unlikely. Present evidence requires us to assume that the Soviet system is going to continue as a tightly operated party dictatorship, though less personalized in a deified dictator. Its new leadership, which prefers to call itself "collective" for sound Soviet reasons, displays striking qualities of realism and flexibility. If this is so, then the challenge and the dangers which Soviet power and purposes present to the strength, cohesion and survival of the free world are definitely not on the wane, but are increasing. These dangers can be increased still more only if responsible opinion within the free world indulges in daydreams of the "inevitable" self-destruction of the Soviet dictatorship.

:16:

SOVIET POLICY IN THE TWO-WORLD CONFLICT: SOME PROSPECTS[1]

[*January 1954*]

FOR the next few years the central fact in Soviet world policy will be the steady growth in Soviet atomic and hydrogen power and in the ability to deliver this power against vital industrial and urban areas of the free world. Despite the obscurities which surround the piling up of these portentous new weapons, especially on the Soviet side, there is a fairly wide area of agreement on some of the significant political implications of this development. For one thing, it is generally agreed that any all-out war would be fought from or almost from the beginning against the adversary's principal concentrations of industrial power, urban population, and political controls, and that on both sides no weapons or methods of defense now available could prevent massive destruction. In the second place, it seems to be accepted that "equality" in total quantity

[1] *Journal of International Affairs*, Vol. VIII, No. 1 (1954), pp. 107–13. Copyright 1954 by the Board of Editors of the *Journal of International Affairs.*

of atomic power has little meaning, once both sides have achieved a certain undefined but attainable level of atomic build-up. And in the third place, it is assumed that there are no inherent obstacles, either in the accumulation of atomic and hydrogen power or in the production of engines of delivery, which will prevent the Soviet Union from achieving strategic if not numerical equality in this field.

This new factor of power, unprecedented in threat, also contains certain limitations which may influence its use by either or both sides. For one thing, the nature of the power means that it must be applied in a "one-blow" attack, not in the literal sense of a "single strike," but in the sense that an atomic war may be waged and won or lost within a very short time and only by using up those weapons and engines which are available at the moment when hostilities begin or which survive a surprise attack. Both the First and Second World War, which were primarily land wars fought on the European continent, were won by man power and engines of war which were trained or produced largely after the outbreak of hostilities. In fact, it can be argued that those powers which had prepared most strenuously for the wars which began in 1914 and 1939 were afterwards capped by military obsolescence and that the technological race was won by those who started later but not too late! In any case, American participation in both wars was based on the assumption that, even after a major war had begun on another continent, the American nation still had time to decide whether it would participate in the war and to prepare the means of warfare. This assumption is now reversed. In case of an atomic war it would be a Soviet necessity to strike at the central sources of strength and will power of the free world, the United States and Canada, rather than to scatter its blows against secondary targets.

A corollary of the "one-blow" strategy is that the willingness to trade atomic blows may, granted an "equality" of striking power, be determined by the relative effectiveness and reliability of the defensive systems, both military and civilian. The ability of one side to impose a relatively high or low rate of attrition upon the attacking force may prove to be decisive in determining a willingness to risk such a war, or, if it came, might decide which side could absorb horrendous destruction and still go on to win. Similarly, the ability of the civilian population to absorb terrific destruction and still go on with its national life, and the estimate by the respective government of the ability, organizational and psychological, of its people to accept both the risk and the full realization of it, might determine its decision whether to stand up to an atomic threat or to surrender the capacity to exert its own political will thereafter.

Finally, the willingness to exercise the atomic threat may be determined by an estimate of the power of retaliation which would remain to the other side, even if the first exchange of blows should achieve the maximum effect predicted for it. This uncertainty, added to the other critical uncertainties listed briefly above, adds great vagueness to the problem of making reliable estimates of relative strategic power and hence to the political problem of arriving at a decision whether or not to use it. In this phase of strategic-cum-political estimate two further factors come into play.

Faced with the responsibility of making estimates and recommendations of a technical military character which may be followed by decisive victory or by national annihilation, military leaders normally play for the widest possible margin of safety. In a sense, no military establishment considers itself ready to guarantee victory or even survival against an "equal" adversary. Thus it is possible that the strongest advocates of political alternatives to atomic warfare may be the very people who are most directly responsible for its development and potential application.

Another and countervailing factor is the increasing difficulty of estimating the technological, military, and political consequences of an atomic conflict. When military technology has been developing gradually and the political consequences of victory or defeat are measured, as Franz Josef put it after his defeat in 1859, by "paying for defeat with a province," estimates of relative strength can be made with some degree of reliability, although, even under relatively predictable conditions of traditional warfare, there have been many instances of miscalculation. When the factor of uncertainty in calculation increases from, say, twenty per cent, to one hundred per cent, it is transformed into absolute unpredictability. At this point, implying a high degree of unpredictability of outcome, political doctrines and emotional rigidities may take the place of sober technical calculations. Thus, the impossibility of making "scientific" calculations may lead to decisions based upon "unscientific" assumptions and conclusions. The scientific caution natural to the military technician when operating in his own sphere may, because of the growing inability of the technician to document his doubts in a politically convincing way, transfer even more of the weight of decision to the sphere of political hopes or fears. The uncertainty of estimate which derives from the new forms of power does not work automatically either to reinforce caution or to discard caution at a moment when the political situation compels the political leadership to decide to run the risk of either threatening to use them or of rejecting a threat of the adversary to use them.

A factor, both of general knowledge and of general uncertainty, is the rate of development of the capability of intercontinental atomic-hydrogen warfare. On this score, about all that a layman can guess is that the capability is being developed rapidly and that it can be developed, perhaps not at the same technological rate, by both sides. Politically speaking, the important factor is that the intercontinental capability may emerge within the next five to ten years as the decisive element of national power and survival. When it has become a workaday reality of international life, the intercontinental factor will presumably lead to a reassessment of both military and political assumptions which have in the meantime become "traditional" in the pre-intercontinental period of atomic power.

For one thing, the relative role of western and central Europe, already greatly diminished by two world wars, may shrink even further. It may then mean that, for the United States and Canada, possession of advanced bases in western Europe and North Africa will cease to be a decisive factor in the ability to deliver atomic-hydrogen power against vital targets of Soviet power, and for the Soviet Union the assumption that the United States can exert its power only from a wide range of advanced bases located in allied territories will no longer be as crucial as it is now.

For an interim period of five to ten years, on the other hand, the ability of the United States to operate from European and European-owned advanced bases will continue to be the greatest single element of weakness in the over-all Soviet military position. During that period the Soviet leadership will continue to make every effort to break up the solidarity of the Western nations and thus to deprive the United States of the possibility of utilizing advanced bases and to remove from western Europe, the Near East, and Japan the protective umbrella of United States retaliatory power. Thus, it can be assumed that over the next few years the principal aim of the Soviet leaders will be to destroy any form of western European consolidation, to break up the North Atlantic Treaty Organization, and to push back American strategic power and its local land defenses beyond the oceans. In seeking this basic goal the post-Stalin leadership has shown that it is willing to mingle the bludgeoning tactics of Stalin's later years with a somewhat more flexible arsenal of political weapons.

One of the most potent weapons for promoting

Western disunity has been provided by the emergence of the Soviet atomic-hydrogen potential, against which western Europe has no defense except the prospect of American retaliation. As Soviet atomic "equality" grows and is made more evident by demonstrations and gestures, the Soviet leadership can play up this direct threat to the peoples of western Europe. It can say, in effect, that, while America may survive an atomic war in the pre-intercontinental period, Britain, France, and Germany will not, and it can offer western Europe a choice between certain destruction as allies of America and possible survival as "neutrals" in a war which would be decided, not by western Europe, but by combat between the two greatest atomic powers. The campaign of atomic intimidation need not be waged by Kremlin voices. It can be picked up and magnified by western European fears and despairs. The same threat is, if anything, even more ominous for Japan.

A first intimation of this campaign to frighten western Europe into "neutrality" was given by Ilia Ehrenburg shortly after the Malenkov announcement of the Soviet hydrogen experiment. Ehrenburg warned the people of Paris and London that, while New York and Washington might avoid annihilation in an atomic war, their capitals could not escape it and urged them to break loose from the American alliance before it was too late. This theme has, however, not been developed systematically by the Soviet propaganda system. For this silence there may be two major reasons.

One reason may be the risk that a campaign of direct atomic intimidation would boomerang against the Soviet aim. Instead of reacting by alarm and by flight into "neutrality," the western European peoples might react to Soviet threats by reinforcing their ties with the United States, feeling that henceforth their only protection against Soviet bludgeoning and blackmail would be the American capability of strategic retaliation. While they would not like the greater degree of dependence on America which this would imply, they might well adjust their policies to it rather than bow to the Soviet demand that they remain disunited and defenseless against still further threats, continually renewed. Another reaction might be simply to take flight from atomic realities and to go forward in the course of Western co-operation, feeling that the nature of the atomic age is too horrible to absorb into practical thinking.

Another and even stronger reason for the Soviet failure after October 1953 to press the Ehrenburg line of propaganda may be that the Kremlin believes that the same aim—the disunity and defenselessness of western Europe and of Japan—can be achieved by other and more traditional political weapons and that it should not prematurely try out the weapon of direct atomic intimidation. According to the Soviet way of thinking, as set forth again in Stalin's last analysis of world forces, the non-Soviet or "capitalist" world is incapable of prolonged and effective political unity of action. Rivalries for markets, for raw materials, for colonies, make it impossible, in the Soviet analysis, for the advanced industrial countries to strengthen or even to work together over an indefinite or extended period of time. The effects of economic nationalism and cut-throat rivalry, inevitable under the "profit system," are only lessened somewhat during a period of full employment and production; they become difficult of control, Moscow believes, during a recession, and are absolutely unmanageable during a major depression. Looking hopefully for a major economic crisis in the free world, the Soviets think that Japan and Germany are especially vulnerable, economically and socially, to its effects, that economic rivalry will put an end to American-British political partnership, and that a major decline in prices of raw materials will exacerbate the struggle for "national liberation" within the underdeveloped "one-crop" countries. Since the costs of rearmament set up great strains within the countries of the free world and military power is considered to be in direct competition with demands for improved welfare, the Kremlin can hope that its relative military and political power will grow during a period which, they hope, will combine economic decline with intensified economic and political nationalism in the non-Soviet world.

During a period of "over-production" and competition for markets within the free world, the Soviet Union can hope to mount a modest but "helpful" economic offensive of its own. By offering to buy part of the marginal production of the non-Soviet countries, the Soviet government may hope to exert a political leverage disproportionate to its small economic weight in international trade. It regards Germany and Japan as especially vulnerable to enticement. Foreseeing a period of increased economic rivalry within the non-Soviet world, the Kremlin has been actively throwing out trade offers, without directly attaching political conditions to them. Assuming that a somewhat more relaxed international atmosphere, combined with competition for markets, will result gradually in a relaxation, from within the free world, of present barriers to trade in strategic commodities, the Soviet leaders have recently refrained from raising a direct demand for the scrapping of the existing free world agreements to regulate East-West trade in such goods. Another reason for this more flexible approach is that it is better for the Soviet leadership to rebuild a substantial body of East-West trade before it attempts to use this bargaining power to modify the policies of the Western governments.

Still another motive for holding in abeyance the atomic threat against western Europe lies in the Soviet belief, supported by much evidence, that no real European unity will develop from the long campaign, inaugurated in October 1950, to establish a European Defense Community. By playing on German and French suspicions, by utilizing the negatively strong French and Italian Communist parties to promote weak governments and "no governments" in those countries, the Soviet government can hope to nullify the efforts to bring about a concerted land defense of western Europe stiffened by a German "contribution."

It can hope for more than that. Since NATO requires the unanimous actions of its members, and since its operative power is centered primarily in France, the real effectiveness of NATO can be undermined from within, through political division and paralysis of two of its most important members. If this happened, it would not be the first time that the substance of an alliance was eroded from within, leaving only an appearance of strength behind it. From the Kremlin's point of view, there is a great opportunity to work for this goal, and it is its political duty to exploit the opportunity, with its familiar weapons rather than to embark prematurely on an untried technique of atomic blackmail.

The "dynamics" of power in its new dimension thus argue, from a Soviet point of view, for a maximum effort to relax the present international tensions through political gestures and without abandoning any positions or weapons of Soviet strength, for a more flexible policy of improving the relative Soviet position through avoiding a repetition of new Berlin threats and new Korean blunders, and for an intensive effort to promote the disunity and defenselessness of the free world. The Soviet leadership must estimate that it is leading from a position of increasing atomic strength. Without abandoning its deep-seated conviction that the two-power world is engaged in a desperate contest for survival and domination, the Soviet leadership continues to seek to avoid an all-out strategic war, in which the outcome would today be uncertain, and to press the application of its armory of political and economic weapons, in a struggle which is waged within each country and not merely along a rigid periphery defined by military power.

:17:

HOW "NEW" IS THE KREMLIN'S NEW LINE?[1]

[*February 1955*]

HAS the struggle for top place within the Soviet hierarchy come to a more or less orderly conclusion with the dramatic resignation, on February 8, of Premier Georgii Malenkov and his replacement, on nomination of Nikita Khrushchev, by Marshal Nikolai Bulganin? Is the Soviet government scrapping its post-Stalin program, advertised with much fanfare, for relieving the harsh lot of the great bulk of its citizens? Has it come to the conclusion that it must go all-out in preparation for an early showdown with the growing strength of the free West? Has a "soft" line, both at home and abroad, widely attributed to Malenkov, succumbed to a "hard" line, promoted by Khrushchev and the military?

The startling events of February 8 provided only a small dose of hard facts and can be interpreted varyingly to support a rather wide range of projections and speculations. One firm fact is that Malenkov has been demoted from the position of chairman of the Council of Ministers and assigned to the ministry of electric

[1] *Foreign Affairs*, Vol. XXXIII, No. 3 (April 1955), pp. 376–86. Copyright 1955 by the Council on Foreign Relations, Inc.

power, an important but not decisive post. Its importance, incidentally, has been greatly diminished by the creation, by decree of November 22, 1954, of a separate ministry of electric station construction. However, if the ministry of electric power is responsible for the atomic power industry, Malenkov will continue to occupy a key position in Soviet military programs, as well as remaining, so far, as deputy chairman of the Council of Ministers.

A more important question is whether Malenkov will remain a member of the Presidium of the Communist party of the Soviet Union, the real center of power and decision. Meetings of this all-powerful body are rarely mentioned in print, and in the past members have been appointed and dismissed without any immediate announcement being made. Even the composition of the highest party organ can remain concealed from public view for many months. For example, from the Nineteenth Party Congress, in October 1952, until after Stalin's death, in March 1953, real authority within the enlarged party Presidium was actually exercised by a small "bureau" of the Presidium. Even the existence of this "bureau" was made known only after Stalin's death and after the bureau had again been transformed into a small Presidium, patterned after the former Politburo! Under the rule of a conspiritorial dictatorship it is entirely possible for Malenkov to be dropped from the party Presidium, or to be excluded from its meetings, without any indication reaching either the Soviet public or the outside world for many months.

The detailed work of the party Presidium appears to be carried on by a network of active committees dealing with foreign affairs, the international Communist movement, defense, industry, agriculture, ideology, and perhaps other topics. Some scanty and not very firm information about the interlocking memberships of these operating committees has occasionally become known retrospectively, but nothing can be said currently about their composition and assignments. Within the Presidium, Malenkov's role would be strongly affected by any changes in his position in the committee structure, but nothing is likely to be known of this except after the fact.

On balance, the evidence currently available points to a probable early elimination of Malenkov from the seat of power. The terms of his letter of resignation, read to an astonished Supreme Soviet on February 8, are without recent precedent in Soviet practice. "I see clearly," he wrote, "that the carrying out of the complicated and responsible duties of chairman of the Council of Ministers is affected negatively by my insufficient experience in local [administrative] work and also by the fact that I have not had occasion, in a ministry or an economic organ, to exercise direct administration of individual branches of the national economy."

This admission of inadequacy deliberately writes off Malenkov's long experience in the work of central administration and decision making. From March 1939 he served as a secretary of the Central Committee of the party, and as a member of its Organizational Bureau, which, until October 1952, exercised detailed authority over the entire range of executive appointments in the party, in the governmental, military, and economic structure and, though perhaps not at all times, in the secret police. During World War II, Malenkov was a member of the extremely powerful State Committee on Defense. From February 1941 an alternate member of the Politburo, he became a full-fledged member of it in March 1946, and he became chairman of the Council of Ministers on March 7, 1953. The terms of Malenkov's self-excoriation hardly hold water, for the central bodies in which he has held high posts for almost fifteen years make a tremendous number of detailed decisions and exercise a constant supervision over a vast range of "local" and "economic" activities. Sooner or later, no part of the Soviet system escapes their direct attention. The listing of Malenkov's party and official posts, furthermore, leaves out of account his extensive experience, during the 1930's, as an increasingly powerful and experienced member of Stalin's own secretariat.

The wording of Malenkov's resignation resembles the "negotiated" self-flagellations and abject recantations by which Stalin gradually wore down and discredited those Old Bolsheviks whose early claims to authority were no less weighty than his own. How often did Rykov and Bukharin, Piatakov and Sokol'nikov, and many others, confess their "mistakes," in agreed formulas, only to drift lower and lower in the hierarchy of power! In the Stalinist practice, in which both Malenkov and Khrushchev are past masters, the step from admitting "inadequacy" to confessing "sabotage" and "treason" is a short one.

If Malenkov thought to survive and save part of his influence by his letter of resignation, he accepted, in any case, extremely unfavorable terms of partial surrender. He has left the way open to make him the scapegoat for the poor showing of Soviet agriculture. ". . . I see especially clearly my guilt and responsibility for the unsatisfactory state of affairs that has developed in agriculture, since for several years prior to that I had been entrusted with the duty of supervising and directing the work of the central agricultural organs and the work of the local party and Soviet organs in the sphere of agriculture." Will the world be told, within a few months, that this "guilt and responsibility" were inspired by Malenkov's role of a "restorer of capitalism" and a "hireling of the imperialist intelligence services"? The answer to this rests in the personal relations within the top Soviet leadership, the most secretive group of rulers in the world.

If Malenkov's resignation is, as it may be, but the first step toward discrediting and eliminating him completely, why was this not carried through at once?

While an abrupt downfall might satisfy the human yearning for drama, a sudden shock would have many negative effects for the Soviet system of control, for it would raise havoc with higher personnel in all branches of the Soviet administration. Since 1939, Malenkov has had a leading part in appointing and promoting leading officials, and his complete removal would leave them exposed to the threat of a sweeping and highly disruptive purge. By receiving a clear indication of Malenkov's decline, the men whom he has appointed or favored are given time to shift their allegiance, to realign their loyalties with the new "boss," and thus to avoid "panic" and "wavering." Indeed, if the leadership turns the wheel toward the complete elimination of Malenkov, his former friends can be expected to supply the necessary incriminating evidence, thereby proving that they put "party unity" above "personal relations."

A further step toward "amalgamating" his present rivals for power with the "traitors" of an earlier period of struggle may have been foreshadowed by Khrushchev's speech of January 25 (published on February 3). Arguing that the forced development of heavy industry must continue in order to provide the basis for building up production of both agriculture and consumer goods, Khrushchev attacked in strong terms the contrary argument that ". . . at some stage or other of Socialist construction the development of heavy industry, supposedly, ceases to be the main task, and light industry can and must overtake all other branches of industry. . . . This is a belching of the Right deviation, a belching of views which are hostile to Leninism and which, in their time, were preached by Rykov, Bukharin, and their ilk." True, this revived "right deviation" was attributed in Khrushchev's speech to obscure "would-be economists," not directly to his rivals for power. But, obviously, the question of the continued hegemony of heavy industry would not have been agitated so strenuously during the past few weeks unless it has been occupying the attention of the decision makers at the top.

Khrushchev's speech of January 25 was preceded by a detailed attack on the proponents of a balanced development of both heavy and light industry. An article of January 24, on "The Party General Line and the Vulgarizers of Marxism," signed by D. Shepilov, editor in chief of *Pravda*, condemned the new "right-wing" theory that "the policy, pursued by the party, of forced development of the branches of heavy industry has allegedly entered into conflict with the basic economic law of Socialism, since the forced development of the branches of heavy industry retards public consumption."[2] Much has been made of the obscure status of the economists whom Shepilov attacked by name. This argument cannot be pressed very far. Persons named by Shepilov as "candidates for the Ph.D. in economics" may, in Soviet practice, actually be fairly influential experts and advisers in various planning and other economic bodies.

Is the struggle over heavy versus light industry also reflected in the dismissal of Anastas Mikoyan as Minister of Trade (by decree of January 22, published on January 25)? This is one of the four ministries most closely concerned with the flow of consumer goods. However, the probability of a drastic change may be lessened by the fact that Mikoyan's successor, Dimitri Pavlov, had been First Deputy Minister under Mikoyan. It is possible that Mikoyan has now joined a number of other "deputy chairmen without portfolio," including Kaganovich, Pervukhin, Tevosian, and Kosygin. If so, this emerging pattern would resemble in part the administrative structure which was applied during Stalin's last years.

As the operative ministries, mainly economic, grew in number to over fifty, they were grouped under the su-

[2] Cited from *Current Digest of the Soviet Press,* Vol. VI, No. 52 (February 9, 1955), p. 4.

pervision of Stalin's close subordinates, who served simultaneously as members of the Politburo and as deputy chairmen of the Council of Ministers. Immediately after Stalin's death the ministries were consolidated into one half the previous number, and the senior party people again took over direct responsibility for them. During the past year many ministries have again been subdivided, and co-ordination among their competing claims appears again to be vested in deputy chairmen of the Council of Ministers who are also members of the party Presidium. Whether Mikoyan, who has served since the 1920's as an economic administrator and who has gained a high reputation for efficiency, has fallen prey to an inner dispute over basic economic policy, or whether he has been relieved of detailed administrative responsibility and given broader responsibility for policy making, cannot be determined from the evidence now available.

Has there been a real fight at the top between the supporters of heavy industry and those who, allegedly, favor putting "butter" before "guns"? An examination of the public statements of Malenkov, Khrushchev, and Mikoyan since Stalin's death shows that all Soviet spokesmen have continuously stressed the basic role of an expanding heavy industry, as the necessary foundation for the strengthening of both light industry and agriculture.

Has the decline of Malenkov been followed by a real change in emphasis between heavy industry and light industry? What evidence there is gives some slender support to this interpretation. Among the few indices available are the relative rates of investment in heavy and light industry. For 1954, the planned investment in heavy industry from the state budget was just over 90 billion rubles; for 1955 it is 101 billions. Light industry, including food and local industry, received 7.6 billion rubles in 1953, and an estimated 14 billions in 1954, and is to receive 10.6 from the budget in 1955. However, light industry is expected to receive an additional 15.4 billions available from its profits for investment, making a planned total of 26 billions for both permanent and turnover capital. The figures given above are not exactly comparable, for the 1955 budget figures do not distinguish between permanent investment and turnover capital. The conclusion is, then, that in 1954 a modest extra effort to stimulate the development of light and food industry was carried out, and that a slightly smaller assignment of investment funds will be made in 1955. This is, however, a far cry from the widely held assumption of a sudden swing, in 1953, from heavy industry to light industry, and again, in February 1955, from light industry back to a stress on heavy industry. The fact is that the principal stress has been placed on the forced development of heavy and military industry and the major resources have been devoted to it. All that really happened in 1953 and 1954 is that a small marginal shift of resources was effected to strengthen light industry somewhat. Even in 1954, however, the rate of growth in heavy industry was far higher than that in light industry, as it has been ever since 1928.

What is more important is the new and urgent emphasis on raising agricultural production, and on the choice of programs to achieve that. Since September 1953 the new leadership has had two main programs, with conflicting claims on resources, in this field. One has called for raising production in the long-settled farming regions. To achieve this the government has simplified and reduced taxes on the personal household plots and the livestock of the collectivized peasants, has cut back deliveries by the collective farms, at low fixed prices, has promised improvements in farming techniques, equipment, seeds, and supply of fertilizer, and has strengthened its apparatus of control over the peasantry. Most of these measures are aimed at providing stronger incentives for better production. But increasing the return to the peasants for their work creates an increased demand for most types of consumer goods.

The economic report claims that in 1954 the real income of the Soviet population, in comparable prices, increased by eleven per cent over 1953, and that the turnover of goods increased by eighteen per cent, in comparable prices. Even if these figures must be discounted substantially, it is clear that, if the government expects to provide further incentives in the form of improved standards of living, it would have to step up the development of consumer goods even more than it has done in 1954.

While the Kremlin has been increasing slightly the size and attractiveness of the carrot held out to the hard-pressed collective farmers, it has also been increasing the size and weight of the stick. During 1953 and 1954 the number of "labor days" required of the collective farmers was substantially increased. If the individual member fails to meet the "norm" set for his labor on the collective, the taxes on his privately owned market garden and livestock are doubled, in effect confiscating the product of his private labor. In addition, the party's decree of January 31, 1955, on raising the output of animal husbandry, places in the hands of the state-owned machine and tractor stations close control over the work and deliveries of the collective farms.

The other half of the new program in agriculture is more spectacular, and more risky. The new leadership has embarked on a plan for plowing up from 67 to 72 million acres of virgin and long-fallow lands. In 1954 tens of thousands of tractors and several hundred thousand young workers were assigned to this program. In his report of January 25, Khrushchev claimed that the additional grain reaped in the new areas even in 1954 made up for the losses from drought in the Ukraine, North Caucasus, and Volga regions. Significantly, no total figures for grain have been published for 1953 or 1954, and the assumption must stand that the crop for each of the last two years was at least no better than that of 1952.

Khrushchev's speech also contained the first admission that the Kremlin's concern for a larger grain supply is due, in part, to the growth of the population, estimated at 3 million per year. Previously, Soviet leaders have boasted of the high Soviet rate of natural increase as a factor of strength, rather than of worry.

The virgin lands program is designed to increase the cultivated area by one fourth and to increase the marketed grain supply by one third. The Kremlin is making a big investment in this gamble. Total agricultural investment from the state budget amounted to 12 billion rubles in 1953 and 21 billions in 1954, and is to jump to 55 billions in 1955. This budget allocation can be compared with 101 billions for heavy industry and 10.6 billions for light, food, and local industry. The major part of the investment in agriculture is being directed to the virgin soil program.

Clearly, the new leadership has decided that it can make greater short-run gains by putting these large resources into the virgin soil scheme rather than by concentrating the same effort and sacrifices on raising production in the older cultivated areas. If the newly plowed marginal lands of southern Siberia, Kazakhstan, and Altai receive adequate rainfall, and receive it at the right time of the year, the gamble may pay off handsomely. If the rainfall cycle swings against it, as it now has against dryland farming in many parts of Texas, Colorado, Kansas, and other states, no amount of whipped up enthusiasm or mechanization of work will see the program through to success.[3]

Increased farm production has become a vital issue for the Soviet leadership, and its plans to raise incentives for better work will stand and fall with it.

[3] Chauncy D. Harris: "Growing Food by Decree in Soviet Russia," *Foreign Affairs*, Vol. XXXIII, No. 2 (January 1955), pp. 268–81.

Food represents about seventy per cent of the average urban budget in the Soviet Union, and other farm products—cotton, wool, leather, linen, tobacco—supply the necessary raw materials for the most needed consumer goods. It is partly because of the failure to increase the supply of cotton and leather more rapidly that cotton cloth and footwear have shown increases of only between three and six per cent in 1953 and 1954.

The rapid development, by the growing season of 1956, of a new grain area of 67 to 72 million acres is now coupled with a new program, announced on February 2, for raising the output of livestock and animal products. As new lands are sowed to wheat, older lands, especially in the Ukraine, are to be turned over to raising corn and livestock. The acreage of corn, amounting to 8.3 million acres in 1953, is to be raised by 1960 to 67 million acres, and the supply of meat products of all kinds, as well as milk and eggs, is to be doubled by 1960. Speaking enviously of the great advances made by American animal husbandry over the past twenty-five years, Khrushchev has called for the wholesale adoption of American techniques, including the use of hybrid corn, the extensive building of silos, and the ensilage of milk corn. Khrushchev paid no attention to one of the most important aspects of the American revolution in animal husbandry—the specialization of each region in particular stages of breeding, raising, and fattening cattle.

It is probable that the real conflict within Soviet policy making has hinged on the choice between these two main programs of raising agricultural production. The victorious side must have argued that only the virgin soil program for wheat would provide the necessary margin of food and allow a more intensive development of animal husbandry. The defeated side may have maintained that the "new lands" scheme was a gamble and that much more could be achieved by investing the same resources in the improvement of labor incentives by increasing the flow of consumer goods.

The clash has been over means, not ends. Is it more profitable to provide some slight relief for the Soviet consumer, some slight improvement in labor incentives? The primacy of heavy and military industry has never been questioned. The immediate issues, involving the use of marginal resources amounting to two or three per cent of the Soviet budget, have become entangled in the personal struggle for control of the Soviet power machine.

Has the Khrushchev-Malenkov rivalry involved basic issues of Soviet foreign policy, or, again, are only questions of tactics involved? In many parts of the world the post-Stalin actions of the Soviet government inspired a belief, born of wishful thinking, that a new and moderate era of "coexistence" had begun. The abandonment of territorial claims which, if fulfilled, would destroy Turkey, the release of a few Russian wives of American citizens, the admission of a few foreign tourists—these unaccustomed gestures were blown up out of all proportion as harbingers of a co-operative, even friendly, approach to the non-Soviet world. During these two years, however, the Soviet government has not given up a single "position of strength." It has continued to denounce each defensive effort of the non-Soviet world as "preparation for aggression." It has fought hard and cleverly to delay the strengthening of western Europe and the rearmament of Western Germany. Its position on the liberation of Austria has hardened. Molotov now declares openly that his government will agree to a treaty for Austria only if it first secures major concessions in Germany. By "persuading" the Chinese Communists to be satisfied at first with acquiring control over the northern half of Vietnam through negotiation, it has posed as a defender of peace.

In the two years since Stalin's death there has not been the slightest evidence of any substantial change in the objectives and methods of Soviet foreign policy. The recent cautious "normalization" of Soviet-Yugoslav relations, like other minor gestures, represents the removal of an irritating issue which, continually harped upon, brought only disadvantages to Soviet policy and prestige. The most significant recent change in Soviet tactics is the grudging recognition of India's role as the principal "uncommitted" power in Asia, after several years of denouncing the Nehru government as a "tool of the imperialists."

In his speech of February 8, Molotov boasted that one half the population of Europe and Asia is now within the Soviet-led camp of "socialism" and "people's democracy" and predicted that it is only a matter of time before the Americas, so far recalcitrant to the Soviet example, would begin to move in the same direction. He went on to speak flatteringly of India's role. "The fact that there is no longer a colonial India, but the Republic of India, has great historical significance. . . . The international authority of India as a new and important factor in the cause of strengthening peace and friendship among nations is growing more and more." *Pravda*, of February 5, published excerpts from a speech by Mr. Menon, Indian Ambassador to Moscow: "The Soviet government, striving for peace, is fully conscious of its strength. . . . The government and people of the Soviet Union . . . value highly India's independent foreign policy and its role in the cause of preserving peace. Russia . . . understands that it is very essential to its own interests to assure a prolonged period of peace."

The absence of any real change in Soviet policy has been emphasized by the extensive and unusually frank interviews which Khrushchev, Molotov, and Zhukov gave to prominent American journalists before and after Malenkov's dismissal. Totaling many columns of

Pravda's limited space, these statements were longer and more detailed than the total interviews given by Stalin during his entire period of rule. Attacking the Marshall Plan, the North Atlantic Treaty Organization, German rearmament, American bases abroad, the South East Asia Treaty Organization, and the United States' defense of South Korea, Japan, and Formosa, Khrushchev reaffirmed the Kremlin's view that any building of strength and unity in any part of the free world is equated to "preparation for unleashing a new war." He made clear the Soviet preference for making gains through "cold war" while avoiding the risks of a "hot war." "It is good that the war in Korea has been ended, that the fire has been put out there, and the Soviet Union would not want it to break out again anywhere."

Khrushchev was equally frank in reaffirming the Kremlin's long-range ambitions. Arguing that "capitalists" believe in the ultimate triumph of capitalism and that Communists believe in the ultimate triumph of "communism," Khrushchev went on to urge the "capitalists" to abandon all thought of building "positions of force" (the Soviet translation renders "positions of strength" as "positions of force" and propagates this version through all available channels) and to open up "advantageous trade" with the Soviet bloc. "The future," he declared flatly, "is for the Communist system."

Pressed to explain how long "coexistence" would continue, Khrushchev replied with the traditional Bolshevist double talk to the effect that this "depends on historical conditions, historical development." For Khrushchev, as for Malenkov, "coexistence" is a temporary tactic, an episode within an all-embracing, inescapable struggle between hostile and irreconcilable systems of power. Quarrels within the secretive circle of the Soviet dictatorship are concerned with persons and with tactics: at home, a little more butter or a few more guns, a slight relaxing or tightening of the girths on their hard-pressed people; abroad, a few forced smiles or a slightly fiercer brandishing of Soviet armed might.

:18:

CAN MOSCOW MATCH US INDUSTRIALLY?[1]

[*February 1955*]

THE second anniversary of the death of Stalin is a fitting time for a careful reappraisal of the position of the Soviet Union in the world picture, and for a fresh evaluation of the Kremlin's long-run objectives and methods of going after them.

Have the Soviet leaders since Stalin's death turned seriously to the refurbished slogan of "coexistence"? Are they working for a genuine relaxation of tensions and therefore a slackening of the armaments race with the free world and, in particular, with its ultimate citadel, the United States? Do they really want a long period of peace in order to try to match the United States at its strongest point—production?

Or does the ascendance of the Khrushchev group now—following aggressive maneuvers in Asia and revived diplomatic pressures in western Europe—indicate that the post-Stalin period of consolidation was merely a temporary phase which ended with the installation

[1] *Harvard Business Review*, Vol. XXXIII, No. 2 (March-April 1955), pp. 101–8. Copyright 1955 by the President and Fellows of Harvard College.

of Bulganin as Premier, and that a tough, new regime is now installed in the Kremlin?

Various answers are being given to these questions, and the weight of these answers is different in western Europe from what it is in the United States. That is one reason for the different assumptions, made on the two sides of the Atlantic, about whether it is as urgent now as it was before 1953 to get ready to meet and, if necessary, to defeat any new Soviet move to expand the Communist empire.

When the Malenkov government during its first months in power made a few inexpensive gestures toward conciliating the West and providing the Russian people with improvements in their low standard of living, Winston Churchill summarized widespread British reaction:

> I do not find it unreasonable or dangerous to conclude that internal prosperity rather than external conquest is not only the deep desire of the Russian peoples but also the long-term interest of their rulers.

In June 1954, a few days before becoming Premier of France, Mendès-France declared:

> Without neglecting their armament, they [the Soviet leaders] have shifted the center of gravity of their efforts to the economic and social fields.

Though less responsible and less cautious spokesmen went much further, it is clear now that the Kremlin at no time had any intention of abandoning its long-term goals of industrial and military might. During the period of transition following Stalin's death the Soviet leadership was testing its own ability to hold the country on a steady keel. The replacement of Malenkov poses a question as to the Kremlin's real policies for the future.

As of February 8, a detailed examination of the Soviet economy and of the Kremlin's apparent pattern of future growth sheds considerable light on Russia's real "intentions." And because all plans for the future so obviously hinge on massive economic growth, it is of special importance that businessmen in the United States know the magnitude of the program and have some yardsticks for judging the degree of success with which Moscow is able to carry it out.

Since 1928 Russia has become the second strongest industrial power in the world. Thus, from about 4.5 million tons[2] of steel in 1928, it has pushed its output to 45.5 million tons in 1954. Future plans call for a production of 48.4 million tons in 1955, and 66 million tons in 1960. By comparison, United States production was 88.2 million tons in 1954 (with a capacity of 120 million tons).

In coal output the Soviet Union reached between 374 and 379 million tons in 1954; United States production was around 385 million tons. Pig iron production for 1954 reached 31.9 million tons for the Soviet Union, compared with 55 to 60 million tons for the United States. Soviet output of electricity was 147.6 billion kilowatt-hours in 1954; for the United States, 520 billion kilowatt-hours.

Obviously, the Soviet Union's basic economy is strong (and, as we shall see, is growing stronger at a rapid pace). But Russia's strength for war is greater than the bare figures imply. In peacetime, more than one half of American steel production goes into durable consumer goods, housing, roads, and other uses that add up to the highest standard of living in the world. In the Soviet economy, it is estimated that 80 per cent of all steel produced goes into building more heavy industry, more military industry, and more armaments. Thus, the Soviet Union, though currently producing only one half as much steel as the United States, is probably putting an approximately equal quantity of

[2] Throughout reference is to U. S. short tons of 2,000 pounds, rather than to metric tons of 2,200 pounds.

steel into military industry and perhaps somewhat larger amounts into military end products.

And, despite all the hullabaloo about improving the supply of food and consumer goods, there is no firm evidence that the Soviet leadership ever had any intention of diverting, even temporarily, any substantial proportion of its steel from heavy industry and armaments.

What seems to have happened is that between 1950 and 1952 the Soviet Union upped steeply the construction of military industry and military goods. The Kremlin's calculation of an easy conquest in South Korea was upset in June 1950. A worldwide struggle seemed imminent, and, without the Allied aid in supplies which had helped to make up its deficits in World War II, Moscow felt obliged to go all-out for increased military production and enlarged military capacity. It also imposed stepped-up industrial plans and quotas on its European satellites.

By 1952, and even more in 1953, the Soviet leaders decided that the threat of an immediate war or a challenge to war had diminished. They were then able to reduce the frantic flow of military end products, but continued to strengthen their military industries.

What actually happened in 1953 and 1954, then, is that the Soviet leaders, having completed the 1950–2 "crash program" of building up military production, reverted to a more gradual and, for the long run, better balanced program of expanding the national economy. Malenkov promulgated programs—in agriculture, consumer goods, and housing—to correct, in part, the imbalance and inefficiencies which showed up during the crash program. Nevertheless, the Soviet leaders pressed relentlessly to expand basic Soviet production toward the objective of industrial might which has been at the root of all Kremlin planning since the First Five-Year Plan was framed in 1928.

Since Moscow's maneuverings outside her own borders hinge in large part on the country's growing military and industrial strength, the answers to several questions are of paramount importance to the free world: How fast is the Soviet economy growing? How does this rate of growth compare with that in the United States? Can the Soviet Union maintain or increase its present rate of industrial expansion?

There is a wide range of disagreement over the rate of Soviet economic growth, even if we disregard the exaggerated Soviet claims. Serious and critical Western students come up with calculations of an annual increase in national income ranging from 5 to 8 per cent, in terms of fixed values or real increases.[3] From the viewpoint of American security, this range of obscurity is a serious matter. If the annual rate of increase is 7 or 8 per cent, the Soviet government will be able to divert a substantial part of each annual increment into strengthening agriculture, consumer goods industries, and housing, maintain a stable or even rising level of military output, and continue its rapid expansion of heavy industry. If, on the other hand, the annual rate of increase is only 5 per cent, the Soviet leadership will not be able to effect any real improvement in agriculture and consumer goods without cutting back *either* military production *or* the rate of expansion for heavy industry.[4]

But even an annual rate of increase of only 5 per cent would not mean, as many commentators and political leaders in western Europe assume, that the Soviet leadership had suddenly decided to scrap "guns" in order to provide "butter." All it would mean is that the government was going to provide some more "butter," but far less than had been promised. In fact, it is verified by close study of output statistics from Moscow that the Soviet leadership, in the face of mounting eco-

[3] Abram Bergson, editor: *Soviet Economic Growth* (Evanston: Row, Peterson & Company; 1953), especially the chapter, "National Income," by Gregory Grossman, pp. 1–23.

[4] This analysis has been suggested and developed more fully by Dr. Oleg Hoeffding, of the RAND Corporation.

nomic strength outside the Communist bloc, has been proceeding full steam ahead with the basic program of building up armaments and heavy industry.

If the Kremlin aims to push ahead with the expansion of Soviet national income at a rate of 5, 6, or even 7 per cent a year, what does this mean to relative United States-Soviet power by 1960, or by 1970? Is the Soviet economy going to catch up with and outgrow the United States economy? And can its growth be slowed down, from within or without?

In the best years of growth since 1945 the rate of increase in the United States national income has, at best, been 6 per cent; and 4.3 per cent has been the average annual rate since World War II. (The rate of growth of the American gross national product between 1929 and 1950, deflated for changes in the value of the dollar, averaged just under 3 per cent per year.)[5] If, for the purposes of calculation, we assume that the Soviet economy is going to expand at the rate of 6 per cent and the United States economy at the rate of 3 per cent for, say, twenty years, this looks quite serious.

We must, however, make some allowance for the fact that percentages can be deceiving. Even 3 per cent of the United States national income is far larger today, in absolute terms, than 6 per cent of the Soviet national income. Assuming these rigid rates of increase and assigning an arbitrary but plausible comparable dollar value to Soviet national income, it works out that the annual *absolute* increment of United States national income would be greater than the Soviet *absolute* increment for the next twenty-eight to thirty years. *Only then,* when the real gap between Soviet and United States national incomes has become far greater than it is now, would the, by then, enlarged Soviet annual increment enable its economy to begin closing the gap and overtaking our lead.

[5] U. S. Department of Commerce: *National Income—1951 Edition, A Supplement to the Survey of Current Business* (Washington, D. C.: Government Printing Office; 1951), p. 146.

Needless to say, this is a simplified calculation, and not to be taken as a prediction. It is useful here only to point up the caution needed in drawing conclusions from the superior rates of annual increase achieved by the Soviet Union during the period of industrialization since 1928.

The fact remains that if the Soviet Union continues, over the next thirty years, to achieve a cumulative annual increase of 6 per cent, it will have far outstripped all industrial countries except the United States in economic growth, and *will have forced these other countries irrevocably into a position of complete dependence on either the Soviet or the American industrial and power complex*. So to a very great extent American business and political decisions in the years immediately ahead will determine whether the non-Soviet world is consolidated around the American power core, or whether important parts of it are driven or attracted into the Soviet complex.[6] This realization is undoubtedly a factor behind the new emphasis which the Eisenhower Administration has, since the beginning of the year, been placing on foreign economic policy.

The most important result of Russia's new position as the second strongest industrial power is that *the Soviet method of industrialization offers an alternative to the Western or American method*. The Bolsheviks have shown what can be accomplished in a backward country, rich in raw materials and man power and poor in capital and technology, under the ruthless drive of Communist dictatorship. China, with a similar set of conditions, is following the Soviet path. Moscow believes that other capital-poor nations will eventually be forced to do the same unless the United States devises some bold new investment and development program within the democratic, capitalist pattern.

A fact which many are reluctant to face is that the

[6] See, for example, George Waldstein: "Showdown in the Orient," *Harvard Business Review* (November-December 1954), p. 113.

Soviet system of industrialization has a built-in capacity for further rapid expansion, and that this expansion and its rate can hardly be influenced from without. The Soviet Union has the man power, the technological know-how, the resources, and the political system of control to continue a high rate of expansion. That rate of expansion may be slowed down by domestic factors or decisions, but the actions of the outside world have only an insignificant effect on it.

Population statistics are kept secret in the Soviet Union, but a widely accepted estimate for 1955 is 213 to 216 million, with a probable increase of 3 million. The rate of annual increase is declining as Russia becomes industrialized, and is now estimated at 1.49 to 1.67 per cent, as compared with more than 2 per cent before 1928. Between 1955 and 1960 the annual additions into the work force will be unusually small because of the shortage of births during the war years, but after 1960 there will again be a large annual increment. It therefore was good sense for the post-Stalin regime to make a try for increased productivity based on better incentives through rising consumption, in order to man its growing industries without reducing the large forces which it has kept under arms ever since the war.

Population alone does not give strength in an industrial age, and the Soviet Union has made tremendous exertions to spread education, especially technical education. At present, it is estimated, more scientists, engineers, and technicians are being trained in the Soviet Union than in the United States. The level of the best scientific and technical training is very high, but the average level must be assumed to be below that provided in the United States. Still, in Communist as in capitalist countries important scientific and technological advances are usually made by a relatively small number of the top people.

American estimates of Soviet scientific capabilities have recently been revised sharply upwards. It is probable that the Soviet Union was ahead of us in developing the hydrogen bomb. The quality of its aircraft, tanks, and artillery is rated high by Washington defense officials. American experts have been greatly impressed by Soviet advances in alloys, traditionally a Russian strength, and in electronics, in which they were thought to be far behind. The unpleasant fact is that we can no longer safely assume that Soviet science and technology are "incapable" of doing whatever our side can do.

This has profound implications for both government and business. Whatever else we sacrifice or limit, we cannot afford to slacken the pace of research and development on the comforting assumption that what we don't do the Russians won't do either. For United States security, the important thing is not going to be whether government or business pushes ahead with research and development on a tremendous scale, but that the necessary job be done by both together.

Mineral supplies are available for further Soviet expansion. Until two years ago, it was assumed that limited access to uranium sources might restrict the expansion of Soviet atomic power, but in recent months revised estimates assume that Russia has all the uranium she could expect to need. Industrial diamonds are a bottleneck, judging by widely reported Soviet smuggling operations. Zinc, lead, natural gas, molybdenum, bismuth, borax, cadmium, and cobalt are reported to be in relatively short supply.[7] Except for the rarer alloys, however, and perhaps in their case also, the "short supply" may prove only temporary, in absolute terms.

What may prove more important is that many of the rare minerals and many of the best resources are located in remote parts of the country, and access to them, even under Soviet conditions of forced settlement and forced labor, will require large expenditures

[7] For fuller information, see D. B. Shimkin: *Minerals—A Key to Soviet Power* (Cambridge: Harvard University Press; 1953).

to create minimum living and transportation facilities. As better-quality and more accessible minerals are used up, the Soviet Union, insistent on finding its basic resources within its own military perimeter, will then have to use lower-grade ores, expend more on meliorating them for industrial use, or develop more remote sources. These additional expenditures may not affect the rate of national income growth, but they may well tend to reduce somewhat the effectiveness of additional investments in terms of both production and military power.

The Soviet management concept has tended, especially since the mid-1930's, to lodge very great power in an elite corps of administrators, chosen both for political reliability and production achievements, and the competition to get into the top managerial ranks and to stay there is a ruthless one. So long as he meets the demands of the government, the Soviet business administrator exercises a range of power far greater than is generally supposed.[8] And his rewards are correspondingly high.

Furthermore, while the Communist "businessmen" have received added recognition from the post-Stalin leadership, and many of the new programs probably reflect their recommendations on how to make the system work better, the ultimate dominance of party objectives clearly continues. The recent campaign to discredit and discourage anonymous denunciations of managers and of officials strengthens the authority of this influential group of industrial managers.

By improving the incentives for better production and by regularizing the flow of raw materials and equipment, industrial output can be speeded, and Soviet leaders have emphasized these programs. The Russian trade press currently carries an increasing flow of editorials on the need for adequate reserves of materials and spare parts, to avoid periods of shutdown, followed

[8] David Granick: *Management of the Industrial Firm in the U.S.S.R.* (New York: Columbia University Press; 1954).

by desperate campaigns to meet the monthly or quarterly plans. It can be argued that the Soviet system, always pushing against material and manpower limitations, achieves its goals by keeping up an inhuman pressure upon its managers, but the managers are no doubt right in arguing that they can achieve better and less expensive production if they are assured of a better flow of materials and have to expend less effort and money and "nerves" in overcoming one bottleneck after another.

There is no sign that the rate of investment—estimated at 20 to 23 per cent of the annual national income, as compared with 12 to 13 per cent in the United States—is going to be appreciably slackened. One of the key factors in the Soviet industrialization has been the ability of the regime—through collectivization of agriculture, restriction of consumption, and direct and indirect exploitation of man power—to squeeze out regularly about one fifth of the national income for new investment.

Where this new capital is invested confirms the fact that the Kremlin's pattern of industrial growth is completely dominated by the expansion of the heavy and defense industries: Between 1929 and 1952, 64 per cent of all new capital invested went into heavy industry, including military industry; 19.4 per cent to transport; 9.4 per cent to agriculture; and only 7.2 per cent to consumer goods industries. In 1929, the first year of the great industrialization drive, 57.6 per cent of industrial output went directly into consumption; in 1952, only 27.8 per cent of industrial output consisted of consumer goods. In 1954, out of a gross investment of 160 billion rubles, only 16 billion rubles have been allocated to the three ministries of food products, light industry, and trade.

While the Soviet leadership did initiate a substantial increase in the flow of certain consumer goods during 1953 and 1954, as part of its campaign to raise the incentives for better production, performance to date has been very uneven and to a degree, at least, has been achieved through the *importation* of sizable quantities of food and consumer novelties. Presumably Malenkov is the scapegoat.

Cotton cloth is basic in Soviet consumption, but in the first half of 1954 production increased only 3 per cent over the same period of 1953. Meat and meat products, perpetually scarce and high-priced, increased 2 per cent. On the other hand, durable consumer goods, produced in small quantities and largely accessible only to the upper 10 per cent of better-paid people, showed large increases *percentagewise*—for instance, vacuum cleaners, 350 per cent; television sets, 188 per cent; and household refrigerators, 216 per cent. Indeed, part of the materials, factory space, skilled man power, and lathes assigned for military products have been turned to producing television sets for the top managerial and party groups.

What does all this add up to, in terms of the Soviet standard of living?

According to an important new estimate, based on very detailed calculations, Soviet real wages for the urban population in 1952 were substantially below the level of 1928—somewhere between 63 per cent and 90 per cent of real wages in 1928, depending on whether the measurement is made in terms of what the consumer could buy back in 1928 or what went into the "market basket" in a later period.[9] Taking the more favorable comparison, it is possible that the increase in supplies and reduction of prices since 1952 have closed the gap. But this still means that the average Soviet citizen has little in the way of personal property or amenities to show for his pains; twenty-five years of intense effort—for industrialization, collectivization of agriculture, World War II and its devastation, and

[9] Janet G. Chapman: "Real Wages in the Soviet Union, 1928–1952," *Review of Economics and Statistics* (May 1954), pp. 134–56.

postwar reconstruction—have merely brought the average urban standard of living "up" to where it was in 1928. And now, apparently, consumer goods will be subordinated further.

The fact that the increase in basic consumer goods has been much slower than hoped for points directly to the problem of agriculture.

Moving with large promises and jerky performance to correct in some small measure the severe imbalance between heavy and light industry, the Soviet leaders have looked to the farm program to provide the greater volume of foodstuffs and raw materials that are so badly needed. However, the rural population, which has been starved for consumer goods longer and worse than the urban population, can in turn be given incentives for better production only through better provision of those very boots and calico which are still only trickling through the production lines.

Though agriculture has been the weakest link in the Soviet planned economy, there is no evidence at all that the leaders in the Kremlin have the slightest intention of abandoning the collectivization of agriculture or of extending to the long-suffering peasants more than the smallest sop in the way of increased supplies of consumer goods.

What the government does seem to have tried to do is to raise the peasant's incentives for better work by giving him more money income—with which to buy more consumer goods that are not yet available. The agricultural reforms of 1953 reduced and simplified the taxes on the products of the peasant's own kitchen plot and his privately owned cow or pig. They reduced the amounts of produce collected by the government at absurdly low prices; and they raised these prices somewhat, especially for cotton, tobacco, livestock, and flax (but *not* for wheat).

But these reforms do not mean, as some observers have rashly assumed, that the collective farm system is being thrown overboard. On the contrary, the Soviet leaders have always aimed at the complete collectivization of agriculture that was outlined by Stalin in his last testament, "Economic Problems of Socialism," when he declared that "the private holdings of collective farmers must be replaced by completely collective control of all agricultural production." Indeed, a closer look at some of the first moves of the post-Stalin regime which seemed to nullify this program—particularly the very ones increasing the income the peasant gets from the private farming he does—can be interpreted as part of an attempt to strengthen the collective system of farming.

During 1954 Moscow carried on a systematic campaign to raise the annual number of labor days performed by the collectivized farmers, thus tying the peasant even more closely into the collective system. Even the small gains granted the collective farm peasant in using the product of his private garden and cow are used to discipline him into working longer and harder on the collective fields. If a member of a collective farm fails to work the required—and now increased—number of days for the collective, the taxes on his personal garden and livestock are to be doubled.

Actually, it is only by raising the production of the collectives that the government can later afford the risk involved in eliminating the private farming which, on 2 per cent of the cultivated land, raises 23 per cent of the total food supply. Moscow has not hesitated to make the concessions it deems necessary to achieve the ultimate goal, but they should be recognized for what they are: small and reversible at will, their purpose is to make the peasants produce more when working for the collective, and thus help to pave the way for ending the Kremlin's reluctant dependence on the whims of private production.

Far-reaching as this measure is, Moscow has supplemented it with another move (credited to Khrushchev) which has caused fewer repercussions in the Soviet Union though it is likely to produce more striking results.

In order to find a quick way out of its agricultural blind alley, Moscow has embarked upon a bold and ambitious program of plowing up virgin land, especially in Kazakhstan and southern Siberia. The program, launched in March 1954, called for 31 million acres to be plowed in 1954 and 1955; of these more than 5 million were to be sowed and harvested in 1954. Recent reports claim that 9 million acres were sown, and the total program has been increased to 66 million acres to be plowed up before the end of 1956. Compared with a sown acreage of 384 million acres in 1952, this represents a promised increase of 17 per cent in sown area.

How this "virgin land" campaign will work out is hard to predict. Presumably, it is bringing into cultivation much fertile land afflicted with periodic drought, and over a number of years it may create a new and vast dust bowl. It is probably more significant for the moment that these lands have been usurped from Kazakh nomads who used them for grazing. Since Russia, despite its vast increase in population, has fewer head of livestock than it had in 1916 (before the revolution) or in 1927 (before the famous Five-Year plans were inaugurated), this can lead to fresh dissatisfactions among the workers. The government is apparently willing to take the gamble for the sake of the increased grain it expects to collect from the newly plowed lands. It must reckon that it can get a better immediate return from its virgin soil program than by putting the same resources into other parts of the agricultural program.

What about the possibility of Moscow bolstering its supplies of short materials through foreign trade? It is doubtful that the government can start a major drive now to get what it wants from the countries which are not already obligated to supply what is asked for. (Of course it might be possible for Soviet exports to dominate the market of some small and weak country that is not now recognized as a satellite, but this assumes that Moscow will first have established its political and military domination.)

The total foreign trade of the Soviet Union, estimated in dollar values, was probably $5 billion in 1952, and $6 billion in 1953, and $7.5 billion in 1954. In 1952, 80 per cent of Soviet trade was with its satellites in eastern Europe and with China, and trade outside the Soviet bloc amounted to about $1 billion. During 1954 trade outside the Soviet bloc may have increased to $2 billion, after strenuous Soviet efforts to increase the range and volume of the goods exchanged. In relation to Soviet national income, however, foreign trade is a very small item, even when imports are stimulated by sales of gold, as they were last year to the tune of $250 million.

The goods which Russia can supply are limited in range. On balance the country is now importing foodstuffs, and its exports of timber, pulp, and ores have declined. Interestingly, industrial equipment has come to play an increasing part in Soviet exports, primarily to Soviet-dominated countries which must take what they can get in return for their politically dictated exports to the Soviet Union. (While Moscow has offered industrial equipment to India, Egypt, and Indonesia, and has delivered small quantities to Afghanistan, it has not been able to sell its industrial goods in markets which are free to choose the products of the West.)

If foreign trade is, for Russia, a very weak economic weapon, it nevertheless has considerable propaganda and political appeal. The Soviet government has used incessant talk about trade to drive wedges into the political solidarity of the West. Wherever an opportunity occurs to exploit economic weakness, Soviet delegations appear and talk up the advantages of a "stable" long-term exchange with the Soviet Union with its "planned" imports. They talk especially about the disadvantages of depending on the United States for a market.

It is important to keep the Soviet Union from benefiting from new industrial advances of the West which can add to its military potential. In the August 1954 agreement of the Western powers and Japan to cut down the definition of black-listed "strategic" goods, both this factor and the importance of permitting an expansion of nonstrategic trade between the non-Soviet and Soviet blocs were recognized. An over-rigid insistence on a very extensive definition of "strategic" goods would be increasingly difficult to enforce, since America's economic aid to western Europe is rapidly coming to a close. If a general disregard for the embargo developed, more of the really crucial items might slip through than would be the case with a carefully defined and enforced list of strategic goods. Thus the wider embargo would defeat its own purpose and weaken America and its allies.

Moreover, a total embargo on trade with the Soviet Union would have only a very limited effect on its over-all economic development, which is self-propelled by "built-in" factors. Such an embargo would, however, cause significant economic difficulties to many countries of western Europe, and it would greatly increase the political frictions within the non-Soviet world.

During 1950–2 Soviet economic programs aimed at maximizing preparation for war or for a possible diplomatic showdown. Since 1952, and especially after Stalin's death in March 1953, the Soviet leadership went through a transition period of strengthening the Soviet economy, with continued emphasis on heavy and military industry, and some increased attention to such weak sectors as agriculture, consumer goods output, and transportation.

Malenkov called for a partial redressing of the imbalance which has marked the forced industrialization for twenty-five years, and for easing the girths which have worn saddle sores into the Soviet consumer and citizen. By showing slightly better manners in diplomacy, yet without conceding a single point of strength, he temporarily allayed the immediate fears of many nations in the non-Soviet world and thus facilitated a substantial cutting back and postponement of rearmament programs in the free world. Naturally, it is to Soviet advantage to bring about a substantial cut in the arming of the free world, rather than to have to offset additional free world military strength by equivalent stepped-up demands on its own constantly strained resources.

Basic to the decision to relax pressure on the free world was the realization that Russia needed more time to offset the atomic-hydrogen potential of the United States. Given this respite, it could concentrate on expanding its conventional armaments and modernizing its own forces and those of its satellites and China. Thus, in the near future it could hope both to neutralize the atomic-hydrogen potential of retaliation (already a declining asset of United States power) and to expand its power and that of its allies to wage piecemeal campaigns of peripheral conquest as in Indochina.

Also, while taking the needed time to develop more fully the resources of its satellites and to integrate them into its own economic potential, it could continue its campaign to divide its opponents by seeking out and magnifying the issues which divide governments or peoples. For the Soviet leadership, a major war is a terrible gamble. Since Moscow presumably has no definite timetable of expansion, it has preferred to use the more familiar weapons of political and psychological warfare including, wherever practicable, the threat of its great military power.

But now we must reckon with the possibility that this period of easement is over.

In 1939 we could not foresee the emergence of a bipolar world, based on two major and truly independent centers of power, America and the Soviet Union.

We could not anticipate that this process of bipolarization would be speeded up tremendously by the new post-1945 weapons of atomic-hydrogen power and the new means of delivering them. Even if Russia and America shared a common ideology, it would be difficult to manage the problem of a bipolar division of power; but since the Soviet leadership foresees and works unceasingly for the destruction of all competing power centers, we are involved, whether we like it or not, in a contest for survival.

For the American people, and especially for American businessmen, the Soviet challenge is a more complex one than we have ever faced before. We must maintain our lead as long as possible in strategic power, and at the same time we must strengthen our friends, economically as well as militarily, in order to deter Soviet-inspired local aggressions. We must develop a more flexible political and propaganda arsenal, in order to build up the unity of the free world and its ability to plan and act together. And we must back this up with an expanding economy, in order to support large continuing expenditures for military power and to bind the free-world nations more closely together in a general upward movement of their economies.

The Soviet challenge is primarily military and political in its impact today, but it is buttressed by a rapidly growing economy. The answer to that challenge requires a vigorous and inventive American economy as well as military skill and political wisdom.

:19:

THE SOVIET UNION AND THE UNITED STATES: PROBLEMS AND PROSPECTS[1]

[*October 1955*]

STALIN'S successors have modulated somewhat the bad manners of Soviet policy and have refurbished its arsenal of diplomatic and psychological weapons. The new flexibility of their tactics has brought important gains and promises more for the future. Stalin's threats and bludgeonings—the pressures against Greece and Turkey, the attempt to starve West Berlin into submission, the Communist attack on South Korea—forced the threatened countries of the free world into countermeasures and new defense arrangements and made the United States, reluctantly, the chief bastion and promoter of resistance to further Soviet expansion. At first timidly, since 1954 with growing self-assurance, the new Soviet leadership has shifted and varied its tactics. Has it changed its basic strategy?

Since Stalin's death there have been numerous and clashing estimates of the Soviet power position. Some

[1] *Annals of the American Academy of Political and Social Science*, Vol. CCCIII (January 1956), pp. 192–8. Copyright 1956 by the American Academy of Political and Social Science.

commentators have pictured a Soviet leadership disrupted by the danger or reality of mutual destruction. They have inflated the execution of Beria or the demotion of Malenkov into a harbinger of the imminent downfall of the Soviet system and have overlooked the basic persistence of the Stalin-erected apparatus, which rules through massive and all-embracing institutions that in turn are regulated and propelled by the Communist party. They have often confused the struggle for power within the system—a struggle which is always bitter and often fatal within a totalitarian regime—with a crisis of the system itself.

Stalin's successors have been franker than he was in admitting defects in Soviet economic plans and achievements and have taken some fairly substantial steps to raise agricultural production, improve housing, increase economic incentives, and raise somewhat the standard of living. From this fact many foreign commentators have drawn contradictory but usually comforting conclusions. The new leadership, some say, has abandoned its world-wide ambitions and is primarily interested in promoting the welfare of its own people. Or, contrariwise, the leadership is, others assert, unable to cope with its accumulated economic problems and is therefore interested in achieving a genuine basis of understanding and coexistence with the outside world, even to the point of making major political and territorial concessions.

Within the framework of the basic drive to build heavy industry and military strength, the new leaders have made substantial but still minor concessions to strengthen the lagging fields of food, housing, and living standards. But actual investments in military strength have continued to increase since March 1953, and heavy industry has maintained its remarkable rate of growth. The prospect is strong that the Soviet economy will continue the race to outstrip all other economies except that of the United States. Ten years from now the American and Soviet economies will overshadow even more ominously those of all other countries.

The prospect is strong for a continued bipolarization of military as well as economic power. True, some analysts predict the widespread development, within a few years, of "cheap" atomic-hydrogen power and the emergence of the intercontinental guided missile as a "poor man's weapon." If these forecasts prove true, the present bipolarization of the newest forms of power may be followed by a new distribution of strength among countries, and by new dangers, too. Until these predictions have been tested, however, one basic factor of great importance is the trend toward ever more complex and costly systems of modern weapons. In this race, which is both technological and economic, only three major countries are now able to stand the pace. In both technology and resources the Soviet Union continues to demonstrate great and growing military strength.

Stalin's policies had, as he boasted, extended the Communist system to one third of the population of the world, but they had also aroused hate and fear outside the realm of his writ. His successors turned their hands to liquidating the political liabilities which they had inherited, thereby recovering greater freedom of political action. In 1953 Moscow dropped Stalin's stubborn insistence that Turkey surrender one fourth of its national territory. In 1955 it returned to the Finns the Porkkala enclave, a base outmoded in the age of atomic warfare. It abandoned its grip on eastern Austria. It persuaded the Yugoslav leadership that the independence and survival of their country were no longer threatened by Soviet enmity. Except in the case of Austria, each of these "concessions" was a recognition of facts which could not be changed except at the risk of war. None of them cut into any Soviet positions of strength. However, for many people fearful of war and yearning for more hopeful omens, the new trend offered "proof" of an entirely new Soviet policy, a permanent policy of live and let live.

In Germany, which the Soviet leadership regards as the key to Europe, it has made no concessions. The two Geneva conferences of 1955 demonstrated the Kremlin's persistent belief that it can exploit the desire of the German people for reunification in order to detach it from its alliance with the West. The fear of Soviet preponderance may deter the West Germans for some years from accepting Soviet terms for reunification. Will it be effective indefinitely?

The Soviet leaders look to a new depression in America, with its repercussions throughout the free world, to force West Germany to seek markets in the Soviet bloc, to detach itself from the West, and to accept Soviet terms for national reunification. Meanwhile, it has made abundantly clear that it has no notion of sacrificing East Germany, its most valuable colony, for the sake of any paper assurances of "security."

Soviet smiles and token concessions have given new currency to Moscow's proposals for a European security pact. At the two Genevas the Kremlin proposed a series of stages by which the Western North Atlantic Pact and the Eastern Warsaw Pact would be fused into an over-all European security agreement. If achieved, this result would completely eliminate the role of the North Atlantic Treaty Organization as a framework of Western defense. On the other hand, through its control of the party, secret police, and military apparatus in the satellite regimes, the Soviet-led groupings in eastern Europe, now including East Germany and Albania, would still remain a fully effective, ever-ready instrument of Soviet purposes.

Of course, the Soviet spokesmen did not expect the NATO governments to swallow the bait, but at no cost to their own strength or programs they have promoted a greater sense of security in the West and a growing reluctance to make sacrifices for the strength of the Western bloc, and have contributed to slow down the rate of NATO's military build-up. If the NATO countries reduce their military efforts by, say, five or ten billions of dollars a year, the relative gain to the Soviet bloc, with its steady increase in military resources, will be well worth a small diplomatic effort.

As a symbol of its new flexibility of tactics, the place of the remote and cryptic Stalin has been taken by the eager and voluble travelers Bulganin and Khrushchev. While their appearance in Belgrade may have had relatively little effect upon the cautious and strong-willed Yugoslavs, with their recent memories of Russian interference and menaces, it is more difficult to appraise the impact of their visits to India and Burma. There the flattering attentions of the leaders of a great power have apparently reinforced the feeling that the Soviet Union represents a remote and presumably beneficient power. Other visits have been foreshadowed, to Britain, France, and Egypt. In each mission the Soviet spokesmen emphasize, crudely but not ineffectively, those interests and emotions which may draw other peoples to support specific Soviet policies and, above all, those prejudices and fears which may turn them against the United States.

Under Stalin, Soviet policy concentrated its pressure against its immediate neighbors along the periphery. Under his successors, Soviet policy reaches farther afield. To the Arab countries, which do not feel Soviet pressure directly, as have Turkey and Iran, it offers political support against Israel and promises of economic assistance and military supplies, to enable them to escape from one-sided dependence on the West. To India, which is more interested in its struggle with Pakistan over Kashmir than in any seemingly remote Soviet ambitions, it offers political support for the annexation of the Portuguese enclaves and remarkably favorable terms for constructing a large steel mill. To Burma, which may see the usefulness of direct

Soviet interest as a potential offset to possible Chinese Communist pressure, it offers industrial equipment and technical assistance in exchange for its embarrassing rice surplus.

Within the United Nations the new Soviet diplomacy has also shown an unaccustomed sureness and flexibility. On more and more occasions is has found its positions supported not only by the Asian-African bloc but also by a substantial number of Latin American states. It can no longer complain of the "mechanical majorities" rolled up in support of United States proposals. Instead of insisting rigidly upon its one-sided proposals for disarmament, it has flexibly adopted the Western proposal for over-all numerical limitations on defense forces and has pushed hard for the acceptance of early limitations on the use of the atomic bomb, while resisting the insistence of the West on the need for establishing effective controls. Still, in many countries the Soviet tactics in the question of control of armaments have greatly lessened suspicion of Moscow's intentions.

Perhaps the Kremlin's persistent rolling of the "anti-colonialist" drums has been its most effective instrument. The "West" is easily identified as the bogeyman for peoples recently emancipated from alien rule, or still seeking their emancipation, and the Soviet leaders are working hard, as they have since 1917, at attuning these deep-seated emotions to their own interests.

While the Soviet leadership continues the strenuous pace of economic development at home and pursues the consolidation of the Soviet sphere, it looks hopefully for signs of economic decay and political disruption in the non-Soviet camp. True, the Soviet picture of American and Western economic life is no longer so grossly oversimplified as it was in Stalin's last years. Delegations of farm experts and housing administrators have admitted that there are new and valuable ideas to be gleaned from Western innovations, and *Pravda* has condemned technicians who claim that everything

Soviet is best. On the other hand, Soviet periodicals are predicting an early economic depression in the American economy, which, they maintain, has been sustained only by the armaments race. They point out that the crash of 1929 came ten years after World War I, implying clearly their hope for a new depression, scheduled to begin ten years after the close of World War II.

Even without the long-awaited economic crisis, the Soviet press eagerly picks out each new evidence of "imperialist rivalries" within the non-Soviet world. As Stalin explained in his "Economic Problems of Socialism" (October 1952), these conflicts are bound to undermine any efforts to consolidate the free world and must even lead to new wars within it, wars which could only redound to the advantage of the Soviet Union. Of course, all programs of United States economic assistance, in this view, are designed only to "export unemployment," to weaken foreign competitors, and to establish "control by the dollar" over underdeveloped areas. As in Stalin's time, Soviet commentators believe that Germany and Japan are especially vulnerable to a new depression and to American competition, and therefore especially susceptible to being wooed away from the American-led bloc of "imperialists."

Without waiting for a major depression or a "general crisis of capitalism," the Soviet leadership is working hard to break up those links of solidarity which Stalin's policies did so much to forge within the non-Soviet world. Both by direct diplomatic and not-so-diplomatic appeals and by indirect appeals to pride, fear, and envy, Soviet policy and propaganda endeavor to exploit the inevitable disagreement and dissensions within the free world. Against American policies Soviet propaganda appeals in France to deep-seated fears of a rearmed Germany, in Germany to the suspicion that it is France, rather than Russia, which seeks to keep Germany divided. Soviet policy and propaganda have intensified their main effort, which aims to divide the United States from its allies, and thus to bring about the retraction of American power to North America.

The principal aim of the Soviet leaders, now as under Stalin, is to eliminate the system of bases which, in case of conflict, might support American pressure against the Soviet Union. The United States and the Soviet Union have been approaching "atomic parity," in terms of their capacity to inflict punishment on each other. Soon the principal advantage which the United States and its allies may still enjoy will be the geographical one of being able, in case of Soviet attack, to effect or threaten convergent retaliation from many directions. It would be a long time before the Soviet leadership would, under such conditions, be confident of the ability of their regime to survive, even if they succeeded in destroying the major American cities.

American and Soviet strategic power may soon enter a stage in which each can destroy the other without the use of intervening bases. However, if American policy, at that stage, discards its alliances or disregards its allies because it need no longer rely on bases outside North America, Soviet policy will be encouraged to increase its pressure on the countries lying in between. As the arm of strategic power is lengthened, the United States will need to build the community of interest within the free world not less actively but more actively than it has done so far.

Since World War II Soviet policy has failed in Europe to expand its sphere of control beyond the line of its military penetration; in fact, it failed to secure control of Austria and Finland, and in 1948 it drove Yugoslavia into a desperate assertion of its independence. As after World War I Soviet Communism failed in Europe to win any new country by voluntary conversion to its creed.

In Asia the victory of the Chinese Communists, achieved after many years of political and military struggle, marked the beginning rather than the end of a desperate and crucial wrestling for the future of Asia. The stalemating of the Communist forces in the Korean War and the temporary pause in the military struggle for Southeast Asia offer no inherent assurance of the long-continued stabilization of contesting forces. One of the main purposes of post-Stalin Soviet policy is to prepare favorable conditions for the renewal of Communist expansion in Asia.

By cultivating a renewed sense of security and relaxation among America's Western allies, Soviet policy hopes to avoid a repetition of the dangerous experience brought on it by Stalin's Korean adventure. At the time of the Korean War many countries directly menaced by Soviet threats rallied to support American counteraction in Korea, feeling that this would in turn strengthen their own security in the future. Soviet propaganda was largely unsuccessful, outside the Soviet bloc, in picturing the Korean War as a spontaneous "civil war," in which the United States and the United Nations were gratuitously interfering. In promoting an atmosphere of relaxation, Moscow hopes now to reinsure itself and Communist China against a new risk of this sort. Any stepped-up demand for "elections" in Vietnam or any revival of guerrilla warfare in South Vietnam will, it hopes, be regarded generally as a purely local affair, to be settled by local forces without interference by outside powers, especially by the United States.

If the Kremlin expects a new period of tensions, risks, and opportunities for Communist expansion to unfold in southeast Asia, it is entirely logical for it to work hard at strengthening its "peace-loving" posture elsewhere throughout the world. Thereby it can, in effect, hold the ring for the Chinese Communists and their local allies in southeast Asia while making sure that no threat of major retaliation is directed toward the Soviet Union. If the United States and its allies should then disagree concerning the desirability or necessity of blocking further Communist expansion in Asia, the Soviet leadership might succeed in its aim of separating the United States from its allies and thus dismantling the American-led security and bases system of the free world.

Faced by the more subtle strategy and the more flexible tactics which are being pursued by Stalin's successors, American opinion has shown a wide variety of reactions. The initial assumption that the Soviet regime was about to collapse or, alternatively, that it would now devote all its energies to the welfare of its people encouraged a natural desire to limit military expenditures and to cut down economic aid to friendly nations. At the same time, in accepting the Soviet challenge to negotiate, President Eisenhower narrowly escaped the position of being forced to "prove" America's peaceful intentions. Instead, he reaffirmed dramatically the American desire to avoid recourse to war and the American willingness to accept a drastic form of arms inspection for itself as well as for others, as a means of building confidence in the prospect of reducing the threat of war.

After the narrow limits of Soviet "concessions" had been made clear, American opinion recognized that it was the manner rather than the substance of Soviet policy which had changed. The question still remained: In the somewhat changed atmosphere, would time work for Soviet aims or for American and free world purposes?

As many peoples and groups begin to feel less directly menaced by Soviet pressures, the task of maintaining a broad range of understanding and co-operation within the free world becomes more difficult. It will no longer be sufficient to say that the United States is willing to aid other peoples because keeping their "real estate" in friendly hands contributes to United States security. No people likes to feel that its survival or its economic development is going to depend indefinitely on the "generosity" of a more powerful state.

In the long run, interests must be mutual in order to be strong. In order to preserve and strengthen its alliances the United States must make clear the mutual interest of itself and its allies in maintaining the widest possible area of political freedom and economic opportunity within the world. The element of mutuality and joint decision making within the American-led alliance system must be strengthened constantly and systematically. Rather than allowing the United States to "go it alone," the early arrival of the stage of intercontinental combat will give a new urgency to that common interest in joint survival.

The Soviet leadership is endeavoring to deal separately with European and Asian affairs and thus to probe the weak points of American policy. It is in the American interest to combat this Soviet effort. Instead of treating the Communist-bloc demand for early elections in Vietnam as a purely localized matter, American policy would do well to link it with the free world's demand for genuinely free elections in Korea and East Germany. This would make it clear that the United States is working actively to overcome the division of all three nations. Instead of pursuing a completely separate policy with respect to the offshore islands, the United States would be well advised to draw a clear and defensible line through the Formosa Strait and to rally as wide a political support as possible for the defense of Formosa.

The industrial development of the Soviet Union is now largely self-generating, and the race in military technology is becoming closer all the time. The competition for new break-throughs in military technology cannot be halted or slowed down. This means that the only important—if crude—instrument by which Soviet decisions can be influenced is the maintenance of a very large United States military budget.

When Soviet policy makers feel uncertain about the rate of progress in American military technology, their willingness to use their own very great power in a reckless manner may be restrained. In addition, while very large and growing, the Soviet economy is hard pressed to meet the competing demands for improved and costly armaments, for domestic expansion of heavy industry, and for some rise in Soviet living standards, not to mention the demands of Communist China for Soviet aid to its industrialization. American policies can do little or nothing to influence Soviet decisions regarding domestic growth or aid to China, but its actions do have a direct effect on Soviet decisions in the military field. A continuing large American military budget is almost the only way of compelling the Soviet leadership to face the competing claims on its economic resources and to consider from time to time the feasibility and the desirability, from its own point of view, of taking on new risks in the pursuit of its world-wide aims.

At the same time the United States must demonstrate that free world assistance in economic development and in political and cultural progress, offered with freedom and dignity, is both more attractive and more efficacious than the Soviet counteroffers. As far as possible, such assistance to nations eager to develop their productive resources must be offered on a continuing basis and must be co-ordinated with the development of world-wide trade opportunities rather than offered as an emergency response to Soviet blackmail or enticements. Instead of relaxing and forgetting about the needs and aspirations of underdeveloped and ambitious countries, Americans need to think now in terms of longer-range, persistent, and shared programs of economic development.

Above all, in the new phase of Soviet smiles, Americans must realize even more fully that the dangers through which we are passing are not of short-term character. No one policy, no one appropriation, no one administration, can be expected to cope with them once and for all. Whether Americans like it or not, what they do or do not do will be one of the two determining factors in shaping the world of tomorrow. If Americans are sorely tried by the too great predictability of Soviet aims and tactics, probably Kremlin analysts are constantly fuming over the unpredictability of American opinions and actions. A strong, stable, and predictable American position in world affairs is now the most important element in an increasingly unstable equation of forces.

:20:

SOVIET FOREIGN POLICY: NEW GOALS OR NEW MANNERS?[1]

[*May 1956*]

WILL the dismantling of the Stalin myth, the most startling result of the Twentieth Congress of the Communist party of the Soviet Union, be followed by the modification or abandonment of the basic goals of Stalin's foreign policy? Or merely by a change in Soviet manners and methods? Nikita Khrushchev's bitter attack on Stalin, delivered to a secret session of the congress on February 25, has now been published in America, at least in part, in what appears to be an authentic version.[2] It gives evidence of substantial changes in the "style" in which the post-Stalin party Presidium proposes to exercise its dictatorial power at home, while pursuing the same basic goals of building heavy industry and military power. But it gives no evidence of doubt as to the correctness of Stalin's basic foreign policy.

[1] *Foreign Affairs*, Vol. XXXIV, No. 4 (July 1956), pp. 541–53. Copyright 1956 by the Council on Foreign Relations, Inc.

[2] A large number of details concerning the Khrushchev speech were given by the Moscow correspondent of the Belgrade *Borba*, March 20, 1956, pp. 1, 3. For the fuller but still probably incomplete version see *The New York Times*, June 5, 1956.

True, Khrushchev attacked Stalin bitterly for his blind faith in Hitler's word and for his refusal to believe Churchill's warnings against the impending German attack on the Soviet Union. The available extracts depict Stalin as a bullheaded and uninformed meddler in military strategy and, by implication, enhance the military stature of both Khrushchev and the army command. Stalin is also accused of "an incorrect position with respect to the nationality question." "He undertook a whole series of reprisals against several nationalities and national minorities." Most striking is the downgrading of the *Short Biography of Stalin*. "The short Stalin biography, which appeared in 1948, is an expression of that uncontrolled self-praise, an attempt by Stalin to show himself as 'an infallible genius.'"

The Khrushchev speech condemns Stalin (but no others) for his stubborn efforts to "break" Tito "with his little finger." (This passage was not included in the version published in the Belgrade *Borba* on March 20.) Since then the Yugoslav Communists have received a double satisfaction, through the disbanding of the Cominform in April and the resignation of Molotov as Foreign Minister on May 31. Apart from the obeisance to Tito, the Khrushchev speech does not question a single one of Stalin's foreign policies, his methods or his achievements. So far as foreign policy is concerned, the key to the current changes in tactics may be concealed rather than revealed in Khrushchev's reference to "the tremendous damage which Stalin caused to the Soviet Union and the international working-class movement."

True to their ingrained Stalinist discipline, the non-Soviet Communist parties have hastened to repudiate their previous groveling obeisances to Stalin's leadership and nervously promise to return, like the Soviet party, to "true Leninist principles." In Bulgaria, Chervenkov has been demoted, at least outwardly, while in Hungary, Rakosi continues in control of the Communist party. Changes in the Polish party have been more far-reaching than in the Czechoslovak party.

These and other maneuvers provide the basis for a wide range of speculation. The retention of Rakosi in Hungary may be due to the relative scarcity of Moscow-trained Communists. Or perhaps the Bulgarian and Polish Communist parties were much more closely affected by the Stalin purges of the late 1930's, and therefore the reaction against "Stalin's methods" of "the crudest physical pressure" may have made it necessary to rearrange the "pecking order" within the satellite leaderships.[3]

Only a Soviet leadership supremely confident of the stability of its rule within the Soviet Union could have undertaken such a drastic operation as the direct repudiation of the Stalin myth. In the European satellites de-Stalinization offers some minor risks to Soviet goals. While it may not be an easy or quick process to rehabilitate "Leninist" methods of operation and control at home, within the Soviet Union the more senior Communist cadres remember vividly the pre-Stalinist or pre-1935 "methods of party work," and the refurbished leadership can therefore appeal to a genuine Leninist myth. In the satellites, the Stalinist system, with all its paraphernalia of multiple controls and terror, was imported in the baggage trains of the Soviet army. It did not develop out of a previous Leninist tradition. To modify the simple command of "Eyes on Moscow!" is a difficult matter.

In Poland, where the attacks on Stalinist methods have gone farthest, considerable confusion and uncertainty have been evident. Loyal Polish Communists must now proclaim that their leaders were wrong in claiming that everything Soviet was best and in deny-

[3] The rehabilitation of the Polish Communist party, dissolved by Stalin in 1938 (*Pravda*, February 21, 1956), may have undermined the seemingly impregnable position of Jakob Berman, long regarded as Stalin's agent in liquidating the pre-1938 leadership. The simultaneous restoration of Béla Kun to posthumous favor (*Pravda*, February 21, 1956) may not have any similar consequences for Rakosi.

ing the importance of Poland's special conditions and traditions. The resistance heroes of the Polish Home Army, after years of being condemned as "agents of Western imperialism," are now praised for their valiant if "misguided" attempt to liberate Warsaw in mid-1944. In literature, "socialist realism," itself subject to some redefinition and stretching in the Soviet Union, is no longer offered to Polish writers as the sole way to please their political masters.

With the continued rapid expansion of the Soviet economy, the satellites' resources and production seem no longer to be needed so desperately by the Soviet Union as in the years of reconstruction and the Korean War. If the satellites are now to carry on an increasing proportion of their trade with the non-Soviet world, many of them may envy the Yugoslav Communists their ability to trade freely with both East and West and to secure direct assistance from the West, and particularly from the United States. If somewhat more flexible forms of economic and cultural relations are to be developed between the Soviet satellites and the non-Soviet world, the problem of defining and conforming to a wavering line of Soviet demands may cause many uncertainties, both in Moscow and in the satellite capitals. Moscow will certainly retain the essential controls, through its penetration of the satellite parties, armed forces and secret police, but the task of its apparatus of control and of the satellite Communists will be a more complex and ticklish one than it was in the "good old days" of Stalin's commands.

For Communist China, the effects of the de-Stalinization are likely to be less noticeable. For one thing, it is very hard to say how far Stalin went in trying to penetrate the control channels of the Chinese dictatorship. Since the Khrushchev-Bulganin visit to Peking of mid-October 1954, the outward and hierarchical position of Chinese Communism has been made more and more equal to that of Soviet Communism. Whether the "tremendous damage which Stalin caused to the . . . international working-class movement" has any reference to Sino-Soviet relations remains obscure.

Since the close of the congress in Moscow the Chinese Communist Politburo, without blaming Stalin directly, has spoken out strongly against ". . . some of our comrades mechanically applying Stalinist formulas in the Chinese revolution," from 1927 to 1936, and their "dogmatic errors."[4] Some further hint of dissension between Moscow and Peking perhaps may be read into or out of the speech made at the party congress by D. T. Shepilov, since appointed Foreign Minister:

> The progress of the socialist revolution in China has been even more unique. . . . From the point of view of pedant Marxists such an approach to the question of transforming exploitative ownership into socialist ownership almost amounts to flouting the principles of Marxism-Leninism. But in reality this is creative Marxism-Leninism in action, a masterly application of Marxist dialectic to the specific conditions of China, boldly and wisely carried out by the heroic Communist party of China. (*Stormy applause*).[5]

Does this laudatory reference to the path chosen by Chinese Communism reflect or veil a recent struggle between the two major centers of Communism over Mao's insistence on pursuing a "Chinese path to socialism?" More recently, rumors have seeped out from satellite capitals of a speech by Khrushchev, during his visit to Warsaw in March for Bierut's funeral. He is said to have attacked Stalin for subjecting Sino-Soviet relations to a dangerous strain by attempting to clamp his control on the Chinese party and economy.

[4] "Concerning the Historical Experience of Dictatorship of the Proletariat," editorial in *Jen Min Jih Pao*, summarized in *Pravda*, April 7, 1956; cited from *Current Digest of the Sovet Press*, May 16, 1956, p. 5.

[5] *Pravda*, February 17, 1956; cited from *Current Digest*, March 28, 1956, p. 19. Shepilov, formerly editor of *Pravda*, is a candidate-member of the party Presidium and a member of the party secretariat.

Among the Communist parties of the non-Soviet world the effects of the de-Stalinization campaign are likely to be slight. These parties are too weak and insecure to do more than switch abjectly to the new Soviet line. Perhaps they will lose some of their fringe followers, but the leadership cores have been jumping obediently through the hoop held up for them by the rejection of "Stalinist methods." However, over the next few years, the Moscow leadership must reckon that any minor losses of following or of prestige caused by the repudiation of the "father of the peoples" will be more than offset by the greater flexibility in tactics now gained through rejecting Stalin-worship and by broadening the Communists' opportunities to enlist the co-operation of other political and social forces behind slogans of "peace," Soviet-style, and anti-Americanism.

In his public speech of February 14, Khrushchev proclaimed three important "principles" of Soviet foreign policy, leaving it to foreign commentators to describe them as "new." These are: the principle of "peaceful coexistence" of two systems, the rejection of the "inevitability" of war, and the approval of various forms of transition to "socialism," the term by which Communists describe their own dictatorship.

Khrushchev rejected the allegation that the Soviet Union puts forward the principle of peaceful coexistence purely from tactical considerations and proclaimed it as "a basic principle of Soviet foreign policy." Repeating the standard Stalinist interpretation of the nature of war, he attributed the origin of all wars and all threats of war solely to the unfortunately prolonged survival of the capitalist system and again claimed that only the Soviet system, in the long run, supports and guarantees peace.[6]

> When we speak of the fact that in the competition of the two systems—capitalist and socialist—the social-

[6] *Pravda*, February 15, 1956.

> ist system will triumph, that does not mean by any means that victory will be achieved through armed intervention by the socialist countries in the internal affairs of the capitalist countries.

Both the meaning and the implicit limitations of Khrushchev's standard restatement of the principle of "peaceful coexistence" were clarified by Shepilov's elaboration:

> The fact that the prerequsites for the transition to socialism mature at different times in different countries, the fact that individual countries break away from the capitalist system at different times, means that the simultaneous existence of both capitalist and socialist states is *inevitable* on our planet.

Shepilov then went on to warn the Communist parties against the idea of a genuine or lasting reconciliation:

> The capitalist and socialist outlooks cannot be reconciled. . . . We are convinced that the final victory in the historical competition between the two systems belongs to socialism as the higher, more progressive, social system.[7]

The second "principle," as refurbished by Khrushchev, is that "war is not inevitable at the present time." In support of this assertion, Khrushchev cited the formation of a Soviet bloc of 900 million people, the formation of a very large uncommitted "peace bloc," and the growth of "pro-peace" and anti-imperialist forces within the imperialist world.

This "new" principle received further elaboration in a speech by Suslov, one of the Kremlin's most trusted theorists:

> The balance of forces in the world arena has now changed radically in favor of the supporters of peace and not the supporters of war. It stands to reason

[7] *Pravda*, February 17, 1956; cited from *Current Digest*, March 28, 1956, p. 19.

> that, in so far as imperialism remains, the economic basis for the outbreak of wars also remains, and danger of the unleashing of military adventures by the more reactionary monopolistic circles, particularly against the countries of socialism, does not disappear. . . . Now, under the new historical conditions, there are mighty forces possessing considerable resources for preventing the imperialists from unleashing a war and, if they try to start one anyway, for crushing the aggressors and for burying forever both war and the capitalist system. . . .[8]

This formulation, stated somewhat more fully than in Khrushchev's speech, repeats almost word for word one of the basic "principles" as set forth by Stalin in his "Economic Problems of Socialism," published in October 1952. Neither Khrushchev nor Suslov credits the "imperialists" with any positive contributions to the preservation of peace. At best, the capitalists' "subjective" protestations of their desire for peace are still regarded in Moscow as a sign of "reasonableness" inspired by fear of the powers of the Soviet bloc; at worst, as a camouflage for preparations to launch a war against it.

Khrushchev's third "principle," endlessly repeated and lauded by other speakers at the congress, dealt with "the forms of transition of various countries to socialism." Khrushchev cited with approval Lenin's assertion of mid-1917 that "All nations will come to socialism, that is inevitable, but not all will come in the same manner, each will introduce its own peculiarity into one or another form of democracy, into one or another variety of the dictatorship of the proletariat. . . ."

To buttress Lenin's prediction, Khrushchev cited the appearance of the "people's democracies" and of Communist China.

[8] Speech by Suslov, *Pravda*, February 17, 1956; cited from *Current Digest*, April 4, 1956, p. 23. M. A. Suslov is a full member of the party Presidium and a member of the party secretariat.

> The leadership by the Communist party of China, by the Communist and Workers parties of the other countries of people's democracy, of the great cause of socialist reconstruction, taking into account the peculiarity and particularities of each country—that is creative Marxism in action. . . . It is true that we recognize the necessity for the revolutionary reconstruction of capitalist society into socialist society. That distinguishes revolutionary Marxists from reformers, opportunists.

Khrushchev went on to deny that the only "path to socialism" is through civil war. He pointed out that civil war had not been necessary for the triumph of the "people's democracies" in eastern Europe after 1944. He failed to mention the decisive role of the Soviet armies, the secret police and the Communist party apparatus in imposing Soviet control on them. In some countries, Khrushchev said, there might even develop a "parliamentary path" to socialism. The working class may gain "a firm majority in parliament and transform it from an organ of bourgeois democracy into an organ of true popular will. (Applause)." He continued:

> Of course, in those countries where capitalism is still strong, where it has in its hands an enormous military-police apparatus, there the serious opposition of the reactionary forces is inevitable. There the transition to socialism will take place in conditons of sharp class, revolutionary struggle.
>
> Under all forms of transition to socialism the indispensable and decisive condition is the political leadership of the working class headed by its progressive part. Without this, the transition to socialism is impossible.[9]

Khrushchev's "new" principle is simply a briefer restatement of the position set forth by Stalin in October 1952, and in many previous declarations. At that time Stalin went into even more graphic detail,

[9] *Pravda*, February 15, 1956, p. 4.

pointing out that in some countries where capitalism and the *bourgeoisie* were weak the people, led by the vanguard of the "toiling masses," the Communist party, would be able to seize power through elections and without civil war. Whether the "transition to socialism" is to be peaceful or bloody is, for Stalin and Khrushchev alike, determined by the will and capacity of the "capitalists" to resist. The will and the duty of the Communist party to seize power and thereafter to exercise complete control are, for them, not in question. So much for Khrushchev's alleged "conciliatory" revision of Stalinist doctrine!

In order that Communists would not be misled into relaxing their "Bolshevik vigilance" against "compromisers" and "opportunists," Suslov spelled out further Khrushchev's statement of the Kremlin's view:

> The enemies of Communism portray the Communists as advocates of armed uprisings, violence and civil war at all times and under all conditions. This is an absurd slander of the Communists and the working class which they represent. The Communists and the working class, of course, prefer the most painless forms for the transition from the one social system to the other. . . . Whether the methods are more peaceful or more violent depends, not so much on the working class, as on the extent and forms of resistance of the exploiting classes which are being overthrown and which do not wish to part voluntarily with the vast property, political power, and privileges they possess.

And Suslov also stated clearly the traditional Soviet view that only the Communist party can be relied upon to "build socialism."

> . . . Insuring a transition to socialism requires the establishment of political leadership of the state by the working class, headed by its vanguard. . . . Political leadership of the state by the working class is necessary in order that over a shorter or longer period, depending upon the specific conditions, the capitalist class be deprived of ownership of the means

> of production and that the means of production be made public property, that all attempts by the overthrown exploiting classes to restore their rule be repulsed, and that socialist reconstruction be organized.[1]

In other words, the Kremlin's position remains unchanged. Just as Stalin wrote in 1952, the Communist parties are willing to achieve power by parliamentary means, but only in order to destroy the parliamentary system and to establish the dictatorship of the Communist party.

Despite this uncompromising insistence upon the future "hegemony" and monopoly of power by the Communists, the Twentieth Party Congress also emphasized the desirability of re-establishing co-operation with the moderate Socialist and labor parties. Immediately after reaffirming the aim of the Communist parties to achieve dictatorial power, Shepilov went on to appeal to the non-Communist Socialists.

> The attractive force of the idea of socialism has grown so much that—besides the proletarian Marxist revolutionaries—politicians, groups, and parties who do not interpret socialism in accord with principles of revolutionary Marxism, but who are ready to fight against imperialism and for the vital interests of the working class and all the working people, declare themselves supporters of socialism. This is why in many instances the existing differences and viewpoints can be relegated and are relegated to the background when it is a question of common interest in fighting against the capitalist yoke, for freedom and democracy. Communists are opponents in principle of sectarian narrowness. They advocate that all the efforts of all kinds and varieties of mass movements of the present day must be merged into an anti-imperialist stream.[2]

[1] Suslov, *Pravda*, February 17, 1956; cited from *Current Digest*, April 4, 1956, p. 23.

[2] Shepilov, *Pravda*, February 17, 1956; cited from *Current Digest*, March 28, 1956, p. 20.

In his speech Suslov spelled out somewhat further the new line of seeking rapprochements with the Social Democratic parties:

> Unquestionably, the split of the international workers' movement, when all the forces of the people should be united to fight the menace of a new war, is doubly intolerable. Life has raised a number of important questions on which we have points of agreement with the social Democrats. . . . In today's situation the workers' movement faces such cardinal tasks as defense of peace, national freedom and democracy. In many capitalist countries the working masses are obviously swinging strongly to the Left. The vast majority of the rank-and-file members of the socialist parties, Christian trade unions, and other organizations favor peace. It is to be presumed that the idea of unity will take stronger and stronger hold among the various groups of the working class and lead to practical results. But this will not happen of itself, it will depend largely on us Communists, on our efforts along this line.[3]

Since the Twentieth Party Congress the Soviet leadership has made intensive explorations of the attitudes of the leaders of the Social Democratic parties in western Europe. Outstanding leaders of the Norwegian and Swedish Socialist parties have visited Moscow. Khrushchev and Bulganin have met with the leaders of the British Labor party, and the visit of Guy Mollet to Moscow was prematurely advertised as a step toward a Socialist-Communist *rapprochement*. The bearlike courting of the sophisticated Western Socialists by the Kremlin has not so far increased the prospects for a revival of a "united front from above," similar to the alliance achieved in France of the mid-1930's.

If anything, the arrogance of the Soviet leaders, the obvious dangers concealed in their new attempts to

[3] Suslov, *Pravda*, February 17, 1956; cited from *Current Digest*, April 4, 1956, pp. 23–4.

embrace the Socialists in a death hug, has worked against the Kremlin's immediate aims. Whether the more discontented local organizations of the Socialist parties will be equally adamant in resisting pressures for a "united front from below" is less certain. Perhaps the Kremlin is counting on a falling off in the present prosperity of western Europe and on the growth of popular resistance to military expenditures to promote electoral and other forms of co-operation between Socialists and Communists "from below." Their present gestures, however futile for the moment, may pay political dividends in case of an economic crisis, which, they declare, has been postponed only by the armaments race.

In the underdeveloped countries prospects for developing co-operation between Communists and Socialists are far better than in Europe. The level of sophistication concerning the real aims of the Communist parties is far lower. In Burma, India, and Indonesia, popular understanding of the differences between Socialists and Communists is vague, and the Communists can hope, by vigorous propaganda for the united front, to absorb some of the more impatient following of the Socialist parties. Pursuit of a "united front" policy in the underdeveloped and newly parliamentary countries of Asia can be facilitated by the overtures now being made to the Socialist parties in western Europe, for the Kremlin's new tune may blunt the warnings which the Western Socialists have so often given to their neophyte colleagues in Asia. Whether President Tito's confidential descriptions of his treatment by the Kremlin, given to selected leaders during his visits to India and Burma, will have any lasting effect is doubtful.

A more novel feature of the new Soviet line is the strong insistence on cultivating close relations with the so-called "peace bloc," made up of "those countries which are not permitting themselves to be drawn into military blocs." Khrushchev, and other orators, constantly cited India, Burma, Indonesia, Afghanistan, Egypt, and Syria as the principal countries making up this third force in world politics. As during his visit to India and Burma in November and December 1955, Khrushchev spoke at the congress in support of the "five principles" advanced by Nehru and strove to emphasize the common aims of the Soviet-led bloc and the "uncommitted bloc." In effect, the Soviet leaders have been saying since mid-1955 that, in the absence of war, the future of the world may be determined by the third force which has been taking shape in Asia. Instead of the traditional Soviet slogan that "whoever is not with us is against us," the Kremlin spokesmen are now saying "whoever is not against us is with us."

When Khrushchev praises those countries which remain aloof from military alliances, he glosses over completely the greatest military bloc of all, the Sino-Soviet alliance, buttressed by the Warsaw alliance of May 1955. In many countries, apparently, the inconsistency of his boasting of the "indestructible" Soviet-led bloc and its great military power, while simultaneously praising those countries which remain uncommitted, is scarcely noted.

By laying stress upon the "peace bloc" comprising two thirds of humanity, the Soviet leadership can also hope to secure widespread support for particular goals: the seating of Communist China in the United Nations; the condemnation of the United States for the military support which it has accorded to the Nationalist Chinese regime on Formosa; the denunciation of the refusal of South Vietnam to accept Communist-rigged elections. The spread of a "neutralism" which prevents the consolidation of non-Soviet forces brings many benefits for Soviet policy. Neutralism, as the Soviet leaders have emphasized constantly, remains a commodity for export beyond the periphery of the Soviet bloc, not for toleration within it.

The Kremlin's claim to be "leading the forces of

peace" has been reinforced, in many parts of the world, by the broad appeal of its offers to accept a limitation on the numbers of conventional forces and by the unilateral reductions, claimed or promised, in the size of the Soviet forces. With that, Moscow has continued to press for the prohibition of nuclear weapons, thus attempting to deprive the opposing forces of their best means of resistance to any revival of direct Soviet threats. With the turning of Dairen over to the Chinese Communists and of Porkkala to Finland, the Soviet leadership can proclaim that it no longer has any bases beyond its own territory and has thus strengthened, as in Iceland, demands for the withdrawal of American and North Atlantic Treaty Organization forces from bases located in other countries.

During the past year the Soviet leadership has also added the instrument of long-term economic development programs to its armory of political warfare. The Soviet agreements with Afghanistan, India, and Burma, and the offers to Egypt, Syria, and Pakistan, have made a strong impression. They provide important and dramatic evidences of Soviet economic achievements and thus enhance the prestige of local Communist and pro-Communist forces. Offered ostensibly without political strings, the Soviet trade deals, initially at least, strengthen the independent bargaining power of the beneficiaries. An especially attractive feature is, of course, that the development assistance is given through long-term loans, at low interest, and with provision for repayment from the export surpluses of the recipient country.

All told, the offers which the Soviet bloc has made under these programs may now amount to about $900 million. Except in Afghanistan, the prospect that the Soviet Union would, in the next few years, be able by economic pressure to take over political control of any of its beneficiaries seems remote. If the Soviet leadership fails to gain direct political domination through this program, will it continue it? Probably, but on a modest scale. With a steel production of about 50 million tons in 1956, scheduled to grow to 75 million tons in 1960, and with one of the two largest machine-tool industries in the world, the Soviet Union will be, increasingly, in a position to divert a small percentage of its capital goods output to support its political objectives in non-Soviet parts of the world. Its ability to fix terms and interest rates by government fiat and its capacity to absorb almost any form of imports give it certain advantages. In general, Moscow's assistance programs, based on "aid through trade," are likely to be used primarily to strengthen its political influence in the uncommitted third of the world and particularly to weaken the influence of the West.

By 1949 the Soviet leadership had seen free Europe consolidated, slowly and painfully, but nonetheless consolidated against the Soviet military menace. If the Soviet Union had achieved its goal in Korea, in 1950, by swift conquest, it would probably have switched rather quickly, even under Stalin, to a campaign for stabilization and relaxation, in order to slow down the arming of the West. The United Nations opposition to the Communist seizure of South Korea plunged the Kremlin into a severe case of war jitters and led it to adopt drastic, hasty and wasteful revisions of economic and armaments programs, in both the Soviet Union and the satellites.

The Soviet leadership was at first fearful that the resistance of the free world in Korea was but a first step toward organizing a concentric attack against the new and not yet consolidated Soviet empire. After the MacArthur hearings, held in the spring of 1951, had given clear proof of the American desire to confine the war to Korea, the Kremlin began gradually to relax its tense nerves and its strained efforts. In the economic field the shift was visible by the summer of 1952. The Nineteenth Party Congress, in October 1952, laid stress on competitive coexistence, on the development of a long-range effort to undermine the stability and security of the free world by measures short of war. This program was doubtless implemented somewhat hesitantly because of Stalin's physical and mental decline.

Almost as soon as Stalin died, the new leadership began exploring at a gradually quickened tempo various minor steps for relaxing international tensions. A major review of Soviet foreign policy and its methods appears to have taken place in January and February 1955, following the displacement of Malenkov from the leading role. This resulted in the partial eclipse of Molotov by the new Khrushchev-Bulganin leadership in the conduct of Soviet diplomacy, even prior to his replacement by Shepilov. There followed, during the rest of 1955, a series of dramatic steps designed to melt or break up the ice pack which Stalin's policies had formed around Soviet policy: the treaty with Austria, the evacuation of Porkkala, the Soviet leaders' pilgrimage to Belgrade, the Geneva conferences, the establishment of relations with the German Federal Republic, the military supplies for Egypt, new disarmament proposals, negotiations with Japan for a peace treaty, the Khrushchev-Bulganin visit to India, Burma, and Afghanistan.

As so often in the conduct of Soviet policy, the public stocktaking provided by the Twentieth Party Congress has confirmed and systematized trends which were already strongly evident in the preceding months. Khrushchev's restatements of Soviet goals, enlivened by new and flexible tactics, and flavored by the denunciation of Stalin's methods of rule, are, at bottom, an expression of continuity of basic goals in Soviet policy. As under Stalin, the Kremlin seeks to slow down and reverse the consolidation of the free world, to promote neutralism beyond its own orbit, to get rid of all strategic limitations on East-West trade, to confine American power to North America, and to await new targets of opportunity. Above all, it sees in Asia a promising field for Communist expansion.

Since Soviet strategic planning is now shifting its primary attention from continental wars to intercontinental nuclear warfare, the Kremlin may well prefer to develop a lengthy period of lower-key diplomacy, while waiting to see which side will first have available a decisive stockpile of the intercontinental missile. During the period of the race for the long-range missile the Soviet leadership may seek to avoid menacing talk and alarming acts and may endeavor, by using a flexible armory of political, economic and psychological weapons, to improve its position vis-à-vis the principal obstacle to its ambitions, the United States. If the Soviet Union is the first to achieve the missile in decisive quantities, it may then feel free to revert to the Stalin method of threats and force. So far as the results of the Twentieth Congress go, it is clearly the manners rather than the goals of the Kremlin that have changed since Stalin's death and posthumous dethronement.

:21:

RUSSIA REVISITED: MOSCOW DIALOGUES, 1956[1]

[*August 1956*]

MANY of the American tourists who are pouring into the Soviet Union this year are surprised by the evidences on every hand of economic vigor and large-scale construction. "From our papers," said one, "I thought everything would be in a mess. Things look pretty good here; they have built a lot." Another tourist: "People are very free here. I took as many pictures as I wanted in the Kremlin and no one stopped me."

The new rulers are obviously gaining credit with the people at large through making one minor adjustment or accommodation after another. Many Soviet people commented favorably to me on the shortening of the sixth day of work, on Saturdays and on the eve of holidays, from eight to six hours. "This will be a great help in my weekly shopping." Many individuals mentioned this change with pleasure and then asked whether people in the United States work six or eight hours on Saturday. They were amazed to learn of the normal five-day work week in America and in many other Western countries.

[1] *Foreign Affairs*, Vol. xxxv, No. 1 (October 1956), pp. 72–83.

Much satisfaction was expressed over the recent restoration of free tuition for students in high schools and universities, a reversion to the pre-1940 arrangement. Since education is the major channel for social advancement, this is an especially welcome improvement. Again, no one I spoke with had any realization that in the United States tuition in high schools has long been free and also includes free books and school supplies. On the other hand, the multifarious system of free, partly free, and paid tuition and scholarships in our colleges and universities was much too complicated for most listeners to grasp.

There was much favorable comment on the improved pension system, which was adopted by the Supreme Soviet in July. Many people remarked that the raising of the minimum pension would now make it possible for older people actually to give up work without becoming a direct burden on their grown-up children. Through these and other measures the new rulers appear to be paying closer attention to raising the living conditions of their people and have won much credit and a great extension of patience. The assertions of the regime that only the rapid growth of the economy has made it possible to provide these alleviations seem to be accepted in good faith. If there were people who questioned whether these beneficent actions could not have been taken earlier, their comments did not come to the ears of a foreign visitor. As one casual acquaintance said: "We had an evil-hearted ruler; now our rulers are closer to the needs of the people."

Another general impression was one of relief following the slackening of obvious and active forms of terror. On every hand people seem to feel that the political police are now less active, but that they are continuing to observe and to note down actions and attitudes which might be "interesting." In general, people over thirty-five, having lived through previous periods of "relaxation" and then of revived terrorism, do not believe today in the permanent abandonment of these methods of rule. Perhaps those under thirty, who have grown up since the tightening of the screws after the end of the war, will be more inclined to believe that the "bad old days" are gone, never to return.

Perhaps just because of the great impact of the Stalin apparatus of unpredictable terror, the new rulers can now relax the pressure somewhat and still receive the same or even better obedience to their commands. The effects of Stalinization, which has left a firm imprint of caution and conformity, make it possible for Stalin's successors to carry through a small percentage of de-Stalinization.

When offered opportunities to comment on Stalin and his posthumous demotion, ordinary citizens were not inclined to blame Stalin for more than "excesses" and "mistakes." Perhaps their caution was due to the realization that it is not possible to go far in criticizing Stalin without seeming to question some of the basic policies of the regime, such as forced industrialization, drastic collectivization, intellectual conformity to a line determined from above, and other continuing features of the regime. It may also be due to the feeling that the criticism so far leveled at Stalin deals only with his ruthless handling of the upper ranks of the Communist party, and the ordinary Soviet citizen is reluctant to mention, much less discuss, people in these lofty positions of power.

In any case, while attacking Stalin's methods more and more openly, the new rulers are, in other respects, applying procedures and pursuing aims which were characteristic of Stalin's program. For example, this summer the Kremlin decided that the raising of private livestock, often by the use of purchased bread, was distorting the economy and creating too large a private sector. New decrees, issued in July, promptly put a stop to this revival of the bad old capitalistic Adam of private profit. However, it is typical of the new methods of rule that, instead of simply confiscating the excess of private livestock, particularly marked in suburban areas, the government offered to buy it back from its owners at rates pretty close to the market price. The reduction in the size of the private plots of the collective farm members is also proceeding apace. This is in line with Stalin's dictum of October 1952 that the private sector in agricultural production must eventually be eliminated completely. The vigorous campaign for the establishment of boarding schools on a widespread, ultimately universal basis marks a revival of the doctrinaire Communist belief that the education of children must be taken away from the parents and concentrated in the hands of the government and party.

Because of the wide range of abuses and discomforts which have been suffered by the Soviet population, the opportunities for the new rulers to provide one alleviation after another are extensive. Each new removal of pressure or discomfort is greeted with genuine gratitude. It would be a mistake to underestimate the ability of the regime to provide more and more of its members with a genuine stake in its expanding economy without slackening the build-up of heavy industry and military power.

A minor part of the de-Stalinization program has been to reopen intellectual and scientific contacts with non-Soviet countries. During the past year several hundreds of Soviet delegations have attended congresses abroad, or have paid visits to associations and other bodies with professional interests similar to their own. Very few Soviet tourists travel abroad alone, but during the past summer at least two cruises of Soviet tourists have followed the route from the Black Sea to the Baltic or the reverse, with brief trips to major cities in western Europe.

The Soviet government has admitted large numbers of foreign travelers, in a drastic reversal of Stalin's policy of careful political screening of all visitors. In addition to delegations from European satellites, North

Korea, and Communist China, visits were paid this summer by delegations of social security workers from Sweden, three hundred Finnish partisans of peace, former Italian partisans, English experts in metallurgy, Italian political leaders, a parliamentary delegation from Pakistan, and two boatloads of French tourists. It was reported that some 2,500 visas had been issued to American tourists. During one period of four weeks, the Soviet Union received extended visits from the Shah of Iran, Prince Norodom Sihanouk of Cambodia, as well as a brief visit from Dag Hammarskjold, the Secretary-General of the United Nations. All this, of course, in addition to the visits by the leaders of the Communist parties of France, Italy, Belgium, and Great Britain, following the publication of the Soviet party decree of June 30 on de-Stalinization. In general, the Soviet authorities prefer to receive organized delegations, which enjoy well-planned hospitality and follow tightly packed programs. However, individual tourists are also admitted readily and find it relatively easy to secure interviews with people in the fields of science and letters.

Contacts of Soviet citizens with foreign visitors are not unrestricted or unsupervised. A foreign visitor is informed politely but firmly that he is not permitted to consult a Moscow telephone directory, although any numbers required are furnished to him at his request. When a visitor approaches the building of the United States Embassy, for example, to collect mail, he is greeted by the piercing stares of one, two, or three security officers; when they are addressed in English, their gaze softens and turns away. Certain other unwritten limitations are discovered only by accident. On returning to their hotel on foot from the theater one evening, two recent tourists lost their way and, seeing a lighted and open doorway, entered a dormitory to ask for directions. Their appearance aroused great interest and, through the use of French, they had a lively exchange of information and opinions for about two hours. On leaving, they were urged to return the next evening. On the second occasion, having arranged to take along an *Intourist* interpreter, they found the entrance to the building guarded by several firm characters in leather jackets; some of the same people with whom they had chatted innocently and vivaciously the evening before passed in or out of the door without a sign of recognition. In some cities away from the capital, the supervision of foreigners is more obvious and more easily detected than in Moscow.

When Westerners think about the Soviet Union, they often forget that the regime has been in power for nearly forty years and that a very detailed system of supervision and direction of thought has been enforced for more than twenty-five years, despite periodic shifts in the details of the party line. Over this period of time the present generation of "leading intellectuals" has had ample opportunity and incentive to become adjusted to the concept that "truth," though it may vary in content from time to time or may even be reversed, is a definite doctrine to be ascertained and applied but not to be questioned except at grave risk. Since all intellectual activities are organized from above and regulated by the party doctrines, there is obviously a large number of "officials for science" who can now be "licensed" to meet with foreign visitors and can be fully relied upon to exchange permitted information and to state with conviction and apparent spontaneity the official and party view. Persons who do not feel secure and at ease within the system or in their loyalty to its dogmas are likely to avoid contacts with foreigners. Experience has shown them that no good can come to them from such meetings, whether casual or planned. In addition, most contacts with non-Communist foreign visitors are carried on in groups, an arrangement which provides the protection of witnesses.

In Moscow, certain standard questions about Soviet-American relations, based on the flow of information which Soviet thought-control transmits to its own people, were brought up with great regularity and with apparent sincerity. "Why does the American press tell lies about the Soviet Union?" To this, the obvious answer was that under our cherished freedom of the press a wide variety of facts and opinions are presented. Certainly, serious newspapers and periodicals make strenuous efforts to provide well-rounded information, but many parts of the press are likely to publish only news stories which have a vivid, sometimes a sensational, news interest. In any case, the difficulties which the Soviet government places in the way of securing accurate information concerning the Soviet Union are a major handicap. For example, I pointed to the failure, from 1939 until April 1956, to publish such a simple fact as the total size of the Soviet population. "Why doesn't the American government punish those who spread false information?" My interlocutors seemed baffled by the notion that the government should reflect the basic desires of its people, based on freedom of information and discussion, rather than imposing selected information and its own views on the people.

"Why does the American government subject Soviet visa applicants to fingerprinting, which is the mark of a criminal?" Some Soviet interlocutors assumed that fingerprinting was required only of Soviet applicants, and were surprised to learn that it is required of all foreign visitors except those bearing diplomatic or official passports. They found it hard to understand that, being a government of laws and not of individuals, the United States government could not make exceptions without appropriate Congressional action. It was easy to point out that Americans coming to the Soviet Union accept Soviet requirements as a matter of course, including internal passports and numerous permits equipped with photographs, as well as registration with the police at each change of address. Soviet listeners found it incredible that none of these requirements exist in the United States; once they had absorbed this concept, some were ready to understand that fingerprinting, in American practice, is a partial substitute for the much larger number of Soviet identification papers.

The question of "Why does the United States not have a social security system?" was answered readily by taking my social security card from my wallet and passing it around. Soviet people were amazed to learn that despite the greater size of the Soviet population a larger number of persons are covered by the United States social security system, and a far larger proportion are currently receiving benefits under it.

Soviet journalists, in particular, were informed in detail, and were indignant, about the demonstrations by former displaced persons against the seven Soviet journalists who toured the United States a year ago. To the comment that "no such demonstrators or pickets would be allowed to annoy a visitor to the Soviet Union," I could only reply that this was a great pity, for I would welcome demonstrations for and against myself. They found it hard to understand that private citizens can freely picket the President of the United States or anyone else so long as they refrain from physical violence. My quoting of the American saying "Words do not kill" left them shaken but unconvinced.

To the complaint that "the Soviet Union is cutting down its troops by 1,840,000 men, and why doesn't America cut back too?" I gave the easy rejoinder that we had cut back our forces very completely at the end of World War II and had rearmed only as a result of Soviet aggressions and threats. Furthermore, we do not know how many troops the Soviet government is maintaining today, nor how many it will have after it has carried through the cutback. Soviet interlocutors admitted freely that they also had no idea how large the Soviet forces were. It was my turn to be somewhat embarrassed when pressed to explain why the United States, having proposed a ratio of fixed ceilings for conventional forces, was now attaching new conditions to its own proposal after it had been accepted by the Soviet government in July. It was easier to explain why the Soviet proposals for setting aside limited and fixed areas for inspection of troop and material movements would not remove the uncertainty over actual Soviet strength and therefore would not eliminate the distrust of the West concerning Soviet armaments.

My Soviet interlocutors were well informed about statements by individual Americans concerning the possible use of the hydrogen bomb in case of war. It was not easy to get across to them that not only individual citizens and journalists but even congressmen and high military officials are accustomed, according to American tradition, to state their individual views, even when they are at variance with the policy of the government. They could only shake their heads over this in incredulity.

Soviet people frequently asked: "Why don't you Americans trust the Soviet Union?" To this my reply was that for ten years—in Greece, Iran, Czechoslovakia, Berlin, and Korea—Soviet policy had been beating us over the head with a crowbar and our head was naturally still aching. I suggested that if they showed a genuine willingness over the next ten years to resolve many unsettled questions, including the acceptance of free elections in divided countries, they would gradually restore the level of confidence which they had enjoyed in America in 1945.

From these and many other conversations one thing which stood out was a sense of "unrequited love" toward America: the tendency to measure each of their own achievements against American achievements and a sometimes pathetic desire to receive some favorable recognition from Americans. "Isn't there anything we do that you admire?" If Americans wish to promote greater receptivity to fuller cultural exchanges with the Soviet Union, they must be prepared to speak favorably of Soviet achievements, wherever they exist, in order to overcome this deep-seated feeling among

Soviet intellectuals that Americans look down upon them and talk down to them.

Another factor which the American cultural approach must take into account is that the Soviet picture of the United States has been carefully shaped over many, many years by the information which is pumped through Soviet channels. True, a very few "intellectual workers" have access to a wider range of information. In general, however, the Soviet citizens' picture of America is that given by Soviet printed sources. In order to broaden and correct this picture, one must start from it. If the information given is too sharply in contrast with what is known and accepted by the Soviet citizenry, it meets with incredulity, alarm, and rejection. The higher people rise in the Soviet system, the more information they generally have available—though selected and organized according to the Soviet pattern—and the more confidence they have in it. If the picture painted for them is too directly in contrast to what they have been taught, this makes them uncomfortable and fearful of losing their grip on the pattern which has been set for them, and thus of coming into political conflict, even though unspoken, with the Soviet line.

The strength of American culture is that it is, aside from a basic acceptance and enthusiasm for freedom, "unpolitical," whereas Soviet information and science are based on a rigid political line. American information and cultural policy should turn this unpolitical factor to advantage by appealing to the professional, cultural, and scientific interests of specific Soviet audiences. Physicians, musicians, writers, architects, farm experts, and others can be reached through their intellectual interests, provided political differences are not thrust into the foreground.

In the early 1930's a large majority of Soviet intellectuals were well aware of the inner meaning of a free and democratic system, either through their knowledge of the West or through their memories of the earlier struggles for freedom within Russia. Opposing them stood a fanatical minority of Communist party liners on whom the regime relied in its ruthless campaign to shape all intellectual life to a pattern of conformity. By now this struggle of twenty-five years ago has ended. Several generations of intellectuals have been recruited, indoctrinated, and promoted to positions of responsibility under the pressures and ruthless vigilance of the party controls. Today intellectual life is staffed from top to bottom by Communist-trained intellectuals, but since the struggle for domination is over, the latter have much less reason to be fanatical than had their "red professor" prototypes of twenty-five years ago. They have gone through so many changes of line within the basic dogma that they now seem to be "bureaucrats of culture," eager to satisfy the regime, proud of Soviet strength and Soviet achievements, alert to detect forthcoming changes in party policy, and, in Western eyes, distressingly at ease within the rigid system of Soviet ideology.

Today it is second nature for Soviet-trained intellectuals to accept the assumption that all questions should be and are decided by the dicta of political authority, sometimes handed down in a flash of lightning from on high, rather than being settled or left unsettled through a continuing clash of free opinions. In one group in which I raised the question of how Soviet scholars set about analyzing the desirable balance between the production of consumer goods and capital goods within the Soviet economy, the reply, presented with great earnestness, was: "Some months ago a few isolated individuals set forth an incorrect position to the effect that, with the maturing of the economy, a larger share of production would be devoted to consumer goods, but their mistakes have been corrected." With that dictum, the "discussion" came to an end.

In general, a visit to Moscow leaves the impression that people over thirty-five are not going to forget the rigidity and ruthlessness with which the party line, in its changing aspects, has been enforced upon several generations of intellectuals. They accept gratefully the present relaxation of the direct pressure of doctrine upon their minds, but they do not assume that the present relaxation will necessarily be either extensive or permanent. The steel helmet has been pulled back a quarter inch, to their great relief; but it is still there.

While at the Twentieth Party Congress of last February the Soviet leadership criticized its scholars for their "mania for quotations" from Marx and Lenin, there has been no change in the basic assumption that there is a single "truth," and that that truth is defined ultimately by the party leadership. There is taking place a slight broadening of access to evidence and facts. Scholars are being urged to exercise some independence in their analysis, but they will remain timid about using it, for sharp reprimands are still being issued from on high whenever the findings of research conflict with party policy or prejudice. Sometimes one has the impression that the party leadership is exhorting its scientists to display more initiative, whereas the scholars remain reluctant to abandon their comfortable reliance on established and familiar doctrines. Whether younger scholars, who have reached intellectual activity during the most recent period of stringent control since 1946, will come to believe in a permanent relaxation and will endeavor to stretch somewhat the realm of permitted analysis and speculation is too subtle and difficult a question to be answered after a brief visit.

Unrest among writers and critics, which has been manifested sporadically since Stalin's death, suggests that literature and the theater may prove the first fields of creative activity to feel the benefits of a partial broadening of the limits of what is permitted. The recent and posthumous rehabilitation of the famous theatrical innovator, Meyerhold, may be merely a belated gesture of contrition, or it may foreshadow a renewal of the search for new forms of creativity in the dramatic arts. Last spring architects and engineers were severely criticized for the "wedding cake" style of architecture which has monopolized the Soviet scene since 1937. How far architecture will now enjoy a wider freedom of experimentation remains uncertain. Will the "line" in architecture merely shift its course, or will it be broadened to accommodate several varying schools of thought? There may be some significance in the remark that "if the buildings of the new Moscow University were being planned today, they would be executed in a different style."

What does the incipient "intellectual thaw" denote for Soviet Russia's relations with the West? To weigh its significance with care, we must keep certain basic facts in perspective. First, it is being carried out by a regime which is supremely confident, even arrogant. The Soviet leaders and Soviet intellectuals of today emphasize with great pride the fact that the Soviet system is the dominant force for one third of the world's population, that it has built up the second largest economy in the world and that it is one of the two greatest military powers. Second, despite the criticisms of Stalin's "excesses," this amazing development is attributed to the Soviet leadership and its "correct" doctrine. Third, by now several generations of intellectuals have been trained to implement the canons of Soviet dogma. Today there is almost no trace left of the former Russian deference for the science and culture of the West; it has given way to self-confidence, boasting, and arrogance. Soviet intellectuals now desire to acquire useful facts from the West, not to borrow basic values, and they are pleased that the leadership has opened the door a crack. They want to improve their professional equipment, but to do so within the over-all structure of dogma. Within this new attitude of intense pride and intellectual self-sufficiency, the Soviet leadership can now permit a wider range of contacts with the West with relatively slight risk that Western cultural values will be understood, much less accepted, by the thin layer of intellectuals "licensed" to carry on cultural relations.

A somewhat widened intercourse with the West is also welcomed, with caution, by many Soviet intellectuals. Among them there is a real curiosity about the West, which is partly due to their having been denied direct access to it for many years. There is also a desire to receive from the West recognition of their achievements. Even more important is their belief that the current partial relaxation of tension, which they see reflected in the exchanges of cultural visits, means, to them, stronger prospects for a continuing improvement in the conditions of intellectual work and in material conditions within the Soviet system.

For Soviet people, the status of intellectual relations with the West is also a barometer of general prospects of peace. As many commented: "A year ago we could not have sat down at the same table; it is good that we can talk now." Until recently the order was: "Turn your back on the West." The instruction has now gone out: "Face the West." If the order should go out tomorrow again to ignore and attack the West, the order will be obeyed, even though at the cost of some silent resentment and loss of *élan*, and especially of a revived fear of war. The relaxation has been decreed by the Soviet leadership as a means to reinforce its claim to be seeking a relaxation of tensions in all fields. It gratifies a deep-seated aspiration of many Soviet intellectuals, but it is not due to "pressure" or "demand" on their part.

Is the present relaxation of intellectual barriers going to be an interlude, or is it the beginning of a continuing process, a movement toward ever wider freedom? Some analysts feel that the movement of "liberalization" is reaching or will reach a "point of no return." Others regard it as an effort to remove certain abuses and to improve the workings of the system, a strictly controlled development and one that can be reversed whenever the leadership decides to do so. In any case, the relaxation has been greeted with considerable caution by the Soviet intellectuals, ever mindful of the possibility of new reversals of line from above.

Whether or not the relaxation turns out to be long continued, the West should respond with sincerity. It should be prepared to meet with and co-operate with Soviet intellectuals on their own grounds of professional, scholarly, and technical competence, without putting political questions directly in the foreground. Closer acquaintance with the cultural and scientific achievements of the West may help to demonstrate pragmatically the advantages of gradually broadened areas of intellectual freedom. We cannot require Soviet-trained people of today to subscribe to the abstract principle of intellectual freedom as a precondition for developing intellectual contacts and exchanges. The West does have an opportunity, a better one than at any time in the past two decades, to demonstrate empirically the soundness and vitality of its tradition of freedom of the mind, freedom of inquiry. It should grasp the opportunity.

The Soviet leadership is confidently challenging the West to compete with it for the future allegiance of the awakening peoples of Asia and Africa. One important aspect of the challenge is in the intellectual field. If free Western thought is to maintain and develop its great advantages in this competition, it must also be prepared to enter into closer if probably not intimate relations with Soviet scientists and scholars. An ounce of example will count more than a balloonful of exhortation.

Any sign of Western shrinking from the new Soviet challenge resounds throughout the Soviet-controlled world and also has unfavorable consequences among the intellectual leaders in Asia and Africa. The slight and somewhat tentative swing of Soviet policy toward the limited development of intellectual and scientific relations with the West is a challenge and an opportunity which cannot be brushed aside. It must be faced by the West, with confidcncc in the vitality of free science and free culture.

:22:

THE MOSCOW-PEKING AXIS IN WORLD POLITICS[1]

[*November 1956*]

WORKING in close co-operation since October 1949, the Moscow and Peking centers of Communism have been firmly linked together by a shared system of political values and aims and by a shared interpretation of the movement of history which, they believe and proclaim, will bring about the triumph of Communism throughout the world. They have taken great risks together, navigated difficult twists and turns of policy in outward harmony, and chalked up a number of important gains, though less than they aimed for. Moscow has not received from Peking, and probably has not demanded, the automatic response to its commands which it has until recently been able to exact from the satellite leaderships in eastern Europe.

Since 1949, Moscow and Peking have presumably had to negotiate out a large number of concrete decisions, and between them there may well have been divergences in detail over the advantages and disadvan-

[1] *Moscow-Peking Axis: Strengths and Strains*, by Howard L. Boorman, Alexander Eckstein, Philip E. Mosely, and Benjamin Schwartz (New York: Harper, for the Council on Foreign Relations; 1957), pp. 198–227. Copyright 1957 by the Council on Foreign Relations, Inc.

tages of specific steps. They have also had to work closely together in the field of economic co-operation. In doing so, the traditional Communist primacy of politics over economics has led them to accept some important disadvantages and even some substantial sacrifices. The cement which holds together their alliance and makes it one of the two most powerful blocs in the world is primarily a shared system of political ideas and aims, and behind these aims, whether immediate or of longer range, is the basic purpose of expanding Communist power politically, militarily, industrially, and territorially.

Perhaps the ideological community between the two leaderships has not been complete at all times. The paths which non-Soviet Communist leaderships have to tread are not always simple or safe. Hints of past divergences over dogma have been expressed somewhat more plainly since the dethroning of the Stalin image in Khrushchev's partially published speech, on February 25, 1956, to the Twentieth Congress of the Soviet party. After the close of the congress, the Chinese leadership, without attacking Stalin head-on, spoke out strongly against ". . . some of our comrades mechanically applying Stalinist formulas in the Chinese Revolution" from 1927 to 1936, and their "dogmatic error." [2] Some further hint of continuing controversies in Moscow inner sanctums over the path followed by the Chinese Communist party, of disputes over its Leninist purity, may perhaps be detected in the speech at the Twentieth Congress by Dimitri T. Shepilov, who, at the end of May 1956, was appointed Foreign Minister:

> The progress of the socialist revolution in China has been even more unique. . . . From the point of view of pedant Marxists such an approach to the question of transforming exploitative ownership into socialist

[2] "Concerning the Historical Experience of Dictatorship of the Proletariat," editorial in *Jen Min Jih Pao* (People's Daily) (Peking), summarized in *Pravda*, April 7, 1956; cited from *Current Digest of the Soviet Press* (New York), May 16, 1956, p. 5.

ownership almost amounts to slighting the principles of Marxism-Leninism. But in reality this is creative Marxism-Leninism in action, a masterly application of Marxist dialectic to the specific conditions of China, boldly and wisely carried out by the heroic Communist party of China. (*Stormy applause.*) [3]

In mid-1956 rumors began seeping out from satellite capitals of a speech which Khrushchev had made to party circles in Warsaw in March 1956.[4] He was quoted as having attacked Stalin for subjecting the Kremlin's relations with Peking to a dangerous strain, particularly through his insistence upon establishing Soviet-controlled joint-stock companies. These devices, which seemed to many in Peking to constitute an unexpected revival of imperialism, were abolished only some months after Stalin's death.

The increasing emphasis, at least on paper, by Khrushchev and Bulganin on Moscow's new toleration of "different paths to Socialism" seemed designed to reduce or eliminate the likelihood that ideological divergences would place an intolerable strain upon the alliance. Perhaps Peking is satisfied with Moscow's formal recognition of its ideological autonomy and, therefore, as in the dramatic events of October and November 1956, it is content to affirm its support of Moscow's grudging acceptance of the Nagy path for Hungary. At the end of December, at an extraordinary session, the Chinese Politburo reaffirmed its unequivocal support of Soviet policies toward the East European satellites and denounced Tito for following a course which "can only lead to a split in the Communist movement." [5]

Certainly, by acknowledging Peking's autonomy in matters of Communist ideology, the present Kremlin leadership runs less risk of alienating Mao and his

[3] *Pravda*, February 17, 1956; cited from *Current Digest*, March 28, 1956, p. 19.

[4] *The New York Times*, June 4, 1956.

[5] Peking broadcast, December 28, 1956; summarized in *The New York Times*, December 29, 1956.

followers than they would by insisting on Moscow's sole right to determine what constitutes true Communist dogma and to define the "correct path" to Socialism. And conceivably Peking's underwriting of Soviet policies toward the satellites in eastern Europe, reaffirmed in the declaration of January 18, 1957, may have its counterpart in Moscow's leaving to the Chinese party the direct responsibility for "guiding" several of the Communist parties and regimes in Asia.

Perhaps the growing emphasis since 1953 upon the enhanced stature of Peking as an autonomous center of Communism reflects, in the ideological sphere, the reality of a self-contained and self-propelled system of power, a center which has been built up from within by the Chinese Communists and which is fully capable of dealing on a basis of independent decision, if not true equality of power, with the Moscow center. Granted that Moscow will retain for several decades a great superiority of industrial and military power, and that this inequality of strength will continue to influence profoundly the manner and the speed with which Peking pursues its purposes, the fact also remains that the Soviet leadership must henceforth pursue its vast goals in Asia with and through the new Chinese regime, not without it or against it.

Shared political and strategic objectives provide the strongest incentive for both partners, senior and junior alike, to bridge over even major conflicts of ideological outlook or economic interest. Those who believe that Moscow and Peking can be separated from each other must, it would seem, prove either that their goals are incompatible or that each of the two centers may judge itself better able, in separation or even in conflict with the other, to achieve its own goals. The evidence of their visible actions indicates, thus far, that each partner sets a high value on their close co-operation and will make great efforts to assure its continuation.

Judging by the policies which the Chinese Communist regime has followed ever since 1950, it has a definite range of immediate and longer term objectives. Peking is intensely interested in overthrowing the Nationalist Chinese regime on Formosa and thus in rounding out its victory in what both it and the Nationalists regard as a civil war between opposing Chinese forces. The Nationalist occupation of the offshore islands, in the view of the Communist Chinese regime, impinges even more directly upon its security.

The fact that the United States regards its strategic frontiers as including Formosa and the Pescadores, and as involving the protection of the offshore islands against attack, raises this issue to a level of power politics which makes it impossible for mainland China at present to resolve it by its own military strength. Obviously, without the active military backing of the Soviet Union, Peking cannot undertake to force a military decision against the main strength of the United States. Peking now counts on undermining the Nationalist regime by attrition. Even the desultory United States-Communist Chinese negotiations at Geneva, during 1955 and 1956, were utilized in Peking's propaganda to imply that the Americans were negotiating a "deal" to scuttle the Nationalists.[6]

The Chinese Communists have not abandoned their desire to see the two halves of Korea united under Communist control, and presumably under Chinese hegemony. Similarly, they have pressed constantly for reuniting the two parts of Vietnam, of course, only under conditions which would, they believe, assure Communist control. Beyond that, Communist China looks to strengthening its influence—and, presumably, establishing ultimately its dominance—over the countries of Southeast Asia, and over Burma and Indonesia. For the near future, it prefers to see India and Indonesia pursue their "neutralist" role. It is encouraged

[6] Chou En-lai: "The Foreign Policy of the Chinese People's Republic and the Question of the Liberation of Taiwan," *Pravda*, July 18, 1956.

that those countries' leaders constantly criticize non-Communist alliances but seldom, if ever, mention the most massive and ominous bloc of all, the Sino-Soviet bloc.

Communist China is interested in fostering the spread of "neutralism" and "de-commitment" to Pakistan and Thailand, to Japan and the Philippines, and it favors the "liberation" of Malaya. Both Soviet and Chinese Communist propaganda make it clear that neutralism and noncommitment are policies recommended as the way of salvation for countries outside the periphery of Communist control, but not to be encouraged or tolerated within the Communist bloc. If new evidence of this double standard were needed, it was provided by Moscow's ruthless suppression of the Imre Nagy government's attempt to proclaim the neutrality of Hungary. All these aims of Peking, if they can be achieved without involving the Soviet bloc in a major war, are enthusiastically endorsed and promoted by the Soviet leadership. Divergences, which are apparently resolved by frequent and secret consultations between the two leaderships, relate not to aims, but to questions of means, timing, and judgment of the risks involved.

Let us assume, on the other hand, that Communist China were to seek to co-operate or even to coexist in permanent harmony with the nations which have joined together to resist the expansion of the two major Communist powers. In this case, Mao's government would have to abandon all present goals of its foreign policy. It would have to accept the indefinite existence of the "two Chinas" and abandon any threat to take Formosa by force. It would have to agree to the reunification of Korea and Vietnam through free elections. It would have to tolerate the American alliances with Formosa, Japan, Korea, the Philippines, Australia, and New Zealand, and the continued existence of SEATO (South East Asia Treaty Organization), at least until such time as its own mild demeanor had persuaded China's neighbors that the danger of a future renewal of Communist expansion was gone forever.

In brief, Communist China would have to concentrate its efforts entirely on its domestic reconstruction and pursue an exclusively peaceful competition for the future leadership of Asia. Presumably, it would also have to accept whatever economic terms could reasonably be secured from the major free world powers. While trade barriers would be relaxed promptly, Peking could not expect any large economic sacrifices by the West or Japan to help it along in its program of industrialization. By contrast, the Soviet leadership wishes to see China achieve its far-ranging ambitions, both at home and abroad, though it may well differ in estimating the costs and risks involved in any specific action. Divergences over means may grow into friction and strain, but in practice they are likely, for the sake of larger and shared goals, to result in compromises rather than in a rupture.

Perhaps the basic strain in Sino-Soviet relations arises from the question of the range of power to be applied in any given situation. While Peking and Moscow subordinate their disputes over means to the achievement of shared goals, China is not likely to tear itself loose from Russia. In addition, when an issue moves toward the risk of using large-scale military power, and particularly when it increases the risk of involving the United States and its allies in a direct military struggle, the reponsibilities and the risks of the Soviet partner are drastically enhanced, together with China's dependence on Moscow's backing. So long as primarily political, ideological, and economic means can be employed to promote the cause of "liberation" Communist-style, Peking probably enjoys a wide range of initiative and autonomous responsibility.

Moscow apparently prefers to remain in the background except at points of major crisis. When the Chinese Communists' intervention in the Korean War fell short of its goal of conquering South Korea and expelling the influence of the United States from the Asian continent, the Soviet regime took upon itself, in June 1951, the major responsibility in seeking to bring about negotiations for a cease-fire. The wearisome negotiations over the terms of the truce were, however, left primarily to the Chinese Communist negotiators. In March and April 1955, when the Chinese Communists' preparations for seizing the offshore islands had reached a threatening stage, and American opinion seemed to be sharply divided over the question of whether or not to use force to defend them, Moscow, it has been widely surmised, exerted its influence to deter Peking from pressing the issue to a military showdown and thus prepared the way for the Geneva Conference between East and West, held in July 1955.

Are there potential or actual divergences of interests between the two partners? Or is there merely a division of roles within the alliance? Have Moscow and Peking agreed on assigning to one or the other regional priorities or spheres of influence in their dealings both with governments and with Communist parties in the various countries of Asia? Are there divergences in their respective estimates of the risks which any given course may involve? Because of the extreme secrecy which surrounds Communist policy making, any answers to these central questions are bound to be highly speculative and tentative, but, even at a more than normal risk of being refuted by future events, the questions cannot be evaded.

Do Moscow and Peking believe that the conquest of Formosa can conceivably be carried out without involving the United States? The refusal of Peking, during the prolonged Sino-American discussions at Geneva in 1955 and 1956, to renounce the use of force against Formosa, and its persistent demands that the United States renounce the use of force to defend Formosa, indicated clearly its insistence on maintaining its right, at some future opportunity, to use force to overthrow the Chinese Nationalist regime. Since the crisis in the spring of 1955, however, Moscow and Peking have presumably agreed that the direct use of force by mainland China would, at this stage, seriously undermine Peking's claim to support the policy of coexistence and that destructive American reprisals might leave China in a weaker position than it now enjoys.

Both Peking and Moscow now assume that Formosa may fall to mainland attack either as one segment of a much vaster program for driving the United States from all of eastern Asia, in other words, through a major and decisive war, or, more likely, through American naval and air forces being withdrawn from the western Pacific to parry a Soviet threat to western Europe or the Middle East, or both. In any case, the acceptance by Peking, and Moscow, perhaps not without some severe friction, of the fact that it was not worth risking a direct and presumably unsuccessful engagement with the United States over Formosa was followed by a new emphasis on political rather than military pressure against Formosa. Of course, as part of this political pressure, the Chinese Communists have carried through an intensive build-up of air and land power and supporting facilities on the mainland opposite Formosa. In the future, if the Soviet leaders should conclude that an early showdown with the United States was both unavoidable and desirable, a mainland attack on Formosa would be a convenient initial move designed to pin down a large part of available American forces in a war in which a quick local decision would be unlikely.

The policy of coexistence, proclaimed by Chou En-lai at Bandung in April 1955, has promised Peking increasing opportunities to extend its influence and has opened the way for more active relations with many countries of Asia and the Middle East. Thus, in November 1956, Peking hastened to offer Nasser contingents of Chinese "volunteers." Each time that a new government extends recognition and establishes relations with Peking, the Nationalist regime loses ground, politically and morally, even though its immediate security remains unimpaired. As a consequence of Bandung, followed up by the Soviet campaign, dramatized by the Geneva Conference of July 1955 for a "relaxation of tensions," Peking, for some time to come, will have to be satisfied with extending its political influence by the normal channels of international negotiations and propaganda. It hopes thus to place its claim to Formosa on a stronger footing, if or when it should decide, at a later stage, to revert to the use of force.

The Soviet and Chinese Communist campaign, waged persistently since late 1949, to secure for Peking China's seat in the United Nations, would, if successful, greatly strengthen its claim that the future of Formosa is an internal, purely Chinese, question and that in using force to prevent the conquest of Formosa by Mao's forces the United States would be guilty of "aggression." The seating of Communist China in the United Nations, if accomplished by Moscow and Peking without some action by the West to consolidate Formosa's separate international status, would tend to promote the disintegration of Nationalist hopes of survival and might eventually make it unnecessary for Communist China to conquer Formosa by force. The "peaceful" subversion of Formosa would almost certainly inhibit the United States from using force to defend it. If, as is possible, Moscow was not really eager in 1950–3 to see Peking actually seated in the United Nations, since 1953 and particularly since 1955, they have both been pressing, with increasing prospect of success, for this major accretion of prestige and freedom of maneuver.

The period of relaxation of strain, which followed the crisis of March and April 1955, offered an opportunity for new political thinking and action. Peking has utilized the lull intensively to extend its political influence and to continue its compaign for discrediting the Nationalists and attempting to undermine their morale. British policy has supported the "two Chinas" proposal. American policy has been to stand pat.

Even if Peking and the Soviet bloc remain adamant in refusing to recognize the permanent existence of the Formosa regime, it has been suggested that United States policy could gain a valuable initiative by taking up the advocacy of the "two Chinas" solution. This step, while disheartening to any remaining Nationalist hopes of recovering control of the mainland, would perhaps rally the backing of many active supporters in the free world coalition, and would win the approval of many uncommitted states. India, for example, recognizes Peking's claim to sovereignty over Formosa, but strongly opposes any use of force to seize it.

A mainland attack on Formosa, coming after a strong United States effort to secure the adoption of the "two Chinas" solution, would probably result in India and other uncommitted countries throwing their weight against this act of aggression. The present American policy in this question tends to lend plausibility to the Communist-propagated image of Formosa as being of interest to the United States primarily as a potential springboard for mounting an invasion of mainland China.[7] Active American advocacy of a "two Chinas" policy, without changing the strategic outlook in any essential respect, would put the Communist bloc on the political defensive.

The question of the Chinese offshore islands is in quite a different status. Almost everywhere outside the United States and Formosa, there is a general assumption that Quemoy, Matsu, and the lesser offshore islands have no historic connection with Formosa and are constituent parts of the nearby mainland territories. Here a local military attack by the Chinese Communist forces would almost surely be successful, unless

[7] For a fuller statement of the alternatives, see Arthur H. Dean: "United States Foreign Policy and Formosa," *Foreign Affairs*, Vol. XXXIII, No. 3 (April 1955), p. 360–75.

the United States intervened with strong military force against mainland air bases. An American declaration in advance that it would use its strategic power to resist their seizure through retaliation against the mainland would most probably serve as a deterrent. But if this failed and the United States retaliated, by atomic bombardments of the mainland, against the Communist seizure, without using atomic weapons, of the offshore islands, this step would profoundly alarm public opinion throughout the world. It might well result in mobilizing a great many countries, including many of the best friends of the United States, behind political efforts to put a stop to hostilities before they had caused serious damage to the mainland government or had forced it to break off its aggressive action. Under these circumstances, tremendous political and moral pressure, backed by Soviet atomic threats against Japan and western Europe, would be organized to halt the American retaliation in mid-course. As one result, the offshore islands would probably remain in Communist hands and the military resources and political prospects of the Nationalist regime would be seriously damaged.

In the second half of 1955 and throughout 1956, the attention of the world was seldom drawn to the offshore islands, but the Communist military build-up has proceeded apace. By carrying on its intensive campaign to promote "coexistence" and the "five principles," the mainland regime may now have put itself in a stronger political position to undertake a seizure of the islands. If successful, this action might shatter the morale of the Nationalist forces, of whom some forty per cent have been concentrated in the offshore islands. It might drive a wedge between the Nationalists and the native Formosans. And it might induce a serious panic among America's allies in eastern Asia and a panicky flight to "neutralism." Although the United States government has officially reserved the right to determine for itself whether or not it would take direct military action to protect the offshore islands, the passage of time, the massing of American-supplied equipment on the islands, and the presence there of American military advisers have tended to link American prestige, as well as the ambitions of the Chinese Nationalist leaders, to the maintenance of Nationalist possession of them.

So long as the Chinese Nationalists claim, and most of the world believes, even though mistakenly, that the offshore islands are primarily of importance as a staging area for invading the mainland, the United States government, through its policy of deliberate ambiguity, leaves itself open to a political flanking attack. Perhaps the United States would be better advised to utilize the period of quiescence in this question to decide definitely, and without immediate pressure on it, how it can best defend Formosa over a long, perhaps an indefinite, future.

Would it be wiser to support a plainly defensive posture, such as would be forcefully advertised to the world by its adopting the "two Chinas" policy, even if it were not accepted by either Chinese government? A corollary to this would be to induce the Nationalists to withdraw their forces intact from the offshore islands, to secure wide political support for Formosa as a "second China," and perhaps to place Formosa under a United Nations guarantee prior to its giving up possession of China's permanent seat in the Security Council of the United Nations. The other alternative appears to be for the United States to wait passively, to see what may happen next. Meanwhile, the prospects for the Nationalists to control the offshore islands indefinitely can be expected to worsen, and Formosa's political isolation to be deepened, while Peking continues to push home its propaganda advantage.

It is hardly necessary to linger over the Chinese Communists' persistent ambition to unify Korea under their control. As a consequence of the serious setback administered to this ambition in the Korean War, the issue has been subordinated since 1953 to a wider pattern of Communist-bloc interests.

Can United States striking power be jockeyed out of its bases in Japan? Can the defense partnership between the United States and Japan be undermined by Soviet-bloc blandishments and Japanese Communist pressure, thus eventually depriving the United States of the use of a base system in Japan? Without a strong partnership with Japan and the use of strong bases in Japan, can American power again protect South Korea against a new local attack launched by the re-equipped Chinese Communist forces, except by the threat of all-out retaliation against both Russia and China? And would an American withdrawal from Japan, and perhaps Okinawa, weaken decisively the threat of retaliation? One final question is whether the United States will continue for as long as may be necessary to assist the economic development of South Korea, and whether it will succeed in stabilizing its economy at a viable level. For the time being, any Chinese Communist action against South Korea is subordinated to the longer range questions of the degree of the American determination to strengthen South Korea and its ability to maintain its defenses in Japan.

During the current partial relaxation of tension, Peking's attention has been centered primarily on its ambition to complete the Communist conquest of Vietnam. Ever since the Geneva Conference on Indochina, of May-July 1954, it has been clear that the Communist bloc has strong hopes of being able to take over South Vietnam, Laos, and Cambodia by peaceful and gradual means. During the first year following the partition, the Communist bloc must have been extremely hopeful that South Vietnam would fail to achieve inner stability and external security and would fall sooner rather than later under Communist control. While it is hazardous to make long-range predictions in these matters, South Vietnam has certainly achieved major successes since mid-1955. With American military support and economic assistance, its new government has done far more than many had predicted was possible to solve its political, military and economic problems.

It must not be forgotten that, despite similar predictions of domestic collapse, South Korea had also begun, between 1948 and June 1950, to achieve a more satisfactory level of stabilization, and that it was at this time that the Sino-Soviet bloc, presumably at the lengthy Moscow consultations of January and February 1950 between Mao and Stalin, decided to resort to direct force in order to conquer it. With respect to South Vietnam, the degree of certainty over the extent of United States commitment is today substantially greater than it was concerning South Korea in June 1950. Through SEATO the United States has joined with several allies to declare South Vietnam within the area to be defended by that organization. While the United States has no forces, aside from an advisory group, in South Vietnam and has no direct military commitment toward it, the intensive efforts which it is making to strengthen South Vietnam should be adequate, for some time, to deter the Communist bloc from a direct resort to military force and from yielding to any temptation to turn the North Vietnamese army loose for a march south.

The Moscow-Peking axis has been relentlessly pressing its political warfare against South Vietnam, ceaselessly denouncing United States military and economic aid as a new form of "colonization." Taking advantage of the frictions between South Vietnam and Cambodia, both Moscow and Peking have showered attentions on the latter. In 1956 Prince Norodom Sihanouk, temporarily out of the government but still powerful, paid lengthy visits of state to both Russia and China, both of which have extended aid to Cambodia in the form of long-term credits and grants, technical assistance and scholarships. Isolated Laos, still partitioned since the abortive Geneva agreement of July 1954, has also carried out exchanges of ceremonial visits and signed agreements with Peking, as gestures designed to assert its status of noncommitment.

Despite the plain fact that neither South Vietnam nor the United States is bound by the Geneva Convention to support the holding of nation-wide elections which were scheduled under that agreement for July 1956, the Soviet-bloc press and radio never tire of denouncing them for their obvious unwillingness to have South Vietnam participate in some sort of elections to "reunify" the country. Both Communist China and Soviet Russia have gone to great lengths to secure from many other governments endorsements of their claim that elections must be held at once throughout Vietnam to elect an all-Vietnamese government. For example, during their visit to India and Burma, Khrushchev and Bulganin succeeded in pocketing joint declarations in support of elections, without any hint that genuinely free elections, if difficult in South Vietnam, would be entirely out of the question in North Vietnam under the control of the Vietminh. In addition, the slightly larger population of North Vietnam, when marched to the polls under Communist discipline, would be able to vote a Communist regime into power over the entire country, even if South Vietnam was completely opposed to it.

Through these and other steps Moscow and Peking are laying the groundwork for a strenuous political campaign against the United States on this issue, within and outside the United Nations, accusing it of "increasing tensions" and "violating agreements." While this campaign may not actually bring about elections, whether free or not, its persistence and its vehemence do a great deal to keep opinion uncertain and fearful in South Vietnam, Laos, and Cambodia. After all, China is an ancient and close neighbor of the peoples of Southeast Asia. The United States, on the other hand, is far away, has been involved only recently in the affairs of the region, and may not be presumed to have an equally persistent interest in its future, especially in view of the many claims on its attention and resources in other parts of the world. At the very least, then, the Soviet-bloc agitation for elections serves to encourage uncertainty, fence sitting, and secret currents of timorous pro-Communist appeasement within South Vietnam, and thus to make the efforts of the Free Vietnamese and the United States less fruitful. And all this, at the cost of mere words!

United States policy need not remain on the defensive in this issue, which is being made a touchstone of the good faith of its concern for the future of the peoples of Southeast Asia. It can accept the general proposal for an election in both North and South Vietnam, provided it is first satisfied that genuinely adequate safeguards for a free choice will be determined in detail and then enforced. It can go further. It can insist that genuinely free elections be held simultaneously in all three partitioned nations—Germany, Korea, and Vietnam. This stand, in clear support of a basic principle of liberty, would compel the Soviet bloc to explain why it urges "free" elections in Vietnam and rejects them in Germany and Korea. Again, a stand taken on broad principle would clarify the basic contrast between Communist and democratic attitudes toward freedom of decision by the peoples directly concerned and would rally wide backing outside the Soviet bloc for this basic principle.

Communist China seems to have assumed not only a priority of political direction, but also the principal burden of economic aid, with respect to both North Korea and North Vietnam. Itself a recipient of large-scale Soviet assistance for its development programs, Peking has extended, or has promised to extend, substantial aid of a similar type, based only in part on China's low production, to assist in the reconstruction and development of its two satellites. Presumably, the provision of supplementary Soviet aid to both areas still leaves the Chinese Communists with the principal position of influence. Similarly, Peking has taken on substantial obligations for training and equipping the armed forces of the two regimes, although, obviously, aircraft and other heavy equipment, which have been reported in large numbers in North Korea, are of Soviet origin. To what extent North Korea and North Vietnam are able, through exports, to compensate mainland China for its military and economic support remains highly obscure.

Within the countries of Southeast Asia, the Communist Chinese must reckon that they possess substantial and growing assets. Most important of these, perhaps, is the large Chinese population.[8] As Communist China has grown in political and military strength, the national pride of the overseas Chinese and their resentment of the inferior position to which they have generally been relegated by the nations among which they reside, have tended to focus their loyalties on mainland China, now admired as a major power.

Peking has also undertaken to build up its economic relations with the area. Since a great deal of both local and international commerce is in Chinese hands, this in turn provides an additional channel for the expansion of Communist Chinese influence, both directly, through their dealings with governments, and indirectly, through stimulating and financing the efforts of the local Communist parties. In Thailand, for example, Peking has engaged in an extensive campaign to sell its new manufactured goods, including small electric motors, sewing machines, and bicycles, as a demonstration of its rapid economic growth. In June 1956, Peking signed an economic assistance agreement with Cambodia, reportedly providing an unconditional grant of aid for purchases in China during 1956–8. The ability of Communist China to absorb some of the tradi-

[8] Cf. Walter H. Mallory: "Chinese Minorities in Southeast Asia," *Foreign Affairs*, Vol. XXXIV, No. 2 (January 1956), pp. 258–70.

tional exports of the region, particularly rice and rubber, works in its favor. The slow recovery of Japanese trade in Southeast Asia and the almost complete breakdown of its trade with Indonesia also tend to leave open wide channels of commercial penetration for the trade of mainland China.

Above all, there is the power factor. Traditionally, a strong China, prior to the early nineteenth century, exerted a strong influence—political, commercial, and cultural—within these countries. During the nineteenth century China lost its position, but its present recovery of strength tends to reactivate both the fears and the attractions of superior power among the peoples of Southeast Asia. In many ways, their bonds with each other are weaker than their traditional bonds with China, and, unfortunately, they show little desire to take a common stand. Certainly, over the next several years the Chinese Communist aim will be to deal separately with each of them, to encourage noncommitment and to undermine SEATO, which they attack as a "Trojan horse" for the "reimposition of the white man's imperialism."

Much criticism has been leveled at SEATO because it has only two members—Thailand and Pakistan—on the Asian mainland. To this, the only reply is that, in their present view of the world, neither India nor Burma would be willing or able to join in an intraregional grouping, even a neutralist one which excluded non-Asian powers, for their mutual defense. Of the island states in the area, the Philippines belong to SEATO, and Indonesia takes a neutralist position, patterned on that of India. Therefore, SEATO, even in its present form, is merely the best grouping that can be worked out among those states which are willing to combine their efforts for their common defense. Against SEATO, it has been argued that its very existence tends to drive the nonmembers to search out reasons for opposing it and to justify their abstention by praising Communist China and Soviet Russia.

Whether Burma's recent experience in attempting to persuade Peking to withdraw its troops from the contested border areas will make its leaders more happy or less happy about entrusting its entire security to China's good will remains uncertain.

SEATO exists. Its disbandment would be a serious blow to future attempts to organize resistance to a renewal of Communist expansionism and would be generally interpreted as a withdrawal of American interest from the mainland countries of Southeast Asia and a reversion to the peripheral strategy of building its defense on the island chain. The only choice, then, is to make SEATO work as well as possible, so that the advantages of belonging to it will become clear to both members and nonmenbers.

The proponents of SEATO also urge, and rightly, that the SEATO concept must be enlarged beyond the military sphere, to provide the basis for geographically wider nonmilitary programs of economic and cultural development. These programs are necessary in themselves and they may serve to make clear to present nonparticipants in SEATO the basic values of national independence and democratic progress which it is designed to safeguard. How far nonmembers may prove willing to take part in its nonmilitary programs is at present not at all clear. In any case, economic and cultural progress in Southeast Asia requires confidence in the future security of the area. As Communist China becomes more powerful and more active, the only potential barrier to its pressure is represented by SEATO. It is a hopeful concept which must grow in strength or else wither on the vine.

Is Communist China likely, in the near future, to resort to direct military force in order to extend its power throughout the arc from Burma to Vietnam and Indonesia? Probably not, for at least two other and less risky paths are open to it. It can continue its present campaign, launched at Bandung, to win over the governments in the area, binding them more closely through trade agreements, playing on their memories and fears of Western and Japanese imperialism, and discouraging them from seeking military support or economic aid from the non-Soviet world. Peking may come to believe that it can achieve its negative aims of excluding United States and Western influences from Southeast Asia without resorting again to force, especially as its growing strength carries with it the increasing ability to use the threat of force as a political weapon.

By following this path, the Chinese Communists would avoid arousing fear and resentment in India. While the Indian government has shown a definite interest in securing and exchanging promises of nonintervention and of abstention from force, it does not possess the political economic strength to provide a counterforce of attraction, in resistance to the pull toward China. So long as independent though weak governments were voluntarily pursuing policies of ever closer co-operation with China, India would have no grounds for mobilizing opinion at home or abroad to resist this pull. The main risk to Communist China in pursuing this path is that at some stage the governments of Southeast Asia and Indonesia might prefer to form a larger uncommitted bloc under Indian leadership, and in opposition to both major power blocs. To Peking, this risk must seem slight, for India has gone far to underwrite China's benevolent intentions in Asian eyes and India itself would be the last to feel the direct consequences of a Chinese policy of indirect and gradual expansion over its smaller neighbors.

A second path, which is also available to China, is not incompatible with the first and may even run parallel with it. This involves the building up of Communist parties and pro-Communist movements, working toward the establishment of "united front" governments, within which the Communists would aim to gain control of several "commanding heights," such as defense, information, and education. The elections of 1956 in Burma and Indonesia showed substantial gains for the Communists, and in Indonesia they have won many concessions from other parties.

When Khrushchev and other Soviet leaders referred, at the Twentieth Party Congress, to the possibility of a "peaceful and even parliamentary path to socialism," it was presumably countries like Indonesia, Burma, Ceylon, and even India which they had in mind. As Khrushchev pointed out, in some countries the "working class" may gain "a firm majority in parliament and transform it from an organ of bourgeois democracy into an organ of true popular will. (*Applause.*)" "Of course," he went on, "in those countries where capitalism is still strong, where it has in its hands an enormous military-police apparatus, there the serious opposition of the reactionary forces is inevitable. There the transition to socialism will take place in conditions of sharp class, revolutionary struggle."[9] In other words, if the opponents of Communist totalitarianism are willing to surrender power peaceably, the revolution will take place with little or no bloodshed, at least prior to the establishment of Communist rule. If they resist, they will by that very fact be declared solely responsible for the Communists' having to resort to methods of violence in order to seize control.

To those governments which are committed to resisting co-operation with the West and yet are unable to build strong defenses and progressive economies by their own means, Soviet and Chinese Communist offers of "aid-through-trade" present an attractive and seemingly harmless alternative. In addition to the Soviet aid-through-trade agreements with India, Burma, Cambodia, Indonesia, Afghanistan, Syria, and Egypt, Communist China, in June 1956, concluded its first agreement for the outright granting of aid to a non-bloc country, Cambodia, and was reported to have made offers to Burma, Ceylon, and Egypt. Soviet and Chinese programs usually include provision for edu-

[9] *Pravda*, February 15, 1956, p. 4.

cating increasing numbers of young engineers in Russia or China, which can easily appear to young and impressionable Asian intellectuals as representing the acme of social and economic progress. The hosts in Moscow and Peking hope that their guests will return home to reinforce the idea that co-operation with Communists at home against the "imperialists" and their local "hirelings" is as harmless as co-operation with Communist governments.

A third path, one which cannot be excluded from calculation, is that, after a more or less prolonged period of intensive wooing and softening up both at the governmental and "united front" levels, the Communist parties in Southeast Asia would be ready to revert, this time with greater prospects of success, to the strategy of the violent seizure of power which they tried out in each country, except Thailand, between 1948 and 1951. Following a "trade-union conference" at Calcutta, in 1948, and obeying the "tough" line which had been promulgated by Moscow at the founding conference of the Cominform, in September and October 1947, each Communist party in Asia scrapped its previous gradualist program and embarked on a fierce struggle to seize power through armed uprisings and extensive sabotage.

Were these bloody campaigns, which raged on into 1951, designed to assist the Chinese Communists in the final stage of their conquest of the mainland? Or did Moscow believe that, with the departure of the Western "imperialists" from India, Pakistan, Ceylon, Burma, and Indonesia, the time was ripe for the Communists to seize power, before non-Communist nationalist regimes had time to consolidate their control and embark on positive programs of social and economic progress? Whatever the estimates of Moscow, the militant parties had pretty much burned out their strength of revolt by 1951, although they returned fully to the "peaceful" path only in 1955 and 1956.

Today the Communist bloc probably reckons that the prospects of success through violent tactics would be much greater several years from now, particularly if the Western ability to work with the governments of the area had been increasingly blunted in the interim. The past history of the alternation of the Communists between "hard" and "soft" tactics suggests that the major Communist powers can order, and the local Communist parties will carry out, a revival of violent methods whenever the prospects of early success seem favorable to Moscow and Peking, or whenever it suits their political strategy. Whichever tactic, "soft" or "hard," may seem more promising is the one which will be applied.

Since 1951 and particularly since the return, in 1955, of the Japanese Communist party to the "lovable," gradualist policy of Nosaka, Peking seems to enjoy a certain priority of interest over Moscow in the development of close relations with Japan. Chinese spokesmen, who formerly insisted that the Japanese government must withdraw its recognition from the Formosa regime if it hoped to establish relations with Peking, now imply, unofficially, that the establishment of relations between Tokyo and Peking can be effected without requiring this step as a precondition. Aside from the question of Japan's enforcement of the trade controls against mainland China, there are now no difficult questions pending between Japan and Communist China, in contrast to the profound differences which have so long delayed the conclusion of a peace treaty between Soviet Russia and Japan. In general, Japanese opinion, traditionally distrustful of Russia, places great confidence in the ability of the Japanese to work well with the Chinese, whom it regards as primarily "Chinese" rather than Communists. While many of the more optimistic estimates of the value of a revived China trade with Japan have been revised downward of late, Japan's difficulties in opening up markets in other parts of the world would make even a modest revival of trade with China an attractive addition to its economic opportunities.

Peking and Moscow share a common desire to see Japan detached from its alliance and defense agreement with the United States—the alliance concluded in September 1951, and the defense agreement in February 1952. In January 1951, Stalin sent a resounding message "to the Japanese people" urging them to throw off the yoke of their American conquerors, and the theme of "Japan, an American colony" is played up continuously by Peking and Moscow. Since all Japanese parties had promised to negotiate the reestablishment of relations with Russia and mainland China, the Soviet government was able, in the agreement of October 1956, to stand pat on its refusal to discuss the Japanese claim to recover some of the Kurile Islands, even though it agreed to give up the Habomai and Shikotan Islands, long recognized as part of Hokkaido Prefecture, after the conclusion of a peace treaty.

Did Communist China press the Soviet Union to complete its negotiations with Japan? There is certainly no suggestion that Peking would think of urging Moscow to abandon any territorial claims, but probably Peking welcomed the Soviet compromise proposal, of May 1956, for establishing diplomatic relations without a prior settlement of conflicting territorial claims. The reopening of relations, even in this truncated form, between Russia and Japan opened the way for an eventual restoration of relations between Peking and Tokyo and for the further broadening of Chinese Communist contacts with various groups and interests within Japan. Both Peking and Moscow place their hopes in the emergence of a parliamentary majority in Japan committed to bring about the withdrawal of United States forces and installations from Japan, and in a consequent rapid decline in United States diplomatic and economic support for Japan. This, they believe, would make political and economic co-operation with the Communist powers even more attractive and perhaps indispensable for Japan, which would then be more vulnerable to military and economic blackmail by the Communist powers.

Whether the Japanese Communist party is more directly influenced by Peking or Moscow remains obscure and may have tactical rather than strategic importance. Peking and Moscow are both working hard to bring Japan over to a neutralist and "de-committed" position, a shift which might be effected more readily through Chinese Communist blandishments rather than through Soviet pressures. If this can be achieved, the growing strategic threat of the Soviet Union, multiplied by the new and rapid advances in military technology, would in turn make Japan even more vulnerable to a sudden revival of political and military pressure from the mainland. If there is a potential rivalry between Peking and Moscow for dominant control over the Japanese Communist party, this is not likely, short of a victory of Communism in Japan, to prevent them from sharing out the appropriate roles in striving to achieve their common objective.

In India, the first impact of the Chinese Communist revolution was to strengthen the extremists among the Communists. Under the Ranadive leadership, the Communist party resorted to methods of violence, and to all-out denunciations of the ruling Congress party. Large-scale railroad and industrial sabotage was practiced, and an attempt was made to build up "Yenans" in several regions of the country. In a sharp reversal of the party's previous line, Gandhi and Nehru were demoted to the ranks of "hirelings of the imperialists."

The return to peaceful methods was proclaimed with some waverings as early as 1951, more clearly after 1953, and the new line was fully spelled out at the Communist party conference of 1956, following the Khrushchev-Bulganin visit. Since then, the Communist party of India has secured the release of many political prisoners from custody and has proclaimed its support for Nehru's policy of noncommitment. The Communists now concentrate their attacks on Western enterprises and investment in India, while wooing the "national *bourgeoisie*," and glorifying Soviet and Communist achievements as models for India to follow. It has been suggested, but not confirmed, that from 1948 to 1951 the Communist party of India fell within the sphere of direction of the Chinese Communists, who pressed it to launch a civil war against India's "Chiang Kai-shek," and that today the Soviet Communist leadership has asserted its direct interest in the movement in India, brushing to one side the traditional channel of contact, the Communist party of Great Britain.

India is involved in both co-operation and rivalry with Communist China, and many Indians see the next five to ten years as a decisive period in which either India or China will "prove" the superiority of its methods of economic progress. If this is so, then why should Soviet Russia extend economic support to the Indian Five-Year Plan of 1956–60, especially when China has a better claim to all assistance that Moscow can spare? The Soviet support given to India may conceivably be a long-range hedge, designed to build up Russia's influence in India as a potential offset to the preponderant role which China is assuming in Southeast Asia.

Burma, lying uncomfortably close to Communist China and still plagued by Communist insurgents at home and by Chinese pressure and encroachments along an ill-defined frontier, may feel that a direct Soviet interest, as expressed in the Khrushchev-Bulganin visit of 1955 and the subsequent trade agreements, may serve to offset any direct pressure from China. Whether or not an attempt to play off Moscow against Peking, if it is in Burmese thinking, is likely to succeed is doubtful. In a crisis, it is more likely that any influence exercised by Moscow over governments or Communist parties would be used to serve the common aims of both major Communist powers.

For the time being, since neutralism is designed solely for export beyond the periphery of the Soviet bloc, the negative purpose of the axis in strengthening the attachment of India, Burma, Cambodia, Laos, Indonesia, and perhaps of Ceylon to their status of noncommitment can be best served through programs of political, economic, and cultural co-operation. The prestige of India, which gives approval to many Soviet and Chinese Communist demands made in the name of "peace" and of opposition to "blocs," tends, in many parts of Asia and Africa, to underwrite a vague popular trustfulness in the peaceful intentions of the Soviet bloc.

At the Twentieth Party Congress, Soviet spokesmen stressed again and again the great importance of building up co-operation between the "peace bloc" of the Soviet-led "one third of mankind" and the "peace zone," exemplified by India, which influences another one third of mankind, in order to isolate the "imperialist-controlled" remaining third. Both Moscow and Peking affirm on every occasion their support for Prime Minister Nehru's "five principles," although Nehru himself has frequently denounced the Indian Communists as "strangers" who "love Russia more than India." In contrast, he has repeatedly endorsed the "peace-loving" purposes of the two major Communist partners. Even the Soviet suppression of the revolt in Hungary, in November 1956, was denounced by Nehru more in pain than in anger. While he complains frequently against Western-inspired alliances and blocs and, less frequently, has chided Russia for its Warsaw bloc, he apparently has no public misgivings about the powerful Sino-Soviet alliance.

In the Soviet view of political strategy, the "peace bloc" has an important role to play. It can help to restrain the resistance of the non-Communist world to any Soviet actions short of all-out war, and discourage any political or military preparations for facing up to or forestalling such an eventuality. And in the meantime it may serve Moscow's and Peking's purposes by winning away a number of countries from the "imperialist" camp and bringing them over to the ranks of the uncommitted and defenseless nations. Probably the Soviet government now estimates that, despite the trend toward nuclear stalemate, any serious military clash would increasingly run the risk of expanding into an all-out struggle between the United States and the Soviet bloc. Possibly it has decided that it is in its own vital interest to avert or, at least, to postpone such a stupendous conflict and to avoid enlarging its risks beyond politically manageable limits for the next few years, or until the outcome of the present race for superiority in long-range aircraft, atomic power, and guided missiles has been resolved.

In the meantime, while minimizing the risk of all-out war, Moscow hopes to make important political gains through co-operating with the "peace zone," particularly, as in the case of Egypt and Syria, by supporting its members against the "imperialists." If its new and more conciliatory tactics work well, it may hope to weaken or even eliminate the political influence of the non-Soviet bloc from the mainland of Asia. It hopes that the attractions of noncommitment will bring Thailand and Pakistan to abandon their commitments to SEATO, as Ceylon has done with respect to the British bases there. If this should come about, partly through domestic pressures within the two mainland allies of SEATO, it is doubtful that the Indian government would see any purpose to be served by organizing a defensive bloc of its own within the "peace zone." Accordingly, with SEATO's counter-pressure removed, each individual country of the "peace zone" would be increasingly vulnerable to the pressures and blandishments, combined or alternated, which can be exerted by Russia and China. Presumably this policy is compatible with the primary short-run aim of the Soviet bloc, to destroy the Western system of alliances and thus to bring about the retraction of United States political and miliary commitments from the mainland of Asia.

Finally, it must not be forgotten that both in Moscow and Peking policies are shaped by basic Marxist assumptions. Relying on Marxist reasoning, the Communist leaders undoubtedly reckon that methods of development based upon liberal institutions and upon co-operation with the timid venture capital of the West cannot solve the problems of internal economic and social development in the underdeveloped and newly independent countries. It is only a question of time, they believe, before the failure of the liberal democratic path will be made clear, thus opening the way for these peoples to adopt, peacefully or through violence, the alternative path of modernization, represented by the Soviet model of compulsion and dictatorship.

During a period of violent action, from 1945 through 1951, the Communist leaderships drove their own forces to the limit and consolidated their territorial gains in eastern Europe and China, only to overreach themselves in Greece, Berlin, Yugoslavia, and Korea. From 1951 to 1955 they were occupied in disengaging their forces from counterproductive adventures and testing out a variety of tactics, some of them contradictory to others. Since Bandung and Geneva, in 1955, the Soviet leadership, seconded somewhat clumsily and perhaps reluctantly by Peking, has gone all-out for peaceful co-operation with any governments which are or may become hostile to its principal adversary, the United States, and its close allies. Similarly, it has ordered the Communist parties to woo into "united fronts" the parties and regimes they had previously promised to destroy. The broad smile of Moscow and the less gracious grimace of Peking are alike expressions of these new or refurbished "soft" tactics.

Co-operating with any and all regimes for shared goals, tapping a reservoir of resentment against recent colonialism and fear of the "white man's imperialism," the Moscow-Peking axis is actively engaged in extending its political, economic and cultural influence beyond the periphery of the bloc, while respecting outwardly the existing regimes and cultivating their favor. Parallel to their diplomatic efforts, Moscow and Peking are working for the emergence of new "united front" alliances and coalition governments, within which superior Communist discipline and organization may, they hope, effect a further enhancement of Communist power.

As Moscow and Peking look out on Communist Asia, they feel confident that, in a more or less prolonged period of relaxed tension, their growing political, economic and military strength will bring great gains, especially through their efforts to monopolize the emotions released by the waves of anti-imperialism, national liberation, and modernization. If this results in the extension of the area of neutralism, in the retraction of United States and free world commitments and in a diminished willingness of the United States and its allies to make sacrifices or run risks, their immediate purposes will be fully served. The expectation of Moscow and Peking is that, after a period of "peaceful competition," their axis will be stronger, and its opponents weaker, than they now are.

By the Bulganin-Chou En-lai declaration of January 18, 1957, the two major Communist powers proclaimed again "the unbreakable unity" of their countries and their determination to co-operate fully in striving for "victory in the common struggle for triumph of Communism."

For the next few years, the primary challenge of the Moscow-Peking axis is likely to be political, economic, and cultural in character, while the two partners go on building up their military power at top speed, to prepare for future contingencies and opportunities.

This means that programs for the strategic consolidation of the free world must be backed up flexibly through imaginative programs of political, economic, and cultural co-operation, programs which can win the sincere support of the peoples of both committed and uncommitted areas. At the same time the countries of the free world cannot afford to drop their guard or be lulled into falling behind in the race for military power and political cohesion. In Asia, the free world has both handicaps and advantages. It must examine both realistically if it is to meet successfully the new challenge of the Moscow-Peking axis.

:23:

KHRUSHCHEV'S NEW ECONOMIC GAMBIT[1]

[*May 1958*]

IN THE past twelve months Nikita Khrushchev, since March 27 chairman of the Council of Ministers as well as first secretary of the Communist party of the Soviet Union, has pressed forward with a major reshaping of both Soviet industry and agriculture. While engaged in dislodging any serious competitors for political power, he has also been carrying out a far-reaching reconstruction of the vast system of production and management. Was there a really dangerous challenge to his power just before his defeat of Molotov, Malenkov, and Kaganovich a year ago? Or did he deliberately provoke their opposition to his "adventurous" tinkering with the machinery of production in order to wrench their practiced hands from the apparatus of rule?

Which came first, the political goal or the economic one? This remains a matter of dispute and conjecture. If Khrushchev did, in fact, take on a risky gamble in his revamping of industry, he has now compounded it by scrapping one of the main controls over agricul-

[1] *Foreign Affairs*, Vol. XXXVI, No. 4 (July 1958), pp. 557–68. Copyright 1958 by the Council on Foreign Relations, Inc.

ture. But his elimination of the "old guard" has undoubtedly made it easier for him as undisputed boss of the party machine to press ahead with a drastic change in the collective farm system: the elimination or reduction of the machine and tractor stations, the mainstay of Moscow's control over collectivized agriculture for nearly three decades.

For Khrushchev, the new methods of management are an essential means for achieving Stalin's goal, that of "overtaking and surpassing the advanced capitalist countries." Today only one of them—the United States—remains to be overtaken. In his speech of November 6, 1957, on the fortieth anniversary of the October revolution, Khrushchev set a series of ambitious goals for the Soviet economy to achieve by 1972. For example, the target of 100 to 120 million metric tons of steel, as against 51.1 million tons last year, though feasible will be costly.

Actually, this and other targets represent a somewhat lower rate of economic growth than some of those previously attained over the past twenty-five years. Declines in percentage rates of Soviet growth are inevitable, for the most dramatic increases are normally achieved in the earlier stages of industrialization, against a low initial level of output. In most fields, later increments of investment provide a smaller return, measured in percentages. The Soviet economy, like other maturing systems, will have to make larger investments than in the past for the maintenance and replacement of equipment, for rounding out the mechanization of the productive process and for raising the average productivity of a relatively less abundant labor force. The morale of the Soviet people also requires more attention to consumer goods and services and to housing, as Stalin's successors have increasingly recognized.

To some extent the Soviet economy is now forced to pay a higher price, in real terms, for many of its raw materials. In the first spurt of industrialization, the Soviet Union has used up some of its most accessible high quality ores. Last year the Kuznetsk Combine calculated a loss of 50,000 tons of pig iron, due directly to the increased ash content of coking coal over the preceding year. Under the new Seven-Year Plan for 1959–65, the government plans to make large investments either to upgrade poorer ores or to develop more remote high quality sources. When such unfavorable factors as these have been noted, the fact remains that annual additions to Soviet output will become steadily larger, even though the *rate* of growth is gradually declining. The reason is, of course, that the Soviet economy—the base on which the rate of growth is measured—is now a very big one.

One very important way to promote further growth is to reduce waste and inefficiency and utilize more effectively the large and rapidly growing investment fund which each year is squeezed out of a slowly improving standard of living. By late 1956 the search for more efficient and expeditious forms of industrial management was made even more urgent by novel and competing demands on Soviet resources.

These resources, of course, are not unlimited, and the insatiable need for new factories and new facilities comes into competition with other demands upon them. Among the claimants, the new military technology is exceedingly expensive, whether its cost be measured in dollars or rubles, or in scientific and production man-hours. Now that the race for nuclear power has passed into the production stage, it faces the Soviet leaders with vast new requirements for resources. At the same time the promise of credits to Communist China and India, to Egypt-Syria and Yugoslavia, and to many other countries, have set up claims to real resources, and particularly to the relatively scarce supplies of new and complex equipment, which are also in high demand for developing the Urals, Siberia, and Central Asia. The unforeseen assertion of Polish independence in October 1956, Hungary's revolt, followed by new Soviet costs for restarting their economies, and the smaller sops thrown to the more obedient satellites, have piled new and unplanned burdens on Soviet industry.

Toward the close of 1956, it was clear that Soviet investment resources were severely strained. One way to get the maximum effect from them was to strengthen the administration of the economy. The upshot was an attempt in December of that year to improve the central decision-making processes by placing Mikhail Pervukhin in charge of a considerably strengthened State Economic Commission for Current Planning. In retrospect, this move may have been the final spasm of the strictly centralized, traditional approach to the management of the economy. At the same time the plan goals set earlier that year at the Twentieth Party Congress were tacitly revised downward.

On February 14, 1957, Khrushchev proposed a sweeping reorganization of Soviet industry, breaking up many of the industrial ministries and replacing the vertical structure of management with a territorial organization, to be centered in an unstated number of regional councils of national economy. The publication on March 30 of his detailed "Theses" was followed by numerous discussions at meetings in which some glimmerings of doubt and dissent were allowed to show through the mantle of praise. In early May the new structure was enacted by the Supreme Soviet, to take effect on July 1. A review of production goals must also have been proceeding in the inner sanctum of power, for in late September Moscow announced officially that the current Five-Year Plan for 1956–60 had been scrapped and would be replaced after two years of annual plans by a Seven-Year Plan for 1959–65.

Just what are the powers and responsibilities of the new regional councils? Has overcentralization given way to overlocalization? What powers have been retained by the central authorities in Moscow? Has Soviet industry been "decentralized," as has been widely assumed in the West, or merely "reorganized," as Khrushchev insists?

The advantages sought through the change-over can be summarized briefly. The ministries were making decisions in Moscow—or not making them—without an adequate knowledge of the problems or opportunities of the individual plants. The regional councils will be familiar with local resources and will be able to use them better. The Soviet press has been peppered with descriptions of the bad results of remote control by the ministries. Horrendous examples of the waste of compound ores have been cited. At Mizur, because of departmental barriers, only zinc, copper, and lead were extracted, and seven other elements, including sulphur and tin, were discarded as waste. At the Nerchinsk deposits, only lead and tin were extracted; indium and cadmium were thrown away, because they came under the authority of another ministry. At Yaroslavl the new oil refinery is to supply by-products to a new chemical plant; this was allegedly not possible under the regime of the centralized ministries of the oil and chemical industries.

The chairman of the Azerbaijan Economic Council has reported that his new agency has gotten the production of synthetic rubber under way, after it had been delayed during several years of interministerial negotiations; it has organized the by-product utilization of industrial carbon and found unused space in factories formerly controlled by central ministries for setting up the production of cables, electric equipment, insulators, air conditioners, electric stoves and fans, and kerosene heaters. To save on transportation costs, the Krasnoiarsk Economic Council is preparing to shift several factories to the use of local coal and to produce packing materials locally.

While the new regional councils are designed to break down the vertical industrial empires of the former economic ministries, they have shown some tendencies of their own toward empire-building. A. G.

Sheremetiev, chairman of the Cheliabinsk Economic Council and formerly minister of ferrous metallurgy, has complained that very few of the 2,050 officials in his former ministry have shown any desire to exchange Moscow for Cheliabinsk; in building up the new councils it has therefore been necessary to draw upon, and hence weaken, the managerial staffs of the local enterprises. Other former ministers have also turned up in the new regional "command posts."

Each of the 105 regional councils has worked out a substructure, supposedly based on the size and needs of the industries it administers. But according to one complaint, the Arkhangelsk Economic Council, like the ministries it supplanted, is three links removed from actual production. Within the economic councils of Group 1 (apparently those with the most important industries), the number of subdivisions varies from eleven to thirty-five, and the size of the professional staff from 350 to 1,600. The Irkutsk Economic Council, perhaps an average one for Group 1 councils, has a total staff of 520.

The Moscow City Economic Council, responsible for some eight per cent of the country's industrial output, was established with sixteen branch administrations, four trusts, thirty-eight research organizations, thirty-three construction-design bureaus, two main administrations for supply and distribution, eight functional administrations (production, technology, planning), six functional departments (bookkeeping, transportation, arbitration), and a technical and an economic council. No wonder Khrushchev has recently admitted, though in guarded terms, that, ". . . although the new system of administration underwent a period of establishment in the first months, and this undoubtedly affected its work . . . , yet, the management of enterprises has considerably improved. . . . In the future the favorable aspects of the reorganization . . . will be manifested to an even fuller extent. . . ."

One difficult problem facing the regional councils results from Moscow's temptation to cut through the decision-making maze by turning them into direct operating agencies. An example of this is the decree of April 20 on the reorganization of the machine and tractor stations which places ". . . on the chairmen of the Councils of National Economy the personal responsibility for the production of spare parts and ball bearings for tractors, automobiles, agricultural, and earth-moving machines. . . ." Even if the decree presumably applies only to regional councils of provinces in which spare parts and ball bearings are actually produced, rather than to all 105 councils, it is easy to predict that their chairmen will tend, under Moscow's concept of "personal responsibility," to usurp and divide the authority of the managers of the plants, and not merely to supervise them.

The devolution of some measure of economic control to the regional councils points up a further problem: the presence of two "masters" within the same district. For example, side by side with the new Moscow City Economic Council, the Moscow City Soviet also administers a network of nine hundred enterprises with 440,500 employees in the fields of construction, building materials, automobile transportation, garment industries, bakeries, etc. The Kherson Economic Council has complained that, while it has control of wallboard making, granite, and some lime quarries, the executive committee of the province has taken over the brickyards, all gypsum and some lime plants, and sand quarries; it has urged that all construction materials should be brought under the council's own control.

Even more serious has been the outcry against "localism," the tendency of the regional councils to meet the planned and even the "above-plan" demands of "their own" plants ahead of deliveries to "foreign" regions. "Co-operativized deliveries" destined for other areas under the detailed central plan have often suffered. Whether territorial "parochialism" will prove less serious than the ministerial "parochialism" which the new organization is designed to cure, it is impossible to say, at least on the basis of the scattered data available. That the central government is deeply concerned about it is shown by the announcement on May 19 that officials who fail to carry through the planned deliveries to other provinces and republics will be subject to measures of "disciplinary, material, or criminal responsibility," including prison sentences for a second offense.

One of the main complaints against the new system has been the uncertainties which have arisen in the handling of both supply and distribution. Formerly, each centralized ministry had its own mammoth administrations charged with procuring equipment and raw materials, and with distributing the products of its factories more or less according to the central plan. Now, each regional council has been ordered to set up two "main administrations," for supply and distribution, and each of these will have numerous subdivisions to serve its various industries.

Even more striking has been the move of the State Planning Committee (Gosplan) in Moscow to take over the functions and staffs of the former ministries in the fields of supply and distribution. Instead of thirty marketing organizations existing under the former ministries, Gosplan was ordered to set up seventeen new ones, and to turn over the local offices and warehouses to the economic councils. Last month Gosplan was instructed to organize central divisions for inter-republic deliveries.

There have been many complaints against the malfunctioning of supply under the new system. The Azerbaijan Economic Council has raised its voice against the failure of Perm Province and the Georgian Republic to carry out their deliveries to it. The Irkutsk Economic Council has complained that forty-six economic regions had fallen short in their deliveries to it of steel sheets and other products; the Irkutsk heavy machine plant had piled up 3 million rubles' worth of incomplete equipment because of the failure of plants in Kharkov, Cheliabinsk, Stalino, and elsewhere to deliver components according to the plan.

Last December, a deputy from Estonia raised an especially plaintive note: "The U.S.S.R. Ministry of Agriculture used to order and allocate spare parts for equipment; true, not in sufficient quantity; but now one does not even know where to obtain these goods. Several economic councils of the Russian Republic that used to send us these goods report that they are reducing their output and can no longer deliver anything to us." In general, the response to this crucial problem has been to recentralize the control of supply and distribution within the industrial and distribution administrations of the State Planning Committee.

Subject to the final decisions of the Council of Ministers of the U.S.S.R. (and the party Presidium), the State Planning Committee has taken on the main functions of top industrial management. By July 1957, it had twenty-three industrial departments, roughly corresponding to the ministries which had been abolished, and since then it has presumably added to this number, and to its staff. The central ministries of medium machine building, chemical industry, and electric power stations, among others, have survived, but the ministries of aircraft industry, defense industry, radio-engineering industry, and shipbuilding industry have been replaced by state committees of similar names. Presumably, the state committees deal with problems of research and development, and the operational control of the industries has been integrated into the structure of Gosplan.

From this reshuffling, Gosplan has emerged with enormous powers, not unlike the All-Union Council of National Economy of the early 1930's. Its chief, I. I. Kuzmin, is one of the six vice chairmen of the Council of Ministers and seven of its vice-chairmen and directors of departments also have ministerial rank. What is more important, it exercises (subject to higher control) the main authority in making decisions on new investment, in managing the supply and distribution system, and, with the Ministry of Finance, in drawing up both the national and republic budgets. It also exercises a direct supervision over the fulfillment of the plan, both by receiving constant reports and by sending out its own teams of inspectors.

The new regional councils are expected to exercise more responsibility in making full use of local resources, in supervising local enterprises more closely, in making more rapid decisions—but all within the over-all plan laid down at the center. They have a little more elbow room and more responsibilities. But the plans, drawn up by the regional councils and integrated by the republic Gosplans, undergo final decision in Moscow. Aside from the day-to-day control now exercised by the industrial divisions of Gosplan instead of by the former ministries, the regional councils are also under constant supervision by the executive and party committees both of the provinces and the republics. The success or failure of the regional councils is judged on the basis of their record in meeting the national production plans, not by their local popularity. "Decentralization" is a misnomer. There has been a devolution of decision-making functions to strong regional agencies, but all important decisions are still made in the center and are now co-ordinated through an expanded superministry, Gosplan.

A parallel transformation is being carried out in the management of collectivized agriculture. The proposal to eliminate many or most of the machine and tractor stations (M.T.S.) was first presented by Khrushchev in January of this year at an agricultural conference at Minsk. It was implemented on April 20 by a joint decree of the Central Committee of the party and the Council of Ministers. This latest reform means that in many regions of the Soviet Union the state-owned M.T.S. are transferring most of their machinery and their machine operators and a part of their repair equipment to those collective farms which are able and willing to buy them. The basic aim is to do away with a situation in which "the field has two masters"—the collective farm and the M.T.S. The argument is that the collectives, having grown stronger in management and resources since the reforms of 1953 and 1955, will now make better use of the equipment than was possible when they had to "co-ordinate" with the M.T.S. to get their plowing and harvesting done. This, Khrushchev believes, will lead to an increase in the productivity of land and labor and thus "overtake America."

The discussions of the failings of the M.T.S. system have thrown a clear light on many disadvantages of Soviet agriculture. The M.T.S. have not found it to their interest to carry out deep plowing of long-fallow or unused lands, since they were paid according to the amount of "soft plowing" completed. Even when not in use for plowing or harvesting, their machines were often hoarded and were seldom made available to the collective farms for other productive purposes. On the other hand, an M.T.S. had to take whatever assortment of machines was assigned to it by "the center," as in the case of the useless cabbage pickers and potato diggers assigned to the Crimea. Between 1954 and 1957 more than 1 million mechanics were trained at a cost to the government of over nine billion rubles, but sample surveys showed that only a small proportion were subsequently employed at their new skills.

The basis for transferring the farm machinery to the collectives had been prepared by the consolidation of many collective farms into larger units, which Khrushchev pressed for in 1949–51. Between 1949 and 1957, according to Khrushchev's speech of March 27, the average size of collectives, measured in hectares of plowland, had risen from 557 to 1,954; the average monetary income had increased from 111,000 to 1,247,-000 rubles; and the number of collectives had declined from 250,000 to 78,000. In some regions of very large collective farms, as in the Kuban and in Stavropol Province, the experiment of turning over the M.T.S. equipment had, it now appears, been tried out successfully during 1957. In such regions the change will probably work out well; in others, made up of small and scattered collectives, it may be long delayed and have little benefit.

One of the effects of the change is to encourage the absorption of small and weak collectives into their larger neighbors. Many instances of this are being cited in the Soviet press, without making it clear how the two unequal partners to the fusion may feel about it. One manager felt that ". . . there is no need to maintain the M.T.S. for several years, even with reduced staffs, just to serve the weak farms; these collective farms should be advised to merge with large, economically strong farms." On the other hand, in Khabarovsk Province there is no one zone or district in which all the collectives can dispense with the services of the M.T.S. And in the Georgian Republic, the industrial crops—the most valuable ones—are still carried on intensively by hand labor and will benefit least from the sale of the M.T.S. machinery.

One further reason for the change was mentioned casually by Khrushchev in his speech of March 27. The grain and other products by which the collectives pay the M.T.S. for their services have recently been costing the government more than its direct purchases from the collectives. In addition, the government will benefit to the tune of some 20 billion rubles through payments to be made by the collectives for the M.T.S. equipment. By comparison, in 1957 the collectives set aside some 16 billion rubles in their "indivisible funds" (out of a total cash income of 94 billion rubles) to pay for all types of improvements, such as new buildings, purchases of equipment, and livestock.

Many of the collectives are planning to set up small repair stations of their own, but the main reliance for this service will be placed on the repair and technical stations (R.T.S.), which will, where necessary, continue to supply tractor and harvesting services to those collectives which cannot buy the former M.T.S. equipment. But they are to do so on a cost-accouning basis, which will save money for the government but raise the cost to the collectives. The R.T.S. are also to provide repair services through mobile units as well as at the station, and they are to check and report to the government on the condition of the collectives' equipment. After much dispute over what agencies should provide spare parts, fuel, lubricants, and other requirements for the collectives, it was decided in April that the R.T.S. should supply these materials and also fertilizers, insecticides, and other production needs. In addition to the control exercised by the R.T.S., the district soviets are to establish a system of inspectors to watch over and "guide" the work of the collectives, in place of the control previously exercised by the M.T.S.

While there have been many published reports boasting of the smooth transfer of the M.T.S. machinery to the collectives, some new problems have come to light. In many places, the tractor drivers of the M.T.S. would have received a lower wage than before, if paid as members of the collective on the basis of workdays performed; the government has intervened to insist that the collectives provide them with a "guaranteed minimum" equal to their former wages. In some villages the new equipment has been abused or fallen in disrepair. Many collectives have also insisted on buying only the newer machines, and in at least one district they were ordered to take machines they did not want. Large numbers of houses must be built to accommodate the farm experts, veterinarians, mechanics, and tractor drivers as they are transferred to the collectives. The cost of setting up even small repair stations in the collectives will be considerable, and for several years payments for the machinery will reduce sharply the amounts that would otherwise be available for improving farm production directly.

Whether the change will work out favorably for the economy as a whole will not be clear for some time. Its effect should be to strengthen further the productivity and management of the stronger collective farms—those which, in any case, provide most of the marketable crops. Like Stolypin, Khrushchev is "betting on the strong," only this time on the economically strong collective farms and on the tens of thousands of experienced party administrators who have been sent out over the past three years to stiffen the collectives. The M.T.S. represented a steady, reliable channel of control and a sure source of foodstuff deliveries, but they have tended to inhibit the growth of productivity. Now, without releasing the collective farms from the system of centralized planning and centralized pricing, Khrushchev expects to raise farm production rapidly by placing the collectives under unified leadership at the local and district level.

From the discussions of the change-over have come several indications of further problems which worry Soviet leaders. Some have urged the establishment of a pyramid of district, provincial and national "collective farm councils" which would represent the interests of the collective farmers at the various levels of the Soviet administration. A sharp rejoinder to these "populist" echoes was given by one correspondent in *Pravda*. "Some comrades say that collective farm councils will allegedly protect the rights of the collective farmers; but does or can anyone in our country infringe upon these rights?" Instead, the district collective farm councils are to be heavily weighted with soviet, party and administrative officials to watch over the work of the collectives.

For the time being, Khrushchev has rejected the proposal to pay uniform country-wide prices for collective farm deliveries. In order to avoid ruining the weaker collectives and also to force the stronger ones to contribute more to the state, differential prices will continue to be set for deliveries and purchases of farm products. On January 1 of this year the Soviet government abandoned the collection of taxes in kind from the private garden plots and private livestock of the collective farmers, at a cost to itself of three billion rubles, but it had previously raised to fourteen per cent the income tax on the collectives' net cash income (net of production costs and state deliveries). One proposal has been made that the government should provide a stronger incentive to improved work by announcing its deliveries requirements for five years ahead, instead of one year. Another proposal, echoing an abortive reform of several years ago, has been to change the tax on the cash incomes of the collectives into a land tax, based on the area and quality of the arable land. Even though it would provide a strong stimulus to raise production, this proposal has been rejected as involving "great difficulties."

Both of Khrushchev's major gambits point in the same direction. Their purpose is to push operational decision making downward, away from the congested bureaucratic maze of Moscow ministries. Khrushchev is betting on the accumulated experience, administrative judgment, and material ambitions of tens of thousands of party executives in the provinces, republics, and enterprises, and even in the collective farm managements, to take on-the-spot decisions in harmony with a detailed central plan. The central authority, as has happened repeatedly since Stalin's death, is increasing the size of the carrot and reducing the size and visibility of the stick.

Khrushchev, who has had much practical experience away from the "center," appears confident that the machinery of industrial and agricultural production will respond favorably to these new methods of management. At the same time he has taken care to keep the basic levers of plan, investment, supervision, and control in the hands of the central government. For this purpose, he has strengthened the control of the party apparatus over the economy, while tightening his own control over the party.

PART V

The Dual Challenge of Soviet Policy

:24:

THE WORLD IMPACT OF THE RUSSIAN REVOLUTION[1]

[*May 1951*]

THE apocalyptic storm which swept across Russia in 1917, to beat since then against strongly buttressed and poorly battened societies alike, may have blown itself out within the Soviet Union. On that score the evidence is conflicting, and the interpretations of the evidence even more so. But the multiple challenges of its ideology and its military might have not been answered adequately. They are a major preoccupation of men and women everywhere who believe, unlike the Soviet leaders, that there is no justice without freedom, no wisdom without discussion, no social fulfillment without self-generated social initiative.

Bolshevism attained and consolidated its power in Russia because it gave expression to a deeply felt ethical demand of the "oppressed and humiliated." Its manifold appeals evoked, and gave direction to, the support of a militant, dedicated minority, and won the neutrality of the majority of ordinary people during the struggle for power. Bolshevism promised peace

[1] *Religious Faith and World Culture*, edited by A. William Loos (Prentice-Hall: New York; 1951), pp. 143–56. Copyright 1951 by the Church Peace Union.

to the people, land to the peasants, emancipation to the workers, and liberation to oppressed nationalities. It declared itself against war for annexations, against landlord rule in the villages, against arbitrary exploitation of factory workers, and against national oppression. But Bolshevism conquered Russia, not with a program, but through releasing the pent-up energies of protest and revenge against an order of things which was, in any event, about to vanish.

By the time of the October Revolution the peasants held most of the land and were rapidly seizing the rest. The workers had won the right to form trade unions, and many of the nationalities were debating vigorously the nature of their future relationship to Russia. While there was no simple or painless way to end the war at once, Russia, as Lenin said, had never in its history been so free as it was under the provisional government of 1917. The principal aims of the Bolshevist program were likely to be achieved by the Constituent Assembly, elected just at the time of the Bolshevist seizure of power, but the assembly was committed to achieving likewise the widest measure of individual and political freedom.

The prospect of a relatively peaceful reconstruction of Russian society was thrust to one side by the triumph of the October Revolution. In an explosion of accumulated resentments, the peasants took revenge for three centuries of serfdom, the workers for two generations of misrule in the factories. Control over chaos passed into the hands of the most revolutionary, closely knit, and ruthless of the parties which were competing for leadership over the revolution.

The revolutionary ethic with which Lenin and his followers rode the whirlwind was compounded of contradictions. It preached direct, often primitive, revenge for remembered oppressions; it promised a prompt millenium of equality, brotherhood, and freedom under anarchy. It demanded complete self-dedication of its followers; it justified in advance their ruthless repression of all who rejected the aims and demands of the party. Denouncing "imperialist war," it called joyously for a civil war which was to last longer and cause more destruction. Even while the outcome in Russia hung in the balance, Bolshevist dogma proclaimed its possession of the only key to the creation of a unified world society, cleansed of all social and national conflicts. Once in the saddle, the Soviet leaders continued to seek out one "enemy class" after another and to destroy, as "enemies of the people," those whom it regarded as opponents—real, potential, or imaginary. Propagating and increasingly enforcing a monolithic view of the universe, it sought in every way to destroy the spiritual and social activity of the Orthodox Church and of all faiths, and it arrogated to itself the sole power to dictate the form and content of scientific research, of art, music, and literature.

The Soviet regime emerged from the civil war and intervention a highly centralized party-state. All basic decisions were made by party organs and were usually promulgated at party rather than at Soviet congresses. The non-Russian republics, such as Ukraine, Belorussia, and the Trans-Caucasian republics, obeyed the policies laid down by central party organs in Moscow long before the first federative constitution was adopted (almost as an afterthought) in 1924. The "revolutionary" election of officers had quickly given way to centralized command and severe discipline. By 1920, trade unions were controlled by officials chosen by the party, and merely presented for confirmation by their constituents.

In the 1920's, the party still clung to its aureole of a "workers' party." "Proletarian" dress and speech for Communists, "proletarian descent" for those seeking an education or a party career, "proletarian literature," narrow-mindedly militant in contrast to the traditional humanism of Russian letters, were stressed flamboyantly, even while the party apparatus was being transformed into a self-contained instrument of power. The party now became the master of a strong industrial system, and at the same time eliminated the last potential rival for power by organizing the peasants in large, centrally controlled collective farms. Later in the 1930's the party forgot its boast of being "blood and bone" of the working class. It now lavished praise and numerous material favors on the "Stakhanovites," on "leading collective farmers," chiefly administrators, and on "distinguished people" and other "non-party Bolsheviks" singled out from among the "Soviet intelligentsia."

By the mid-1930's, all basic tools of production, both factories and mechanized equipment in agriculture, were owned by the party-state. Few could escape the control of the state over education, employment, and ever-scarce urban housing. Increasingly the non-Russian nationalities found that the relatively broad opportunities of cultural development, which had been theirs in the 1920's, were being curtailed. Uniformity of ideological content was more and more identified with acceptance of the "leading role" of Russian culture within the "Soviet family of nations." During the 1930's, the exclusive control of the Communist party over all "levers of power" was reinforced, in turn, through the drastic purge of all ranks of the party by the political police and the Politburo. Party congresses became rare (the latest ones were in 1934 and 1939) as the leadership no longer needed them even as sounding boards for pre-determined policies.

Centralized control from above continued to be supplemented by manipulation of instruments for displaying or simulating "participation from below." Compulsory attendance at factory, election, and trade-union meetings, compulsory balloting, adoption of pre-fabricated resolutions, the never-ceasing pressure of written and oral propagandizing, went on. Yet Soviet comments on the work of local Soviets, trade-unions, collective farms, and party committees suggest that neither local administrators nor those administered find this "meeting mania" useful or meaningful.

Preparation for World War II intensified central control, and gave it an increasingly military character. On the eve of the war, workers in transport and war industries were placed under military discipline, and nearly all urban employees and workers were forbidden to change jobs without higher permission. These restrictions have remained in force since the end of the war.[2] Collective farmers may not go more than a few miles from the village without permission of an official. The widespread use of forced labor for many types of production and construction has gone on unabated since the middle of the First Five-Year Plan.[3] Under a Politburo, most of whose members have grown old in office over the last twenty years, the Soviet Union has moved full circle from the promises of a quick entry into an equalitarian utopia to the hierarchical rigidity of an armed camp.

War, victory over Germany, and the postwar striving to extend Soviet power to the maximum have further intensified the military strain which has always been present in the regime. Despite the continuing low standards of living, the many forms of compulsion exercised over most Soviet subjects, and the persistent exploitation of slave labor on a large scale, Soviet propaganda asserts that, basically, all domestic problems have been solved; and that the Soviet Union will pass, within a few years, from its present stage of "socialism" to that of "communism." It is not clear in what respects "communism" will differ from the present Soviet society, since the state is to remain all-powerful and striking inequalities of status and income are to persist. Meanwhile, according to Soviet propaganda, the only remaining obstacle to the achievement of Communism within the U.S.S.R., and of peace and well-being throughout the world, is the "war-monger-

[2] (Author's note, 1959) The restrictions on mobility of labor have been relaxed substantially since 1953, and fines have largely replaced criminal penalties as punishment for violations of labor discipline.

[3] (Author's note, 1959) The Khrushchev regime has largely abandoned the use of forced labor.

ing" "ruling circles" of imperialist countries and their striving for "world domination."

Since the war, Russian culture has been proclaimed the only true culture, and this applies not only to Soviet culture, but to prerevolutionary Russia, now considered the life-giving and unique source of art, culture, science, and invention, even under serfdom. The non-Russian peoples of the Soviet Union are forbidden to record or recall any past conflicts with tsarist Russia, or any past cultural relations with peoples outside the Soviet Union. For example, Shamil, who led the Moslems of the Caucasus in their thirty-year fight against Russian conquest, was recently proclaimed a "reactionary," since submission to Russian rule opened the way for his people to learn from Russian culture, the "most progressive" of all cultures, and to learn the language of Lenin (who was not yet born). The non-Russian Soviet peoples have not forgotten the fate of several members of the "family of nations" which were accused of disloyalty to Moscow during the war. The Crimean Tartars, the Volga Germans, Kalmyks, and Chechen-Ingush, totaling over three millions, were uprooted from their homes and scattered to remote parts of the country, thus forfeiting their national identity. The principle of national equality, a great promise of the Russian revolution, has, like the granting of "all the land to those who till it," borne bitter fruit.

Is there any revolutionary enthusiasm left within this regime which uses the most severe sanctions to enforce a rigid uniformity of thought and action and which rejects spontaneity of thought on principle? This is hard to believe. The rhetoric of the original enthusiasm is repeated mechanically, but the spirit is that of rigid discipline and coldly calculated expansion.

Immediately before and after the October Revolution, Lenin believed that backward Russia would be unable to achieve socialism by its own efforts, and he looked to spontaneously generated revolutions, evoked by the Soviet example, in advanced industrial countries, particularly in Germany, to make good the technical and organizational deficiencies of his own country. Almost from the beginning, however, the Soviet leaders supplemented revolutionary appeals by such revolutionary forces as they could muster. In the Finnish civil war of 1918, Russian troops did the greater part of the fighting for the cause of "Soviet Finland." In the armies which established the Soviet regime in Ukraine, some eighty per cent of the man power was Russian. When Soviet and local pro-Soviet forces were driven out of Estonia and Latvia, Stalin remarked grimly that the Red Army would return one day in overwhelming strength. The attempts to impose Soviet rule met with especially strong resistance among the Finns, Ests, Letts, Lithuanians, and Poles, whose cultural traditions had been formed in communion with the Catholic and Protestant West.

Although Lenin protested in 1920 that the Communist International was being organized too much "on Russian lines," and that it was not possible for revolutions elsewhere to follow the Russian model blindly, he pressed for the creation of a tightly organized "general staff of the world revolution," a worldwide version of the Bolshevist party. Once the basic condition of "democratic centralism" had been imposed upon the "national sections" of the "international party," it was inevitable that Russian control over them should become ever more rigid and exacting, for the Russian leaders alone held power. No longer expecting "spontaneous" revolutions in other countries, the Comintern set about organizing them from above. By the late 1920's, all pretense to equality between the Soviet and the foreign parties had been discarded. Those foreign Communists who survived the drastic purges of the Comintern between 1937 and 1939, became, after the dissolution of the Comintern in

1943, instruments of the Soviet party within the satellite states and, elsewhere, leaders of the parties' bid for power.

Immediately after World War II, the equating of the "people's democracies" with unquestioning service to the Soviet Politburo was partially concealed. Most of the newly recruited Communists abroad were not aware of the channels by which instructions were passed on and conformity enforced. The aureole of national resistance to Hitlerism clung to several of the parties, and the Communists became advocates of extreme nationalist claims against neighboring countries, even against other "people's democracies." Leaders of the new regime were even allowed to speak of finding "new paths to Socialism," different from the Soviet path, as the mission of their Communist parties.

When the Soviet government refused, in 1947, to join in the Marshall Plan for European economic reconstruction, it saw with alarm that the Communist leaders in the satellites, confronted with unmanageable problems of reconstruction, of unequal trade with the Soviet Union, and sweeping schemes of industrialization, were hankering after the economic manna of the West. It now dropped the pretense of equality within the Soviet orbit, put through the Sovietization of Czechoslovakia and undertook, at risks greater than it foresaw, to establish its direct control over the army, police, and party in Yugoslavia.

One of the most alarming aspects of postwar Soviet policy is the tremendous emphasis which it places upon military power. This militarist trend in thinking was laid bare by the correspondence between the Soviet Politburo and the Central Committee of the Yugoslav Communist party. A "people's democracy," the Soviet leaders insisted, can be created only by the presence and with the aid of the Red Army. "Unfortunately," the situation at the end of the war did not allow the Soviet Union to create people's democracies in France and Italy, as had happened in eastern

Europe. Accordingly, Yugoslavia could not possibly have created a "people's democracy" by its own efforts, and should gratefully allow Soviet advisers to take control over the party, the political police, and the army.

Postwar experiences have shown that, through applying Soviet techniques of control, propaganda, and intimidation, a Soviet-dominated regime can be established in any country. Long anti-Russian traditions, as in Poland, Hungary, and Rumania, or traditions of pro-Russianism, as in Czechoslovakia, Yugoslavia, and Bulgaria, have made no basic difference. Once the system of all-embracing controls has been put into operation, the victim only tightens the cord by struggling against it. No spontaneous revolution is required or allowed. The technique of the "cold *Putsch*" can wipe out the outward expression of a thousand years of independent cultural and national development. A growing realization of the nature of Soviet expansion has stimulated the efforts of other European nations, beyond the sphere of Soviet control, to regain control of their destinies and to compensate their own military weakness by co-operation with each other and with the United States and Canada.

At the same time that Europeans were coming to realize that the direct Soviet threat to their independence was military in character and must be met with preparation for defense, Soviet ideology was making colossal conquests in Asia. In China, a native reformulation of Soviet Communism, relatively removed from direct Soviet control, profited by the weaknesses of the previous regime and extended its control over the entire country except Formosa. There is some indication that the Soviet leaders were surprised by the rapid sweep of the Chinese Communist armies, and that they had not fully prepared the way for the exercise of close control of the satellite type.

This does not mean that Mao Tse-tung can be, or wishes to be, a second Tito. For a long time to come,

Russia is China's only possible ally in a policy of expansion or "liberation." Russia is also the principal source of military supplies and the furnisher of advisers to the program of industrialization and militarization. In China, the anti-capitalism of Communism finds ready reinforcement in anti-Westernism. Both China and Russia want to get the Western powers out of Asia. Whatever frictions may arise between Peking and Moscow over the resources of Manchuria and Sinkiang, or the ultimate disposition of Korea or control of the resources of Southeast Asia, lie in the future; as long as China pursues goals beyond its frontiers, it depends, strategically and economically, on the Soviet Union.

The European nations offer many obstacles to Soviet penetration. The Soviet boasts of cultural superiority are repugnant to them. They have highly developed political and economic techniques, and are capable of finding military security in a common effort. In Asia the situation is quite different. Habits and techniques of Western democracy are nowhere fully developed or applied. Parties and parliaments have shallow roots. The tradition of personal loyalty is strong. When great political changes have occurred, as in Turkey and India, they have usually been shaped by the personal role of an outstanding individual, interpreting the aspirations of his people at a critical time, rather than through the slow accretion of democratic debate and adjustment.

Because of the piling up of demographic and economic problems, Asian countries lack the margin of safety for rash experimentation. A policy which results in losses or inconveniences in a wealthier country may lead to starvation and breakdown among people living on the margin of subsistence. Tradition and custom make most Asian peoples skeptical of their ability to control or even influence governments. Exploitation of the peasants by the landowners has now been called in question everywhere. But will governments dispossess the very class which, to a large extent, has access to education and time to participate in political life? Many locally owned industries exploit the surplus of labor to keep their workers unorganized and poorly paid. Western-run industries are in some cases more enlightened in their treatment of the workers, but the Westerner remains alien, inaccessibly superior in status, mobility, and income. Westerners, with their attitudes about "natives" and color, have long been respected for their practical abilities, but rarely loved.

This brief and oversimplified sketch of the problem may suggest a few of the reasons why Western democracy has such difficulty in penetrating below the surface of Asian life, and why Lenin and Stalin have both insisted that Soviet Communism has limitless opportunities of expansion in Asia. Unsolved agrarian problems, a primitive and predatory stage of industrialization, a small, partially Westernized class of intellectuals debarred from exercising political power—for what better conditions could the Soviet leaders hope? If to these favorable factors are added the obvious weakening of western Europe and the growing military and technological might of Soviet Russia, seconded by Communist China, the attempt to guide or assist the Asian countries along a non-Communist path of modernization might seem well-nigh hopeless.

Perhaps the Asian picture does not appear so encouraging to the Soviet leaders as it is often painted. The Asian countries may throw up leaders who can bring about a reshaping of the agrarian structure. Perhaps the gradual development of industry can contribute to an enlarged livelihood. Or perhaps the intellectuals, who are trying to merge something of Western concepts of political and social progress with a knowledge of their own peoples and their aspirations, will prefer the ways of gradualism and freedom to the temptations of dictatorial power, which ends by stifling the atmosphere of debate and criticism from which it sprang.

Despite its vaulting claims, the Soviet leadership may not believe that it could, with impunity, extend its control many thousands of miles beyond the limits of Russia, which supplies its man power and shapes its ways of thinking and feeling. The Politburo may wonder how far and how fast it can allow Communist China to penetrate into Southeast Asia, and whether an unlimited advance into Asia may not result in the Atlantic power bloc transforming its present inferiority and potential superiority into actual superiority of power. Believing ever since the October Revolution that "Western imperialism" can most conveniently be destroyed through the spread of revolutions to the East, and that "capitalist encirclement" of the Soviet Union will be replaced eventually by "socialist encirclement" of the remnants of capitalism, how great risks are the Soviet leaders willing to run in order to speed up what is, to them, an inevitable process?

At the present time, Soviet expansion has set no limits to itself in Europe or Asia. In Europe, the Western community of nations has thrown up a fairly definite, though not consolidated line of defense, and thus far Soviet advance has halted at that line. Neither the non-Communist powers of Asia nor the Western countries have drawn a similar line on the mainland of Asia. Nor does it seem possible to do so now. Would western Europe and America prepare and launch an offensive riposte against the Soviet Union in Europe if Communist China joins with the native Communists to seize control of Indochina? Would Burma be able to defend itself against any invading force; and would it invite any Western forces to defend it? Can the Chinese, the majority in Malaya, be expected to transfer their loyalty overnight from China to Malaya?

In the meantime, there is much else that can and must be done to overcome both colonialism and anticolonialism in Asia; and this requires from the West both changes in thinking and provision of material and technical assistance. President Truman's Point Four, the Colombo Plan, the Fulbright Act, the United Nations' program of technical aid, the British Colonial

Development Fund, are signposts along the path which must be followed much more vigorously and purposefully than has yet been the case. Generally speaking, the Asian countries are moving to improve their livelihood, to broaden opportunity through education, to break down religious and caste barriers, and to hasten the emergence of a more modern political system. To them, both the Soviet Union and the Atlantic community are "the West." Which one they will lean toward will depend in large measure on the understanding and the assistance which the West will bring to them. Understanding cannot mean condescension, and assistance cannot be charity.

The West must comprehend not only the partial imitations of itself, but also the deeper originalities and resistances of Asian cultures. It cannot expect Asian countries to imitate its own technical and educational systems wholesale, but must help their leaders to select and apply those innovations which are practicable in their own society. In many parts of the world the introduction of small wheeled carts, made of local materials, would lift great burdens from human backs, and hand sprayers against pests are much more needed than tractors. An Indian village assembly will never be a replica of a New England town meeting, but it can be an effective instrument of social change as well as of social rigidity. Power plants, irrigation projects, major transportation, and extractive facilities are bound to be publicly built and operated; the important thing is to establish the basis of efficient and economical management.

The United Nations may be able to provide aid which Asian peoples would be fearful of receiving directly from America. If Americans are unwilling to work under unpleasant conditions at low salaries and in out-of-the-way places, others are willing. Swedish engineers have a record of outstanding achievement in basing small industrial plants on cheap electric power. Mexican farm experts have learned much about improving the yields of subtropical and semi-arid agriculture. The Danish record in the co-operative movement and in rural education is nowhere surpassed. Declarations and sporadic gestures will not help to solve the problems of the underdeveloped economies. Neither will the indiscriminate scattering of huge electric plants and steel mills. The spadework waiting to be done is enormous. Most of it must be done by young Asians who are willing to abandon the black coat of the newly urbanized intellectual and civil servant, and go out among their own people to help them find a bridge between their problems and the future. Westerners can, with modesty, help them.

Finally, it is worse than useless to help the Asian countries *only* in the name of stemming the advance of Communism. This is, unfortunately, the motive which is presented to the American public and to the Congress in requesting funds. Then the debate turns on whether $4 or $40 billion will turn the trick! The debate is an unavoidable part of decision making, but the notion that the friendship of any country can be bought is nauseating to the people of that country. Apparently, it is a part of the American anxiety to avoid being "made a sucker" that makes us insist upon purely "realistic" motives when we justify our aid to foreign countries. Actually, it would be much more in keeping with American traditions to regard Point Four as a continuation and enlargement of the philanthropy and education which have been supported by the selfless work of thousands, and the contributions of millions of Americans almost from the establishment of our Republic.

Whatever the expressed motives under which we act, it must be said that the implementation of Point Four and of the United Nations' technical assistance program has fallen dangerously short of the anticipations which they aroused, and of the urgency which they express of finding a new and more stable pattern of relations between advanced and underdeveloped countries.

With defeats, delays, and victories strewn along their path, the Soviet leaders have pursued their long-range program for unifying the world under one political control. In the process they have built up a position of very great power in Europe and Asia, but have held their own people on a low economic and cultural level. They have also deprived them of communion with other peoples and cultures in order that the Soviet propaganda structure may not be challenged within their own empire. Despite the development in Russia of the society and culture of an armed camp, the Soviet ideological drive for power still has offensive impetus to some extent in Europe, and potentially even more in Asia. Since it is clear that the Soviet leaders have come increasingly to rely on military might to advance the boundaries of their control, the free nations, if they are to manage their own destinies, must balance Soviet power by voluntary and purposeful co-operation.

But that is not enough. The free nations must also take the ideological offensive, relying on the simple and basic morality common to all the universal religions. They must combine strength with co-operative action, social justice with freedom of choice, international unity of action with mutual tolerance. And, in gathering their moral and material strength, they must not forget that the Russian people have drawn courage and endurance again and again from deep well-springs of brotherhood, mutual help, and kindly tolerance that are in fundamental contradiction to the hatred and lust for domination which drive the Soviet leaders to extend their power outward and upward to limits set by forces beyond their control.

:25:

THE NEW CHALLENGE OF THE KREMLIN[1]

[*June 1959*]

UNDER Khrushchev's leadership, Soviet diplomacy is making bolder use of a wider and more varied arsenal of weapons than in Stalin's last years. At its "peace-loving" extreme the spectrum of diplomatic tools now includes the granting of economic development credits on favorable terms and the lavishing of political support for any form of anti-Western nationalism, no matter how reactionary it may be at home, provided it can serve to weaken the influence of the West. At the other extreme of the spectrum Khrushchev has been making increasingly frequent threats of nuclear and missile destruction against "any point on the globe." The mixture of weapons and tactics has become variegated and kaleidoscopic. What does this portend for the peace of the world? Is this change of tactics due in part to the new dictator's personal ebullience, or does it reflect an extremely serious and long-term shift in the world balance of power?

Before we turn to these most difficult questions, we

[1] *Diplomacy in a Changing World,* edited by Stephen D. Kertesz and M. A. Fitzsimons (Notre Dame: University of Notre Dame Press; 1959), pp. 117–32. Copyright 1959 by the University of Notre Dame Press.

must first consider briefly whether the Soviet regime is changing its character at home, and if so whether these changes are likely to modify its purposes in world politics over the next few years.

The Soviet Union and the United States are now the only powers sufficiently large and powerful, and sufficiently self-contained, to generate their own foreign policies primarily from within. In greater or lesser degree all other governments today tend to adapt their policies to those of one or the other of the two strongest powers, or to the fact of their rivalry. Hence it is essential to consider whether the inner drives of the Soviet leadership are now undergoing any significant changes.

In the past many observers have argued that the psychologically belligerent posture of Soviet policy was due to a feeling of inferior power. Once it had achieved "security," whatever that is, the Soviet leadership would, the argument ran, relax its hostility toward outside powers and would gradually become a more tolerant member of the family of states. As it became more assured of its own permanence, it would also accept the permanence of its own coexistence in a world of differing social and political systems. It would relax its pressure to reshape the entire world in its own image. Today the Soviet Union is one of the two strongest military powers in the world; in some respects, difficult for the layman to measure, it has surpassed the military technology of the West and it also maintains far larger conventional forces. Yet the Soviet leadership, now that it feels vastly secure in its power, appears to be stepping up the frequency and the intensity of the crises that it provokes directly or encourages indirectly in widely separated regions of the world.

The Soviet Union is also one of the two major industrial powers of the world. Its rate of industrial growth, while slackening somewhat, promises to be sustained at a pace more rapid than that of most other countries. So far from feeling inferior in this area of achievement, since 1955 it has been offering large-scale technical assistance and development credits to a wide range of countries. The Seven-Year Plan of 1959–65, like the Five-Year Plans of Stalin's era, places its major emphasis upon the development of heavy industry—power, steel, machine tools, chemicals—and promises only modest improvements for the consumer. Since 1953, it is true, the average standard of living has improved substantially, with special attention to foodstuffs, clothing, and housing, but the economy remains firmly oriented to the industrial and military demands of the state. Khrushchev has committed his regime to overtaking the United States in the basic fields of heavy industry, and this ambition has both symbolic and practical implications in world politics.

So far from pressing their rulers for new concessions and new comforts, the long-enduring Soviet people appear to accept gratefully the modest and gradual improvements in their way of life. They now believe for the first time that the regime seriously intends to carry out its promises of a better life for the people. It can be argued that the improving standard of living, far from arousing new discontents and new demands, has given the people more confidence in the benevolent intentions of their rulers than at any time since the beginning of the Five-Year Plans, in 1928. Formerly, when the Soviet leaders claimed to be promoting the highest standards of living in the world, many Soviet people, on the evidence of their own eyes and memories, could not believe this claim, and this skepticism and hostility sometimes extended to Soviet propaganda claims to be the most "peace-loving" regime in the world. The gap between propaganda and reality was one of the factors which led Stalin's regime to apply massive measures of control and repression.

Since 1953, Stalin's successors have turned to a milder policy. They have relaxed labor controls substantially, granted more adequate pensions, and undertaken a major effort to overcome the great gap in urban housing. They have shortened the work week from forty-eight to forty-six hours and promise further curtailments. They appear to have largely abandoned the prison camp system of forced labor and there is now no evidence of large-scale and arbitrary repression. To all these new advantages Soviet people naturally respond favorably. Rather than demanding further changes, they work hard to please the regime and avoid a return to Stalinist methods. By increasing the size of the carrot and cutting down the weight of the stick, the post-Stalin Soviet leadership has actually, as I see it, gained a much wider freedom of action, politically and psychologically, in pursuing its aims both at home and abroad.

The spread of education, it is argued, is bound sooner or later to lead to a questioning of Soviet doctrine and Soviet propaganda, and this will eventually weaken the government's ability to enforce its highly doctrinaire view of the world, making it more wary of risking its stability and even its survival in foreign adventures. Not all is tranquil, it is true, in the intellectual sphere, as shown by Khrushchev's repeated and forceful interventions against even mild forms of dissent or indifference. The problem of how to develop vigorous thinking and intellectual initiative in order to meet the need of the regime for intelligent and responsible administrators and experts in all fields, while simultaneously maintaining full control over all aspects of thought and expression, has always worried the Soviet leadership and will continue to do so. Stalin's successors have demonstrated repeatedly their uncertainty as to whether to loosen the reins of intellectual control a little, in order to overcome the heritage of fear and apathy, or whether to hold them tight, in order to forestall the growth of diversity and heresy. They have, however, endeavored to carry out this somewhat erratic shift back and forth between "hard" and "soft" lines of thought control without resorting to outright terrorism.

The problem of where to hold the line in the intellectual and ideological field is a difficult one, probably an insoluble one, for a totalitarian regime. But are we justified in leaping from the evidence of these confusions and perplexities to the hopeful conclusion that the spread of independent thinking among influential segments of the apparatus of rule will inevitably lead to basic changes in the system of control and in the purposes of the regime? This is a very long leap, indeed. In order to present a more relaxed and confident posture to the outside world, the Soviet leadership has permitted freer access by foreign visitors, but it keeps a firm grip over all information which reaches its people and over the expression of ideas. If a continuing poverty of economic thought, philosophy, and artistic creation are a part of the price the regime must pay in order to protect its monolithic psychological structure, it seems as willing to pay that price under Khrushchev as it was under Stalin.

Today Soviet feeling and action leave a stronge impression of national pride, even national arrogance. A powerful though intellectually barren type of Soviet chauvinism permeates both the leadership and its active instruments of rule. This emotion, which is fed by industrial achievements and growing military might, by pride in the expansion of the Communist system to eastern Europe and China, and by Khrushchev's bold strokes and threats, is much more widely felt and shared than the earlier Bolshevik commitment to a messianic world-wide mission, but, like it, it recognizes no moral or political barriers to its eventual domination of the world. Khrushchev is in deadly earnest when he boasts that Communism will triumph everywhere by the end of the twentieth century, and many Soviet hearts beat faster when they hear this boast. Meanwhile, on the whole, the claim of the Soviet Communist party to be the sole correct interpreter of history seems much more widely accepted at home than ever before. The chafing of the hard-working, efficient, and curious Soviet youth against taboos on knowledge and thought may worry the leadership; it is not likely to endanger the survival of the Soviet system or lessen the ability of its leadership to pursue its self-appointed course in world affairs.

Under Stalin it could be said with confidence that, although he was willing to exert pressure where it could be exerted without serious risk, and was eager to bring under his control any international real estate which was not adequately protected by countervailing strength, he did not intend to involve his regime in a major war. Indeed, even on those occasions when Stalin raised the risks of war to a high pitch by his miscalculations, as in his imposing of the Berlin blockade, in 1948–9, and in unleashing Communist aggression in Korea, he generally tried to calculate carefully the margin of risks which he could afford to take. Today, the margin of risks open to Khrushchev has been greatly enlarged, and the outside world cannot be sure just where in Soviet calculations that margin of risk lies. Crucial developments in Soviet military technology have contributed to this change. The development of a major nuclear capability was one of Stalin's dominant aims after 1945. Even while he was both denying the decisive importance of nuclear power and making every effort to mobilize the fear of a new war against the only possessor of that new weapon, he was bending every effort to match the West in nuclear power.

The outside world was surprised at the speed with which the Soviet Union achieved an atomic and then a hydrogen capability. Apparently, the non-Soviet world has been even more astounded at the Soviet Union's great technological advances in the field of guided and ballistic missiles. The launching of Soviet sputniks since September 1957 has marked the beginning of a new appraisal of the nature and location of advanced military power. Soviet space achievements demonstrated that Soviet technology had, at least temporarily, outstripped the West in its ability to launch large and heavy space-vehicles and in mastering the intricacies of missile guidance systems. Khrushchev was quick to turn this new weapon to political advantage. Even before he announced the launching of a Soviet intercontinental ballistic missile, he had added a new note of menace to the arsenal of Soviet policy. During the Suez crisis of 1956 he sent notes to many Western capitals, informing them that he was now able to destroy their cities, their industries, and their power of resistance. A year later Khrushchev had expanded his threats to North America and, indeed, "any point on the globe."

Whatever the unauthorized and overenthusiastic boasts of private individuals may have been, no similar threats were ever made by the United States government or its official spokesmen, during its period of monopoly over nuclear power, except as a form of deterrence against clear and direct aggression. Are Khrushchev's threats an over-reaction to the postwar years, when the Soviet leadership felt that its advantages in conventional man power and weapons were being nullified by the nuclear capability of the West? Or do they mark a deliberate heightening of tension, designed to hasten the achievement of definite aims through exploiting the changing shift of power?

Even in its published discussions, Soviet military thinking has undergone a remarkable change in the past four years. It no longer holds to the traditional concept of a defensive war on land begun by an attack on Soviet-controlled territory and to be ended by a victorious counteroffensive by massive conventional forces. Soviet discussions now speak openly of a "pre-emptive blow," designed to defeat a presumed aggressor *before* he can get in the first attack.[2] The new Soviet analyses of strategy emphasize for the first time that a war can be won or lost through the element of surprise. Apparently, the only difference between a "pre-emptive blow" and a "preventive war" is that a pre-emptive

[2] Herbert S. Dinerstein: "The Revolution in Soviet Strategic Thinking," *Foreign Affairs*, Vol. XXXVI, No. 2 (January 1958), pp. 241–52.

blow would be struck only after there was clear evidence that an aggressor was about to attack the Soviet Union, whereas a preventive war would be launched in the absence of such evidence. The difference may loom large in the subtleties of the dialectic, but in a delicately poised situation of strategic balance it might not have much practical significance.

As missiles increase in size and destructiveness, in accuracy and concealment, the question of how each side can evaluate the imminence of an attack becomes almost insoluble. In the age of full-scale missile power—the main reliance for both offense and retaliation—an error of judgment, one way or the other, may result in unleashing an unintended but overwhelmingly destructive war or in suffering the irretrievable elimination of a nation's power. It would surely be no consolation to know that a war of this new type had been let loose only after highly skilled technicians had examined radarscopes and decided that an enemy attack was already on its way.

The most novel and alarming aspect of Khrushchev's apparent view of nuclear strategy is his conviction that the Soviet leadership is now in a stronger position than the democratic West to force a new crisis close to the brink of war and to compel the other side to flinch from this fateful decision. Instead of bringing to the Soviet leadership a greater sense of power and security, the achievement of nuclear parity, combined with some slight and uncertain margin of missile superiority, has raised the level of risks, stepped up the frequency of crises, and increased the danger of war.

In the past it has been assumed that the Soviet leadership wished to avoid an all-out war because it would place in question the survival of its regime. But what if the Soviet leadership now believes, as it appears to, that a nuclear-missile confrontation places in question, not its own survival, but that of its strongest adversary, or, at the very least, the survival of the far-flung Western alliance system? It would be comforting to say that no military expert can assure his political chiefs of a one hundred per cent certainty of success, and that, in the face of this continuing margin of uncertainty, the Soviet leadership will therefore always pull back at the next-to-the-last minute from the final showdown. With so little known in the outside world about this type of Soviet strategic calculus, it would be rash to build a strategy, military and political, on this assumption. The frequency with which the Soviet leadership has in the past misjudged the political and psychological situation in other countries today offers no guarantee that its mathematical and technical calculations of the new balance of power will be less efficient than those on which its post-1945 scientific advances have been based.

Undoubtedly, the Soviet leadership would prefer to utilize its military advantages for political purposes without incurring the risk of resorting to the direct use of force, and it asserts with vehement conviction that no war will henceforth remain a limited one. The Kremlin would surely prefer to see Communist or at least pro-Soviet regimes come into power in areas presently beyond its control. It would then hope, through nuclear threats, to deter any outside intervention into these newly attached areas, without utilizing its conventional forces in a direct invasion. Khrushchev, no doubt, calculates that, if he should succeed through combined political and military means in detaching a number of strategic areas from the opposing bloc, this would destroy the self-confidence and mutual confidence of the opposing alliances, thus greatly increasing the opportunities for the nonmilitary expansion of Soviet influence and control.

With the spread of the new military technology, only two major powers are equipped to carry on an all-out war, and both of them are now vulnerable to attack in their heartlands. Under these new circumstances, a truly farsighted Soviet leadership might be well advised to adopt the recipe of that arch-imperialist, Theodore Roosevelt, who favored "walking softly and carrying a big stick." As the two major powers continue to outstrip more and more astronomically all other powers, it might be to Soviet advantage to promote a prolonged period of international relaxation, to increase the sense of strategic hopelessness among most nations of the world, and to diminish the fears which Soviet policy has periodically revived through its actions and its words.

Viewed from this point of view, for example, the survival of the North Atlantic Treaty Organization is a great advantage to Soviet policy. NATO sets its armament goals as ceilings, not as floors; it lays down its goals of strength for several years in advance; it is not engaged in building more than a minimum of defensive force, perhaps not even a minimum. If the Soviet leadership under Khrushchev, as under Stalin, pursues wholeheartedly its aim of breaking up NATO, this can only be, not because it fears NATO, but because it believes that NATO can be destroyed by threats, and that this event, accompanied by the withdrawal of British, Canadian, and American forces from the continent, would greatly improve the Soviet Union's relative position in pursuing its local and intermediate goals of expansion. A Soviet leadership which sincerely wanted to achieve a continuing relaxation would welcome NATO because it brings former European rivals together in what can be only a defensive coalition. Khrushchev's increasingly vehement efforts to undermine NATO are motivated, not by fear, but by ambition.

Since the consolidation of his power at home, Khrushchev's major miscalculations have occurred within the Soviet bloc. The search for a more flexible and more profitable way of managing the European satellites brought with it several costly setbacks. The Hungarian national uprising of October 1956, and its bloody suppression by Soviet tanks, the achievement of a substantial measure of internal autonomy by the Polish satellite regime, the economic concessions which had to be made to the more obedient satellites, were costly to Soviet prestige and to Soviet economic interests. Khrushchev's efforts to bring Communist Yugoslavia into a renewed obedience to Moscow failed. In controlling the captive countries of East Central Europe it again came to seem psychologically more economical of effort, as it had under Stalin, to blame all resistance on "Titoism," rather than examine objectively the incompatibilities between Soviet demands and the basic feelings of the conquered peoples.

The new break with the Yugoslav Communists coincided with the celebration, in November 1957, of forty years of the Soviet regime and the massive obeisance of other Communist regimes and parties before the shrine of Moscow's primacy. When Tito refused to sign the Declaration of Communist Parties and insisted, despite lavish Soviet promises of economic aid, on maintaining his independent position between the two blocs, on apportioning the blame for the cold war between the two blocs, rather than heaping it all on the West, Khrushchev turned upon the Yugloslav Communist leaders with the anger of a worthy suitor spurned. Did this return to overt hostility to the Yugoslav practice of independent Communism reflect a basic shift in Soviet strategy, a shift provoked by the achievement of great missile power? Or was it primarily an after-reaction to the alarming outburst of national anti-Soviet emotions which had so recently shaken the Soviet domination over East Central Europe?

Western policy has too long assumed that the unrest, actual or potential, in the East European satellites has been due to the refusal of the West to recognize the legitimacy of the Soviet-imposed governments. As a matter of fact, any hopes among the people of this area that the West's symbolic intransigence would have any effect upon their own helpless predicament had faded by 1950. Neither a Western embracing of the satellite regimes, nor a breaking off of relations with them, would have any real effect upon the degree to which each satellite nation adapts or avoids adapting itself to its situation. It is equally an illusion today to assume that the Soviet leadership attaches any value to receiving from the West a "legitimization" of its domination over East Central Europe. The time has gone by when the Soviet leadership would have found any such symbolic act to be of material value to it.

The band of East European satellite regimes has far less immediate strategic value to the Soviet Union today than it had before the emergence of its nuclear-missile capability. The Soviet Union does not foresee any time when the NATO forces would pose an aggressive threat on land to its own very large conventional forces, even if it completly discounts the satellite armies in its calculations. The exercise of Soviet menace and deterrence is now carried out primarily by missile threats. This new type of threat can play on single states, at a great distance, promising immunity to those intervening countries which disassociate themselves from resistance to Soviet demands. Whether or not Soviet forces can be reduced in the satellite areas or even withdrawn from them has become a factor, not of over-all military strategy, but a part of the calculus of political strategy. If a mutual withdrawal led to the isolation of each of the West European states from each other and from North America, while the East European regimes, buttressed by strong Soviet-trained police forces and intimidated by nearby Soviet power, remained in political obedience, the Soviet leadership could accept a considerable range of risks and hope to gain substantially from an exchange of concessions of this character.

Communist China presents a quite different range of opportunities and risks to Soviet policy. Can there develop between Moscow and Peking a range of frictions and suspicions which would render their alliance ineffectual? Or is most of the speculation in the West about these frictions simply another form of political

Micawberism? It is easy to assume that the Sino-Soviet honeymoon has long since been over. In the past several years Soviet credits have been offered and executed in substantial amounts to the benefit of many uncommitted countries, but not to that of Communist China. Embarked on an unprecedented effort of imposed sacrifice and rigid control, Communist China, in its "leap forward," must have special reasons for emphasizing that it is not only paying its own way but is rapidly repaying the earlier Soviet credits. When the Chinese Communist leaders read of Khrushchev's claims to possess an overpowering range of force, they must wonder why it is not exerted directly for the benefit of their own ambitions. Rather than Khrushchev prodding Peking in August 1958 to bombard the offshore islands, it seems more probable that he found it necessary, in person, to co-ordinate the degree of threat and risk which the Soviet leadership was prepared to back. Nor can it be assumed that Moscow and Peking always have the same evaluation of the level of risk which it is desirable for them to run in achieving a particular objective. When all these and other sources of possible friction have been measured, the overweening fact remains that the Soviet Union and Communist China have everything to lose by splitting apart and everything to gain by working together. The differences between them are presumably of degree and timing, not of basic purpose. Without Soviet backing, and even more so in the face of Soviet hostility, Communist China would be a power of medium weight, even in the Far East. Overt dissension between the two major centers of Communist triumph would destroy the psychological gains which they have made together in many parts of Asia.

If Khrushchev believes his own prognostications of the relative power curves, he must believe that the time is fast approaching when, under the cover of the Soviet nuclear-missile deterrent, Communist China may be able to exert its very great conventional strength to expand its power. Its strength, even if it remains without nuclear armaments, is growing much faster than that of all other countries of Asia combined. As this imbalance grows, the only available makeweight for the protection of non-Communist Asia against the might of Communist China is the power and determination of the United States. But if, as Khrushchev asserts, the central, nuclear, factor of that power can be neutralized, the United States and its allies would then lack the conventional forces, in adequate numbers and location, to offset the conventional strength of the Chinese Communists.

In the past Stalin moved slowly and cautiously from one area of crisis to another. The political disputes with Western Allies over the fate of East Central Europe and over the future of Germany were pitched to a nonmilitary key. When his attempt to prevent the integration of West Germany into the Western bloc failed, contrary to many predictions, over the Berlin blockade of 1948–9, Stalin sought a return to the previous *status quo* in Germany and made minor concessions in Austria. Slowly and massively Soviet interest then turned to the Far East and after what must have seemed more than adequate preparations the attempt was launched, in Korea, to drive American influence (there were no American forces there) from the Asian mainland. When, three years later, Stalin's successors decided to liquidate an unprofitable stalemate in Korea, they renounced counterproductive claims against Turkey, Iran, and Yugoslavia and actually withdrew from a militarily useless base in Finland and from an unstrategic eastern Austria, in order to re-establish their good faith as negotiators. Each of these shifts was carried out by many small steps, from each of which withdrawal would have been easy.

Since mid-1958 Khrushchev has turned the "rolling crisis" with dizzying speed from the Arab East to the Chinese offshore islands, and then to Berlin. He has laid the groundwork for other crises against Finland, through severe economic pressure, against Iran, through his protests against the U. S.-Iranian military assistance agreement. Are we approaching a period when, instead of probing cautiously for one weak spot at a time and simultaneously making conciliatory gestures about other disputed questions, the Soviet leadership will feel free to provoke several crises at the same time? In the past Stalin must have feared that to provoke several simultaneous crises might bring on a military showdown, in which his conventional forces were offset by a disparity in nuclear power. Khrushchev may come to feel, at some stage, that it is to his advantage to try to burst apart the American defensive system at several points at once, by raising more challenges than the West can cope with at any one time. Whatever these calculations may be—and we must not presume too far in this murky chamber of Soviet inner thought—the strategic partnership between Communist China and the Soviet Union, greatly revivified since June 1958, is a continuing fact. It is a stubborn fact which cannot be brushed aside by wishful speculation on allegedly fatal frictions between the two powers, united by common ideology, by joint, if not entirely common, ambitions, and by a shared hostility toward those who resist those ambitions.

The most striking innovation in Soviet policy since Stalin has been the new wooing of the uncommitted countries, particularly in Asia, but also persistently in Africa and Latin America. The new development was codified in Khrushchev's statement at the Twentieth Party Congress, in February 1956, that the world was now divided into three blocs; in addition to the Soviet camp of "peace and democracy" and the bloc of "imperialists," there was now a "peace bloc," typified by India. Through state visits, cultural propaganda, technical aid, and credits the new leadership undertook to win the sympathies and, it hoped, the political co-operation of a wide arc of countries, ranging from Egypt to Indonesia. Here Soviet propaganda, pursuing its traditional "anti-imperialist" line, met with a favorable response, for the resentment against Western colonial rule or domination, withdrawn only recently, provided the strongest political motivation of the new nations. The burning issue of destroying colonialism, wherever it still existed, served further to bring many of these countries closer to accepting the Soviet insistence that this issue, rather than the conflict between democracy and totalitarianism, is the only important question of our time. The granting of Soviet aid through trade, through an expressed willingness to purchase any surplus commodities in payment for Soviet industrial equipment, and the extension of credit without careful study and without conditions, further impressed many Asian political leaders with the advantages of co-operating part way with Soviet policy.

Were the Soviet leaders running the risk of strengthening non-Communist regimes in the newly independent countries? After all, before Stalin, Lenin had argued for the need of pre-industrial countries to pass through a minimal stage of economic development, to develop national states, before they could become "ripe" for Communist revolution. Looking at the vast economic and social problems of most of these countries, at the pressure of population on resources, at the difficulty of acquiring adequate capital either through savings at home or through investment from abroad, the Soviet leadership must feel that the political risk of strengthening non-Communist governments, even those which suppress Communist movements at home, is not a great one. In many of the countries, as in India and Indonesia, the Soviet *rapprochement* with the nationalist leaderships was followed by greater freedom of action for local Communist propaganda and organizers, as well as for Soviet propaganda. In addition, the local Communist parties could profit politically both by the prestige of Soviet friendship for their countries and through the rapidly spreading awareness of the growing industrial and military might of the Soviet

Union. Now, underdeveloped countries could, in effect, choose between the Western democratic model of economic modernization and the totalitarian Communist model. It was in line with the Soviet assumption that only Communism can solve basic economic problems for Khrushchev to assert, as he has often since 1956, that in some countries, weakly organized and administered, Communist parties may come to power through parliamentary means; and then, the changing strategic balance will prevent the "imperialists" from intervening to overthrow the new Communist rule.

Several factors have perhaps diminished Khrushchev's enthusiasm for the "peace bloc" and the "parliamentary path" to Communist rule since 1956. In some Asian countries the Soviet reconquest of Hungary left a strong impression, unlike Stalin's more creeping conquest of 1945–7. The Chinese Communist suppression of Tibetan autonomy was a direct shock to many Asians. There have been strong indications that the union of Syria and Egypt was prompted by fear of the growing influence of the Syrian Communist party, and the marked Soviet favoritism for the post-1958 regime in Iraq has led to bitter exchanges between President Nasser and Premier Khrushchev. Even the widespread enthusiasm in Asia for persuading the United States to recognize Communist China, presumably as a step toward the pacification of Asia, has given way, in some circles, to the feeling that it may even be desirable from their point of view, giving them a greater freedom of political action, to have American-backed Chinese Nationalist forces in direct contact with those of Communist China. Whether those Asian countries, such as Pakistan, Burma, and Thailand, and, less directly, Indonesia, which have placed more authority in the hands of the organized military forces have thereby raised enduring barriers to Communist pressures from within and without remains doubtful, but Moscow and Peking have left no doubt of their dislike of this presumed check to the expansion of Communist parties in South and Southeast Asia. The "peace bloc" and "united front" tactics have not brought the political successes which Khrushchev perhaps anticipated in 1955 and 1956. Indeed, his long speech to the Twenty-First Party Congress, in 1959, was remarkably taciturn on this subject.

Behind the kaleidoscope of greater variety and flexibility of tactics, Khrushchev's regime shows a basic continuity with that of his mentor, Stalin. Unlike Stalin, however, Khrushchev shows a less inhibited curiosity about the outside world, a willingness to expose himself to frequent and long conversations with prominent representatives of "imperialism." Perhaps having inherited his ideology ready-made, he has even greater confidence in his dialectical ability to impress on his listeners those arguments which fit the Leninist book. Basically, however, Khrushchev thinks in the same grooves. He believes that the Soviet system has alone resolved the fundamental problems of economic development and social welfare, brushing aside the far greater gains registered by other countries over the same decades. Like Stalin, he finds no contradiction between the ultimate goals of Communism and the ambitions of the Russian state.

Khrushchev's Russia, like Stalin's, rests upon a psychological armature of life-long indoctrination "from the cradle to the grave," upon rapid decision at the top and immediate obedience below, upon a monopoly of information which presses Soviet views outward while admitting as little as possible of outside information and opinion. If the Soviet leadership once lost confidence in the superiority of its ideology, it is doubtful whether Soviet nationalism, even Soviet arrogance, would be an adequate cement. "Relaxation of international tension," which Stalin and his successors demanded constantly from 1952, proved fraught with great dangers abroad and even with minor worries at home. On the other hand, to assure their own peoples and the world that the danger of war had greatly receded required only minor adjustments for democratic leaders, for the essence of democracy is to believe in and act on an assumption of good faith, and this assumption is readily extended from one's own people and their friends to an adversary. For a democracy it is natural to believe that hostility must derive from an unfortunate misunderstanding. For a totalitarian ruler, on the contrary, the vanishing, whether sincere or not, of the dread of war presents great risks. While their precise form could not have been predicted, the events of 1956 in eastern Europe followed logically from the summit conference of 1955, even though the meeting had no concrete achievements to its credit. Under the new strategic balance, however, it is far from clear that Khrushchev has been seeking a second summit meeting in order to bring about a genuine relaxation of tension. Perhaps now, in order to explore certain relative advantages in military power, he would like to confront Western political leaders with the alternatives which they would prefer to ignore.

The past three years, since 1956, have given Soviet policy a wider range of goals, a far greater variety of instruments. The adaptation to the new environment has not been without risks and costs to Soviet policy. All of these, in Khrushchev's eyes, appear to have been compensated by the rapid progress of Soviet strategic power. By 1948 Stalin could write to Tito that the Yugoslav Communists had no right to claim any credit for establishing a Communist regime in their own country, since it was the over-all strategic situation which had made this possible; similarly, the French and Italian Communists, who had been attacked by the Yugoslavs for their passivity, had been unable, so Stalin said, to establish "people's democracies" because "unfortunately," the Soviet armies were unable to help them in this. After a period of experimentation with the wider range of political, economic, and psychological instruments, Khrushchev seems again to be concentrating his main hopes on the deployment of Soviet military power, now arrayed in a new and even more ominous form. He seems determined, in one part of the world after another, or perhaps in several regions at once, to raise a major strategic challenge to the strength and cohesion of the free world.

INDEX

PHILIP E. MOSELY, who was born in Westfield, Massachusetts, in 1905, did both undergraduate and graduate work at Harvard, where he took his Ph.D. in 1933, after studying for the year 1926–7 at Cambridge, England. Now Director of the European Institute of Columbia University, he was Director of Studies at the Council on Foreign Relations New York, from 1955 to 1963, as well as Adjunct Professor of International Relations at the Russian Institute of Columbia University. From 1951 to 1955 he was also Director of the Russian Institute. While engaged in historical research in Moscow, 1930–2, under a fellowship from Harvard, he had an unusual opportunity to get to know Russians and to see Soviet life at first hand. He visited the Soviet Union again in 1943, 1956, and 1959. Between 1943 and 1946 Dr. Mosely spent over two thousand hours negotiating with the Russians on the postwar settlements with Germany, Austria, Italy and the Balkans. From 1942 to 1946 Dr. Mosely was an officer of the United States Department of State, and served as Chief of the Division of Territorial Studies. He was a member of the U.S. delegation to the Moscow Conference in 1943; a representative on the four-power European Advisory Commission, in London, during 1944 and 1945; a U.S. advisor at the Potsdam Conference in 1945, and at the Council of Foreign Ministers in London and Paris in 1945–6. He was also the U.S. representative on the Commission for the Investigation of the Yugoslav-Italian boundary in 1946. This experience of actual negotiation has been supplemented by some thirty years of study of Russian and Soviet policy. Dr. Mosely is married, has two daughters, and lives in New York City.

THE TEXT of this book was set in *Electra*, a Linotype face designed by W. A. Dwiggins. This face cannot be classified as modern or oldstyle. It is not based on any historical model, nor does it echo any particular period or style. It avoids the extreme contrast between thick and thin elements that marks most modern faces, and attempts to give a feeling of fluidity, power, and speed. Composed, printed, and bound by THE COLONIAL PRESS INC., Clinton, Massachusetts.